THREE
CARTESIAN FEMINIST
TREATISES

THE
OTHER VOICE
IN
EARLY MODERN
EUROPE

A Series Edited by Margaret L. King and Albert Rabil Jr.

OTHER BOOKS IN THE SERIES

HENRICUS CORNELIUS AGRIPPA
*Declamation on the Nobility and
Preeminence of the Female Sex*
Edited and translated by Albert Rabil Jr.

LAURA CERETA
Collected Letters of a Renaissance Feminist
Edited and translated by Diana Robin

TULLIA D'ARAGONA
Dialogue on the Infinity of Love
Edited and translated by Rinaldina Russell
and Bruce Merry

CASSANDRA FEDELE
Letters and Orations
Edited and translated by Diana Robin

CECILIA FERRAZZI
Autobiography of an Aspiring Saint
Edited and translated by Anne Jacobson Schutte

MODERATA FONTE
The Worth of Women
Edited and translated by Virginia Cox

VERONICA FRANCO
Poems and Selected Letters
Edited and translated by Ann Rosalind Jones
and Margaret F. Rosenthal

MARIE LE JARS DE GOURNAY
*"Apology for the Woman Writing"
and Other Works*
Edited and translated by Richard Hillman
and Colette Quesnel

LUCREZIA MARINELLA
*The Nobility and Excellence of Women,
and the Defects and Vices of Men*
Edited and translated by Anne Dunhill with
Letizia Panizza

ANNE-MARIE-LOUISE D'ORLÉANS,
DUCHESSE DE MONTPENSIER
*Against Marriage: The Correspondence
of La Grande Mademoiselle*
Edited and translated by Joan DeJean

ANTONIA PULCI
*Florentine Drama for Convent
and Festival*
Edited and translated by James Wyatt Cook

SISTER BARTOLOMEA RICCOBONI
*Life and Death in a Venetian Convent:
The Chronicle and Necrology
of Corpus Domini, 1395 – 1436*
Edited and translated by Daniel Bornstein

MARÍA DE SAN JOSÉ SALAZAR
Book for the Hour of Recreation
Introduction and notes by Alison Weber,
translation by Amanda Powell

ANNA MARIA VAN SCHURMAN
*"Whether a Christian Woman Should Be
Educated" and Other Writings from Her
Intellectual Circle*
Edited and translated by Joyce L. Irwin

LUCREZIA TORNABUONI DE' MEDICI
Sacred Narratives
Edited and translated by Jane Tylus

JUAN LUIS VIVES
*"The Education of a Christian Woman":
A Sixteenth-Century Manual*
Edited and translated by Charles Fantazzi

François Poullain de la Barre

THREE
CARTESIAN FEMINIST
TREATISES

*Introductions and Annotations
by Marcelle Maistre Welch
Translation by Vivien Bosley*

THE UNIVERSITY OF CHICAGO PRESS
Chicago & London

François Poullain de la Barre, 1647–1723

Vivien Bosley is associate professor of French in the Department
of Modern Languages and Cultural Studies at the University of Alberta.
Marcelle Maistre Welch is professor of French in the Department
of Modern Languages at Florida International University.

The University of Chicago Press, Chicago 60637
The University of Chicago Press, Ltd., London
© 2002 by The University of Chicago
All rights reserved. Published 2002
Printed in the United States of America
11 10 09 08 07 06 05 04 03 02   1 2 3 4 5

ISBN: 0-226-67653-6 (cloth)
ISBN: 0-226-67654-4 (paper)

Library of Congress Cataloging-in-Publication Data

Poulain de La Barre, François, 1647–1723.
    [Treatises. English. Selections]
    Three Cartesian feminist treatises / François Poullain de la Barre ; introductions
and annotations by Marcelle Maistre Welch ; translation by Vivien Bosley.
        p.   cm.—(The other voice in early modern Europe)
    Includes bibliographical references (p.) and index.
    Contents: On the equality of the two sexes—On the education of ladies—On the
excellence of men (Preface and Remarks).
    ISBN 0-226-67653-6 (cloth)—ISBN 0-226-67654-4 (pbk.)
    1. Women—Early works to 1800. 2. Equality—Early works to 1800. 3. Women's
rights—Early works to 1800. 4. Women—Education—Early works to 1800.
5. Poulain de La Barre, François, 1647–1723—Views on women. I. Maistre Welch,
Marcelle. II. Bosley, Vivien Elizabeth, 1937– III. Title. IV. Series.

HQ1201 .P664213 2002
305.4—dc21

                                                            2002028639

⊗ The paper used in this publication meets the minimum requirements of
the American National Standard for Information Sciences—Permanence
of Paper for Printed Library Materials, ANSI Z39.48-1992.

CONTENTS

Marcelle Maistre Welch wishes to acknowledge the support of her husband, William W. Welch, whose patience and editorial comments were much appreciated. Vivien Bosley wishes to acknowledge her debt to her husband, Richard Bosley, and to her colleagues Nicole Mallet, Enrico Musacchio, Willi Braun, and Andrew Gow for their prompt responses to questions about philosophy, philology, theology, and religious history. Warm thanks to the Bibliothèque Nationale in Paris for graciously allowing use of materials.

THE OTHER VOICE IN EARLY MODERN EUROPE: INTRODUCTION TO THE SERIES

Margaret L. King and Albert Rabil Jr.

THE OLD VOICE AND THE OTHER VOICE

In western Europe and the United States women are nearing equality in the professions, in business, and in politics. Most enjoy access to education, reproductive rights, and autonomy in financial affairs. Issues vital to women are on the public agenda: equal pay, childcare, domestic abuse, breast cancer research, and curricular revision with an eye to the inclusion of women.

These recent achievements have their origins in things women (and some male supporters) said for the first time about six hundred years ago. Theirs is the "other voice," in contradistinction to the "first voice," the voice of the educated men who created Western culture. Coincident with a general reshaping of European culture in the period 1300–1700 (called the Renaissance or early modern period), questions of female equality and opportunity were raised that still resound and are still unresolved.

The other voice emerged against the backdrop of a three-thousand-year history of the derogation of women rooted in the civilizations related to Western culture: Hebrew, Greek, Roman, and Christian. Negative attitudes toward women inherited from these traditions pervaded the intellectual, medical, legal, religious, and social systems that developed during the European Middle Ages.

The following pages describe the traditional, overwhelmingly male views of women's nature inherited by early modern Europeans and the new tradition that the other voice called into being to begin to challenge reigning assumptions. This review should serve as a framework for the understanding of the texts published in the series The Other Voice in Early Modern Europe. Introductions specific to each text and author follow this essay in all the volumes of the series.

TRADITIONAL VIEWS OF WOMEN, 500 B.C.E. – 1500 C.E.

Embedded in the philosophical and medical theories of the ancient Greeks were perceptions of the female as inferior to the male in both mind and body. Similarly, the structure of civil legislation inherited from the ancient Romans was biased against women, and the views on women developed by Christian thinkers out of the Hebrew Bible and the Christian New Testament were negative and disabling. Literary works composed in the vernacular language of ordinary people, and widely recited or read, conveyed these negative assumptions. The social networks within which most women lived—those of the family and the institutions of the Roman Catholic Church—were shaped by this negative tradition and sharply limited the areas in which women might act in and upon the world.

GREEK PHILOSOPHY AND FEMALE NATURE. Greek biology assumed that women were inferior to men and defined them merely as childbearers and housekeepers. This view was authoritatively expressed in the works of the philosopher Aristotle.

Aristotle thought in dualities. He considered action superior to inaction, form (the inner design or structure of any object) superior to matter, completion superior to incompletion, possession superior to deprivation. In each of these dualities, he associated the male principle with the superior quality and the female with the inferior. "The male principle in nature," he argued, "is associated with active, formative and perfected characteristics, while the female is passive, material and deprived, desiring the male in order to become complete."[1] Men are always identified with virile qualities, such as judgment, courage, and stamina, and women with their opposites—irrationality, cowardice, and weakness.

Even in the womb, the masculine principle was considered superior. The man's semen, Aristotle believed, created the form of a new human creature, while the female body contributed only matter. (The existence of the ovum, and with it the other facts of human embryology, were not established until the seventeenth century.) Although the later Greek physician Galen believed that there was a female component in generation, contributed by "female semen," the followers of both Aristotle and Galen saw the male role in human generation as more active and more important.

In the Aristotelian view, the male principle sought always to reproduce itself. The creation of a female was always a mistake, therefore, resulting

1. Aristotle *Physics* 1.9.192a20–24, in *The Complete Works of Aristotle*, rev. Oxford trans., ed. Jonathan Barnes, 2 vols. (Princeton, N.J., 1984), 1:328.

from an imperfect act of generation. Every female born was considered a "defective" or "mutilated" male (as Aristotle's terminology has variously been translated), a "monstrosity" of nature.[2]

For Greek theorists, the biology of males and females was the key to their psychology. The female was softer and more docile, more apt to be despondent, querulous, and deceitful. Being incomplete, moreover, she craved sexual fulfillment in intercourse with a male. The male was intellectual, active, and in control of his passions.

These psychological polarities derived from the theory that the universe consisted of four elements (earth, fire, air, and water), expressed in human bodies as four "humors" (black bile, yellow bile, blood, and phlegm) considered respectively dry, hot, damp, and cold and corresponding to mental states ("melancholic," "choleric," "sanguine," "phlegmatic"). In this schematization, the male, sharing the principles of earth and fire, was dry and hot; the female, sharing the principles of air and water, was cold and damp.

Female psychology was further affected by her dominant organ, the uterus (womb), *hystera* in Greek. The passions generated by the womb made women lustful, deceitful, talkative, irrational, indeed—when these affects were in excess—"hysterical."

Aristotle's biology also had social and political consequences. If the male principle was superior and the female inferior, then in the household, as in the state, men should rule and women must be subordinate. That hierarchy does not rule out the companionship of husband and wife, whose cooperation was necessary for the welfare of children and the preservation of property. Such mutuality supported male preeminence.

Aristotle's teacher Plato suggested a different possibility: that men and women might possess the same virtues. The setting for this proposal is the imaginary and ideal Republic that Plato sketches in a dialogue of that name. Here, for a privileged elite capable of leading wisely, all distinctions of class and wealth dissolve, as do, consequently, those of gender. Without households or property, as Plato constructs his ideal society, there is no need for the subordination of women. Women may, therefore, be educated to the same level as men to assume leadership responsibilities. Plato's Republic remained imaginary, however. In real societies, the subordination of women remained the norm and the prescription.

The views of women inherited from the Greek philosophical tradition became the basis for medieval thought. In the thirteenth century, the supreme scholastic philosopher Thomas Aquinas, among others, still echoed

2. Aristotle *Generation of Animals* 2.3.737a27–28, in *The Complete Works*, 1:1144.

Aristotle's views of human reproduction, of male and female personalities, and of the preeminent male role in the social hierarchy.

ROMAN LAW AND THE FEMALE CONDITION. Roman law, like Greek philosophy, underlay medieval thought and shaped medieval society. The ancient belief that adult, property-owning men should administer households and make decisions affecting the community at large is the very fulcrum of Roman law.

Around 450 B.C.E., during Rome's republican era, the community's customary law was recorded (legendarily) on twelve tablets erected in the city's central forum. It was later elaborated by professional jurists whose activity increased in the imperial era, when much new legislation, especially on issues affecting family and inheritance, was passed. This growing, changing body of laws was eventually codified in the *Corpus of Civil Law* under the direction of the Emperor Justinian, generations after the empire ceased to be ruled from Rome. That *Corpus*, read and commented on by medieval scholars from the eleventh century on, inspired the legal systems of most of the cities and kingdoms of Europe.

Laws regarding dowries, divorce, and inheritance pertain primarily to women. Since those laws aimed to maintain and preserve property, the women concerned were those from the property-owning minority. Their subordination to male family members points to the even greater subordination of lower-class and slave women, about whom the laws speak little.

In the early republic, the *paterfamilias*, or "father of the family," possessed *patria potestas*, "paternal power." The term *pater*, "father," in both these cases does not necessarily mean biological father but rather head of household. The father was the person who owned the household's property and, indeed, its human members. The *paterfamilias* had absolute power—including the power, rarely exercised, of life or death—over his wife, his children, and his slaves, as much as his cattle.

Children could be "emancipated," an act that granted legal autonomy and the right to own property. Male children over fourteen could be emancipated by a special grant from the father or, automatically, by their father's death. But females could never be emancipated; instead, they passed from the authority of their father to a husband or, if widowed or orphaned while still unmarried, to a guardian or tutor.

Marriage under its traditional form placed the woman under her husband's authority, or *manus*. He could divorce her on grounds of adultery, drinking wine, or stealing from the household, but she could not divorce him. She could neither possess property in her own right nor bequeath any to her children upon her death. When her husband died, the household property passed not to her but to his male heirs. And when her father died, she had no claim to any family inheritance, which was directed to her brothers or more remote male relatives. The effect of these laws was to exclude women from civil society, itself based on property ownership.

In the later republican and imperial periods, these rules were significantly modified. Women rarely married according to the traditional form but according to the form of "free" marriage. That practice allowed a woman to remain under her father's authority, to possess property given her by her father (most frequently the "dowry," recoverable from the husband's household in the event of his death), and to inherit from her father. She could also bequeath property to her own children and divorce her husband, just as he could divorce her.

Despite this greater freedom, women still suffered enormous disability under Roman law. Heirs could belong only to the father's side, never the mother's. Moreover, although she could bequeath her property to her children, she could not establish a line of succession in doing so. A woman was "the beginning and end of her own family," said the jurist Ulpian. Moreover, women could play no public role. They could not hold public office, represent anyone in a legal case, or even witness a will. Women had only a private existence and no public personality.

The dowry system, the guardian, women's limited ability to transmit wealth, and total political disability are all features of Roman law adopted, although modified according to local customary laws, by the medieval communities of western Europe.

CHRISTIAN DOCTRINE AND WOMEN'S PLACE. The Hebrew Bible and the Christian New Testament authorized later writers to limit women to the realm of the family and to burden them with the guilt of original sin. The passages most fruitful for this purpose were the creation narratives in Genesis and sentences from the Epistles defining women's role within the Christian family and community.

Each of the first two chapters of Genesis contains a creation narrative. In the first "God created man in his own image, in the image of God he created him; male and female he created them" (New Revised Standard Version, Gen. 1:27). In the second, God created Eve from Adam's rib (2:21–23). Christian theologians relied principally on Genesis 2 for their understanding of the relation between man and woman, interpreting the creation of Eve from Adam as proof of her subordination to him.

The creation story in Genesis 2 leads to that of the temptations in Genesis 3: of Eve by the wily serpent and of Adam by Eve. As read by Christian theologians from Tertullian to Thomas Aquinas, the narrative made Eve responsible for the Fall and its consequences. She instigated the act; she deceived her husband; she suffered the greater punishment. Her disobedience made it necessary for Jesus to be incarnated and to die on the cross. From the pulpit, moralists and preachers for centuries conveyed to women the guilt that they bore for original sin.

The Epistles offered advice to early Christians on building communities of the faithful. Among the matters to be regulated was the place of women. Paul offered views favorable to women in Galatians 3:28: "There is neither Jew nor Greek, there is neither slave nor free, there is neither male nor female; for you are all one in Christ Jesus." Paul also referred to women as his coworkers and placed them on a par with himself and his male coworkers (Phil. 4:2–3; Rom. 16:1–3; 1 Cor. 16:19). Elsewhere, Paul limited women's possibilities: "But I want you to understand that the head of every man is Christ, the head of a woman is her husband, and the head of Christ is God" (1 Cor. 11:3).

Biblical passages by later writers (though attributed to Paul) enjoined women to forgo jewels, expensive clothes, and elaborate coiffures; and they forbade women to "teach or have authority over men," telling them to "learn in silence with all submissiveness," as is proper for one responsible for sin, consoling them, however, with the thought that they will be saved through childbearing (1 Tim. 2:9–15). Other texts among the later Epistles defined women as the weaker sex and emphasized their subordination to their husbands (1 Pet. 3:7; Col. 3:18; Eph. 5:22–23).

These passages from the New Testament became the arsenal employed by theologians of the early church to transmit negative attitudes toward women to medieval Christian culture—above all, Tertullian ("On the Apparel of Women"), Jerome (*Against Jovinian*), and Augustine (*The Literal Meaning of Genesis*).

THE IMAGE OF WOMEN IN MEDIEVAL LITERATURE. The philosophical, legal, and religious traditions born in antiquity formed the basis of the medieval intellectual synthesis wrought by trained thinkers, mostly clerics, writing in Latin and based largely in universities. The vernacular literary tradition that developed alongside the learned tradition also spoke about female nature and women's roles. Medieval stories, poems, and epics also portrayed women negatively—as lustful and deceitful—while praising good housekeepers and loyal wives as replicas of the Virgin Mary or the female saints and martyrs.

There is an exception in the movement of "courtly love" that evolved in southern France from the twelfth century. Courtly love was the erotic love between a nobleman and noblewoman, the latter usually superior in social rank. It was always adulterous. From the conventions of courtly love derive modern Western notions of romantic love. The phenomenon has had an impact disproportionate to its size, for it affected only a tiny elite, and very few women. The exaltation of the female lover probably does not reflect a higher evaluation of women or a step toward their sexual liberation. More likely it gives expression to the social and sexual tensions besetting the knightly class at a specific historic juncture.

The literary fashion of courtly love was on the wane by the thirteenth century, when the widely read *Romance of the Rose* was composed in French by two authors of significantly different dispositions. Guillaume de Lorris composed the initial four thousand verses around 1235, and Jean de Meun added about seventeen thousand verses—more than four times the original—around 1265.

The fragment composed by Guillaume de Lorris stands squarely in the courtly love tradition. Here the poet, in a dream, is admitted into a walled garden where he finds a magic fountain in which a rosebush is reflected. He longs to pick one rose, but the thorns around it prevent his doing so, even as he is wounded by arrows from the God of Love, whose commands he agrees to obey. The remainder of this part of the poem recounts the poet's unsuccessful efforts to pluck the rose.

The longer part of the *Romance* by Jean de Meun also describes a dream. But here allegorical characters give long didactic speeches, providing a social satire on a variety of themes, including those pertaining to women. Love is an anxious and tormented state, the poem explains, women are greedy and manipulative, marriage is miserable, beautiful women are lustful, ugly ones cease to please, and a chaste woman, as rare as a black swan, can scarcely be found.

Shortly after Jean de Meun completed *The Romance of the Rose*, Mathéolus penned his *Lamentations*, a long Latin diatribe against marriage translated into French about a century later. The *Lamentations* sum up medieval attitudes toward women and provoked the important response by Christine de Pizan in her *Book of the City of Ladies*.

In 1355, Giovanni Boccaccio wrote *Il Corbaccio*, another antifeminist manifesto, though ironically by an author whose other works pioneered new directions in Renaissance thought. The former husband of his lover appears to Boccaccio, condemning his unmoderated lust and detailing the defects of women. Boccaccio concedes at the end "how much men naturally surpass women in nobility" and is cured of his desires.[3]

---

3. Giovanni Boccaccio, *The Corbaccio, or, The Labyrinth of Love*, trans. and ed. Anthony K. Cassell, 2d rev. ed. (Binghamton, N.Y., 1993), 71.

WOMEN'S ROLES: THE FAMILY. The negative perceptions of women expressed in the intellectual tradition are also implicit in the actual roles that women played in European society. Assigned to subordinate positions in the household and the church, they were barred from significant participation in public life.

Medieval European households, like those in antiquity and in non-Western civilizations, were headed by males. It was the male serf (or peasant), feudal lord, town merchant, or citizen who was polled or taxed or succeeded to an inheritance or had any acknowledged public role, although their wives or widows could stand on a temporary basis as surrogates for them. From about 1100, the position of property-holding males was enhanced further: inheritance was confined to the male, or agnate, line—with depressing consequences for women.

A wife never fully belonged to her husband's family, nor was she a daughter to her father's family. She left her father's house young to marry whomever her parents chose. Her dowry was managed by her husband and normally passed to her children by him at her death.

A married woman's life was occupied nearly constantly with cycles of pregnancy, childbearing, and lactation. Women bore children through all the years of their fertility, and many died in childbirth before the end of that term. They also bore responsibility for raising young children up to six or seven. That responsibility was shared in the propertied classes, since it was common for a wet-nurse to take over the job of breast-feeding, and servants took over other chores.

Women trained their daughters in the household responsibilities appropriate to their status, nearly always in tasks associated with textiles: spinning, weaving, sewing, embroidering. Their sons were sent out of the house as apprentices or students, or their training was assumed by fathers in later childhood and adolescence. On the death of her husband, a woman's children became the responsibility of his family. She generally did not take "his" children with her to a new marriage or back to her father's house, except sometimes in artisan classes.

Women also worked. Rural peasants performed farm chores, merchant wives often practiced their husband's trade, the unmarried daughters of the urban poor worked as servants or prostitutes. All wives produced or embellished textiles and did the housekeeping, while wealthy ones managed servants. These labors were unpaid or poorly paid but often contributed substantially to family wealth.

WOMEN'S ROLES: THE CHURCH. Membership in a household, whether a father's or a husband's, meant for women a lifelong subordination to others.

In western Europe, the Roman Catholic church offered an alternative to the career of wife and mother. A woman could enter a convent, parallel in function to the monasteries for men that evolved in the early Christian centuries.

In the convent, a woman pledged herself to a celibate life, lived according to strict community rules, and worshipped daily. Often the convent offered training in Latin, allowing some women to become considerable scholars and authors, as well as scribes, artists, and musicians. For women who chose the conventual life, the benefits could be enormous, but for numerous others placed in convents by paternal choice, the life could be restrictive and burdensome.

The conventual life declined as an alternative for women as the modern age approached. Reformed monastic institutions resisted responsibility for related female orders. The church increasingly restricted female institutional life by insisting on closer male supervision.

Women often sought other options. Some joined the communities of laywomen that sprang up spontaneously in the thirteenth century in the urban zones of western Europe, especially in Flanders and Italy. Some joined the heretical movements that flourished in late medieval Christendom, whose anticlerical and often antifamily positions particularly appealed to women. In these communities, some women were acclaimed as "holy women" or "saints," while others often were condemned as frauds or heretics.

In all, though the options offered to women by the church were sometimes less than satisfactory, sometimes they were richly rewarding. After 1520, the convent remained an option only in Roman Catholic territories. Protestantism engendered an ideal of marriage as a heroic endeavor and appeared to place husband and wife on a more equal footing. Sermons and treatises, however, still called for female subordination and obedience.

THE OTHER VOICE, 1300 – 1700

When the modern era opened, European culture was so firmly structured by a framework of negative attitudes toward women that to dismantle it was a monumental labor. The process began as part of a larger cultural movement that entailed the critical reexamination of ideas inherited from the ancient and medieval past. The humanists launched that critical reexamination.

THE HUMANIST FOUNDATION. Originating in Italy in the fourteenth century, humanism quickly became the dominant intellectual movement in Europe. Spreading in the sixteenth century from Italy to the rest of Europe, it fueled the literary, scientific, and philosophical movements of the era and laid the basis for the eighteenth-century Enlightenment.

Humanists regarded the scholastic philosophy of medieval universities as out of touch with the realities of urban life. They found in the rhetorical discourse of classical Rome a language adapted to civic life and public speech. They learned to read, speak, and write classical Latin and, eventually, classical Greek. They founded schools to teach others to do so, establishing the pattern for elementary and secondary education for the next three hundred years.

In the service of complex government bureaucracies, humanists employed their skills to write eloquent letters, deliver public orations, and formulate public policy. They developed new scripts for copying manuscripts and used the new printing press for the dissemination of texts, for which they created methods of critical editing.

Humanism was a movement led by males who accepted the evaluation of women in ancient texts and generally shared the misogynist perceptions of their culture. (Female humanists, as will be seen, did not.) Yet humanism also opened the door to a reevaluation of the nature and capacity of women. By calling authors, texts, and ideas into question, it made possible the fundamental rereading of the whole intellectual tradition that was required in order to free women from cultural prejudice and social subordination.

A DIFFERENT CITY. The other voice first appeared when, after so many centuries, the accumulation of misogynist concepts evoked a response from a capable woman female defender: Christine de Pizan (1365–1431). Introducing her *Book of the City of Ladies* (1405), she described how she was affected by reading Mathéolus's *Lamentations:* "Just the sight of this book . . . made me wonder how it happened that so many different men . . . are so inclined to express both in speaking and in their treatises and writings so many wicked insults about women and their behavior." These statements impelled her to detest herself "and the entire feminine sex, as though we were monstrosities in nature."[4]

The remainder of the *Book of the City of Ladies* presents a justification of the female sex and a vision of an ideal community of women. A pioneer, she has not simply received the message of female inferiority but, rather, she rejects it. From the fourteenth to the seventeenth century, a huge body of literature accumulated that responded to the dominant tradition.

The result was a literary explosion consisting of works by both men and women, in Latin and in the vernaculars: works enumerating the achieve-

---

4. Christine de Pizan, *The Book of the City of Ladies*, trans. Earl Jeffrey Richards, foreword by Marina Warner (New York, 1982), 1.1.1 (pp. 3–4), 1.1.1–2 (p. 5).

ments of notable women; works rebutting the main accusations made against women; works arguing for the equal education of men and women; works defining and redefining women's proper role in the family, at court, in public, describing women's lives and experiences. Recent monographs and articles have begun to hint at the great range of this phenomenon, involving probably several thousand titles. The protofeminism of these "other voices" constitutes a significant fraction of the literary product of the early modern era.

THE CATALOGS. Around 1365, the same Boccaccio whose *Corbaccio* rehearses the usual charges against female nature wrote another work, *Concerning Famous Women*. A humanist treatise drawing on classical texts, it praised 106 notable women, ninety-eight of them from pagan Greek and Roman antiquity, one (Eve) from the Bible, and seven from the medieval religious and cultural tradition; his book helped make all readers aware of a sex normally condemned or forgotten. Boccaccio's outlook, nevertheless, is unfriendly to women, for it singled out for praise those women who possessed the traditional virtues of chastity, silence, and obedience. Women who were active in the public realm, for example, rulers and warriors, were depicted as usually lascivious and as suffering terrible punishments for entering into the masculine sphere. Women were his subject, but Boccaccio's standard remained male.

Christine de Pizan's *Book of the City of Ladies* contains a second catalog, one responding specifically to Boccaccio's. Where Boccaccio portrays female virtue as exceptional, she depicts it as universal. Many women in history were leaders, or remained chaste despite the lascivious approaches of men, or were visionaries and brave martyrs.

The work of Boccaccio inspired a series of catalogs of illustrious women of the biblical, classical, Christian, and local past, among them Filippo da Bergamo's *Of Illustrious Women*, Pierre de Brantôme's *Lives of Illustrious Women*, Pierre Le Moyne's *Gallerie of Heroic Women*, and Pietro Paolo de Ribera's *Immortal Triumphs and Heroic Enterprises of 845 Women*. Whatever their embedded prejudices, these catalogs of illustrious women drove home to the public the possibility of female excellence.

THE DEBATE. At the same time, many questions remained: Could a woman be virtuous? Could she perform noteworthy deeds? Was she even, strictly speaking, of the same human species as men? These questions were debated over four centuries, in French, German, Italian, Spanish, and English, by authors male and female, among Catholics, Protestants, and Jews, in ponderous volumes and breezy pamphlets. The whole literary phenomenon has been called the *querelle des femmes*, the "woman question."

The opening volley of this battle occurred in the first years of the fifteenth century, in a literary debate sparked by Christine de Pizan. She exchanged letters critical of Jean de Meun's contribution to the *Romance of the Rose* with two French royal secretaries, Jean de Montreuil and Gontier Col. When the matter became public, Jean Gerson, one of Europe's leading theologians, supported de Pizan's arguments against de Meun, for the moment silencing the opposition.

The debate resurfaced repeatedly over the next two hundred years. *The Triumph of Women* (1438) by Juan Rodríguez de la Camara (or Juan Rodríguez del Padron) struck a new note by presenting arguments for the superiority of women to men. *The Champion of Women* (1440–42) by Martin Le Franc addresses once again the negative views of women presented in *The Romance of the Rose* and offers counterevidence of female virtue and achievement.

A cameo of the debate on women is included in the *Courtier,* one of the most read books of the era, published by the Italian Baldassare Castiglione in 1528 and immediately translated into other European vernaculars. The *Courtier* depicts a series of evenings at the court of the duke of Urbino in which many men and some women of the highest social stratum amuse themselves by discussing a range of literary and social issues. The "woman question" is a pervasive theme throughout, and the third of its four books is devoted entirely to that issue.

In a verbal duel, Gasparo Pallavicino and Giuliano de' Medici present the main claims of the two traditions. Gasparo argues the innate inferiority of women and their inclination to vice. Only in bearing children do they profit the world. Giuliano counters that women share the same spiritual and mental capacities as men and may excel in wisdom and action. Men and women are of the same essence: just as no stone can be more perfectly a stone than another, so no human being can be more perfectly human than others, whether male or female. It was an astonishing assertion, boldly made to an audience as large as all Europe.

THE TREATISES. Humanism provided the materials for a positive counterconcept to the misogyny embedded in scholastic philosophy and law and inherited from the Greek, Roman, and Christian pasts. A series of humanist treatises on marriage and family, on education and deportment, and on the nature of women helped construct these new perspectives.

The works by Francesco Barbaro and Leon Battista Alberti—*On Marriage* (1415) and *On the Family* (1434–37), respectively—far from defending female equality, reasserted women's responsibilities for rearing children and managing the housekeeping while being obedient, chaste, and silent. Nevertheless, they served the cause of reexamining the issue of women's nature by placing domestic issues at the center of scholarly concern and reopening the pertinent classical texts. In addition, Barbaro emphasized the companionate nature of marriage and the importance of a wife's spiritual and mental qualities for the well-being of the family.

These themes reappear in later humanist works on marriage and the education of women by Juan Luis Vives and Erasmus. Both were moderately sympathetic to the condition of women, without reaching beyond the usual masculine prescriptions for female behavior.

An outlook more favorable to women characterizes the nearly unknown work *In Praise of Women* (ca. 1487) by the Italian humanist Bartolommeo Goggio. In addition to providing a catalog of illustrious women, Goggio argued that male and female are the same in essence, but that women (reworking from quite a new angle the Adam and Eve narrative) are actually superior. In the same vein, the Italian humanist Maria Equicola asserted the spiritual equality of men and women in *On Women* (1501). In 1525, Galeazzo Flavio Capra (or Capella) published his work *On the Excellence and Dignity of Women.* This humanist tradition of treatises defending the worthiness of women culminates in the work of Henricus Cornelius Agrippa *On the Nobility and Preeminence of the Female Sex.* No work by a male humanist more succinctly or explicitly presents the case for female dignity.

THE WITCH BOOKS. While humanists grappled with the issues pertaining to women and family, other learned men turned their attention to what they perceived as a very great problem: witches. Witch-hunting manuals, explorations of the witch phenomenon, and even defenses of witches are not at first glance pertinent to the tradition of the other voice. But they do relate in this way: most accused witches were women. The hostility aroused by supposed witch activity is comparable to the hostility aroused by women. The evil deeds the victims of the hunt were charged with were exaggerations of the vices to which, many believed, all women were prone.

The connection between the witch accusation and the hatred of women is explicit in the notorious witch-hunting manual, *The Hammer of Witches* (1486), by two Dominican inquisitors, Heinrich Krämer and Jacob Sprenger. Here the inconstancy, deceitfulness, and lustfulness traditionally associated with women are depicted in exaggerated form as the core features of witch behavior. These traits inclined women to make a bargain with the devil— sealed by sexual intercourse—by which they acquired unholy powers. Such bizarre claims, far from being rejected by rational men, were broadcast by intellectuals. The German Ulrich Molitur, the Frenchman Nicolas Rémy, and the Italian Stefano Guazzo all coolly informed the public of sinister orgies and midnight pacts with the devil. The celebrated French jurist, historian, and political philosopher Jean Bodin argued that because women were especially prone to diabolism, regular legal procedures could properly be suspended in order to try those accused of this "exceptional crime."

A few experts raised their voices in protest, such as the physician Johann Weyer, a student of Agrippa's. In 1563, he explained the witch phenomenon thus, without discarding belief in diabolism: the devil deluded foolish old women afflicted by melancholia, causing them to believe that they had magical powers. Weyer's rational skepticism, which had good credibility in the community of the learned, worked to revise the conventional views of women and witchcraft.

WOMEN'S WORKS. To the many categories of works produced on the question of women's worth must be added nearly all works written by women. A woman writing was in herself a statement of women's claim to dignity.

Only a few women wrote anything prior to the dawn of the modern era, for three reasons. First, they rarely received the education that would enable them to write. Second, they were not admitted to the public roles—as administrator, bureaucrat, lawyer or notary, or university professor—in which they might gain knowledge of the kinds of things the literate public thought worth writing about. Third, the culture imposed silence upon women and considered speaking out a form of unchastity. Given these conditions, it is remarkable that any women wrote. Those who did before the fourteenth century were almost always nuns or religious women whose isolation made their pronouncements more acceptable.

From the fourteenth century on, the volume of women's writings crescendoed. Women continued to write devotional literature, although not always as cloistered nuns. They also wrote diaries, often intended as keepsakes for their children; books of advice to their sons and daughters; letters to family members and friends; and family memoirs, in a few cases elaborate enough to be considered histories.

A few women wrote works directly concerning the "woman question," and some of these, such as the humanists Isotta Nogarola, Cassandra Fedele, Laura Cereta, and Olympia Morata, were highly trained. A few were professional writers, living by the income of their pen—the very first among them being Christine de Pizan, noteworthy in this context as in so many others. In addition to *The Book of the City of Ladies* and her critiques of *The Romance of the Rose,* she wrote *The Treasure of the City of Ladies* (a guide to social decorum for women), an advice book for her son, much courtly verse, and a full-scale history of the reign of King Charles V of France.

WOMEN PATRONS. Women who did not themselves write, but encouraged others to do so, boosted the development of an alternative tradition. Highly placed women patrons supported authors, artists, musicians, poets, and learned men. Such patrons, drawn mostly from the Italian elites and the courts of northern Europe, figure disproportionately as the dedicatees of the important works of early feminism.

For a start, it might be noted that the catalogs of Boccaccio and Alvaro de Luna were dedicated to the Florentine noblewoman Andrea Acciaiuoli and Doña María, first wife of King Juan II of Castile, while the French translation of Boccaccio's work was commissioned by Anne of Brittany, wife of King Charles VIII of France. The humanist treatises of Goggio, Equicola, Vives, and Agrippa were dedicated, respectively, to Eleanora of Aragon, wife of Ercole I d'Este, Duke of Ferrara; to Margherita Cantelma of Mantua; to Catherine of Aragon, wife of King Henry VIII of England; and to Margaret, Duchess of Austria and Regent of the Netherlands. As late as 1696, Mary Astell's *Serious Proposal to the Ladies, for the Advancement of Their True and Greatest Interest* was dedicated to Princess Ann of Denmark.

These authors presumed that their efforts would be welcome to female patrons, or they may have written at the bidding of those patrons. Silent themselves, perhaps even unresponsive, these loftily placed women helped shape the tradition of the other voice.

THE ISSUES. The literary forms and patterns in which the tradition of the other voice presented itself have now been sketched. It remains to highlight the major issues around which this tradition crystallizes. In brief, there are four problems to which our authors return again and again, in plays and catalogs, in verse and in letters, in treatises and dialogues, in every language: the problem of chastity; the problem of power; the problem of speech; and the problem of knowledge. Of these the greatest, preconditioning the others, is the problem of chastity.

THE PROBLEM OF CHASTITY. In traditional European culture, as in those of antiquity and others around the globe, chastity was perceived as woman's quintessential virtue—in contrast to courage, or generosity, or leadership, or rationality, seen as virtues characteristic of men. Opponents of women charged them with insatiable lust. Women themselves and their de-fenders—without disputing the validity of the standard—responded that women were capable of chastity.

The requirement of chastity kept women at home, silenced them, iso-lated them, left them in ignorance. It was the source of all other impedi-ments. Why was it so important to the society of men, of whom chastity was not required, and who, more often than not, considered it their right to vio-late the chastity of any woman they encountered?

Female chastity ensured the continuity of the male-headed household. If a man's wife was not chaste, he could not be sure of the legitimacy of his off-spring. If they were not his, and they acquired his property, it was not his household, but some other man's, that had endured. If his daughter was not chaste, she could not be transferred to another man's household as his wife, and he was dishonored.

The whole system of the integrity of the household and the transmission of property was bound up in female chastity. Such a requirement only had an impact on property-owning classes, of course. Poor women could not expect to maintain their chastity, least of all if they were in contact with high-status men to whom all women but those of their own household were prey.

In Catholic Europe, the requirement of chastity was further buttressed by moral and religious imperatives. Original sin was inextricably linked with the sexual act. Virginity was seen as heroic virtue, far more impressive than, say, the avoidance of idleness or greed. Monasticism, the cultural institution that dominated medieval Europe for centuries, was grounded in the renunci-ation of the flesh. The Catholic reform of the eleventh century imposed a similar standard on all the clergy and a heightened awareness of sexual re-quirements on all the laity. Although men were asked to be chaste, female un-chastity was much worse: it led to the devil, as Eve had led mankind to sin.

To such requirements, women and their defenders protested their inno-cence. Furthermore, following the example of holy women who had escaped the requirements of family and sought the religious life, some women began to conceive of female communities as alternatives both to family and to the cloister. Christine de Pizan's city of ladies was such a community. Moderata Fonte and Mary Astell envisioned others. The luxurious salons of the French *précieuses* of the seventeenth century, or the comfortable English drawing rooms of the next, may have been born of the same impulse. Here women might not only escape, if briefly, the subordinate position that life in the fam-ily entailed, but they might make claims to power, exercise their capacity for speech, and display their knowledge.

THE PROBLEM OF POWER. Women were excluded from power: the

whole cultural tradition insisted on it. Only men were citizens, only men bore arms, only men could be chiefs or lords or kings. There were exceptions, which did not disprove the rule, when wives or widows or mothers took the place of men, awaiting their return or the maturation of a male heir. A woman who attempted to rule in her own right was perceived as an anomaly, a monster, at once a deformed woman and an insufficient male, sexually confused and, consequently, unsafe.

The association of such images with women who held or sought power explains some otherwise odd features of early modern culture. Queen Elizabeth I of England, one of the few women to hold full regal authority in European history, played with such male/female images—positive ones, of course—in representing herself to her subjects. She was a prince, and manly, even though she was female. She was also (she claimed) virginal, a condition absolutely essential if she was to avoid the attacks of her opponents. Catherine de' Medici, who ruled France as widow and regent for her sons, also adopted such imagery in defining her position. She chose as one symbol the figure of Artemisia, an androgynous ancient warrior-heroine, who combined a female persona with masculine powers.

Power in a woman, without such sexual imagery, seems to have been indigestible by the culture. A rare note was struck by the Englishman Sir Thomas Elyot in his *Defence of Good Women* (1540), justifying both women's participation in civic life and prowess in arms. The old tune was sung by the Scots reformer John Knox in his *First Blast of the Trumpet against the Monstrous Regiment of Women* (1558), for whom rule by women, defects in nature, was a hideous contradiction in terms.

The confused sexuality of the imagery of female potency was not reserved for rulers. Any woman who excelled was likely to be called an Amazon, recalling the self-mutilated warrior women of antiquity who repudiated all men, gave up their sons, and raised only their daughters. She was often said to have "exceeded her sex" or to have possessed "masculine virtue"—as the very fact of conspicuous excellence conferred masculinity, even on the female subject. The catalogs of notable women often showed those female heroes dressed in armor, armed to the teeth, like men. Amazonian heroines romp through the epics of the age—Ariosto's *Orlando Furioso* (1532) and Spenser's *Faerie Queene* (1590–1609). Excellence in a woman was perceived as a claim for power, and power was reserved for the masculine realm. A woman who possessed either was masculinized and lost title to her own female identity.

THE PROBLEM OF SPEECH. Just as power had a sexual dimension when it was claimed by women, so did speech. A good woman spoke little. Excessive speech was an indication of unchastity. By speech, women seduced

men. Eve had lured Adam into sin by her speech. Accused witches were commonly accused of having spoken abusively, or irrationally, or simply too
much. As enlightened a figure as Francesco Barbaro insisted on silence in a
woman, which he linked to her perfect unanimity with her husband's will and
her unblemished virtue (i.e., her chastity). Another Italian humanist, Leonardo
Bruni, in advising a noblewoman on her studies, barred her not from speech
but from public speaking. That was reserved for men.

Related to the problem of speech was that of costume—another, if silent,
form of self-expression. Assigned the task of pleasing men as their primary
occupation, elite women often tended toward elaborate costume, hairdress-
ing, and the use of cosmetics. Clergy and secular moralists alike condemned
these practices. The appropriate function of costume and adornment was to
announce the status of a woman's husband or father. Any further indulgence
in adornment was akin to unchastity.

THE PROBLEM OF KNOWLEDGE. When the Italian noblewoman
Isotta Nogarola had begun to attain a reputation as a humanist, she was accused of incest—a telling instance of the association of learning in women
with unchastity. That chilling association inclined any woman who was educated to deny that she was or to make exaggerated claims of heroic chastity.

If educated women were pursued with suspicions of sexual misconduct,
women seeking an education faced an even more daunting obstacle: the assumption that women were by nature incapable of learning, that reason was
a particularly masculine ability. Just as they proclaimed their chastity, women
and their defenders insisted on their capacity for learning. The major work
by a male writer on female education—that by Juan Luis Vives, *On the Education of a Christian Woman* (1523)—granted female capacity for intellection but
still argued that a woman's whole education was to be shaped around the requirement of chastity and a future within the household. Female writers
of the next generations—Marie de Gournay in France, Anna Maria van
Schurman in Holland, Mary Astell in England—began to envision other
possibilities.

The pioneers of female education were the Italian women humanists
who managed to attain a Latin literacy and knowledge of classic and Christian literature equivalent to that of prominent men. Their works implicitly
and explicitly raise questions about women's social roles, defining problems
that beset women attempting to break out of the cultural limits that had
bound them. Like Christine de Pizan, who achieved an advanced education
through her father's tutoring and her own devices, their bold questioning
makes clear the importance of training. Only when women were educated to
the same standard as male leaders would they be able to raise that other voice

and insist on their dignity as human beings morally, intellectually, and legally equal to men.

THE OTHER VOICE. The other voice, a voice of protest, was mostly female, but it was also male. It spoke in the vernaculars and in Latin, in treatises and dialogues, in plays and poetry, in letters and diaries, and in pamphlets. It battered at the wall of prejudice that encircled women and raised a banner announcing its claims. The female was equal to (or even superior to) the male in essential nature—moral, spiritual, intellectual. Women were capable of higher education, of holding positions of power and influence in the public realm, and of speaking and writing persuasively. The last bastion of masculine supremacy, centered on the notions of a woman's primary domestic responsibility and the requirement of female chastity, was not as yet assaulted— although visions of productive female communities as alternatives to the family indicated an awareness of the problem.

During the period 1300–1700, the other voice remained only a voice, and one only dimly heard. It did not result—yet—in an alteration of social patterns. Indeed, to this day, they have not entirely been altered. Yet the call for justice issued as long as six centuries ago by those writing in the tradition of the other voice must be recognized as the source and origin of the mature feminist tradition and of the realignment of social institutions accomplished in the modern age.

We would like to thank the volume editors in this series, who responded with many suggestions to an earlier draft of this introduction, making it a collaborative enterprise. Many of their suggestions and criticisms have resulted in revisions of this introduction, though we remain responsible for the final product.

PROJECTED TITLES IN THE SERIES

Chiara Matraini, *Selected Poetry and Prose*, edited and translated by Elaine MacLachlan

Olympia Morata, *Complete Writings*, edited and translated by Holt N. Parker

Isotta Nogarola, *Selected Letters*, edited and translated by Margaret L. King and Diana Robin

Jacqueline Pascal, *"A Rule for Children" and Other Writings*, edited and translated by John Conley, S.J.

Eleonora Petersen von Merlau, *Autobiography* (1718), edited and translated by Barbara Becker-Cantarino

Alessandro Piccolomini, *Rethinking Marriage in Sixteenth-Century Italy*, edited and translated by Letizia Panizza

In Praise of Women: Italian Fifteenth-Century Defenses of Women, edited and translated by Daniel Bornstein

Madeleine and Catherine des Roches, *Selected Letters, Dialogues, and Poems*, edited and translated by Anne Larsen

Oliva Sabuco, *The New Philosophy: True Medicine*, edited and translated by Gianna Pomata

Margherita Sarrocchi, *La Scanderbeide*, edited and translated by Rinaldina Russell

Madeleine de Scudéry, *Orations and Rhetorical Dialogues*, edited and translated by Jane Donawerth with Julie Strongson

Madeleine de Scudéry, *Sapho*, edited and translated by Karen Newman

Justine Siegemund, *The Court Midwife of the Electorate of Brandenburg* (1690), edited and translated by Lynne Tatlock

Gabrielle Suchon, *"On Philosophy" and "On Morality,"* edited and translated by Domna Stanton with Rebecca Wilkin

Sara Copio Sullam, *Sara Copio Sullam: Jewish Poet and Intellectual in Early Seventeenth-Century Venice*, edited and translated by Don Harrán

Arcangela Tarabotti, *Convent Life as Inferno: A Report*, introduction and notes by Francesca Medioli, translated by Letizia Panizza

Francesco Buoninsegni and Arcangela Tarabotti, *Menippean Satire: "Against Feminine Extravagance" and "Antisatire,"* edited and translated by Elissa Weaver

Arcangela Tarabotti, *Paternal Tyranny*, edited and translated by Letizia Panizza

Laura Terracina, *Works*, edited and translated by Michael Sherberg

Katharina Schütz Zell, *Selected Writings*, edited and translated by Elsie McKee

THREE
CARTESIAN FEMINIST
TREATISES

INTRODUCTION:
POULLAIN DE LA BARRE'S
CARTESIAN FEMINISM

THE OTHER VOICE IN POULLAIN'S FEMINIST WORKS

During a short three-year period at the end of the *Querelle des femmes*, as the "Woman Question" debate was known in French society in the seventeenth century, François Poullain wrote three treatises on women's nature and destiny that departed noticeably from the traditional discourse on women's fate in a patriarchal society. Bringing Cartesian objectivity to gender issues, he published *On the Equality of the Two Sexes: A Physical and Moral Discourse which Shows the Importance of Getting Rid of One's Prejudices* anonymously in 1673, which addressed cultural inequalities between the sexes.[1] The following year, he published *On the Education of Ladies: For Training the Mind in the Sciences and in Moral Judgment*, in which he advocated an enlightened education, soundly grounded in Cartesian philosophy, for women of leisure. Then in 1675, and in spite of its misleading and incomplete title, *On the Excellence of Men: Against the Equality of Sexes*, he applied the concept of equality between the sexes to a refutation of misogynist scholastic discourse. By systematically employing Cartesian methodology Poullain rejected tradition as a means of dealing with the issue of feminism.[2]

In spite of the development of an urban, polite society that fostered the idea of some intellectual activities among ladies of quality, by and large throughout the seventeenth century attitudes toward women's learning persisted in reflecting the old axiom of female mental inferiority, which in turn justified women's subordination.[3] Notably, with the rise of the regime of Louis XIV a stricter adherence to social conformity evolved into a self-

---

1. François Poullain de la Barre, *De l'Egalité des deux sexes* (Paris, 1984).

2. Madeleine Alcover, *Poullain de la Barre: Une aventure philosophique* (Paris, Seattle, and Tübingen, 1981), 24–30.

3. Linda Timmermans, *L'Accès des femmes à la culture (1598–1715): Un débat d'idées de Saint François de Sales à la Marquise de Lambert* (Paris, 1993), 63–132.

censoring ideology of the elite. By the time Poullain came of age, the ever-powerful rules of *bienséance* had proclaimed "the indecency of knowledge" for the weaker sex.[4] One has only to read Molière's satires on women's intellectual endeavors to comprehend the magnitude of Poullain's task.[5] Members of the worldly society that characterized French classical culture regarded with contempt the display of knowledge from both sexes. In this *mondain* social context, most of the women salon-holders known as *salonnières* seemed satisfied with the powers derived from their more traditional "women's virtues." Suspicion of pedantry could ruin anyone's reputation. By the last quarter of the century, their sexual "difference" would entitle them only to exert a superficial influence within the boundaries set by the mondain order. Women with intellectual inclinations had to face expulsion from the group (as in Molière's *Les Femmes savantes*) or comply with the status quo of silence and hide their knowledge.[6] A third alternative seemed to be safer, to choose ignorance.

Poullain believed otherwise. Driven by Descartes's unequivocal certainty found in the *cogito* that established the supremacy of mind over body, Poullain extended the challenge of rational thinking to the polemics of sex and gender. He deduced that since the "mind has no sex" (*Equality*, 82), discrimination between the sexes could not, rationally speaking, be accepted as the truth whether enshrined by tradition or not. The female gender carried as much intellectual potential as its male counterpart because a lack of physical strength had no correlation with a weaker mind. Descartes's *good sense* explained it all, and his maxims provided Poullain with the means to unmask prejudices. Women should not be denied the benefit of scholarship because of their presumed flawed nature. On the contrary, men themselves were responsible for maintaining women in a state of ignorance for fear of losing their own advantage. Customs and traditions, terms Poullain often uses to refer to cultural idiosyncrasies, have predetermined women's subordinate status. In this premise of natural rights resides the core of Poullain's original stand for the recognition of equality between the sexes: men created laws that benefited themselves while subjecting women to a lesser role. In our own day, Simone de Beauvoir was prompted to recall along with Poullain that "whatever men wrote about women should be suspect as they are both judges

4. Madeleine Alcover, "The Indecency of Knowledge," *Rice University Studies* 64 (1978): 25–39.
5. *Les Précieuses ridicules*, 1659, and *Les Femmes savantes*, 1672, which triggered Poullain's response.
6. Timmermans, *L'Accès des femmes à la culture*, 319–86. Erica Harth, *Cartesian Women* (Ithaca, 1992), 17: "It is true that over the centuries there have been few, if any, French institutions in which women have been so central. However, when we turn the lens back to the seventeenth century and its male-dominated intellectual institutions, the salon appears in a new light."

and interested parties."[7] Thus, any reasoning on the theory of female inferiority could only lead to a self-fulfilling devalued outcome that in a perverse way conformed to biased masculine expectations. In Poullain's Cartesian quest for absolute certainty, female nature had little to do with women's intellectual infirmities.

As a true believer in the power of reason over the authority of tradition, Poullain advanced intellectual, political, and social theses on gender equality that foreshadowed the achievements of centuries to come. For some philosophers like Montesquieu and Rousseau, Poullain's theories merged with their own, whereas many other minor authors simply used his ideas without proper attribution during the Enlightenment. More significantly, Poullain formulated the question of knowledge and power for women in terms of absolute equality that in retrospect could only be implemented within the legal apparatus of our contemporary institutions.[8]

Probably unknown to Poullain himself, his claims for gender equality sought to put on trial the foundations of French patriarchal ideology at a time of increasingly tense repression from the monarchy. Beginning in 1661, Louis XIV had consolidated the power of the state in his own hands. The Sun King embodied absolute law and order aimed at the preservation of the nation's social stability. By choice or for social survival, especially among feminine circles, French readers therefore remained vastly indifferent to Poullain's first awakening call in 1673.

POULLAIN'S LIFE AND WORKS

Poullain de la Barre was born in Paris in July 1648, "of an honorable Catholic family sufficiently wealthy to permit him to study with ease and distinction for the priesthood and a doctorate, both of which he was destined for from childhood," according to Moréri's *Grand Dictionnaire historique*.[9] However, Poullain was not to submit easily to this prescribed path. Contrary to family expectations that he would rise to high clerical office, he married, sired two children, and was a Calvinist when he died in Geneva in May 1723. Long before, he had abandoned the Roman Catholic Church without achieving the ultimate scholar's goal of a doctor's degree in theology. Seemingly not a rebellious man by nature, two significant events occurred that had serious na-

---

7. Simone de Beauvoir quoted this sentence from memory as an epigram to the first volume of the complete French version of *Le Deuxième Sexe* (Paris, 1949).

8. Geneviève Fraisse, "Poullain de la Barre ou le procès des préjugés," *Corpus* 1 (1985): 28–29.

9. Alcover, *Poullain*, 111, citing Louis Moréri, *Le Grand Dictionnaire historique ou le Mélange curieux de l'histoire sacrée et profane* (Basle: Jean Brandmuller, 1733), 6:1101.

tional consequences for France's absolute monarchy and that also shaped Poullain's choices. The first factor that led to his quiet defiance of gender conventions was the dissemination and popularization of Cartesian philosophy among Parisian salons, notwithstanding the church's censure in the 1660s. The second catalyst that ultimately triggered his rejection of his social background was Louis XIV's Révocation of the Edict of Nantes in 1685, prohibiting religious freedom and more generally freedom of expression.

Until his fortuitous discovery of Cartesian philosophy, probably in some undocumented social setting around 1667, Poullain had followed the conventional path for students of scholastic philosophy of becoming a Catholic priest. Under the guise of Stasimachus, the "Philosopher" in his *On the Education of Ladies,* Poullain recalled "studying from nine to twenty with great zeal and considerable success for a student" (245). Madeleine Alcover's biographical research on his formal academic training has established the following chronology: (1) Poullain received the level of "Maître ès Arts" on July 15, 1663, just around his fifteenth birthday; (2) immediately after, he joined the College of Theology at the Sorbonne, which adhered strictly to Saint Thomas Aquinas's teachings; (3) he completed his bachelor's degree in three years instead of the usually required five years of study and at a much younger age than the normal twentieth birthday. However, in spite of his remarkable achievements, young Poullain was ready to abandon completely the secure realm of academic conformity. Seven or eight years later, in his treatise on women's education, he would reflect upon the reasons and circumstances of his withdrawal. Generally speaking, his writings remained rather scarce in autobiographical insight. It is therefore significant that his fifth, and last, chapter in *On the Education of Ladies* recorded precisely his state of mind leading to the crisis. Whether moved by the desire to vindicate his own defection from scholasticism or determined to rally others to the modernist camp, Poullain proceeded to explain his general disaffection for the old school of thought:

> As far as my age allowed, I rose to the highest scientific degree our classics-dominated system awards to those who have studied the opinions it teaches. Then I started to think about what I had learned. I was appalled to realize that I'd been wasting my time and that my only qualifications were on parchment and titles. . . . I realized that everything I knew was of no use in the world except to make my way along a path I had no intention of taking.
> (*Education,* 245)

Thus, by the time he received his bachelor's degree in late 1666, Poullain was already considering abandoning further studies for the priesthood. Years of training in the Aristotelian tradition had left him "with nothing to say" (*Education*, 245).

His encounter with Cartesian rationalism became his intellectual salvation. It was love at first sight:

> When, one day, I found all the sciences of the Schools particularly distasteful, by a great stroke of luck I allowed myself to be taken off by a friend to hear a Cartesian lecturing on a subject concerning the human body. . . . I confess that I was astonished to hear nothing but what was clear and intelligible, to realize that he was reasoning on the basis of principles that were so simple and so true that I could not fail to agree with them, and to hear him draw conclusions from them that clarified in a few words certain mysteries that had completely baffled me. The more he spoke, the more I became convinced that he possessed reason and good sense.
>
> (*Education*, 245)

In all probability, Poullain had been attending the sort of public lectures that Cartesians like the physicist Jacques Rohault gave in Paris about that time.[10] Descartes's philosophy had become a fashionable subject of discussion in the *salons* of Paris and in the French provinces, appealing equally to learned gentlemen and highborn ladies. Like many other private academies that had flourished in France since the middle of the century, the conferences offered an interesting informal alternative to the more erudite, but pedantic and outmoded, setting of the university. For one thing, the discussions were conducted in the vernacular rather than in Latin; second, as in the case of Rohault's scientific experimentation, the questions addressed had the ring of novelty and good sense; and third, women were a welcome audience. The fact that the Roman Catholic Church had placed Descartes's works on the Index of Forbidden Books since 1663 did not deter his followers from embracing modernity. Undoubtedly, some element of snobbism explained the feminine response to the Cartesian fad of the 1660s, though, in the final analysis, Wendy Gibson is right to point out that their motives "matter less

---

10. Antoine Adam, *Grandeur and Illusion: French Literature and Society 1600–1715*, trans. Herbert Tint (New York, 1972), 129: "The Academies that came into being around 1660 were Cartesian. . . . Cartesianism had begun to conquer the highest positions of French society. Even the salons opened their doors to the new philosophy, and the ladies of society proclaimed that they were both learned and Cartesian. This was not merely because they wanted to be in fashion. Cartesianism had confidence in reason, and consequently in the inspiration of personal taste." See also Wendy Gibson, *Women in Seventeenth-Century France* (New York, 1989), 33: "The decision of professional philosophers, men of science and mathematicians to propagate the fruit of their research from the public rostrum was a momentous one for women. Philosophy, and mathematics beyond simple arithmetic formed no part of their school timetable. Sciences were generally neglected even in boys' educational establishments in favor of a predominantly literary culture."

than the fact that they made the effort to go there and that their minds were consequently exposed to forms of education elsewhere denied to them."[11] Poullain converted to Cartesianism just about the time Descartes's remains were brought back from Stockholm to Paris for burial, in 1667.

On the precise circumstances of Poullain's change of heart, Alcover has made the point that Poullain could not have met Cartesianism while frequenting another sort of popular public conference given at Jean de Richesource's Académie des Orateurs. On the contrary, the subject matter and format of the weekly debates there were still very much modeled after Aristotle's maxims and Saint Thomas's method. Would-be male orators seeking a career in law or in the church could practice public speaking in front of a real audience and mingle with ladies and gentlemen of the upper class.[12] Several speakers would argue in the affirmative and negative fine points of casuistry before Richesource gave his ruling on the matter under consideration. Among the topics debated were "Whether women's passions are more violent than men's," or "Whether the study of sciences and letters is suitable for ladies and whether it is useful to them."[13] Consequently, Poullain's presence in such mondain assemblies had to expose him to the gamut of recurring prejudices that defined the "Woman Question" in lay culture while remaining true to academic practice. Asked about his "view of women during that time," his answer was simple enough: "You can guess that as long as I was a scholastic I considered them scholastically, namely, as monsters, and very much inferior to men, because that's how Aristotle and some of the theologians I'd read considered them."[14] Thus, this part of Poullain's social life, coinciding with the Académie des Orateurs's high days in Paris between 1664 and 1666, had to precede his encounter with the new Cartesian philosophy.

Adherence to the logically self-evident truth expressed in the *Cogito ergo sum* had rendered questionable any knowledge based strictly on the authority of experts. *Bachelier* from the Sorbonne at the age of twenty, and by then utterly repelled by his former masters' obscurantism, Poullain left the Sorbonne, never to complete his final degree in theology. As he became committed to Cartesian methods, "allowing my memory to forget everything I had learned" (*Education*, 246), only six months of independent think-

---

11. Gibson, *Women in Seventeenth-Century France*, 34.

12. Marie-Louise Stock, "Poullain de la Barre: A Seventeenth-Century Feminist" (Ph.D. diss., Columbia University, 1961), 10, 13.

13. Alcover, *Poullain*, 14.

14. *Education*, 245. However, according to Siep Stuurman, "he made good use of his theological knowledge during the rest of his life" ("From Feminism to Biblical Criticism: The Theological Trajectory of François Poulain de la Barre, " *Eighteenth-Century Studies*, 33 [2000]: 368).

ing in the company of "reasonable people" sufficed to obliterate the sum of six years of bookish instruction. However, his Cartesian awakening also took him temporarily away from his former ecclesiastical goal.

One can only speculate on Poullain's secular activities during the following decade. For one thing, at the time he wrote *Education* in 1674 he had not "read any philosophy for three years now" (246). Marie-Louise Stock traced back to him a modest textbook, published anonymously in 1672, but later attributed to him, *Les Rapports de la langue latine avec la françoise pour traduire élégamment et sans peine. Avec un recueil étymologique & méthodique de cinq mille mots françois tirez immédiatement du latin.*[15] Essentially, he wrote a student handbook made of helpful hints on translation from Latin to French and vice versa, while he was earning a living in some teaching capacity.

What then could have prompted this radical cleric to publish in August 1673 *On the Equality of the Two Sexes?* Once he had severed his ties with the Ancients' school his intellectual quest for truth had found its perfect ground for testing the validity of Cartesian principles. On the basis of clear and distinct innate ideas Poullain launched a systematic attack on the faulty reasoning that had legitimated cultural bias against women: "Our choice fell on the question of the equality of the sexes, which is more prone to prejudice than any other subject" (*Equality*, 50).

His attempt was not an exercise in gallant eloquence designed to dazzle the fair sex accustomed to witty praise.

Just as his next two books on the subject would thoroughly justify his beliefs, there is no reason to doubt the sincerity of his personal commitment to the cause of women when he undertook his initial project in 1673. In fact, there were risks involved in taking to task the official discourse of the church and the university on women's equality issues. Although Descartes died in 1650, and although his philosophy still dominated the intellectual life of the Continent in the second half of the seventeenth century, in 1669, in France, doctoral candidates hoping to receive a degree in philosophy could only support anti-Cartesian theses. In 1671, the Archbishop of Paris considered eliminating any teaching adverse to the philosophy of the Schools.[16] Therefore, in the years 1673–74, Poullain was very much aware of the forces of censorship he chose to confront head on when he claimed to discover the truth by himself. In all the universities in France "Cartesians are in such bad

15. Stock, "Poullain de la Barre," 19–20.

16. Louis XIV forbad the popular physicist Pierre-Sylvain Régis from giving public lectures (with some spectacular demonstrations of Cartesian mechanism) because of the threat that Cartesianism posed to the very foundations of Aristotelian science, to the church's authority, and possibly to the divine right of the French monarchy.

odor that people won't even listen to them," he noted plainly in *On the Education of Ladies* (244), all the while eager to defend his controversial choice. In this climate of intellectual repression, any reference to Cartesian philosophy took on a particularly symbolic significance, especially for someone like Poullain who lived in a precarious social limbo. One should not underestimate his polemical tendencies in choosing to expose with great fortitude the weaknesses of the Ancients' schools of thought. For him, the state of ignorance and submission in which women were maintained had become just cause for redress. Yet, he had dropped out of the university. His livelihood as a language teacher in a Parisian school depended on the good will of the ecclesiastical authorities as well as on Poullain's good standing in the church: thus, the cover of anonymity for the first editions of his three essays, in 1673, 1674, and 1675.

It is highly probable that Molière's satire *Les Femmes savantes* bears responsibility in the actual timing of Poullain's involvement in the public arena. Performed for the first time in March 1672, the play attacked with a vengeance women's intellectual pursuits. Although Poullain never mentioned Molière by name (he rarely mentioned any author with the exception of the scholarly reading list that concludes his essay *On Education*), it is remarkable that so many of the arguments he presented in *On the Equality of the Two Sexes*, reprised and expanded in the other two treatises, refuted so convincingly the playwright's traditionalist discourse.[17] Obviously, Poullain wrote for, and in defense of, intelligent women he wished to distinguish from precisely the most extremist and misguided partisans of feminine emancipation, the kind of social misfits that Molière ridiculed so convincingly. Molière's comedy was at the expense of Cartesian ladies derelict in their domestic functions for science's sake. They were guilty of destructive female solipsism, making them an easy target for the proponents of patriarchal values. In this satire, educated women transgressed the prerogatives of their sex the instant they expressed an interest in matters of the mind. Feminine erudition beyond the realm of a rudimentary education was easily perceived as a threat to moral order. Laughter made light of learning that was conveniently confused with grotesque pedantry. Molière's ideas needed not to be new to be entertaining. He only reflected the consensus of the majority. His successful criticism of the *précieuses'* agenda went back to 1659 with his farce *Les Précieuses ridicules*. However now with his more sophisticated comedy in five acts, *Les Femmes savantes*, he struck a severe blow to the cause of women's intellectual emancipation, a blow from which it would take more than a generation to recover.

17. Marcelle Maistre Welch, "La Réponse de Poullain de la Barre aux *Femmes savantes* de Molière," *Ordre et contestation au temps des Classiques*, ed. Roger Duchêne and Pierre Ronzeaud, Biblio 17 (Paris, Seattle, and Tübingen, 1992), 1:183–91.

Witness Père Rapin's comment that *Les Précieuses ridicules* and *Les Femmes savantes* brought so much shame to the ladies that within fifteen days of Molière's latest production, women would rather be reputed for bad morals than distinguished for their knowledge.[18]

Poullain must have strongly enough regretted this turn of events to engage in a full-fledged defense of gender equality. The satire built on prejudices that coincidentally provided him with a worthy subject of critical thinking, a "clear-cut, obvious example that is of interest to everyone" (*Equality*, 50). By using the immemorial *topos* of a loathsome world-turned-upside-down for his domineering "learned ladies," Molière had played on misogynist fears that Poullain set out to denounce as not founded on reason.[19] Women's access to knowledge did not have to lead to social chaos, and learning did not have to breed feminine disruptive behavior. Certainly, *On the Equality of the Two Sexes* was meant to bring radical change to the dominant ideology of his times. By placing the blame for women's failings squarely on societal predicaments rather than innate attributes, Poullain extricated the old "Woman Question" from its abstract frame of reference.[20] The question had become socio-political and could hope for resolution only through socio-political changes. Remarkably, his Cartesian refusal of any authority except reason itself when asserting women's rights necessarily implied the broader, even riskier, thesis of individual rights for everyone in an egalitarian system. However, in 1673, very few, if any, readers perceived the revolutionary ideal that undergirded Poullain's feminist standpoint.

Despite his having given due warning of his "serious intent so that people do not get the wrong idea of it and reject it as frivolous" (*Equality*, 51), that is exactly what happened to the reception of *On the Equality of the Two Sexes* in 1673. To its author's greatest disappointment, few people paid serious attention to him, and those who read him failed to understand. The few précieuses remaining in the open applauded his general sense of equity, grateful to have another champion, but everybody else appeared to reduce his line of logic to another mere paradox that had more gallantry than truth.

Still, the following year, Poullain provided the blueprint for the founda-

18. Stock, "Poullain de la Barre," 173: "Madame de Lambert, writing in 1727, claims that by ridiculing women's intellectual preoccupations, the play had a pernicious effect on morals." In *Réflexions nouvelles sur les femmes, par une dame de la Cour de France* (Paris, 1728), 4.

19. Pierre Ronzaud, "La Femme au pouvoir ou le monde à l'envers," *XVIIe siècle* 108 (1975): 9–33. Natalie Zemon Davis, *Society and Culture in Early Modern France* (Stanford, 1975), 124–51; Marc Angenot, *Les Champions des femmes: Examen du discours sur la supériorité des femmes, 1400–1800* (Montréal, 1977), 148–49.

20. Alcover, *Poullain*, 45. Daniel Armogathe, "De l'Egalité des deux sexes, 'la belle question,'" *Corpus* 1 (1985): 23. Siep Stuurman, "Social Cartesianism: François Poulain de la Barre and the Origins of the Enlightenment," *Journal of the History of Ideas* 58 (1997): 617.

tion of a modern feminine education in his *On the Education of Ladies*. His initial intention was twofold: first, to train the minds of "mistresses" (i.e., women as professional educators), according to Cartesian methodology; and second, to "go into detail about the education of children" (*Education*, 141) with another treatise which, apparently, he never produced. *On the Education of Ladies* was the necessary companion book to *On the Equality of the Two Sexes* for guiding women toward individual emancipation. Poullain was well aware that social equity would not be realized without a profound transformation of women's self-image, so he set out to show all women in his first book that there are no great achievements of which they are not just as capable as men. Women could be their own worst enemy in conformity to the patriarchal status quo. Poullain's second treatise intended to give them the means, and the will, to overcome their inferiority complex. "By laboring mightily to overcome the inertia into which custom has reduced them and by employing part of the peace and leisure they enjoy in serious study, which would give them a solid understanding of what is necessary for the happiness and conduct of their lives" (*Education*, 140), what Poullain really proposed was an awakening of women's minds to their own condition.

Whereas *On the Equality of the Two Sexes* brought to trial the omnipotence of the masculine tradition, *On the Education of Ladies* was meant to be a manifesto for the feminine *cogito*. Given the opportunity to exercise the power of their sovereign reason, freethinking women could finally break the cycle of female alienation. Knowledge would be power. Poullain exhorted his readers (of both sexes interestingly) at the end of his essay to "observe everything, look at everything, and listen to everything without scruple. Examine everything, judge everything, reason about everything—about what has been done, what is being done, and what you foresee will be done" (*Education*, 288). His strategy moved in absolute opposition to any pedagogical doctrine in which gender predetermined individuals' access to truth, "there being but one way to teach both, since they are of the same species" (140). Fundamentally speaking, his egalitarian discourse on education was striking at the core of the basic postulate on gender difference. Since for him the two sexes shared intellectually one essential identity—same mind, same brain—logically only education could bear responsibility for the "difference."[21] The most respected reformers of women's education, however, continued to treat women's knowledge as if it were specific to women. The last quarter of the seventeenth century would bring about a renewal of interest on the general subject. However, when Fleury, Fénelon, or Mme de Maintenon deplored

21. Elisabeth Badinter, "Ne portons pas trop loin la différence des sexes," *Corpus* 1 (1985): 13.

the sorry state of girls' education, their point of departure for improvement remained rooted in the concept of female imperfection. Their programs taught feminine compliance—not a change in the patriarchal ideology.[22]

In 1674, Poullain's ideas went once again unnoticed. Overall, the principle of personal freedom, which Poullain linked to issues of feminine promotion, clearly ran counter to the contemporary structure of society. A polite review article of *On the Education of Ladies* appeared in the *Journal des sçavans* on April 8, 1675. When reading this editorial on Poullain's essay, one realizes the degree of cultural blindness he struggled to overcome. Reporting that "there is no science that the author of these Conversations docs not believe the ladies incapable," repeating after him that "truth does not have any greater enemy than prejudices," and concluding that thus one has to exercise one's reason on everything, the critic paraphrased correctly the Cartesian substance of *On the Education of the Ladies.* However, in conclusion, he limited his personal comments to the pleasing style of the author.[23]

Poullain expected an intellectual debate, at least from the traditional feminists he chastised for gallant condescension in the First Conversation of *On the Education of Ladies.* With no reply forthcoming, he persisted alone in a solitary "dialogue" in which he borrowed temporarily the voice of the opposition to argue what seemed to be two sides of a rhetorical question. Accordingly, in September 1675 he published *On the Excellence of Men.* In a manner similar to "the précieuses's inclination to turn full circle and argue any side of a given cause when it suited their tastes,"[24] he wrote in this third essay a complex series of rebuttals to his own *On the Equality of the Two Sexes* that he framed between a two-part defense of women's equality. The incomplete title was confusing, and the origin of much confusion in Poullain's feminist legacy. Not surprisingly, Pierre Bayle recognized in Poullain's maneuver the marks of a soulmate:

> He [Poullain] expected to have been written against, and indeed was threatened with an answer, but finding that no reply was likely to appear, he wrote against his own book himself. . . . Upon careful exami-

22. See Maité Albistur and Daniel Armogathe, *Histoire du féminisme français, du Moyen Age à nos jours* (Paris, 1977), 1:219–22. Carolyn C. Lougee, *Le Paradis des Femmes: Women, Salons, and Social Stratification in Seventeenth-Century France* (Princeton, 1976), 174–87.

23. See Magné's introduction to Poullain, *De l'Education des dames* (Université de Toulouse, n.d.), pages not numbered. Magné quotes the *Journal des sçavans,* April 8, 1675: "Tout cela lui fournit des très belles choses à dire et il en parle d'une manière fort agréable" (All of that leads him to talk about very interesting things in a highly pleasing manner).

24. Michael Seidel, "Poulain de la Barre's *The Woman as Good as the Man," Journal of the History of Ideas* 35:3 (1974): 501.

nation of all that he says, it appears that he had no design to refute his first work, and that his view was rather to confirm it indirectly.[25]

As a matter of fact, his devil's advocate tour de force consisted in strengthening the merits of his previous position on the universality of prejudices against women. He called it "the fair question" (*Excellence*, 265), because he believed that its resolution would lead to the betterment of human life in an egalitarian society. In order to reach that level of understanding, one had to be aware not only of prejudice but also to know how to fight back. In his essay of 1673, *On the Equality of the Two Sexes*, Poullain aimed at awakening people's consciousness to the fact that humans shaped cultural outcomes. Two years later, in *On the Excellence of Men*, he uncovered the ontological bases of the debate. Because they granted legitimacy to questionable patriarchal institutions, Poullain dared to deconstruct the scholastics who had built their rationale for law and order on the Holy Scriptures and the beliefs of ancient philosophers. Thus, Poullain expressed his desire to "provide women with powerful arguments to defend themselves against those who use the Scripture to humiliate them." However, in doing so, he led the initial dialogue to "many other complex questions, mainly those of ethics, jurisprudence, theology, and politics, which cannot be discussed freely in a book" (*Excellence*, 266 and 265).

In truth, the principle of personal freedom was at the base of Poullain's solution to the "Woman Question," for he subscribed to the greater ideal of a social contract in a civil society. Poullain's political theories were obviously premature. "If one wonders why Poullain felt so alone in his struggle to widen the scope of feminist thinking so that it might include problems of natural and human rights, the answer is in one sense very simple. Few in the age were willing to link the issue of feminine intellectual and cultural aggrandizement in aristocratic circles to the more unsettling matter of the justice or injustice of European social structure."[26]

This endeavor would have to be a task for future generations, for at this point in his career Poullain abandoned the field altogether. Stock detects in the final pages of his "Remarks" in *On the Excellence of Men*, "a certain disillusionment, an almost misanthropic attitude towards life under the Grand Monarch, whose reign was in 1675 not yet past its apogee. This contrasted with the calmer, more detached tone of *On the Education of Ladies*, where Poullain speaks with enthusiasm of the happiness and satisfaction that result from

25. Seidel, ibid., 502, cites Bayle's entry in *A General Dictionary, Historical and Critical*, trans. into English by several Hands (London, 1738), 8:448.

26. Seidel, "Poulain de la Barre's *The Woman as Good as the Man*," 502.

the search for truth."[27] There were also two other books that he appears to have considered, but never wrote: (1) the pedagogical treatise for children he intended to make a companion to his leading essay on ladies' education, probably aborted following the poor reception of the first volume, and (2) presumably, a book on the principles of French grammar, "from the premise that grammar is based on self-knowledge, stressing the importance of clear thinking as a prerequisite for clear expression."[28]

Documents suggest that by 1679 Poullain had been properly ordained a priest. He was lodging at the College de Fortet, one of many colleges grouped about the Sorbonne, and was probably teaching junior students within the jurisdiction of the university. This unexpected turn of events in Poullain's life needs scrutiny. Around the time of his conversion to the ideal of modernity in late 1666, he had realized that scholastic orthodoxy would lead him "along a path I had no intention of taking" (*Education*, 245). Why then did he return to the theology that he had so intently rejected, especially when one takes into account the nature of his relentless drive for societal change? How could the church dismiss his reputation for being a freethinker, based on its reading of his treatises? "The interval between 1675 and 1679, when he finally decided to take priestly orders, must have been a period of great moral stress for Poullain. He had frequently been called upon to defend himself for having abandoned the philosophy of the Schools for that of Descartes. The new philosophy was continuing to meet with opposition from the authorities," writes Stock. She suggests that "Poullain had apparently acquired a reputation among a certain group of free thinkers," in view of his marginal involvement in the editing of a subversive book on faith by Jean-Patrocle Parisot.[29] In 1685, in reference to Parisot's book's accomplices, Bayle's news article pointed to the author of the book on the equality of the sexes published in Paris in 1673, but fortunately misquoted Poullain's name as "Frelin." So it was likely that at the time of this affair, the cover of anonymity still protected Poullain from any church sanction. Ironically, for the same reason, his disappointing writing career had failed to bring him any solid assurance of earning a living. Financially, Poullain had no choice but to

27. Stock, "Poullain de la Barre," 54.

28. Ibid., 43, 44.

29. Stock, "Poullain de la Barre," 44–45: "Under the heading 'Touchant les livres que l'on s'étonne qui ne soient défendus en France,' the *Nouvelles de la république des lettres* reviews a book entitled *La Foi dévoilée par la raison*, published in 1681 by Jean-Patrole Parisot, Conseiller du Roi en ses Conseils, et Maître des Comptes, which apparently cost its author a very fine church benefice." Of special interest to the reviewer is the fact the Poullain "received remuneration for listening to Parisot's manuscript and discussing his ideas" (October 1685, 1145–46).

take advantage of the privileges attached to his theological credentials. In fact, a powerful relative of his family in the church hierarchy, Gabriel de Flexelles, facilitated his return by granting him a lifetime annuity that enabled him to take holy orders. "His beliefs could no longer have conformed to those of the conservative elements of the clergy, but still he must in all sincerity have felt capable of ministering to his flock and instructing them in Christian principles."[30] At least he probably thought so.

At the end of 1680, Poullain was attached to the small parish of La Flamengrie in Picardy. It was a modest assignment of 826 inhabitants, located in a province that still counted one thousand Protestant families in 1681, some of them in Poullain's village. As conditions worsened for this religious minority in the years preceding the Révocation, Poullain had to witness the physical violence and mental abuses perpetrated to obtain forced conversions. Certainly, Poullain must have found the persecutions revolting, but there is "no record of any recalcitrance on his part. On the contrary."[31] The report in Moréri's historical dictionary assured that during that time Poullain behaved with great wisdom, implying that great prudence was warranted, without a doubt. The Révocation of the Edict of Nantes was signed on October 18, 1685, formally ending freedom of religion in the French kingdom. However, since April 1685, Poullain had been assigned to the much poorer, smaller curacy of Versigny. "In spite of Moréri's assurance to the contrary, could he have expressed himself too freely, with the result that he was removed to a new charge? Such cases were not uncommon."[32] Disciplinary measures were taken against priests with liberal inclinations, be they Cartesians, Jansenists, or Calvinists.

Then, some two and half years later, Poullain disappeared from his parish without a trace. It was more like a flight from intolerance. According to Moréri's account, Poullain had reason to fear one of those arbitrary *lettres de cachet* from his bishop, who may have been disposed to have him incarcerated for suspicious belief. After a brief passage through Paris, Poullain was allowed to settle in Geneva in December 1688 as an *habitant* of the Republic.[33] No biographer has been able to ascertain the actual time of his conversion to the Reformed Church, whether before or after his departure from Ver-

---

30. Ibid, 48.

31. Ibid, 54.

32. Ibid, 55. Stock quotes the *Nouvelles de la république des lettres*: "L'on assure qu'il s'y comporta avec une grande sagesse de conduite" (It is said that he behaved very wisely).

33. Ibid, 57, 63: "The ambition of all foreigners who settled in the city was to be received as 'habitants' as soon as possible" (57). "As 'habitants' they and their descendants had the right to remain permanently" (63).

signy.[34] Nonetheless, Stock reflects accurately on certain early signs in Poullain's disposition that could explain his final decision:

> Undoubtedly it was Poullain's study of Cartesian philosophy that ultimately brought him to leave the Church. At first he tried to remain within the limits Descartes had set himself regarding his religion. This is evident in his three feminist treatises. But in these books, written between 1673 and 1675, we already see the germs of Protestantism in his distrust of tradition, his declaration of the right to disagree with Saint Jerome, his insistence that the individual should read and study the Scriptures by himself. In 1679 he had returned temporarily to the bosom of the Church . . . but his career as a priest was of short duration. The dangers inherent in the study of Cartesianism, dangers which caused Bossuet such great concern, were realized. His own temperament must also have played a considerable part in his decision. . . . The spirit of tolerance is everywhere evident in his works. . . . Far from trying to impose his opinions, he was more likely to conceal them. There are times when it is unwise to say what one thinks, *when one should speak folly to the fool.* His discretion no doubt accounts for the fact that he was able to slip away without incident.[35]

Embracing a new religion in a new country, François Poullain also embraced a new identity. In some legal documents in Geneva, he signed Poullain de la Barre, but he would be more often called F. P. de la Barre or Delabarre. Two factors facilitated his immediate integration into the upper class of Genevan society. First, he had connections with the prominent Perdriau family, whose protection vouched for Poullain's background and breeding, no doubt helping him to secure a respectable marriage with the daughter of a member of the Conseil d'Etat, Marie Ravier, on January 5, 1690.[36] Second, the Calvinist Republic considered him also a good acquisition because Poullain was able to produce a certificate of "good behavior," luckily written by his former bishop in the early part of his stay at La Flamengrie. "In spite of

---

34. According to Bayle, Poullain's conversion occurred at the time of his arrival in Geneva; but according to Stock, Poullain had secretly converted when he was still residing in Versigny (61). See also Alcover, *Poullain,* 129.

35. Stock ("Poullain de la Barre," 59–60) could be referring to Bossuet's *Premier avertissement aux Protestants,* 1689: "A heretic is one who has his own opinion. What does having an opinion mean? It means following one's own ideas, one's own particular notions. Whereas the Catholic, on the other hand, is what the name means, that is to say, one who, not relying on his own private judgment, puts his trust in the Church, and defers to her teaching." Quoted in Paul Hazard, *The European Mind, 1680–1715* (New York, 1963), 199.

36. A daughter was born in 1690 and a son in 1696.

his favored position as compared to that of many other refugees, life must have been difficult for Poullain during his first years in Geneva. . . . To supplement his income, he gave French lessons to members of the foreign nobility."[37] In fact, in 1691, he had published a sixty-page book, *Essai des remarques particulières sur la langue françoise pour la ville de Genève*, with the desire to protect his native language from the linguistic impurities he heard in Geneva. Always a Cartesian, Poullain stressed the faculties of reason and speech that distinguished humans from beasts. Therefore, a good command of the French language was a mark of distinction that should not have been overlooked by the exiled community. Speaking himself as a true French Parisian of the seventeenth century, he noted also that the proximity of the kingdom of France should motivate the people of Geneva to emulate the best qualities of their powerful neighbor. This book did not sell well, but it helped raise Poullain's local reputation as a scholar.

He had come to Geneva in search of religious freedom but soon ran into a climate of intellectual restrictions that again jeopardized his career. In January 1696, Calvinist authorities brought the serious accusation of Socinianism against the "Sieur de la Barre" in association with the trial of a certain Delorme. Professing a very liberal kind of Protestantism, Socinians rejected the dogmas of the Trinity and of Christ's divine nature. It appears that Poullain's propensity for philosophical inquiry had taken a new turn in his adopted country. But he was cleared of any charge of heresy the following month. Nevertheless, a cloud of suspicion would persist over Poullain's orthodoxy long enough to delay his assignment to an official teaching position in the city of Geneva for ten more years.[38] Poullain was finally appointed "régent de la seconde classe" (professor in today's equivalent tenth grade) at the Collège de Genève in 1708, a position he held until his death in 1723. "The program of studies had changed little since Calvin's day. Consequently, we may assume that . . . he taught boys history, rhetoric, and dialectics from Latin and Greek authors; also to read in Greek Homer and the Gospel according to Saint Luke."[39] In spite of the usual problems of discipline he encountered occasionally with a class of fifteen-year-old pupils, Poullain's performance must have been appreciated. He was offered, free of charge, the

---

37. Stock, "Poullain de la Barre," 63–67, 72.

38. This episode has been well studied by Alcover, who stresses the seriousness of this accusation against Poullain (*Poullain*, 18–19). See also Stuurman's analysis in "From Feminism to Biblical Criticism," 373–74, in which he concludes that "Poulain's profession of orthodoxy was almost certainly a dissimulation of his true opinions. All the same, he must have been thoroughly frightened, which may explain why he did not publish anything for over twenty years."

39. Stock, "Poullain de la Barre," 77.

title of "bourgeois de Genève" in 1716. This was a much sought after honor that recognized Poullain's good service to the Republic.[40]

His teaching may have conformed to a Calvinist curriculum, but his independent mind again strayed from Protestant orthodoxy. In 1720, Poullain published *La Doctrine des protestants sur la liberté de lire l'Ecriture Sainte, le Service Divin en langue entendue, l'Invocation des Saints, le Sacrement de l'Eucharistie. Justifiée par le MISSEL ROMAIN et par des Réflexions sur chaque Point. Avec un Commentaire philosophique sur ces Paroles de JESUS CHRIST, Ceci est mon corps; Ceci est mon sang, Matth. Chap. XXVI, v. 26.* Poullain was offering a meditation "on the differences between the Roman Catholic Church and Protestant doctrines, and at the end of his life we find him attempting to reconcile the faith he had abandoned with the one he had espoused."[41] Cartesian methods of inquiry continued to justify his personal interpretations of authoritative pronouncements, an approach that then, at the age of 72, he extended to matters of the faith. However, Stock has made the point that "in his plea for rational interpretation of the Scriptures he did not go so far as to apply the unrestrained rationalism of the later Enlightenment."[42] Nevertheless, his last book was written in defense of religious tolerance, a concept that did not go unnoticed by the Protestant authorities. Quite to the contrary. Instead of the expected financial reward traditionally attached to scholarly essays of quality, the Genevan State Council conveyed Poullain its coolest acknowledgment in a few words of thanks.

Poullain died in his bed on May 4, 1723. To his children, he wanted to be remembered as a "Christian philosopher: that is to say a man who, content

---

40. Ibid., 78. Stuurman, "From Feminism to Biblical Criticism," 375: "One of Poulain's pupils was his own son, Jean-Jacques, who went through the highest classes of the College in 1709–11, entered the Academy in May 1711, and graduated in philosophy in 1714 and in theology in 1717. His doctoral theses exhibit so many parallels and textual affinities with his father's writings that we may regard them as a result of a close collaboration between father and son." His son was also admitted "citizen of Geneva," though he had to pay a portion of the regular fee. See Stock, "Poullain de la Barre," 80–81.

41. Stock, "Poullain de la Barre," 82.

42. Ibid., 84. See also 86: "Poullain seems to be aiming at a synthesis of Catholic and Protestant viewpoints which are in line with the modern ecumenical spirit. Theologians would not rate Poullain as a profound Christian thinker, nor would philosophers consider him a profound philosopher. His originality consists rather in his tolerance and charity in an age of theological rigidity." And see Stuurman, "From Feminism to Biblical Criticism," 369: "The focus in all of Poullain's writings was a quest for a rational Christianity purged of all supernaturalism. . . . The audacious theological opinions formulated in 1670 were the product of the conjunction of his egalitarian views with his philosophical ideas. . . . However, his Genevan book, written almost a half-century later, goes far beyond his early writings in its extensive discussion of Biblical interpretation, centered on the issue of the Eucharist. . . . In a way, his last book reads like a settling of accounts with himself."

with his fair destiny, and serene, prefers the tranquility of his soul, and the calm of his conscience, Truth, Religion, and Peace, to all the greatness of the world."[43] He had found his peace in the country of his choice. His three feminist treatises belonged to his youth, a turbulent, soul-searching period of his life, that in retrospect remains somewhat enigmatic in relation to the rest of his life.

POULLAIN'S INFLUENCE IN HIS OWN TIME AND SINCE

Poullain's radical position in regard to feminine intellectualism made him the precursor of the theory of the equality between the sexes.

Twentieth-century researchers have conducted a far-reaching reassessment of the terms on which women's access to knowledge was defined in the seventeenth century.[44] Scholars have addressed issues ranging from theological discourse on feminine ontological inferiority to the concept of female domesticity that persisted in clouding the debate over the advancement of women. Clearly, questions surrounding the merits of women's intellectual endeavors had an impact on the social relevance of her intellectual pursuits.[45] In the seventeenth century, "the question whether women should be allowed to cultivate their minds [was] not new."[46] Nevertheless, the question confronted the resistance of a timeless tradition well-entrenched in French patriarchal society. Cohorts of Aristotle's students had defined the female sex as a subspecies of the human race, a kind of freakish, "incomplete" sexual being diverging from the universal (masculine) norm.[47] For centuries, the lopsided debate on feminine characteristics had focused on love and marriage and on such questions as whether one could "prove" woman's goodness or, inversely, whether one could confirm her devious nature in relation to her rightful alter ego.[48] The general discourse on feminine virtue was often a pretext for the most virulent attacks against women's capacity for honor at all

43. See his will in Stock, "Poullain de la Barre," 231–32. He signed it "François Poullain de la Barre." His widow died in 1742, his daughter Jean-Charlotte in 1716, and his son Jean-Jacques, a Calvinist minister, in 1751.

44. See Select Bibliography.

45. Timmermans makes the point that women's adversaries contested even more the suitability for women to study than their actual intellectual capacities (*L'Accès des femmes à la culture*, 23).

46. Ian Maclean, *Woman Triumphant: Feminism in French Literature, 1610–1652* (Oxford, 1977), 53.

47. Harth, *Cartesian Women*, 2.

48. Davis, *Society and Culture in Early Modern France*, 124: "The female sex was thought the disorderly one in early modern Europe. *Une beste imparfaicte*, [according to one adage] *sans foy, sans loy, sans craincte, sans constance*" (An imperfect beast, faithless, lawless, fearless, and fickle).

levels of society.[49] Ian Maclean has observed that "at the base of this distrust of women's nature lies the assumption that, from the outset, the female sex has a more difficult task in controlling passion because the world, the flesh and the devil have a greater hold over women than over men."[50]

However, on the eve of the Renaissance, the debate regarding the value of the female gender had gained momentum as advocates of women re-framed the "Woman Question" in terms of feminine intellectual capacity. In 1405, Christine de Pizan had published her *City of Ladies*, in which she exam-ined the performances of intelligent and educated women in history. In her footsteps, subsequent writers of the Renaissance found new grounds from which to argue in favor of women's access to knowledge. De Pizan had al-ready noticed that female intellectual inferiority had its roots in tradition, as it was customary to isolate girls from the benefits of their brothers' formal in-struction.[51] Still, in the first half of the seventeenth century, feminist writers did not fully exploit the sociological consequences of the rhetorical power of the antithesis of nature versus culture. None of them explicitly rejected the fallacious premise of some disorderly female sensuality that obfuscates women's reason. A remarkable exception to this was Marie Le Jas de Gournay, whom Montaigne eulogized as his *fille d'alliance*.[52] She was a self-educated woman who did not hesitate to flaunt her exceptional erudition, at the risk of losing the support of the very women for whom she wrote. She published in 1622 a short treatise, *Egalité des hommes et des femmes*, in which she demanded respect for the female sex. In her view, instruction in the humanities should be made available equally to both sexes. She bristled at the condition of ignorance in which women were kept against any notion of human dignity.[53] She had per-sonally experienced disparaging treatment from male scholars as well as anti-

49. Angenot, *Les Champions des femmes*, 47–49, credits Jacques Olivier's incendiary *Alphabet de l'im-perfection et malice des femmes* (Paris, 1617) for rekindling the "Woman Question" in seventeenth-century French society. See also Maclean, *Woman Triumphant*, 55.

50. Maclean, *Woman Triumphant*, 66.

51. Timmermans, *L'Accès des femmes à la culture*, 20, 24.

52. As his adopted daughter, Gournay edited, after his death, the first complete edition of Mon-taigne's *Essays*, in 1595. See *Marie de Gournay* in this series.

53. Gournay, cited by Lougee, *Le Paradis des Femmes*, 16: "Is there a greater difference between men and women than among women themselves, according to the institution [i.e., station in life] they have taken, according to whether they have been brought up in a city or in a village, or according to nations? And why would not their institution or education in affairs and letters equally with men fill this void which ordinarily appears between the heads of men and women? . . . Why truly would not education strike this blow and fill the distance which now sep-arates the understanding of men and women?"

intellectual salonnières who mocked her resolve.[54] Unfortunately, her passionate plea for feminine scholarship was perceived as an intrusion into a domain traditionally controlled by men.[55] Even more detrimental to Gournay's
cause, she appeared ideologically mired in prior Renaissance values because
of the old-fashioned language she insisted on using. Also, her humanistic
aspirations collided with the mondain activities sanctioned by the newly
spreading culture of the salons.[56] Given her perceived eccentricity, Gournay
left no noticeable effect on the mentality of her time. Her passionate call for
intellectual equality failed to stimulate any serious feminist dialogue. Rather,
the most ardent advocates for women's education preferred to correlate
women's perceptible mental inferiority with a lack of training in moral philosophy.[57]

Overall, with such little faith in women's virtue, feminist proponents in
the first decades of the seventeenth century came to the "defense" of women
for reasons of their own.[58] No doubt the moralists sincerely hoped to rescue
Eve's daughters with practical advice on social behavior, especially concerning such male-biased preoccupations as infidelity, idleness, and the cult of
feminine beauty. The social reforms rising from the Counter Reformation
granted some rudimentary schooling to girls, inasmuch as such education
formed good Christian wives, but such instruction was a far cry from the humanistic studies available to boys. In France, any feminine intellectual enlightenment that extended women's horizons was to be achieved elsewhere
in the secular world. Mainly three social sites drew women's involvement
away from their customary female territory: the *salon* primarily, with an occa-

54. Dorothy Anne Loit Backer, *Precious Women* (New York, 1974), 116–19.

55. See Mary M. Rowan's remarks about Gournay's professional status at the beginning of the
seventeenth century in "Seventeenth-Century French Feminism: Two Opposing Attitudes," *International Journal of Women's Studies* 3 (1980): 279: "A Woman who contradicted a man, no matter
how discretely, was considered bitter, stubborn, and arrogant. The woman who dared to write
received even swifter condemnation than she who dared to speak, and male writers and critics
scorned those works by women without even reading them."

56. Marie de Gournay, *Egalité des hommes et des femmes: Grief des dames suivis du proumenoir de Monsieur de
Montaigne*, ed. Constant Venesoen (Geneva, 1993), 36: "A notre connaissance aucune précieuse,
même parmi les plus hardies, ne fit appel aux lumières de Marie de Gournay" (To our knowledge,
none of even the most daring of the Précieuses aligned themselves with Marie de Gournay's thesis). See also Angenot, *Les Champions des femmes*, 53.

57. Maclean, *Woman Triumphant*, 67.

58. Angenot, *Les Champions des femmes*, 163: "On a pu se demander pourquoi les défenseurs des
femmes, plutôt que de chercher à prouver l'égalité des deux sexes, ont généralement préféré
soutenir le paradoxe extrême et risqué d'une supériorité des femmes, en prenant le contrepied
absolu de l'opinion triviale" (One must wonder why proponents of the women's cause generally
chose to defend the extremely risky paradox of women's superiority, in absolute opposition to
popular opinion, rather than trying to prove equality of the sexes).

sional visit to a literary *academie* by knowledgeable participants, and an occasional attendance at a scholarly *conférence*.[59] It is now well established that polite society provided exposure to learning for adult highborn women willing to risk being perceived as bluestockings. A kind of indirect "continuous education" took place in conversations (and correspondence) with learned gentlemen of the cloth, philosophers, and writers, for those women willing to engage in intellectual activities.[60] But the nature of the learning in question remained ambiguous as it evolved through the seventeenth century. Most of the feminists' hopes rested on the assumption that, ideally, women's nature could make them arbiters of social behavior through presiding over their salons and other worldly gatherings.[61] Rather than claiming gender equality, these women capitalized on their feminine roles. In an urban civilized environment, their effect could be one of peacemaking among the most aggressive, of course positive, "warring" masculine traits when women were properly educated for this mission.[62] They were expected to set the tone with their good taste and moderation, polite manners, and engaging conversations. The mastering of speech, language, and style constituted emblems of progress for women eager to step out of the domestic sphere. In this instance of women's learning, the tenets of moral philosophy were often reduced to a mere "social polish."[63]

However, it was in this salon context that, in the course of the first half of the seventeenth century, some women aimed at higher ground. Much has been said about the précieuses' desire to escape the predicament of their sex as wards and as wives. With no less contempt for the précieuses' views of achieving marital emancipation than for their determination to rule over literary creation, detractors easily dismissed as female arrogance the précieuses's "yearning to transcend the banality and crudity, linguistic and otherwise, of everyday life for a grander, nobler plane of existence."[64] The same deroga-

---

59. Harth, *Cartesian Women*, 15.

60. Roger Duchêne in Timmermans, *L'Accès des femmes à la culture*, 98–99.

61. This assumption is based on Plato's thesis that only women's influence can bring male-dominated society to a higher plane of civilization. The idea gained ground in seventeenth-century France with the blossoming of courtly life and the salon culture. See Angenot, *Les Champions des femmes*, 142–44.

62. In the first half of the seventeenth century, the Marquise de Rambouillet's salon was much credited for restoring elements of politeness in the upper classes following decades of religious and civil wars. Her salon became the model to imitate for numerous aspiring précieuses. See Backer, *Precious Women*, 70.

63. Lougee, *Le Paradis des Femmes*, 27–28.

64. Gibson, *Women in Seventeenth-Century France*, 181. Timmermans, *L'Accès des femmes à la culture*, 98–99. Christine Fauré, *Democracy without Women. Feminism and the Rise of Liberal Individualism in France,*

tory opinion awaited women's access to more earnest scholarship in the second half of the seventeenth century. The terms *savante* (with negative connotations) and *honnête femme* (a catch-all expression for female decorum) referred to those qualities required to succeed in refined company; they conveyed the sophistication dictated by the mondain code of conduct that in itself circumscribed the premises of any serious study. On the contrary, the word *pédant* expressed "the too serious pursuit of learning to the exclusion of the social graces,"[65] a scholarly attribute to be avoided at all cost by both sides. So, précieuses and savantes had to overcome the social stigmatization intrinsic to their demands for education.[66] In the process the more determined women were caught in a double bind, since their ignorance induced mockery from the (male) scholars while a showing of erudition triggered the mondains' laughter.[67]

It is rather ironic that at the beginning of the century, Gournay had experienced similar discredit from the first salons in Paris. However, her case had been unique, and her flamboyance bore as much responsibility for her social ostracism as the incongruity of her erudite demands for women of her time.[68] After the rise to power of Louis XIV, any notion of emancipation women may have gained tended to be frowned upon by the much more effective ideology of the monarchy. Especially after the civil disorders of the Fronde, a yearning for stricter conformity in the social order translated into a tightening of the power structure between the sexes. The reaffirmation of specific qualities and expected behaviors that had traditionally defined gender identities, and consequently, the renewed assertion of an uncontested hierarchy governing functions and knowledge attributed to men and women, became prevalent among the French elite in the second half of the seventeenth century. Molière's representation of his Cartesian learned women illustrated a transgression of preordained power, a case of *lèse-majesté* within the boundaries of marriage. The ridicule affixed to those women's egalitarian pretensions simply catered to the absolutist ideology of the period.

Thus, in the second half of the seventeenth century, with the exception

---

trans. C. Gorbman and John Berks (Bloomington, Ind., 1991), 64: "To devote oneself to such an ephemeral art as conversation might seem excessive; but in doing so they showed their refusal to acknowledge a history that had always come to the aid of male impudence with its pronouncements against women."

65. Lougee, *Le Paradis des Femmes*, 29.

66. Maclean, *Woman Triumphant*, chap. 5 (119–54).

67. Harth, *Cartesian Women*, 38.

68. This is not to imply that Gournay was some kind of crazy old spinster, but only that she was perceived as such. See Backer, *Precious Women*, 116–19.

of Poullain, no one affirmed the rights of women for intellectual emancipation to the extent of advocating equal standing for females with their male counterparts. The socio-political environment certainly presented a major disincentive to entertain that notion. On the epistemological level, Descartes had encouraged his feminine readership to "understand something" of his *Discourse on Method*, but there is no pertinent evidence that the great philosopher subscribed to a spiritual equality for man and woman.[69] Poullain's deduction that "the mind has no sex" derived logically, but also to his credit, independently, from his master's *cogito ergo sum*. Once it was established that human existence could be deduced from the human mind, Poullain had no trouble proving that women were of the human essence.[70] Furthermore, the fact that the biological differences between the sexes "begins and ends" with the reproduction of the species should have been enough to invalidate the intrinsic discrimination perpetrated by the common belief that gender difference breeds exclusion.[71] Poullain was the first philosopher of the modern age to comprehend clearly the magnitude of that concept in terms of major social inequities.[72] He certainly opened the door for the feminist theories developed in the twentieth century, but in 1673 his conclusions went un heeded.[73]

From a review of the circulation of Poullain's books in this period of his life, we can gain a sense of his contemporaries' limited, and somewhat confused, interest in his work. Alcover has established the complete bibliogra-

69. Timmermans, *L'Accès des femmes à la culture*, 382. Alcover, *Poullain*, 72–73.

70. Fraisse, "Poullain de la Barre ou le procès des préjugés," 33: "Si l'existence humaine se déduit de l'existence de l'esprit, le disciple de Descartes n'a aucun mal à démontrer que la femme est d'essence humaine. C'est ce que j'appelle clôre un débat" (If human existence can be inferred from the existence of the mind, Descartes's disciple can easily demonstrate that a woman is of human essence. That's what I call closing the debate).

71. An outraged Gournay had expressed a similar notion: "L'animal humain n'est ni homme ni femme . . . à bien le prendre, les sexes étant faits . . . pour la seule propagation" (the human animal is neither man nor woman . . . considering that the sexes are only for propagation [of the species]), but without any supporting rational frame of reference for proving her point. See Gournay, *Egalité des hommes et des femmes*, ed. Constant Venesoen (Geneva: Droz, 1993), 49.

72. Fraisse, "Poullain de la Barre ou le procès des préjugés," 28, connects Poullain's with Condorcet's defense of the Protestants and the Black slaves as well as the treatment of women in the eighteenth century. In 1848 Victor Schoelcher, the "author" of the abolition of slavery, also drew a link between the proletariat and the feminine condition. In the twentieth century, woman's status is often considered in the context of colonization, racism, and sexism. See also Margaret A. Simons, *Beauvoir and "The Second Sex": Feminism, Race and the Origins of Existentialism* (New York, 1999), 24–25.

73. In 1883, Paul Rousselot, recognizing that Poullain's clock was running ahead of its time, regretted that the man had not lived in the nineteenth century (*Histoire de l'éducation des femmes en France* [1883; rpt. New York, 1971], 1:273).

phy related to the diffusion and reception of his three treatises.[74] There were three authentic editions of *De l'Egalité des deux sexes*. The first and second editions, of 1673 and 1676, were published in Paris by the Jean du Puis. For the third edition of 1679, Antoine Dezallier, as the new owner of the printing press (and second husband of the deceased's widow), simply substituted the front page of the previous unsold copies with a logo of his own in order to clear his inventory. During the same years, 1673 and 1676, there appeared also two counterfeit, and rather defective, editions that Alcover identified as the work of printers from Lyon. Regardless of their origins, none of these editions displayed the author's name. However, in 1685 Pierre Bayle mentioned the name of "Frelin"[75] but later made the correction to the name "Poulin" in his *General Dictionary* under the article "Lucrèce Marinella." By then two other counterfeit editions, published in Geneva in 1690 and 1692, revealed the "new" name of "Sr. F. P. de la Barre." These latter editions of *On the Equality of the Two Sexes* were particularly interesting because the text was intended to "respond" to the central part of *On the Excellence of Men*, both pieces included in one single volume.

De l'Education des dames was printed in 1674 by Jean du Puis, then reissued in 1679 by Antoine Dezallier. In 1679, there was also a defective, counterfeit edition from Amsterdam, which contained an important variant in the last paragraph.[76] Curiously, while maintaining his anonymity on the title page, Poullain had signed "Poulain" at the bottom of the letter to Mademoiselle de Montpensier, to whom he dedicated his book. Overall, judging from its sporadic record of publication, one may safely conclude that *On the Education of Ladies* hardly gained the intellectual acclaim its author was seeking.

The original version of *De l'Excellence des hommes* was published in 1675, on Jean du Puis's press, in one volume in three parts: a Preface, *On the Excellence of Men*, and "Remarks." Also, in 1675, there appeared in Lyon, and in two volumes, a counterfeit edition. Again, in 1679, Antoine Duzallier proceeded to clean his shelves of the unsold copies with a new title page. Then, in 1690, and based on the 1675 counterfeit version, there appeared in Geneva an interesting edition showing the new name of "Sr. F. P. De la Barre." This peculiar copy of *On the Excellence of Men* claimed to include a "Dissertation or Discourse to be the Third Part to the Book on the Equality of the Sexes." In

---

74. Alcover, "Bibliographie, diffusion et réception des oeuvres féministes de Poullain de la Barre," in *Poullain*, 21–35.

75. In Bayle's article, "Touchant les livres que l'on s'étonne qui ne soient pas défendus en France," *Nouvelles de la république des lettres*, Oct. 1685, 1145–46, in *Dictionnaire historique et critique*, 4th ed. (Amsterdam, 1730).

76. Alcover, *Poullain*, 132, n. 19.

fact, this "Dissertation" was made up of the text of the Preface to *On the Excellence of Men* lifted from the original version of 1675, but the editors skipped the last sixty-two pages comprising the Remarks. This third shorter section in the original edition of *On the Excellence of Men* was probably judged redundant in relation to the ideas presented in *On the Equality of the Two Sexes*, which was instead included in the same volume as an answer to the antifeminist stance of *On the Excellence of Men*. Another publication of *On the Excellence of Men*, sandwiched between *On the Equality of the Two Sexes* and the "Dissertation," was again published on 1692. Stock writes that the *Histoire des ouvrages des sçavans* for September 1691 contained "an account of this volume, an impartial eight page condensation of (Poullain's) views," noting that "the reviewer chose to report in some detail on the final pages of the 'Dissertation' in which Poullain questioned the so-called benefits of the man-dominated civilization in which we live."[77]

According to Alcover, there are strong reasons to believe that in 1690–92 Poullain had not collaborated on the Genevan editions of his feminist essays.[78] But the public acknowledgment of Poullain's authorship remained confusing. In the French period of his life, Poullain had left clues for retracing the lineage of his three books to one single author. First, the philosopher Stasimachus, at the beginning of *On the Education of Ladies*, is recognized to be "the author of our book" by one of the young ladies who had read about "the equality of the sexes" (143). Second, the author introduced his "Remarks" in the last part of *On the Excellence of Men* with the explanation that more details were required to complete the arguments advanced in the book *The Equality of the Two Sexes*. And of course, there was his "Poulin" notation at the bottom of the epistle to Mademoiselle de Montpensier in the second treatise, certainly an endorsement that connected all the pieces. In the 1670s and 1680s, it should have been an easy task to find the author's name, if only there had been sufficient interest in pursuing the question.[79] In other words, his readership must have been rather limited in spite of Antoine Dezallier's purely commercial attempt to revive the sales in 1679. A brief article about *On the Excellence of Men* in the March 16, 1676 issue of the *Journal des sçavans* was at the origin of the misunderstanding concerning the actual content of the volume. It stated that the author (unnamed) "of the book about the equality of the sexes" wanted to provide himself the counter-argument to the same subject,

77. Stock, "Poullain de la Barre," 179.

78. Alcover, *Poullain*, 30.

79. There was also mention of the Privilège du Roy on the last page of *On the Equality of the Two Sexes*, granted on July 1, 1673, to *Le Sieur P****.

but it omitted mention of the last chapter, "Remarks," which emphatically refuted the theses on men's excellence. In addition, Bayle's revision of his own
1685 article concerning Poullain's authorship went unnoticed while readers
of the 1690–92 editions, which were disclosing the author's (new) identity,
F. P. de la Barre, could believe that two books on the equality of the sexes had
been written by two different persons "dealing with the same subject."[80]

Interestingly, in 1677 an anonymous translator had published in London
the first of Poullain's treatises, *The Woman as Good as the Man.* That single complete English edition was not reprinted until Gerald M. MacLean reproduced
the original text in 1988.[81] Reviewing the literary production of that period
in England, MacLean concluded that "several English translations of French
texts were published during 1677, suggesting their marketability that year.
. . . Nevertheless, English readers in 1677 seem to have accorded 'A.L.'s'
translation a reception similar to the one that had greeted the appearance of
the original in Paris four years earlier."[82]

If not under the exact author's name, Poullain's ideas began to receive
recognition in the last decade of the century. Stock notes that, in England,
The Gentleman's Journal for May 1693 contained an article, written by Pierre
Motteux, "The Equality of both Sexes," with this introductory sentence:
"Though several Ingenious Persons have from time to time drawn their pens
to vindicate the Ladies from that Ignoble Servitude which the ungenerous
part of Mankind would subject them to, I hope that the following discussion
may not be improperly placed here, since it endeavors to prove their Equality by such arguments as have not been offered yet."[83] In fact, the English-
speaking reviewer was paraphrasing the French article published the previous
year in *Histoire des ouvrages des sçavans,* with two interesting omissions: (1) The
author's name, Sr. F. P. de la Barre, was not acknowledged, and (2) the passages referring specifically to the *Excellence of Men* were dropped, needless to
say because of their negative bias on women's issues. In October 1693,
Motteux issued *The Lady's Journal,* which "consisted chiefly of 'pieces written
by Persons of the fair sex' or concerning them. One of these is entitled *An*

80. Alcover, *Poullain,* 32–33: In spite of Bayle's correction, Basnage was responsible for prolong-
ing this error into the next century in his *Histoire des ouvrages des sçavans* (Rotterdam, 1689–1709;
Geneva, 1989). Gyonnet de Vertron made the same mistake in 1698.

81. See Note on the Texts, 35.

82. See Note on the Texts: Gerald MacLean's edition, 31–32, 38–45. He proceeds to analyze
the cultural causes at the root of English readers' lack of receptivity for Poullain's ideas at that
time. This situation would explain the reasons why Poullain's other feminist works never
reached an English audience.

83. Cited by Stock, "Poullain de la Barre," 179. Motteux's essay was mentioned by Dorothy Foster in her article, "The Earliest Precursor," *PMLA* (1917): 22–58.

Essay to prove that Women can apply themselves to the Liberal Arts and Sciences. It is made up almost entirely of translated excerpts from *On the Equality of the Two Sexes.* The translation is not taken from that of 1677, *The Woman as Good as the Man*, but is undoubtedly Motteux's own, since he was an excellent linguist and a translator by profession."[84] Customary practice of that time allowed the translator to omit his indebtedness to the author.

In France, Poullain's fame hardly fared better. Notably, in 1693, "the author of the Equality" was mentioned by Gabrièle Suchon in her *Traité de la morale et de la politique, divisé en trois parties,* which she presented as a defense of "the persons of the Sex's" natural capacity for learning.[85] In 1698, Guyonnet de Vertron, in *La Nouvelle Pandore ou les femmes illustres du siècle de Louis le Grand,* referred to "Poulin" as "this illustrious author." But several other writers conveniently omitted their debts to the author of *On the Equality of the Two Sexes:* C. M. D. Noël in *Les Avantages du sexe ou le triomphe des femmes,* 1698; the Abbot Morvan de Bellegarde in *Lettres curieuses de littérature et de morale,* 1701; the Reverent Claude Buffier in *Examen des préjugez vulgaires pour disposer l'esprit à juger sainement de tout,* 1704.[86]

To some degree, young Poullain's theses were gaining public attention thirty years too late in his life to make much difference to his career as a sedate schoolmaster in Geneva. Furthermore, it is conceivable that his past radicalism strengthened the city fathers' misgivings at the time of the Socinian allegations, and further delayed Poullain's teaching assignment until 1708. Nevertheless, the public's surge of interest in Poullain's feminist ideas must be attributed to the climate of polemic discourse that swept the country over the "Ancients and Moderns' Querelle" between 1688 and 1694. On its face, the debate hinged on the relative merits of classical versus contemporary French literature, but the arguments made by the Moderns for the ineluctable continuity of the human spirit in reaction to the perfection of past authority created a "culture war" in which women were asked to play their part.[87] Key issues rested on the worth of feminine taste and how dependable women's judgment was in matters of intellectual significance. "The *Querelle* then," writes Elizabeth Berg, "is not only a literary debate, but also the manifestation of a political position regarding the status of women and their right

---

84. Stock, "Poullain de la Barre," 181.

85. Suchon's treatise will appear in this series.

86. Alcover, *Poullain*, 33; Stock, "Poullain de la Barre," 182–90; Ellen McNiven Hine, "The Women Question in Early Eighteenth-Century French Literature: The Influence of Poullain de la Barre," *Studies on Voltaire* 66 (1973): 65–79, 76, on both Morvan de Bellegarde and Buffier.

87. Joan DeJean, *Ancients Against Moderns: Culture War and the Making of a Fin de Siècle* (Chicago, 1997), 40.

to participate in the culture of their society." Berg concludes that "the repeated alignment of feminism with modernism is inevitable. For modernism
represents a rejection of the patriarchal tradition, a rejection that is necessary
to feminism."[88] Thus, on the one hand, the timing for Poullain's 1690 editions of the restructured *On the Equality of the Two Sexes/On the Excellence of Men*
bound under one cover corresponded to a definite evolution in the mentality
of French autocratic society. The absence of publication of *On the Education of
Ladies* at that time would be all the more puzzling unless we realize the fundamental contradiction between the Moderns' reliance on innate (or natural)
feminine good taste and Poullain's vision for feminine scholarship.

   As the Enlightenment dawned, Poullain's feminist legacy receded into
a state of "ideological palingenesis" on both sides of the Channel. Here is
how Seidel places Poullain's accomplishments in the history of English literature:

> His work is a largely ignored seed-bed of feminist thinking, containing
> in many ways more startling ideas than better known works of more
> renowned feminists. Poullain loses little in comparison with Mary
> Astell or Daniel Defoe in his time, with the *luminaires* in eighteenth-
> century France, or with the libertarian feminists, Mary Wollstonecraft,
> Harriet Taylor, and John Stuart Mill in eighteenth- and nineteenth-
> century England.[89]

However, these meetings of the mind attest more to the evolution of intellectual trends common to both cultures than to direct exposure to Poullain's
work, as certainly was the case with Mary Astell writing her *Essay in Defence of
the Female Sex* two decades after him.[90] Seidel stresses Astell's and Poullain's
mutual interests, as Poullain "believed that the feminist cause was tied to a
human cause outside the boundaries of the salon and within the boundaries
of natural rights and reasoned social equity."[91] However, Astell must not
have read Pierre Motteux's articles. Had she overcome her dislike of the

---

88. Elizabeth Berg, "Recognizing Differences: Perrault's Modernist Esthetic in *Parallèls des Anciens et des Modernes*," *Papers on French Seventeenth-Century Literature* 18 (1983): 137. See also 145: "Yet
modernism, in the case of Perrault or any other modernist aesthetic dominated by men, ultimately serves to pass authority, not from men to women, but from a group of men in power to a
group of men seeking power, women acting as intermediaries. Modernism is an agent of social
transformation which may allow for a temporary manifestation of differences—which in fact
must validate differences in its attempt to transform values—but which eventually solidifies
those differences into a hierarchy."

89. Seidel, "Poulain de la Barre's *The Woman as Good as the Man*," 499.

90. Mary Astell, *An Essay in Defence of the Female Sex* (London, 1696).

91. Seidel, "Poulain de la Barre's *The Woman as Good as the Man*," 507–8.

French feminist tradition, she would have distinguished Poullain's defense of women from the suspicious proclamations of his "gallant" contemporaries she so despised.[92]

In eighteenth-century France, Poullain's work did not sink into total oblivion. The legacies of many minor feminist writers betrayed their unique identifiable source. Among the most noticeable examples, in 1750, Mlle Archambault published in Paris her *Dissertation sur la question: Lequel de l'homme ou de la femme est plus capable de constance? Ou la cause des dames.* Also in 1750, but in London, Philippe Florent de Pusieux, with his wife, Madeleine d'Arsant, published *La Femme n'est pas inférieure à l'homme*, possibly one of the two most blatant cases of plagiarism on Poullain's *On the Equality of the Two Sexes*.[93] The second case of plagiarism belongs to Dom Caffiaux, who produced in Amsterdam in 1753 four volumes on *Défenses du beau sexe, ou mémoires historiques, philosophiques et critiques pour servir d'apologie aux femmes*, in which, according to Stock, he managed to lift between one-third and one-half of the content of *On the Equality of the Two Sexes*. By the third quarter of the eighteenth century, Poullain's corpus had been massaged by so many unscrupulous hands that his theories on the status of women had fallen de facto into the public domain. This would explain the "undeniable" connections Magné assumed between Chodelos de Laclos's and Poullain's own position rather than inferring a direct borrowing from Poullain.[94] As far as his influence on the major philosophers is concerned, there is also a case for an intellectual affinity with Montesquieu and the philosophes espousing natural law that will be analyzed in the Introduction to *On the Equality of the Two Sexes*.

From the eighteenth century "no new ideas on the subject were put forth, nor did anyone expound as forcibly as Poullain those he had advanced."[95] In the nineteenth century, considering the hundreds of names and titles mentioned in the general studies on feminine issues, it seemed that no one referred to Poullain by name or by affiliation.[96] Only one antifeminist scholar, Albert Castelau, in the context of his polemic against the co-editor of *La Revue philosophique*, Jenny d'Héricaurt, ironically recalled Poullain (whom

92. According to Armogathe, "De l'égalité des deux sexes, 'la belle question,'" 24, Mary Wollstonecraft and John Stuart Mill knew Poullain's *The Woman as Good as the Man*. See Fraisse, "Poullain de la Barre ou le procès des préjugés," 39–40, for a comparative analysis of Mill's with Poullain's theories.

93. Stock, "Poullain de la Barre," 186–97. Poullain was also briefly mentioned in L. A. Thomas, *Essai sur le caractère, les moeurs et l'esprit des femmes dans les différents siècles* (Paris, 1772), 107.

94. Alcover, *Poullain*, 34. Note that Laclos's personal ethics is often confused with his protagonists' immorality in *Les Liaisons dangereuses*.

95. Stock, "Poullain de la Barre," 197.

96. Alcover, *Poullain*, 34.

he still called "Frelin") and his "system of feminine emancipation," only to bring ridicule to the woman's presumably novel radicalism.[97] And finally came Simone de Beauvoir in 1949, who in *The Second Sex* acknowledged her debt to Poullain's *On the Equality of the Two Sexes:* "Men, he [Poullain] thought, used their superior strength to favor their own sex, and women acquiesced by habit in their dependence. They had never a fair chance—neither liberty nor education. Thus they could not be judged by past performance, he argues, and nothing indicated that they were inferior to men. He demanded real education for women."[98]

In his translator's preface of *The Second Sex,* Parshley omitted mentioning that Poullain's epigraph appears on the initial page of the first volume of the original edition.[99] He completely missed the significance of de Beauvoir's salute to Poullain,[100] so consistent with his own assessment of Beauvoir. Nevertheless, he wrote that "the central thesis of Mlle de Beauvoir's book is that since patriarchal times women have in general been forced to occupy in the world in relation to men a position comparable in many respects with that of racial minorities, in spite of the fact that women constitute numerically at least half of the human race, and further that this secondary standing is not imposed of necessity by natural 'feminine' characteristics but rather by strong environmental forces of educational and social tradition under the purposeful control of men."[101] In many respects, those words of introduction to Beauvoir's *The Second Sex* underscore the relevance of Poullain's most audacious point of departure for his philosophical quest on behalf of women's emancipation. Societal expectations have allowed women to become who they are, the "second sex." Their cultural conditioning has institutionalized a hierarchy of power, in which the "Other" has been cast in an inferior role by

97. Fraisse, "Poullain de la Barre ou le procès des préjugés," 38: "Jenny Héricourt was one of the most radical feminists of the nineteenth century. She criticized systematically the misogynist theses of such contemporaries as Auguste Comte, Jules Michelet, and Joseph Proudhon." Fraisse cites A. Casteleau, "La question des femmes au XVIIe siècle," *Revue philosophique* (May 1857), and his *La Femme affranchie* (Paris, 1857).

98. *The Second Sex,* trans. H. M. Parshley (New York, 1989), 107.

99. See above, note 7 and related text.

100. Albistur and Armogathe, *Histoire du féminisme français,* 240: "La plupart des idées neuves de Poullain se retrouveront dans *Le Deuxième Sexe:* le conditionnement précoce de la petite fille, le narcissisme et le thème du miroir, la mauvaise foi des mâles à partager leur pouvoir, etc. Les écrits de Poullain ont parfaitement résisté aux découvertes des sciences humaines qui sont le fait du xxe siécle" (Most of Poullain's new ideas will be found in *The Second Sex:* early conditioning of the little girl, narcissism and the theme of the mirror, males' bad faith in sharing their power, etc. Poullain's writings concur perfectly with the significant findings made in the human sciences during the twentieth century).

101. Beauvoir, *The Second Sex,* vii.

the laws of men rather than being the result of a natural order. For Beauvoir, "One is not born, but rather becomes a woman."[102] In addressing the historical conjuncture that led to the "inequality of the sexes," Poullain brought under scrutiny the axiom of cultural specificity inherent in the making of the traditional gender ideology. Beyond Poullain's initial demystification of the "eternal feminine," and Beauvoir's demand for the abolition of that myth, postmodern feminists have continued to interrogate the politics of knowledge governing gender relationships.[103]

The young student in the seventeenth century disenchanted with the teaching of the Schools had found the new philosophy. Without Descartes, there would not have been a Poullain de la Barre. But without Poullain de la Barre, where would the movement for women's liberation be today?[104]

102. Ibid, 267.

103. Helen Longino, "To See Feelingly: Reason, Passion, and Dialogue in Feminist Philosophy," 25, and Jeanne Marecek, "Psychology and Feminism: Can This Relationship be Saved?" 124, both in Domna C. Stanton and Abigail J. Stewart, eds., *Feminisms in the Academy* (Ann Arbor, 1995). Simons, *Beauvoir and the 'Second Sex,'* 145: "Many radical feminist theorists of the women's liberation movement in the 1960s have acknowledged that Simone de Beauvoir's *The Second Sex* (1949) provided a model for them."

104. Albistur and Armogathe, *Histoire du féminisme français*, 84: "Sans Descartes, il n'y aurait pas eu Poullain de la Barre; sans Poullain de la Barre, l'histoire du Féminisme aurait piétiné longtemps encore. Il ne faut pas craindre de voir en lui le doctrinaire de l'émancipation des femmes, le plus important que nous ayions eu depuis le moyen age jusqu'au milieu du XIXe siècle (Without Descartes there would not have been Poullain de la Barre; without Poullain de la Barre, the history of feminism would have gone nowhere for a long time. Undeniably, he must be considered the theoretician for women's emancipation, the most important that we had from the Middle Ages to the middle of the nineteenth century).

NOTE ON THE TEXTS

The story of translating Poullain de la Barre into English is not long, though it is not without its complexities. As far as I know, this is the first time that *On the Education of Ladies* and *On the Excellence of Men* have been translated into English, acknowledging that they are actually the work of their author. The qualification is necessary because of the license common in previous centuries which allowed what we would call cribbing from unattributed sources. Parts of all three of Poullain's works were published anonymously as the *Sophia* pamphlets[1] in 1739. The publication of these was proof that Poullain's works—although not Poullain himself—had remained buried somewhere in the consciousness of English readers. The seeds had been sown there some sixty years earlier when *The Woman as Good as the Man*, a translation of *De l'Egalité des deux sexes*, was published in 1677 by Nathaniel Brooks. The translator was known only by the initials A.L.,[2] and he used the 1676 edition of the French text as his source. The Woman Question was very much on the minds of English readers at the time, and they were most receptive to ideas from France; it would be nice, then, if there were some reference to Poullain de la Barre by some eminent, contemporary feminist like Mary Astell, for example. Unfortunately, although her spiritual mentor John Norris, like Stasimachus in *On the Education of Ladies*, gave her guidance about the books she should be reading, and recommended Malebranche, Antoine Arnauld, and Descartes, there is no mention of Poullain de la Barre; nor does Poullain's name figure in the inventory of books in the extensive library of Astell's good friend, Lady Ann Coventry.[3] After a new edition of *De l'Egalité des deux sexes* ap-

---

1. See Gerald M. MacLean's introduction to the reprint of *The Woman as Good as the Man* for a discussion of these pamphlets (26–27).

2. MacLean identifies the translator as Archibald Lovell; see MacLean's introduction, 14–20.

peared in 1690, parts of it were published in English in *The Gentleman's Journal* and *The Ladies Journal*. It has taken the women's movement of the twentieth century to rekindle interest in Poullain de la Barre. In 1988, Gerald M. MacLean published a reprint of the seventeenth-century translation *The Woman as Good as the Man*.[4] One year later Daniel Frankforter and Paul Morman published the French text alongside their own modern English version, to which they added an introduction and analysis.[5] In 1990, Desmond M. Clarke published a second modern translation of the same text.[6]

Madeleine Alcover has made a detailed study of the various editions of the French texts of Poullain de la Barre's works; her assessment of their relative merits is invaluable.[7] In the case of *De l'Egalité des deux sexes*, there is an additional factor in the choice of original text: the original edition of 1673 was reprinted by Fayard in 1984, though with the "avertissiment" at the beginning rather than the end, and with the note that "since the subsequent editions add nothing to the first, that is the one we are publishing."[8] It makes sense, therefore, to use a text to which there is more general access than one that is available only in the rare book rooms of specialized libraries. The first edition of *De l'Education des dames* (1674) has similarly been used. In the case of *De l'Excellence des hommes*, Mme Alcover's work was particularly useful: of the three editions published in the year of publication, 1675, two contain exactly the same information on the title page: same title, same date, same publisher. The only difference (admittedly rather large) is the central identifying mark: the publisher's monogram on the original, a basket of flowers on the pirated version (probably published in Lyon, despite the legend "À Paris"). It is the first of these that has been used here. In all three cases, the publisher was Jean du Puis, rue Saint-Jacques à la Couronne d'Or, Paris.

3. See Ruth Perry, *The Celebrated Mary Astell: An Early English Feminist* (Chicago, 1986), 339–54.

4. François Poullain de la Barre, *The Woman as Good as the Man, Or, The Equality of Both Sexes*, trans. "A.L.," ed. and intro. Gerald M. MacLean ([1677], Detroit, 1988).

5. François Poullain de la Barre, *The Equality of the Two Sexes*, trans. with an intro. by A. Daniel Frankforter and Paul J. Morman. Studies in the History of Philosophy, vol. 11 (Lewiston, N.Y., 1989). The editors call their own work a "commentary," though it falls short of being one, presenting much more a general introduction to Poullain's life (eleven pages), the Cartesian influence (nine pages), and the argument (twenty-two pages). Nor do they provide any notes.

6. François Poullain de la Barre, *The Equality of the Sexes*, trans., intro., and notes by Desmond M. Clarke (Manchester and New York, 1990). Clarke's edition is far the better of the two modern editions prior to our own (see note 6 above).

7. Alcover, *Poullain de la Barre*, 24–30.

8. François Poullain de la Barre, *De l'Egalité des deux sexes* (Paris, 1984).

ON THE EQUALITY
OF THE TWO SEXES

INTRODUCTION

This treatise comprises two large sections, preceded by a Preface and followed by a Postface, all clearly identified by Poullain with titles.

The Preface introduces the reader to Cartesian analysis. Poullain proposes to subject a common prejudice to rational inquiry. No prejudice is better suited to such a purpose than belief in the inequality of the sexes, the most pervasive of all of human errors of judgment. Applying the "rule of truth," that is, "to accept nothing as true unless it is supported by clear and distinct ideas," he proposes to challenge the views of the vast majority of the unlearned (part 1) and then of the learned (part 2). Anticipating the objection that his inquiry will bring about social disruption, he says his intention is only to draw women out of the idleness to which they have been condemned by encouraging them to study, inasmuch as study is "more or less all they are allowed to do at the moment." Poullain's biography shows that he is not a man of action. In retrospect, his ideas might appear revolutionary because they foreshadow the spirit of reforms that will rise from the age of Enlightenment, but Poullain neither promotes nor expects any profound disruption of the social fabric to result from his inquiry. His intention is rather to bring intelligent readers to a new sense of awareness and to give women enough self-confidence to begin their own intellectual emancipation, for which they are as well equipped as men.

Part One deals with the most prevalent prejudices about women embedded in all cultures since the beginning of time. His treatment falls neatly into three parts.

1. Poullain questions the validity of customs and traditions. Why do most people hold onto common beliefs (e.g., that the sun circles the earth) when scientists have proved otherwise? Why do we believe our country the best and our religion the truest? Self-interest or habit. The same is true of be-

lief in the inequality of the sexes. Men believe that women are fit for the home but not for civic life. Had women been capable of public responsibility, so the argument goes, they would never have been excluded from it in the first place. The argument boils down to saying that "this is the way things have always been done, therefore they *should* be done this way." Men have passed laws to insure their rule, and women have tolerated their situation because they have been raised in a state of dependency and so see things as men do. But to hold to custom and usage because they are sanctioned by time (and male privilege) is pure prejudice. The concept of possibly breaking this cycle never occurs under this line of reasoning.

2. How did this situation evolve? In the manner of the new natural law philosophers, Poullain imagines a prehistorical, basically egalitarian society in which the forces governing human relationships were founded on mutual reliance between the sexes. During those innocent times, the constraints of the female anatomy imposed certain demands on women's activities, but their physical make-up did not mandate their subservience to the stronger sex. Ironically, in this presocietal epoch of the savages (as Poullain imagines humans in this state), women's rights were respected. This ideal status remained as long as marriages were endogamic and the family unit fairly simple. The situation evolved with the sophistication of social organization, especially aggravated by the practice of exogamic marriages. Furthermore, the establishment of the rule of primogeniture gave rise to a social revolt of younger males against their oldest brothers for possession of the family goods. At this point, defenseless women became regarded "as the most desirable part of their booty." Under the tyranny of their husbands and brothers, mothers and daughters internalized their new functions of peaceful homemakers while the males took charge outside. Consequently, "women were not included in the first occupations." For Poullain, they had been robbed of their natural rights.[1] Defeated and scorned by their victors, they found that their physical weakness further diminished their social standing, rendering them subject to the violence and injustices of their masters. Poullain depicts the march of civilization in terms of bloody struggles in which "women's gentleness and humanity" disqualified them from sharing the glory and the spoils of wars. Women's role came to be deemed useless in those primitive societies, where sheer military might determined political control. Long before he

1. Montesquieu also argued that natural law never granted men any superiority over women, and that gender inequality had been established against reason. He probably alluded to Poullain in his remark on a "very gallant philosopher." See Bernard Magné, "Une Source de la Lettre Persane XXXVIII? *L'Egalité des deux sexes* de Poullain de la Barre," *Revue d'histoire littéraire de la France* 3–4 (1968): 407–14.

would act upon his reformist beliefs to break away from the oppressive regime of the French monarchy, Poullain contests the concept of any line of command in which "the external deference shown to those in authority became associated with the idea of power," that is, that the more power a person yields the more respect is due him.

Thus, the initial "usurpation" of women's fundamental freedom of choice led to their exclusion from the dynamics of public life.[2] Why, for example, were women excluded from the ministry in religion or from the sciences? Since the women's sphere of influence had been reduced to the maintenance of their household and the care of their children, they were prevented de facto from partaking in intellectual activities typically the reserved domain of men. Poullain singles out the exclusion of women from the male "academies" which were gathering sites of the French intelligentsia.[3] But his criticism encompasses the tradition that has ostracized female participation from the pursuit of knowledge in any form of encounter. Not only were women placed at a disadvantage by the lack of opportunities to enhance their education, formally or informally, they were encouraged to give "themselves up to frivolity," for which alone they received positive reinforcement.[4]

3. In a discussion as long as both the preceding two, Poullain questions the grounds for accepting common prejudices about women by presenting evidence against them. His evidence comes from two different perspectives.

First, women's *manners* distinguish them. Despite their lack of learning, their virtue and grace generally increase with age. They are discreet in look, expression, bearing, and movement (unlike men). The leadership of women in polite society sets the tone for elegance and style.[5] Poullain praises women's natural talent for bringing into social intercourse a pleasantness devoid of pedantic erudition.

In addition, without being trained in intellectual subjects, women have often demonstrated far more good sense than learned men.[6] Poullain con-

---

2. The rare cases of ruling queens and female regents must be considered cases of political expediency. See also Fauré, *Democracy without Women*, 68: "Within this narrative on the origins of inequalities, Poullain found the state apparatus particularly culpable because of its inherent tendency to divide the population."

3. See Harth, *Cartesian Women*, 15–63.

4. Idleness was a major preoccupation of moralists. See Ian Maclean, *Woman Triumphant*, 69 and 139, regarding Du Boscq's feminist views: "Home economics seems to him a very suitable subject for study," whereas "care must be taken to avoid 'des sciences qui portent à la dissolution.'"

5. Poullain's opinion on the social merit of mixed assemblies was commonplace by 1673. See Maclean, *Woman Triumphant*, chap. 5 (140–54).

6. This premise of feminine untrained but spontaneous good taste will play a major role in the fin-de-siècle polemic between the Ancients and the Moderns.

ducted a survey in which he asked women of various social classes what they believed about God and the soul, but also about more empirical matters like the flow of blood and the erosion of rocks, and he discovered that the obfuscating answers given by scholars were far from their responses, which were concrete and down-to-earth.

Second, Poullain gives greatest attention in this section, however, to proving that women have as much aptitude for learning as do men. He does not appeal to history and its examples of illustrious women—standard fare since Boccaccio's *Concerning Famous Women* (1360). Rather, true to his methodology, he focuses on questions of their rationality. He cites, for example, their quick detection of pretense, their ability to speak eloquently and to present a law case logically and convincingly, their penchant for storytelling, their acumen in finding remedies for illnesses. A point of particular interest is Poullain's crediting women for having intuitively understood the influence of climatic conditions to explain the cultural differences in people's way of life.[7]

As to why women know little of abstract sciences such as algebra, geometry, and optics, Poullain replies that these specialized topics rarely blend into polite conversation, and that because traditional institutions of higher learning like the academies have been closed to women, women have had little exposure to abstract scientific knowledge.

Throughout this discussion Poullain speaks against class distinctions. He asks: How many peasants might have become renowned scholars if they had been given a chance? His survey of women, both ladies and commoners, reveals an attitude that might evoke images of the French Revolution, but in Poullain's time his inclusion of classes below the nobility was too extreme to be taken seriously.[8] He was on safer ground when he praised learning "among ladies." He had natural allies among the salonnières, who aspired to play a positive role in the cultural life of the nation. At the top of his list he distinguishes the feminine "scholars" for having the courage and fortitude "to surmount various public obstacles" in the pursuit of their studies, none more difficult than "the unfortunate opprobrium in which female scholars are generally held." Molière's successful mockery in his *Learned Ladies* the preceding year appears to have motivated Poullain's defense of the intelligent woman.

Poullain concludes by praising the virtue of women—in caring for those who are sick, in maintaining their virginity or their steadfastness in marriage, in the care and education of their children. Since women possess virtue, he

7. See Alcover, *Poullain*, 104, on the debate over Montesquieu's intellectual debt toward Poullain's theory on climates.

8. Henri Piéron, "De l'Influence sociale des principes cartésiens: Un précurseur inconnu du féminisme et de la Révolution: Poullain de la Barre," *Revue de synthèse historique* 184 (1902): 270–71.

suggests, they have the principal advantage of scientific study without the study itself. In attributing virtue without study to women, however, he argues as did his opponents.

In Part Two Poullain turns to the prejudices of learned men and attempts to "show why the proofs that could be used against the equality of the two sexes taken from poets, historians, lawyers, and philosophers are all vain and futile." His arguments can be grouped into three sections, identified in Poullain's original text by an extended heading.

1. Since truth is naturally associated with science, we are inclined, says Poullain, to regard as true the claim of poets, orators, historians, and philosophers that women are inferior to (i.e., less noble and perfect than) men. In fact, however, all these scholars base their view of women on the Ancients, who are their authorities. Hence they, no less than common people, accept custom and opinion.

Take the poets. He cites Sarazin's sonnet on Eve and alludes to Molière's rendition of women's foibles as examples of the influence of the Ancients' views of women on modern writers. But however much such writers *assert* the inferiority of women, we are hard pressed to find in their writings any *reasons* for why they are. Men think this way because they have the power; if women had power, as in the kingdom of the Amazons, ways of thinking about the sexes might be reversed. Thus the profession of judge or soldier is given great respect, while that of housewife is given very little, despite the fact that the work of women—safeguarding our lives—is much more important than that of any public official. Respect is arbitrarily bestowed according to the distribution of power.

Historians also base their work on the prejudices of the Ancients. Even if prejudices against women appeared in a thousand chronicles, they should still be considered prejudices and not authoritative. If historians follow prejudicial opinions, why should we be surprised that their readers concur? If we look at what women actually did in the past, however, we find that they governed great states and empires, meted out justice, led armies, suffered for religious principles.[9] History has been used as a weapon against women, but it could more justly be used to show that women are no less noble than men.

Lawyers have erred just as grievously. Against the law of nature which makes all people equal, they have written laws declaring the perpetual servitude of women to men. No one in fact is perpetually dependent. Children are dependent on their parents only until they become adults; then they are free.

---

9. Poullain does not mention particular famous women of the past who filled any of these roles, unlike many earlier writers who made their defense of women rest largely on such recitals.

Although men have been declared heads of families, what we find in practice is a reciprocal commitment in which good sense and power over the body are equal between the partners. And if the husband is given greater control over possessions, nature gives greater weight of authority over children to the wife. If a woman has to do what her husband wants her to, the reverse is also true. In saying all this, Poullain comes dangerously close to professing a doctrinal heresy with regard to the balance of power in the traditional family. He actually calls for the end of the patriarchal unit, which has placed women in a state of civil subordination. His transvaluation of values with regard to the matrimonial state is without a doubt one of Poullain's most radical solutions to the negative impact of the "historical conjecture" on a woman's life.[10]

Last on Poullain's list of culprits but first in their misuse of intellectual authority are the philosophers, who have an authority greater than poets, orators, historians, or lawyers. By philosophers Poullain means "scholastic philosophers," whom he criticizes as given to abstractions and trivialities of speculation, all based on past authority (or prejudice) and irrelevant to scientific truth.[11] Poullain's definition of science is a restatement of Descartes's methodology, which he demonstrates with a "definition of liquidity,"[12] making the point that it contains nothing ordinary women cannot understand. Indeed, more intelligence is required to learn needlepoint and tapestry than to learn physics. Poullain then proceeds to root out completely the contrary opinion.

2. A consideration of the disciplines just discussed leads to a more general maxim, namely, that "the mind has no sex," or, put differently, that "the mind is equal in men and women." The sameness of the sexes lies in their nature, the differences between them rests in custom and social practice. Poul-

10. Gibson, *Women in Seventeenth-Century France*, 59: "The arbitrary and impersonal nature of the process by which young men and women were matched in the seventeenth century meant that for the bond of mutual affection and understanding which modern generations have come to regard as a vital prerequisite of marriage was substituted at best an initial indifference, at worst an active resentment against the person to whom fidelity had to be vowed until death. The onus for closing this emotional breach rested largely, it was stressed, with the wife." See also Marcelle Maistre Welch, "Les Limites du libéralisme matrimonial de Poullain de la Barre," *Cahiers du Dix-septième* 5 (Fall 1991): 41–52.

11. The situation was changing in Poullain's generation. Stephen Toulmin, *Cosmopolis: The Hidden Agenda of Modernity* (Chicago, 1990), 107–8: "After 1660, there developed an overall framework of ideas about humanity and nature, rational mind and causal matter, that gained the standing of 'common sense.'"

12. Cartesian Jacques Rohault had used water's liquidity in his discussion of form and matter in his *Traité de physique* (1671). See Roger Ariew, *Descartes and the Last Scholastics* (Ithaca and London, 1999), 95.

lain owes this idea to Descartes, though Descartes never specifically addressed women's issues in his philosophical consideration of the *cogito*.[13] Poullain discusses the scientific disciplines, from which he believes women should no longer be barred, grouping them into two categories: theoretical sciences, which he later defines as those areas of knowledge that directly concern men and women, and practical sciences, loosely defined as "sciences that deal with people in their relationship to others in civil society."[14] But as he makes clear in the transitional discussion between these two groups of sciences, a person who can master one group can also master the other, contrary to the view that those fitted for one group are rarely fitted for the other.[15]

The first group includes metaphysics (defined by Poullain in Cartesian terms as the nature of mind), physics and medicine (both based on observation and thus closely allied),[16] the passions (motions of the body and emotions of the soul), logic and mathematics (both having to do with order), and astronomy. In the century of Bacon, Galileo, and Descartes it was still possible to envision an all-encompassing scientific expertise of the human intellect. But to invite women to feed from the tree of knowledge was utopian.

The second group includes grammar, rhetoric (eloquence), moral philosophy, politics, geography, secular and ecclesiastical history, civil and canon law. Women should be allowed to study in the academies[17] to perfect

13. Alcover, *Poullain*, 78: "Savoir, libre-arbitre, volonté, c'est ce qu'il a retenu du message de Descartes Il a vu que cette philosophie, contrairement à l'autre, était une philosophie ouverte et c'est pourquoi il a poussé des portes que Descartes avait laissées closes" (Knowledge, free will, choice, are what Poullain has retained from Descartes's message. He saw that Descartes's philosophy, contrary to every other, was open, and that is why he has pushed open some doors that Descartes had left closed).

14. Poullain follows loosely here Aristotle's differentiation of the sciences in the *Nicomachean Ethics*.

15. In his *Principles of Philosophy*, Descartes visualized all knowledge like a tree, with metaphysics forming the roots, physics the trunk, and mechanics, medicine, and moral philosophy as its branches. See *Philosophical Essays and Correspondence*, ed. Roger Ariew (Indianapolis and Cambridge, 2000), 228. All citations of Descartes are to this volume, hereafter abbreviated *Phil. Essays*.

16. The publication of Isaac Newton's *Principia Mathematica* (1686) establishing physics as a theoretical science based on mathematics was still thirteen years in the future when Poullain wrote this passage.

17. Women, of course, were not allowed to study in the academies. Harth, *Cartesian Women*, 25: "Most of the salonnières had little or no access to the learned writing that circulated in the academies. Even the most educated women of the day, like Mme de Sevigné, Mme de Lafayette, Mme de Sablé, Mme de la Sablière, or Mlle de Scudéry, did not have the same command of classical languages and the depth of specialization possessed by the academicians, who were formed in the male educational institutions."

their knowledge of and help to develop further their mother tongue. Women have a natural ability to persuade and so are given to eloquence, the art of persuasion. They are also given to the practice of virtue, which makes the study of moral philosophy natural to them. The study of politics, geography, history, and law are extensions of the disciplines mentioned before them, through which women would realize the diversity of customs among different peoples and would be qualified to make their own personal judgments regarding these differences (a strong statement of cultural relativism for his time). He extended this privilege also to matters of ecclesiastical history, including the interpretation of Scripture. Male theologians, basing their conclusions on women's mental and moral frailty, had raised their most formidable barriers between the sexes in the domain of religious practices.[18] But Cartesian philosophy removed the obstacles. Poullain's early inclination towards Protestantism is particularly evident in his advocacy of a personal interpretation of Scripture. It must be remembered that at the end of the seventeenth century, the Roman Catholic Church was still very reluctant to allow her faithful direct access to the Bible.[19] The idea that women could be theologians was all the more subversive.[20]

Since women are as well equipped as men to pursue learning, they should do so. Women have as much right as men to the only avenue leading to happiness: true knowledge. Without knowledge, in fact, virtue is impossible. To the charge that learned people are often corrupt, Poullain responds that such corruption is the result of false knowledge, that is, knowledge that confuses the mind. Knowledge that clarifies the mind is true knowledge and is synonymous with virtue. Happiness is only possible with the acquisition of true knowledge and virtue. In Descartes this idea remains secular and potentially dangerous, implying that virtue found in knowledge of oneself is sufficient for happiness.[21] Poullain, however, adds a theological dimension, arguing that the happiness achieved through knowledge is the basis of our hope in the future life when our happiness will be complete.[22]

18. 1 Corinthians 14:34 and parallel passages in 1 Timothy; and Maclean, *Woman Triumphant*, 6: "Women are not allowed to speak in church, to teach doctrine, to administer the sacraments." See Poullain's response to theological antifeminism in the Preface and Remarks of his *Excellence*.

19. Timmermans, *L'Accès des femmes à la culture*, 703.

20. The French expression for describing this occurrence of a world turned upside down is "tomber en quenouille." Poullain's view is similar to that of the Jansenists who promoted feminine intellectual participation in biblical studies. See Timmermans, *L'Accès des femmes à la culture*, 664–700.

21. John Marshall, *Descartes's Moral Theory* (Ithaca and London, 1998), 6–7.

22. Poullain followed Cartesian philosophy closely at the expense of this "light confusion." However, it seems that Poullain either totally misunderstood Descartes's moral theory or played

But if women are as capable of learning as men, and if knowledge is as important to women as to men in the achievement of virtue and happiness, then women are as capable as men of holding positions in state[23] and church, of teaching, of being lawyers and judges as well as generals in the army. Poullain does not go on, as one might expect at this point, to advocate that women *should be allowed* to hold any of these positions. However, his bid for women's intellectual endeavor far exceeds any utilitarian purpose seeking to elevate the level of conversation between men and women. Rather, he aims to integrate the feminine experience into what had, until then, been a male-oriented field of knowledge.

3. Poullain raises the question whether, since there are differences among men, there is some difference between men and women that makes women less fit for study. He explores their imaginations, memories, and brilliance and concludes that there is not. What about differences in their bodies?[24] Bodily behavior and ideas of social decorum depend on the rules of a given society, so that any behavior can be correct or incorrect, depending on its cultural context. But considered in themselves, bodies as created by God were perfect, whether male or female.[25] Their primary purpose is procreation, and for this they are adapted perfectly to one another. Supposed temperamental differences between men and women arise from prejudices regarding social behavior, which are then attributed to the body as something essential to it. For this reason, little attention should be paid to common expressions about the sexes endlessly repeated. Thus, when men say that a woman who has shown great courage or strength has behaved like a man, they speak this way in order to flatter themselves, and such expressions contribute to the high opinion we have of men. We do not recognize that such statements are based on custom and so are contingent and arbitrary.

In truth, only our souls are capable of virtue; the body is merely the or-

---

it safe with regard to church censure by echoing remnants of Aquinas's views on the love of God. See Pièron, "De l'Influence sociale des principes cartésiens," 167.

23. Among the state positions mentioned by Poullain is queen. Maclean, *Woman Triumphant*, 60, remarks that "the issue of Salic Law is much discussed in the reign of Anne of Austria, both in imaginative literature and pamphlets."

24. Poullain had to address the Ancients' thesis of the biological superiority of the male sex, accepted also in Christian theology. In that tradition women are regarded as weaker than men with less capacity for virtue, and so in need of guidance from more rational males (see Maclean, *Woman Triumphant*, 6–7, 40). Cartesianism negated this distinction since, in that tradition, reason is gender neutral.

25. In saying that women's bodies were created perfect by God Poullain is reacting against M. Cureau de la Chambre, *L'Art de connoistre les hommes, où sont contenus les discours préliminaires qui servent de l'introduction à cette science* (Paris, 1667).

gan and instrument of the resolve of the mind. That resolve depends in turn on habit, exercise, and education, as well as external factors like gender and social class. Therefore, if we find fault with one or another person with regard to temperament, for example, it should be attributed to upbringing rather than to nature. The education given to women seems designed to dampen their courage. Thus the attributes often attached to women are purely arbitrary. It is said that they are timid, though many are as fearless as men. But fear is a natural emotion and arises in relation to our strength to resist some immediate danger that arouses it. Since women are not given physical training for attack and defense, they often have to suffer the outrages of the male sex, so prone to excess; fear is an appropriate response in this context. Poullain offers the same kind of analysis of avarice, credulity, superstition, chatter, curiosity, inconstancy, artifice, and malice. Such analysis in each case leads to two conclusions: that the supposed fault is not as grave as public opinion makes out and that the faults attributed to women are the result of the pathetic education they are given.

If philosophers had followed this rule in passing judgment on women they would have spoken more sensibly than they have. Poullain concludes his treatise by briefly examining some of the things—foolish in his view—spoken by the Ancients from Plato (thankful that he had not been created a woman) to Cato (contemptuous of women's ability to keep a secret), taking note in between of Aristotle's contention that women were monsters of nature, among other notions that have poisoned an entire intellectual tradition.[26]

His Postface reaffirms the thesis he has developed with respect to authority and tradition, but it also anticipates his discussion of the Bible in *Excellence* two years later.

Cartesian philosophy provided the basis on which Poullain could argue that men and women were equal in mind and therefore in the possibility of being virtuous. Differences between the sexes, therefore, must be attributable to social evolution. In arguing this way, Poullain's *On the Equality of the Two Sexes* would provide later generations with a social view of inequality that would allow for social solutions.

---

26. In viewing women's inferiority as an outlandish notion, Poullain was an iconoclast in his own time and stands out in that respect.

ON THE EQUALITY
OF THE TWO SEXES

A Physical and Moral Discourse
Which Shows the Importance of Getting Rid of One's Prejudices

PREFACE

Plan and purpose of the discourse.

The subject of women is a very delicate one. If men say anything good about them, they are suspected of having gallantry[1] or love in mind. When people read my title, they'll probably think that I'm dealing with one or the other. Let me put their minds at rest. Here is what I propose.

The best things that could happen to people who are struggling to acquire new knowledge is to question whether the traditional education they have received is valid, and then to try to seek out the truth for themselves. They quickly come to realize that we are full of prejudices[2] and that we have to make a real effort to get rid of them before we can hope to come to a clear and distinct understanding.

---

1. "Gallantry" is a loaded word. During the century, but before Poullain wrote, it meant homage to women because of their inherent excellence, though when Poullain says praise of women is motivated by *galanterie,* he seems to mean the tribute paid by the strong to the weak, or "love." Ian Maclean writes further: "It is not inappropriate to compare this with the feudal attitude that all women should be respected and protected by men. . . . *Galanterie* as it is conceived of in this period goes further than this, however, and aspires to higher rewards than those tokens of consideration with which suitors in contemporary novels are satisfied. There are grave moral problems in the courting of married women, and these are no smaller in the case of the unmarried who are served by gallants who envisage not marriage but physical possession. Du Bosc and Grenaille utter earnest warnings about such 'faux serviteurs,' and recommend to their ideals a 'chaste défiance'" (Maclean, *Woman Triumphant,* 130).

2. In a marginal note Poullain defines prejudice as judgments made without examination.

It seemed that the best way to introduce such an important topic was through a clear-cut, obvious example that is of interest to everybody. We will offer proofs that a very deep-seated universal belief is the result of prejudice and error in order to convince readers to judge things for themselves and not to let themselves be deceived by the opinions of others.[3]

Our choice fell on the question of the equality of the sexes, which is more prone to prejudice than any other subject.

If we look at current attitudes towards men and women, we find that intellectual and professional distinctions are more likely to be made than physical ones. The reason given for this discrimination in most writings is that women are incapable of playing any role in the sciences or in public life because they are not as intelligent as men. They deserve, therefore, their inferior status.

Rule of truth. We, however, propose to examine this idea by applying the rule of truth: accept nothing as true unless it is supported by clear and distinct ideas. Thus we find that the common prejudice is founded on mere popular hearsay, and that the two sexes *are* equal. Women have the same gifts of intelligence and energy as men.

Now to make our point we have to refute two adversaries: the common people and most scholars. The former are limited to the hackneyed, old arguments about how things have always been this way. We plan to answer them with a demonstration of how women have been repressed and deliberately excluded from the sciences and public positions. We will use examples from everyday life to show that women have many advantages that make them the equals of men. This will comprise the first part of the treatise.

The second part will address the arguments of the scholars and will be a refutation of their proofs. We will first give positive reasons to establish the idea of equality, then we will prove that the faults women are accused of are imaginary or unimportant and that they are the result of the appalling education they receive. The so-called faults will be shown to be actually a sign of women's considerable advantages.

Now there are two ways of treating this subject: we could either write a florid piece with elaborate turns of phrase and flowery language, or we could write a clearly reasoned essay that would take the reader from *a* to *b* so that he could follow along to the conclusion. It's

3. See René Descartes, *Discours de la méthode: Pour bien conduire sa raison et chercher la vérité dans les sciences* (Leyden, 1637), in *Phil. Essays.*

not so much that the two styles are incompatible, as that the intent of this kind of treatise, which is to convince and persuade, would be subverted. If the mind is too pleasantly distracted it cannot grasp solid facts.

Since we have such a high regard for women, if we allow ourselves to get carried away with compliments, then the reader will become distracted and will lose sight of the main point. This treatise is most intimately concerned with women, and we are about to make the strongest possible statements in their favor—though we have no intention of offending literary taste. We must, therefore, underline our serious intent so that people do not get the wrong idea of it and reject it as frivolous.

We are perfectly well aware that it will raise hackles in some quarters, and those who have a different agenda will not be slow to criticize it. We should warn our readers, therefore—and especially independent-minded women—that if they pay sufficient attention to what we are saying and to the variety of topics covered, then they will realize that the arguments are based on clarity and evidence. Close reading will help them perceive whether their objections are substantive or not. They will also become aware that the most specious arguments will come from certain people who reject good sense and experience in order to defend their own self-interest.

Let the reader reflect that his worst fears about the possible effects of this treatise may not materialize in the case of one single woman. In fact, there could be a positive outcome. Women might be persuaded to forsake the idleness in which they are forced to languish and take up study (which is more or less all they are allowed to do at the moment) if they think they are as capable of it as men.

As it is only unreasonable men who abuse, to the detriment of women, the advantages custom has bestowed upon them, by the same token it will be only mindless women who will use this work to turn against those men who treat them as equals and companions. Finally, if anyone should take exception to this treatise for any reason, he should lay the blame upon truth and not upon the author. To spare himself any distress, he should tell himself that it is merely a cerebral game. It is certain that this or a similar sleight of imagination, if it prevents truth from taking hold, makes it much less unpalatable to those who have difficulty in accepting it.

PART ONE

In which we show that popular opinion is formed on the basis of prejudice, and if we study with a dispassionate eye the way men and women behave, we have to admit that they are absolutely equal.

That men are filled with prejudices.
       There are all kinds of things that men believe with no justification, since they allow themselves to be duped into conviction by mere superficial appearances. If these appearances and their normally accepted habits were otherwise, then they would be equally convinced of the opposite.

       Apart from a handful of scientists, everyone is convinced beyond doubt that it is the sun that moves around the earth. But anyone who has made a study of the revolution of days and years is equally convinced that it is the earth that moves around the sun.[4] Our view of animals is that there must be some kind of intelligence inside them that makes them work, a bit the way savages, who've never come across springs and machinery, think that there must be a little devil inside watches and machines that sets them in motion.[5]

       If we had been brought up in the middle of the ocean and never approached land, we would surely believe, as we move around a vessel, that it was the land that was moving away from us, which is what children think when ships cast off. Everyone believes his own country is the best because it is the one he is most used to, and that the religion in which he was brought up is the true one, although he may never have thought to examine it or compare it with others. We always feel more sympathy towards our compatriots than towards foreigners in our various dealings, even when right is on the side of the stranger. We are more comfortable with people in the same profession even if they have lower intellectual and ethical standards. The unequal distribution of possessions and positions makes many people realize that men are certainly not equal.

4. Allusion to the Copernican system (1543), demonstrated mathematically by Johannes Kepler in 1610 and confirmed empirically by Galileo Galilei but condemned in 1633 on religious and moral grounds. Descartes withheld publication of his book *The World* (1634) which espoused Copernicus's view of the universe for fear of the Roman Inquisition.

5. Allusion to Descartes's theory of "animal machines": "I know well that beasts do many things better than we do, but I am not surprised at that. For that very fact serves to prove that they act naturally and by springs, like a clock, which tell the time better than our judgment can tell us" (Descartes, Letter to the Marquis of Newcastle, 23 November 1646, in *Phil. Essays*, 276).

If we seek the basis for all these diverse opinions, we find that it is either self-interest or habit. It is incomparably more difficult to talk men out of the opinions they hold through prejudice than those they have embraced through the strength and conviction of reason.

We can set among these opinions the one most commonly held about the difference between the two sexes and everything connected with it. It is the oldest and most widespread. Both the learned and the ignorant are so thoroughly convinced of the idea that women are inferior to men in aptitude and worth, and that they well deserve their inferior status, that to hold a contrary view would seem extraordinarily paradoxical.[6]

This view could be perfectly well maintained, however, without even resorting to formal reasoning, if men were more equitable and less self-centered in their judgments. It would be enough to make clear to them that discussion of the difference between the sexes up till now has been superficial and biased against women. To make a sound judgment about whether our sex is by nature superior to theirs we should study the question seriously and objectively and reject everything we have accepted from second-hand information without examining it further.

Opinion contrary to the one commonly held.

What one has to do to judge things accurately.

It is certain that if a man were to reach such an objective and disinterested state, he would realize, on the one hand, that the view that women are less noble and less excellent than ourselves is the result of hasty and blinkered judgment, and that it is only a few natural indispositions which make them susceptible to the faults and imperfections attributed to them and make so many people despise them. On the other hand, he would see that the very appearances which, superficially considered, deceive people about women would convince him of the truth if he looked at them more closely. Finally, if this man were a philosopher, he would find that there are physical reasons which provide incontrovertible proof that the two sexes are equal in body and in mind.

But as there are very few people able to follow this advice on their own, there is no point in giving it unless we undertake to work with them to help them put it into practice; and since the opinion of those who have no learning is the most widespread, it is there that we will begin our study.

If we were to ask any particular man what he thinks of women in general, and if he were to give an honest answer, he would probably

What men think about women.

6. In a marginal note, Poullain defines paradoxical as contrary to public opinion.

say that they were created exclusively for us, and that their sole function is to look after young children and take care of the household.
Perhaps the more insightful among them would add that many women
are spirited and headstrong, but that even the most extreme cases reveal the mark of their sex if we probe a bit: they lack firmness and deci-
siveness and do not have the depth of understanding that men pride
themselves on possessing. He would go on to say that access to science, government, and state positions is closed to women because of
divine providence and male wisdom, and that it would be a great joke
to see a woman holding a university chair and teaching rhetoric or
medicine as a professor, or striding through the streets followed by po-
lice commissioners and officers to execute justice, or pleading a case as
a defense lawyer before judges, or sitting on the bench to bring down
a judgment, or heading a parliament, or leading an army into battle, or
speaking before republics or princes as head of a diplomatic mission.

  I admit that all this would surprise us, but only because of its novelty. If women had a hand in creating states and setting up their various
institutions, then we would be as used to seeing them in office as they
are to seeing us, and we would be no more surprised to see them in the
seat of justice[7] than to meet them in a shop. If we press people a little,
we find that their most powerful reasons are reduced to stating that
things have always been as they are where women are concerned,
which means that that is how they should be, and that if women had
been fit for learning and high office, they would be enjoying them
alongside men.

False idea of
custom.

  This reasoning derives from the opinion we have of the fair-
mindedness of our sex and from a false idea we have of custom: if something is well established, then we think it must be right. Since we think
that reason plays a role in everything men do, most people cannot imagine that reason was not consulted in the setting up of practices that are so
universally accepted, and we imagine that reason and prudence dictated
them, since these two qualities force us to conform to practices when
we cannot avoid following them without considerable inconvenience.

Why women
are thought to
be inferior to
men.

  Everyone sees women in his own country in such a state of subjugation that they depend on men for everything, with no access to
scholarship nor to any position that is achieved through intellectual
gifts. No one reports ever having seen women in a different situation.
We know, too, that this is how things always were, and that there is

7. The French here is "fleur de lys"; it is a symbol of royal judicial prerogative.

nowhere on earth where women are not treated as they are right here. There are even some places where women are treated like slaves. In China their feet are bound during childhood to stop them leaving the house, where they see virtually only their husbands and their children. They are also shut in in Turkey. They are not much better off in Italy. Almost all the peoples of Asia, Africa, and America treat their women the way we treat servants. Everywhere they are given only what are considered menial tasks, and, because it is they alone who perform the everyday chores of the household and childrearing, people think that they were created expressly for this purpose and that they are incapable of anything else. We find it difficult to imagine that things could be right any other way, and it even seems that we could never change them, however hard we tried.

Even the wisest legislators found no interesting role for women when they founded their republics. All laws seem to have been made to keep men in their present position of power. Men we regard as fonts of wisdom have never said anything good about women. In fact, men's behavior towards women in all places and at all times is so uniform that it seems to be part of an organized movement. Some people have even thought that men are impelled to behave this way through some hidden instinct ordained universally by the Creator of nature.

This view is all the more easily justifiable when we consider the way women themselves tolerate their situation. They see it as being their natural place. Either because they do not think at all about what they are, or because they are born and raised in a state of dependency, they share the male point of view. In all these things, both men and women tend to believe that their minds are as different as their bodies and that the distinctions that necessarily exist between them should be extended to all aspects of life. This opinion, however, like most of the ones we hold about custom and usage, is pure prejudice, and is dictated by superficial appearance rather than close analysis. We would certainly reject it if we took the trouble to go back to its origin. We could find many examples of things that were done formerly that we could compare with the things we do now, and we could weigh ancient customs against present-day ones. If we had followed this rule more often, we would have avoided a lot of mistakes. As far as women's present situation is concerned, we would have realized that it is simply the rule of the stronger that has put them in such a subservient position, and we would understand that it is not through any natural deficiencies that they have been denied the advantages enjoyed by our sex.

How we should judge ancient customs.

Indeed, when we think honestly about human history, both past and present, we realize that there is one common denominator: reason has always been the weakest element in our decisions, and all stories seem to have been made up for the sole purpose of demonstrating what we see in any lifetime, that from man's very origins might has always prevailed. The greatest empires of Asia owe their beginnings to usurpers and brigands, and the inheritors of the ruins of Greece and Rome were upstarts who thought they could resist their masters and dominate their equals. All societies exhibit the same kind of conduct. If men behave in this way towards their equals, then it is most likely that they behaved in the same way first of all towards women. Here, more or less, is how it came about.

How we have always been governed.

Men, realizing they were the stronger and physically superior sex, imagined they were superior in all respects. This was of no great consequence for women at the beginning of the world, when a very different state of affairs prevailed from today. There was no government, no learning, no employment, no established religion; dependence was not considered irksome. I imagine that people lived like children, and winning or losing was part of the game. Both men and women, who were naive and innocent, contributed equally to the tasks of tilling and hunting as savages do today. A man went about his business and a woman hers; the person who made the greatest contribution was the most respected.

Historic conjecture. How men obtained mastery.

Since women's strength was sapped for a time by the indisposition of pregnancy and its aftermath, which made them unable to work as before, the help of their husbands became absolutely essential to them, especially when they had young children. Nothing more came of this than occasional marks of favor and preference when the family consisted solely of the mother and father and a few small children. But when families expanded and there lived in the same household the father's mother and father, the children's children with brothers and sisters, young and old, the dependence became more widespread and hence more perceptible. The wife became submissive towards her husband, the sons gave greater consideration to their father who in turn dominated the children. Since it is difficult for sons to get along well under one roof, we can imagine how easily fights broke out. The oldest, who was stronger than the others, hung on to his privileges. Might forced the youngest to bow to the eldest. And the daughters followed their mothers' example.

One can easily imagine that tasks became specialized in the

household: women, who were obliged to remain indoors to raise their children, took over the inside chores, whereas the men, stronger and more independent, performed those outside. After the death of the mother and father the eldest tried to take over. It did not occur to the girls, who were used to staying indoors, to leave the house. A few discontented younger sons rebelled against this new authority and were forced to withdraw and form a separate group. They met with others in a similar situation and banded together. Realizing they were without possessions, they sought means to acquire some. Since the only ones available belonged to others, they swept down on the most convenient victim, and made sure they retained their spoils by seizing the owner at the same time.

The voluntary dependence that had existed within families disappeared at the moment of this invasion. The mothers and fathers, together with their children, were forced to obey an unjust usurper, and the condition of women became more distressing than before. For whereas in the past they had married members of their family who had treated them like sisters, now they were forced to accept as husbands unknown foreigners who regarded them as the most desirable part of their booty.

The victor usually despises the people he thinks are the weakest among those he has conquered, and since women appeared the weakest because their role required less strength, they were seen as being inferior to men.

Why women were not included in the first occupations.

Some men went no further than an initial act of usurpation, but the more ambitious, encouraged by their success, tried to further their conquests. Since women were too humane to be involved in these wicked plans, they were left at home, and men were chosen for their aptitude for projects which required force. At this point, things were only valued for their suitability for the goal in view; and since the desire to dominate had become the ruling passion, and since it could only be satisfied by violence and injustice, it is not surprising that men, who were its sole instruments, should be preferred over women. It was the men who maintained the territory they had conquered. Only male advice was used to establish tyranny because only men could execute it, and in this way women's gentleness and humanity were the reasons they took no part in the governing of states.

The example of princes was soon followed by their subjects. Everyone tried to dominate his neighbor, and individuals began to rule more absolutely over their families. When a lord found himself master of numerous lands and peoples, he made them into a kingdom. He made laws to govern it, chose some men as officers and rewarded with high office those who had best served his ambitions. There was such a remarkable preference for one sex over the other that women were even less respected, and since their temperament and their roles set them at a distance from carnage and war, it was thought that the only contribution they could make to the perpetuation of the kingdoms was by helping to populate them.

It was inevitable that when states were established distinctions would be made among those who lived in them. Decorations were invented to distinguish certain people, and signs of respect were created to enhance perceived differences. Thus the external deference shown to those in authority became associated with the idea of power.

How women were excluded from the ministry of religion among the pagans.

It is not necessary to explain here how God became known to humankind, but He has been consistently worshiped since the beginning of the world. Public worship, however, has been institutionalized only since people have gathered together to form societies. Since it was customary to honor power with marks of respect, it was thought that God, too, should be honored with certain ceremonies that would be proof of the idea of His greatness. Temples were built, sacrifices instituted, and the men who already held temporal power lost no time in seizing spiritual power; since custom had already taught women that everything belonged to men, they asked for no share in the ministry. Ideas of God were completely corrupted by fable and poetic fiction, so male and female deities were created and priestesses were inducted for the service of those of their own sex, but they depended on the authority and the pleasure of the priests.

It has happened that women have governed great states, but we should not, on that account, imagine that [they were called upon out of a spirit of reparation];[8] it was rather that they were skillful enough to manipulate things so that power could not be wrested from their hands. There exist today hereditary states where females succeed males and become queens or princesses, but there is reason to believe that if these kingdoms have been allowed to fall to the distaff side, it has only been to prevent them from sinking into civil war. If women have been allowed to act as regents, it is only in the belief that mothers, whose love for their children is unquestioned, would take particular care of their states during their minority.

8. Addition in the edition of 1676.

Thus, since women were exclusively concerned with the house- *Why they were*
hold, and had enough to occupy them there, it is no wonder that they *excluded from*
did not make any scientific discoveries, most of which were made by *the sciences.*
leisured and unemployed males. The Egyptian priests, who had little
else to do, spent their time talking about the effects of nature, which
were of particular concern to them. By dint of discussion, they made
discoveries news of which aroused the curiosity of other men who
came to seek them out. Sciences, which were in their infancy at that
point, did not draw women out of the house. In addition, jealousy,
which already clouded the judgment of their husbands, would have
made them imagine that their wives were visiting the priests for the
sake of their personal charms rather than for their learning.

When a number of men had acquired sufficient learning, they assembled in a given place to talk at their leisure. As each of them expressed his ideas the sciences took shape. Academies were created to
which women were not invited; in this way they were excluded from
the sciences as well as from everything else.

Even though they were so severely restricted, there were still a
few women who managed to gain access to the conversations and the
writings of scholars. Very soon they rivaled the cleverest of these, but
because of an unfortunate social etiquette which did not allow men to
visit them, nor other women to meet together for fear of creating difficulties, they had no disciples or adherents, and all their learning died
fruitlessly with them.

When we consider how new fashions are constantly introduced
and refined, we will realize that they did not preoccupy people much
when societies were in their infancy. Everything was simple and crude.
The only concern was with basic necessity. Men skinned animals,
sewed the skins together, and fashioned garments out of them. Then
came style, and with everyone dressing to his own taste, people were
quick to adopt the fashion that suited them best. The subjects of any
given prince were all too eager to imitate him.

Fashion was different from government and learning; it was an *Why women*
area open to women no less than to men. And because men realized *gave themselves*
how much it enhanced women's beauty, they encouraged women's in- *up to frivolity.*
terest in it. Realizing that various accouterments lent luster to their
natural attributes and their powers of attraction, the two sexes vied
with each other over them. But men's greater and more grandiose preoccupations prevented them from giving too much attention to such
things.

Women were thus able to show their skill and taste. They realized that external adornment made men look more kindly towards them, which made their condition more bearable. They took pains, therefore, to exploit anything they thought might lend them charm. They used gold, silver, precious stones as soon as they became fashionable. Since men refused to let them shine through their intellectual qualities, they concentrated exclusively upon making themselves look more attractive. They succeeded superlatively, and their clothes and their beauty have won them greater renown than all the books and all the learning in the world. It is unimaginable that they would change this preoccupation now. It is a tradition that has come down to us, and it seems to be too ancient to be challenged.

*What men
should do to
justify their
behavior
towards women.*

This historical conjecture, which is consistent with men's observed behavior, makes it quite clear that it is exclusively through their superior physical strength that they have kept for themselves all external advantages, from which women are excluded. For them to be able to claim that this is the result of rational behavior, they would have to show that only the most capable among them received their privileges. They would have to: use a wise selection process to appoint people, accept into the universities only those who clearly have aptitude for it, name to high office only those with most talent and exclude all others; in short, every man would do the job he is best suited for.

*How men
obtain their
positions.*

What we see happening is quite the opposite, and men are appointed to public office either by accident or through necessity or self-interest. Children learn their fathers' profession because that's what they have always been familiar with. One son is forced into the law when he would have preferred the army, if given a choice, and the most gifted man in the world will never get the office he deserves unless he can afford to pay for it.

How many people remain in the mire when they might have distinguished themselves if they had been given encouragement? How many peasants might have become renowned scholars if they had been given the chance to study? We would be mistaken in thinking that the most distinguished people of today are the ones who showed most promise among their generation in the area in which they have made their name. And we would also be wrong to suppose that among such vast numbers of people sunk in ignorance there are none who, had they had the same advantages, could not have better fulfilled their potential.

On what grounds then, can we be sure that women are less

capable than ourselves, since it is not chance but an insurmountable impediment that makes it impossible for them to play their proper role in society? I am not for one moment saying that all women are gifted for learning or for higher office, nor that every single one is good at everything; nobody claims that for men, either. My only point is to insist that as far as the two sexes are concerned, there is as much aptitude in one as in the other.

We need look no further than children's games. Girls exhibit more goodwill, more character, more dexterity. If they are not being threatened or ridiculed, they are better and cleverer company; their speech is livelier, freer, more light-hearted, they pick up more readily what is being taught them, as long as they are being taught the same things as boys; they work harder and more painstakingly, and they are more obedient, more modest, and better disciplined. In short, they possess to a greater degree all the excellent qualities which, when found in young men, are taken as proof that they are better suited for great things than their peers. *Comparison of children of both sexes.*

Although ample proof is given by both sexes when they are still in their cradles that it is the fair sex that shows most promise, this fact is nonetheless ignored. Teachers and lessons are for males only. Infinite care is taken to instruct them in everything that can develop their minds, whereas women are left to languish in idleness, inactivity, and ignorance or to limp through the basest, most simple-minded kinds of activities.

But we only need to use our eyes to see that the case of the two sexes is like that of two brothers in a family; the younger one often makes it clear, despite his neglected education, that the only advantage the elder has over him is to have been born first.

Normally, what is the use to men of the education they are given? To the majority it is of no use at all for the purpose it is meant to serve; it neither prevents large numbers of them from falling into dissoluteness and vice, nor others from remaining eternally ignorant or even becoming more stupid than they were before. If they once possessed any decency, any good humor, any civility, they lose it through study. Their manner is offensive and everyone offends them; their manners are so dreadful and unbearable that one would have thought their youth had been spent in a country of savages. Such learning as they have acquired is like smuggled goods which they dare not or cannot put up for sale, and if they plan on going back into society and cutting a good figure, they have to go to a ladies' school to learn politeness *That study is of no use to the majority of men.*

and all the points of etiquette essential today to people of good breeding.[9]

If we thought about it, instead of despising women because they have no learning, we would consider them fortunate: although they are deprived of the means of putting their talents to good use and of the advantages that study would bring, at least they have no occasion to spoil them or lose them. Yet despite this privation, they increase in virtue, in intelligence, and in grace as they increase in age. If we were to make an impartial comparison between young men at the end of their studies and their female counterparts, and if we didn't know the background of either, we would imagine the reverse of their respective educations.

A woman's very appearance, her expression, her look, her bearing, her movements have about them something calm, wise, and straightforward that distinguishes her from a man. Women are fastidious in their observation of good manners; their discretion is unimpeachable.

Differences in the manners of the two sexes.

No double-entendre ever passes their lips. Anything slightly risqué offends their ears and they cannot bear the sight of anything that offends modesty.

Most men's behavior is quite the opposite. Their gait is often too brusque, their movements awkward, their eyes too brazen, and their idea of a good time is to get together and give themselves up to things that are better left unseen and unheard.

Engage in a conversation with one or several women and then with a so-called scholar. You will see the huge difference between them. You get the impression that what men put into their heads when they study serves only to stop up their minds and to spread confusion.

Comparison between women and scholars.

Very few are able to express themselves clearly, and their difficulty in summoning up the right words makes one lose one's taste for whatever they have to say, even if it makes sense. Unless they happen to be very clever and with people from their own group, they cannot sustain an hour's conversation.

Women, on the other hand, state their meaning clearly and sensibly. Their words come effortlessly, their discourse has a beginning, a middle, and an end; and their imagination knows no bounds when they are feeling at ease. They have the gift of expressing their opinions gently in a pleasant, nonconfrontational way, and this contributes as much as reason to their being accepted. In contrast men speak in a harsh and unyielding tone.

---

9. In French, "l'école des dames" referred to the salon culture that glorified women's role in polite society.

If a subject is brought up for discussion among educated women, they are the quicker to get the gist of it. They can see it from several angles. Whatever truths are uttered are more readily accepted in their minds, and if the speaker knows something about the subject and they have no reason to distrust him, then their prejudices are quite clearly less obdurate than men's, so they are less likely to reject the truths that are being put forward. They are far removed from the spirit of contradiction and dispute so rampant among scholars. They do not quibble vainly over words and never use mysterious, technical terms that camouflage ignorance so effectively. Everything they say is intelligible and well thought out.

I have found it a great pleasure to converse with women of all classes whom I have met in town and in the country, to find out their strengths and their weaknesses; and I have found that those who were not stultified by need or work have more good sense than most of the works that ordinary scholars think are so marvelous.

When they spoke of God, not one of them took it into her head to tell me that *she saw Him as a venerable old man!* They said, on the contrary, that they could not imagine Him at all, that is to say, to picture Him as some idea of a man. They took it that there is a God, because they could not accept that they themselves or the things around them came into being by chance or were the work of some created being. And because the way their lives turned out had little to do with their own foresight, and since the outcome was rarely the result of their own decisions, then it must be that divine providence dictated it. *Opinion of a great philosopher.*

When I asked them what they thought of their soul, they did not reply that *it is a most subtle flame, or the disposition of the organs of their bodies, or that it is able to expand or contract.* They replied, on the contrary, that they recognized that it is distinct from their body, and the only thing they could say for certain about it was that it was nothing like anything they could apprehend through their senses, and that if they had studied they would know exactly what it was. *These are the opinions of philosophers.*

Unlike the doctors, not a single nurse said that their patients are better because *the coctric faculty is nobly fulfilling its functions.* The evidence of a great jet of blood spurting from a vein makes them consider absurd those who refuse to believe in the circulation of the blood.[10]

When I asked these women why they thought that rocks exposed

10. Poullain is deriding the Scholastics' jargon laden with circular explanations such as this one on the digestive faculty. He is also poking fun at the medical establishment for denying the theory of blood circulation demonstrated by William Harvey (1578–1657) and endorsed (although with some variations) by Descartes.

to the sun and to the southern rains are more eroded than those in the north, none of them was silly enough to reply *that it's because the moon takes great bites out of them* as some philosophers are pleased to imagine; they replied rather that the heat of the sun dries them out, so that the subsequent rains soften them more easily.

Scholastic question.

I deliberately asked more than twenty women if they didn't believe *that God can bring it about by potentia absoluta*[11] *that a stone can be elevated to the beatific vision,* but I could get nothing more out of them than that they thought I was making fun of them.

What are the advantages of learning.

The greatest advantage that we can expect of learning is to be able to discern and to judge between what is true and evident and what is false and obscure, and thus to avoid the pitfalls of error and deception. We tend to think that men—or at least those we think of as learned— have this advantage over women. However, if we exercise some of the good judgment I just mentioned, we find that it is one of the qualities they lack most. For not only do they hold forth in a confused and obscure way—a ploy they use to dominate and exploit the credulity of ordinary, trusting people—but they even reject what is clear and evident, and mock anyone who speaks plainly and intelligibly as being too facile and too commonplace. They are also the first to believe in obscure theories, as they are taken in by their mysteriousness. If we doubt any of the above we have only to listen attentively, and then try to get them to explain themselves.

Women have discernment of mind.

Women's disposition is totally unlike any of this. Women who know anything of the world cannot bear to have even their children speak Latin in their presence. They are suspicious of those who do, and often say they are afraid that a foreign language might be a mask for rudeness. Not only are they not heard to use technical terms—which are thought by some to be sacrosanct—but they cannot even remember them, though they have heard them often enough, and they have a good memory. And when people speak to them incomprehensibly

---

11. *Potentia absoluta* was an important term in medieval nominalistic theology, usually contrasted with *potentia ordinata.* William of Occam, Duns Scotus, and their late medieval follower Gabriel Biel all defined these terms in the same way. Heiko Oberman writes: "The distinction should be understood to mean that God can—and, in fact, has chosen to—do certain things according to the laws which he freely established, that is, *de potentia ordinata.* On the other hand, God can do everything that does not imply contradiction, whether God has decided to do these things [*de potentia ordinata*] or not, as there are many things God can do which he does not want to do. The latter is called God's power *de potentia absoluta.*" See *The Harvest of Medieval Theology: Gabriel Biel and Late Medieval Nominalism* (Cambridge, Mass., 1963), 30–65, at 37.

they admit honestly that they are not learned or clever enough to understand, or else they realize that people who talk like that have themselves limited learning.

If we are looking for an image for the way men and women communicate, we might see men as laborers struggling with rough and unhewn stones, and women as architects or skilled stone cutters who know how to polish and turn and display what they have in their hands.

Not only do we find that a lot of women judge things as well as if they had had a better education, without either the prejudices or the confusion of ideas endemic among learned men, but there are many who have such wise good sense that they can speak on scientific topics as if they had always studied them.

They speak graciously. They have the art of finding the most elegant turns of phrase and of using a single word as efficiently as men use several, and if language in general is under discussion, they have views about it that they share with the best grammarians. In short, we see that they make better use of the mere practice of language than most men do of practice together with study.

They know the art of speaking.

Eloquence is a talent that they come by so naturally and so exclusively that we have to admit their superiority. They convince us of whatever they want to. They can speak for the prosecution and the defense without studying law, and there are few judges who have not discovered that they are the equals of any lawyer. Is there anything more powerful and more eloquent than the letters various women write on a complete range of topics, but particularly on the passions? Their reflections on the subject are a blueprint for the beauty and secret of eloquence. They treat the subject so delicately and straightforwardly that they convince us utterly, and all the rhetoric in the world would not furnish men with what seems to come naturally to women. Writings on eloquence and poetry, exhortations, sermons, and discourses are in no way above their heads, and the only thing missing from their criticism is presentation in a conventional form.

They understand eloquence.

I fully expect that this treatise will come under their scrutiny. Some women will want to disagree with it, some will find its form inferior to the breadth and dignity of its subject, others will find that its expression is not sufficiently refined, its style not elevated and noble enough. They will say that some areas are not touched upon, and some important points are omitted. But I hope too that my good will and my determination to say nothing but what is true and to avoid the excessive literariness that might smack of the novel will pardon me in their eyes.

Another advantage women have over men is that they are much more animated in the gestures that accompany their speech. We no sooner see from their expression that they mean to touch us than we are won over by them. They have an air of nobility and grandeur, their deportment is easy and majestic, their demeanor straightforward, their movements natural, their manner engaging; they speak easily in a sweet, gentle voice. Their message is accompanied by such beauty and grace that it penetrates our minds and opens our hearts to them. When they speak of good and evil their faces reveal an honesty that makes their arguments more persuasive. When they are carried away on the topic of virtue their heart is on their lips, and what they say about it, enhanced as it is by figures of speech and their own characteristically charming turns of phrase, appears a thousand times more lovely.

*They possess
an eloquence in
action.*

It is a pleasure to listen to a woman plead a legal case. However complicated her affairs may be she is able to unravel them and explicate them clearly. She gives a precise account of her claim and that of the person she represents. She lays out the background of the case, how she plans to proceed, the elements she is going to emphasize, and the dispositions she has taken; and throughout, a gift for the law is revealed which men simply do not possess.

*They under-
stand the law
and its practice.*

All of the above makes me believe that if women studied law they would be at least as successful as men. They obviously love peace and justice more than we do; they dislike quarrels and are pleased to intervene to resolve them successfully. They somehow manage to find extraordinary expedients to reconcile opinions, and in the normal running of their own or others' households they rely upon the chief principles of equity upon which the whole of jurisprudence is founded.

The writings by intelligent women contain a well-ordered narrative, but also a greater felicity which is more persuasive than ours. They are good at picking out what is relevant or irrelevant to the topic, at following the story line, at highlighting the essential details of people's characters, at unraveling plots and following the major and minor ones. This is all clearly demonstrated in stories and novels by learned ladies who are still living.[12]

*They are well
suited to be
storytellers.*

12. The name of Mlle de Scudéry (1607–1701) comes automatically to mind, as the most prolific and successful woman writer of that era. On her and especially on her significance, see Joan DeJean, *Tender Geographies: Women and the Origins of the Novel in France* (New York, 1991).

How many women are there who have learned as much from sermons, conversations, and a few slim works of piety as learned doctors with St. Thomas Aquinas on the shelves of their libraries and in their classrooms.[13] The soundness and depth they bring to discussions on the subject of the greatest mysteries and the whole of Christian morality would allow them to pass as great theologians if they had a cap and gown and could quote a few passages in Latin.

They know theology.

Women would seem to have been born to practice medicine and heal the sick. Their meticulousness and understanding go half way to relieving their patients' suffering. They are good not only at applying remedies but also at finding them. They invent them endlessly—though we underestimate them because they are less expensive than those of Hippocrates and they do not require a prescription.[14] Yet they are all the more reliable and easy because they are more natural. Finally, their observations about medical practice are so accurate and so precisely reasoned, that they often make all the notebooks of the faculty superfluous.

They understand medicine.

Countrywomen who are used to work in the fields understand amazingly well the vagaries of the seasons, and their almanacs are much more reliable than the printed ones by astrologers. They explain in such a simple way the fertility or sterility of a given year, depending on the winds, the rains, and whatever else causes change in the weather, that when you listen to them you cannot help feeling sorry for the scholars who attribute these effects to the aspects, the approach, and the ascendance of the planets.[15] All this makes me think that if women had been taught that the illnesses the human body is susceptible to are often caused by individual constitution, exercise, climate, diet, education, and life's varied patterns, it would never have entered their heads to think that human health is at the mercy of the stars which are bodies millions of miles away.

They know the opposite of the astrologers' illusions.

The provenance of the diversity of habits and inclinations.

It is true that there are some sciences women never pronounce on because they are not social or interactionary sciences. Algebra, geom-

13. St. Thomas Aquinas (1225–74) was the pivotal figure in incorporating Aristotle's theories into Christian theology. In the seventeenth century his name had become synonymous with "Scholastic."

14. In the seventeenth century, Hippocrates still represented the official, albeit ancient, medical science. The whole male Faculté de médecine was still committed to it despite various breakthroughs like the discovery of the ovum and of the circulation of blood.

15. Astrological predictions depended on precise determinations of the position of wandering stars against the fixed heavenly bodies, in order to divine the course of human events. Cartesians rejected astrology, as had many intellectuals at least since the Italian humanists in the fifteenth century.

Why they are never heard to speak of certain sciences.

etry, and optics scarcely ever emerge from laboratories or learned academies to enter the mainstream of conversation. Their main function, however, is to clarify thought, so they should make only a discreet appearance in normal intercourse like a hidden spring that sets a vast machine in motion. What I mean is that they should be applied to topics of conversation to give geometric precision to speech and thought without the speaker having to appear to be a geometer.

That all this is more easily observable among ladies.

All our observations about the qualities of the mind can easily be made about women of any class. But if we go to the court and talk with the ladies there, then we notice something quite different. Their intelligence seems to correspond quite naturally to their status. They not only possess exquisite refinement of manners, but they have disarming, easy intelligence and a very characteristic grace and nobility. Mere men seem to approach them only with great respect. They always have a clear perception of things that gives them a remarkable way of speaking. In short, a man of taste, when shown two letters by two ladies of different classes, will easily be able to tell which is by the lady of quality.

That women scholars, of whom there is no shortage, are more worthy of esteem than male scholars.

How many ladies have there been and how many are there still who should be counted as scholars—or even better than scholars. Our century boasts more than all the preceding centuries put together, and as they have become the equals of men they deserve greater respect for specific reasons. They had to overcome the indolence in which their sex is raised, to give up the pleasures and idleness to which they had been reduced, to surmount various public obstacles that keep them from study, and to rise above the unfortunate opprobrium in which female scholars are generally held, in addition to the normal prejudice against their sex. They have achieved this, and, either because those obstacles have made their minds keener and more penetrating, or because these qualities are natural to them, they have, relatively speaking, outshone men.

It must be recognized that women are, in general, capable of scientific study.

We must say, however, without in any way detracting from the admiration that these distinguished ladies inspire, that it is opportunity and external advantages that have allowed them to achieve this—as is the case with male scholars—and there are countless others who would have done no less if they had had the same advantages. If we are unfair enough to say that all women are indiscreet when we know five or six who are, then, by the same token, we should be fair enough to say that the whole sex is capable of scientific study, since we know several who have risen to the challenge.

Most people imagine that Turks, barbarians, and savages do not have the same capacity as European peoples. If, however, we saw five or six who did have aptitude or the title of Doctor, which is not at all impossible, then surely we would revise our opinion and admit that these people are men like ourselves, can do the same things, and, if they had the training, would be in no way inferior to us.[16] The women with whom we live are surely as good as a barbarian or a savage, to make us think about them neither less favorably nor less rationally.

If, despite all the above, common people stubbornly refuse to consider that women are as well suited to science as we are, then they must at least recognize that such studies are less necessary for them. There are two reasons for studying the sciences: one is to understand the objects in question and the other is to become virtuous through this knowledge. Thus in this life, which is so short, the sole aim of science should be to increase virtue, and since women possess this anyway, they can be said to have, through singular good fortune, the main advantage of scientific study without the study itself.

Merely to watch women in their daily pursuits should convince us that they are no less Christian than men. They accept the Gospel simply and submissively. They practice its teachings in exemplary fashion. Their respect for anything connected with religion has always been so great that no one doubts that they are more pious and devout than we are. Admittedly they sometimes go to excess in their practice, but I cannot see that this excess is all that bad. The reason for it is the ignorance we keep them in. If they go too far in their practice, at least their belief is genuine; clearly if they properly understood the nature of virtue, they would embrace it in a completely different way, since already they cling to it so strongly in their darkness. *That women have as much virtue as we do.*

Women seem to be born to practice charity, which is the virtue of the Gospels. As soon as they learn of their neighbor's plight, their hearts are touched and tears well in their eyes. Are not theirs the hands that distribute most generously in time of public disaster? Is it not women who take care of the poor and sick of the parish, who visit the prisons and help in the hospitals? Have we not given the very name of Sisters of Charity to those pious girls who go to different parts of the *They are charitable.* *Sisters of Charity.*

16. See Montaigne, *Essays*, 1.31, in *The Complete Works*, trans. Donald M. Frame (Stanford, 1958), 152: "Each man calls barbarism whatever is not his own practice; for indeed it seems we have no other test of truth and reason than the example and pattern of the opinions and customs of the country we live in."

town giving out food and medicine at regular hours, and bring such dignity to their task?[17]

Sisters of the Hôtel-Dieu.

And even if these sisters of the Hôtel-Dieu were the only women in the world to practice this virtue towards their neighbors, I do not think that men could claim legitimately to have superiority over their sex. Those are the women we should put in the gallery of strong women;[18] they are the ones whose lives we should celebrate with hymns of praise and whose deaths we should honor with highest eulogies. It is they who exemplify the true Christian religion, namely, truly heroic virtue practiced strictly according to all its commandments and counsels. These girls have renounced the world and themselves, they have taken vows of perpetual poverty and chastity in order to take up their cross—and the harshest cross imaginable—and to place themselves under the yoke of Jesus Christ for the rest of their days, dedicating themselves to a hospital where all kinds of patients, of whatever country or religion, are admitted indiscriminately. They tend them without making distinctions between them, and, following the example of their Bridegroom, they take upon themselves all the infirmities of mankind, without flinching when their eyes are constantly assailed by the most terrible sights, their ears by curses and screams of the sick, and their noses by all the infections of the human body. As a sign of the spirit with which they are infused, they carry the sick in their arms from bed to bed, and encourage the dispossessed not with empty words but by the convincing and personal example of an invincible patience and charity.

Can anything greater be conceived among Christians? Other women are no less ready to help their neighbors. They simply lack opportunities or are distracted by other occupations. I find it as insulting to deduce from this, as many do, that women are naturally men's servants, as to claim that those whom God has endowed with special talents are the servants and slaves of those in whose interest they employ them.

How they live celibate lives.

Whatever kind of life women choose, there is always something remarkable in their behavior. If they remain single and live in the

17. With the help of Louise de Marillac, Vincent de Paul (1581–1660), canonized in 1737, organized several charitable foundations. The religious community of the Filles de la Charité (created in 1633) was dedicated to the sick and the poor and worked in the hospital called the Hôtel-Dieu.

18. Poullain's tone is reminiscent of Pierre Le Moyne's book, *La Gallerie des femmes fortes* (Paris, 1648), which exalted traditional feminine virtues in terms of heroic abnegation.

world, they only stay there to act as an example to others. Christian modesty appears on their faces and in their dress. Their virtue is their chief ornament. They keep away from company and worldly entertainments, and they prove by their strict attention to pious observances that they avoided the responsibilities and commitment of matrimony only to enjoy more complete spiritual freedom and to have as their sole obligation that of pleasing God.

There are as many religious houses run by women as by men and their life is no less exemplary. They live in greater isolation and practice equally austere penitence; abbesses are in no way inferior to abbots. They administer the rules with enviable wisdom and rule the girls with such prudence that there is no disorder. The fame of nunneries, their vast possessions, and their sound establishment are a tribute to the firm control that the mother superior exercises over each one.

How they live in convents.

Matrimony is the most natural state for most men. Their commitment to it is life-long. They spend in the married state those years that should be entirely governed by reason. Marriage with its ups and downs presents a challenge to the two partners and tests their fortitude. We don't have to look far to realize that women are better fitted for it than we are. Girls are capable of running a household at an age when men still need a tutor, and the most frequent remedy for a wayward youth who has gone off the rails is to give him a wife who will calm him down with her example, moderate his excesses, and rescue him from debauchery.

How they live within marriage.

What conciliatory tactics do women not employ to live in harmony with their husbands! They submit to their orders, they do nothing without asking their advice, they restrain themselves in many ways to avoid their displeasure, and they often forego the most innocent entertainments to avoid arousing suspicion. We know which sex is more faithful to the other, which puts up more cheerfully with the setbacks that occur during a marriage and generally shows greater wisdom in dealing with them.

Most households are governed exclusively by women to whom their husbands have yielded all authority. The care with which they raise their children is of greater importance than the managing of their material possessions both to the families themselves and to the state. They devote themselves entirely to their well-being. Women often lose sleep worrying that some harm will come to their children. Mothers gladly go without even the most basic things so that their offspring do not want for anything. Their children's slightest sufferings bring

How they raise their children.

them acute misery, and their greatest sorrow is to be unable to alleviate their offspring's woes by taking them upon themselves.

The care they take over their education.

Who does not know of the care they take in instructing their children in the rudiments of virtue as soon as they are able to understand it? They try to make them know and fear God and teach them how little children can worship Him. They pass them on to a tutor as soon as they are ready for one and pay careful attention to their choice, so that the children will have the best education possible. What is even more admirable is that women set a good example for their children to follow.[19]

That greater detail would show women to even greater advantage.

If we were to go into the full details of the various events of their lives and examine how they use them as an occasion to practice virtue, then the most significant items would lead us to a full-scale panegyric. We would be able to show their sobriety in eating and drinking, their patience in time of adversity, their strength and courage in the face of misfortune, fatigue, fasts, and sleepless nights, their moderation in pleasures and passions, their readiness to do good, their prudence in business, their honesty in all things; in short we could show that they possess all of our virtues, whereas there are many grave faults which are found only in men.

These, then, are a few general and ordinary observations about women from the point of view of qualities of the mind, and it is only the use of the mind which should be considered when we discuss the differences between individuals.

Since there are few situations in which people's inclinations, characters, vices, virtues, and talents do not reveal themselves, anyone who wishes to disabuse himself of misconceptions about women has ample opportunity to do so in public places, particularly at court or in the convents, at public entertainments or at church, with the rich or the poor, in whatever state the women may be. If we judge sincerely and without prejudice, we find that if there are few situations which do not flatter women, there are many more in which they shine. And if their status is not equal to ours, it is most certainly not because they do not deserve it but because of lack of fortune or strength, and because public opinion is a popular prejudice without basis.

19. Maclean, *Woman Triumphant*, 50: "The assertion that as women are mothers, sisters, and wives, and as they care for men throughout their lives in these capacities, they do not deserve the ingratitude embodied in the antifeminist writing, is a commonplace found in most feminist works."

PART TWO

In which we show why the proofs that could be used against the equality of the two sexes taken from poets, historians, lawyers, and philosophers are all vain and futile.

Popular opinion about women is confirmed by the views of the learned. If the public pronouncements of those whose power rests on people's credulity coincides—to women's disadvantage—with general appearance, then it is no wonder that women have such a bad image in the minds of simple, uneducated people. As is so often the case, one prejudice is reinforced by another.

Since the idea of truth is naturally associated with that of science, we are inclined to believe the theories of those with a reputation for erudition. Moreover, since there are many more who are more learned in name than in fact, ordinary people, who are impressed only by numbers, take the side of the former, accepting their opinions with even more alacrity since they coincide with the views they already hold.

This is why, since poets, orators, historians, and philosophers proclaim that women are inferior to men and less noble and perfect, the public is even more convinced that this is true because they do not realize that the learning of the experts—albeit more diffuse and sophistical—is based on the same prejudice as their own, . All scholars do is add to the impression of custom the views of the Ancients, whose authority is the basis for their conviction. What I have found where the question of women is concerned is that those who are educated and those who are not fall into the same error, which is to accept as truth the opinion of those they respect because they already anticipate that they are right, instead of reserving their judgment until after they actually ascertain that they are saying nothing but what is true.

The notion of popular science.

Since it is the aim of poets and orators to give pleasure and to persuade, most people ask nothing more of them than the appearance of truth. As exaggeration and hyperbole are compatible with this aim, they inflate ideas according to their purpose and enlarge and diminish good and evil at will, and, using an all-too-familiar ploy, they attribute to women in general what they have observed only in a few in particular. It is enough, for example, for them to have come across one or two female hypocrites to state that this is the flaw of the whole sex. The flourishes they use to embellish these pronouncements provide a wonderful incentive for belief to those who are not on their guard. They speak fluently and gracefully, using various original figures of rhetoric,

Against the authority of poets and orators.

which, because they are attractive, seductive, and original, dazzle the mind and prevent it from discerning the truth. Many seemingly sound works are published against women, and we are persuaded by them, unaware that their power and truth come merely from figures of speech, metaphors, proverbs, descriptions, similes, tokens. Since these kinds of works are usually inspired and skillful, they are accepted as true.

Someone who has read Sarazin's sonnet on the fall of the first woman, who according to the poet, only fell because she listened to the Devil's sweet murmurings, will believe that women enjoy being flirted with. The invention is, indeed, amusing, the device attractive, the argument persuasive, and the fall seductive, but if one examines the work carefully and reduces it to prose, then it becomes completely false and insipid.[20]

Some people are foolish enough to imagine that women are driven to fury more easily than men because they have read that the poets represent the Furies as women. They do not stop to consider that this is mere poetic imagination and that the artists who depict the Harpies with women's faces also depict the Devil in the guise of a man.[21]

I have seen some people try to prove that women are inconstant on the grounds that a famous Latin poet said that they are subject to constant changes of mood, and because a Frenchman playfully compared them to a weathervane that turns with every wind; and all because they forget that this form of expression is a playful diversion rather than a means of instruction.[22]

20. See Jean-François Sarasin (or Sarazin, 1615–54), "A Monsieur De Charleval," *Les Oeuvres de M. Sarasin* (Paris, 1656). Here is a verse translation of the sonnet in question:

When Adam saw the tender beauty near,
A gift to him from Heav'n's immortal hand
He fell in love and—for mankind's good cheer—
She too was held by love's supreme command.

It seems, dear Charleval, as we would guess,
She kept her vows, nor is this strange at all,
For easy 'twas to live in faithfulness
When only on one man her gaze could fall.

But friend, how wrong, how wrong we both can be!
For Adam, though in full vitality
With gentle mind and body strong and young
Did not possess the Devil's flatt'ring tongue;
So she, who craved a woman's rightful part
Of gossip, thus preferred his fiendish art.

21. Latin poets (Juvenal, Catullus, Tibullus, Propertius, and Lucretius primarily) considered woman's nature to be destructive and dangerous for the masculine *animus*.

22. The simile comes from Molière's farce, *Le Dépit amoureux*, 4.2.266–67 ("The woman's head is like the weathervane on the top of a house, and turns at the first gust of wind"). But the expression existed at least since the 1640s.

Common speech is a talking lens that gives objects whatever form and color one chooses, and there is no virtue that it could not represent as a vice.

Nothing is more commonplace than to find authors who say that women are less perfect and less noble than men, but when it comes to the reasons, we are hard put to find them. These authors seem to be as convinced as the general public. Women do not share with us the advantages of high visibility offered by the sciences and administration, which provide the normal standards for judging perfection, so they are not as perfect as we are. To be seriously convinced of this, one would have to prove that they are not admitted to these functions because of incompetence. But this is not as easy as one would imagine, and in what follows we will have no difficulty in proving that the opposite is true and that the error is due to our confused notions of perfection and nobility.

All the arguments of those who affirm that the fair sex is neither as noble nor as excellent as ours are based on the fact that since men are the masters they imagine that everything is for their use. I am convinced that we would believe the contrary with even greater conviction, namely, that men are exclusively for women's benefit, if the latter exercised complete authority, as in the empire of the Amazons.

It is true that they are engaged only in what we think of as the lowliest occupations; it is also true that they are none the less worthy of our admiration in terms of religion and reason. Nothing is base except vice, nothing lofty except virtue, and since even in their minor occupations women display more virtue than men, they are even more deserving of our admiration. It may indeed well be that simply taking into account their usual occupation, which is to nourish and tend men in their infancy, they deserve the highest rank in civil society.

If we lived in isolation and without collective government, the only purpose of forming societies would be to preserve our lives better so that we could enjoy in peace the things we need most. We would give greatest consideration to the people who make this possible. Thus we usually see princes as the foremost members of the state because their good offices and their prescience are the most far-reaching, and they provide the yardstick by which we measure their subjects. Most people have a greater respect for soldiers than for judges, because it is the soldiers who are engaged in combat to preserve our very lives, and everyone judges people according to their usefulness. Therefore women seem to be the most admirable because their contribution is infinitely greater than anyone else's.

That women are more admirable than men in respect of their occupation.

*In what does
women's worth
consist?*

We could do without princes, soldiers, and tradesmen as we did at the beginning of the world and as savages do now. But we cannot do without women in our childhood. When states have been pacified, most of those who possess public authority are of no more use and might as well be dead. Women never cease to be necessary to us. Ministers of justice are there merely to safeguard the wealth of those who possess it; women are there to safeguard our lives. Soldiers act on behalf of grown men, capable of defending themselves; women on behalf of men before they know who they are or whether they have friends or enemies and when their only arms against their attackers are their tears. Masters, magistrates, and princes often act only for their own glory and out of their own self-interest; women act only for the good of the children they are raising. The pains they take, the care they give, their endless concern and unremitting vigilance are unequaled in public life.

That they receive insufficient recognition is the result of arbitrariness. We offer great rewards to a man who can tame a tiger, admire those who can train horses, monkeys, and elephants, and praise to the skies the author of some modest work that has demanded a small amount of time and attention. Yet we neglect women who have spent years and years nourishing and educating children. If we look for the reason, we find it is because the latter is far more commonplace than the former.

*Against proofs
drawn from
history.*

The historians' criticisms of women make a deeper impression on our minds than the speeches of orators. Since they seem not to put forward any views of their own, their testimony is less suspect, and it also confirms already received opinions, namely, that women's situation in the past was as we imagine it should be now. But all the authority they bring to bear is merely the effect of a commonly held prejudice about antiquity, which is represented in the guise of a venerable elder who, because of his wisdom and experience in life, cannot possibly be wrong and can tell only the truth.

The Ancients, however, were no less men than we are, nor less subject to error, and there is no more reason to trust their opinions today than there was during their lifetime. Women were judged in former times as they are today and with as little reason, so whatever men say about them should be suspect as they are both judges and defendants. Even if the charges brought against them are backed by the opinions of a thousand authors, the entire brief should be taken as a chronicle of prejudice and error. There is as little fidelity and exactness in these ancient stories as there is in folk tales where, as we all know perfectly well, there is practically none. The writers have brought to bear their personal feelings and their own self-interest, and the majority of them had only vague ideas of virtue and vice and hence often confused the two. Readers with normal biases will make the same mistake. Given their prejudices, they made a point of exaggerating the virtues of their own sex, and of belittling and minimizing the merits of women because of a contrary bias. All this is so easily recognizable that there is no need to give examples.

If we have some inkling of how to interpret the past, however, we find evidence to show that women have in no way yielded to men and that the virtue they have shown is all the more excellent if we examine it in all its manifestations. We see that they have given no small indication of intelligence and ability in all kinds of situations. Some have governed great states and empires with matchless wisdom and moderation. Others have meted out justice with the integrity of the Areopagus.[23] Several, through their prudence and counsel, have restored peace to a kingdom and a throne to a husband. We have seen them at the head of armies and at the defense of fortifications displaying more than heroic courage. How many women have there been whose chastity has remained inviolate despite horrific threats or lavish promises, and who have, with remarkable valor, suffered the direst agonies in the cause of religion? How many have become as skilled as men in all branches of knowledge, or have mastered the most arcane secrets of nature, the greatest subtleties of politics and the most solid precepts of moral science, and have reached the greatest heights of Christian theology? This history, which has been used as a weapon against women by their enemies, can be seen by those with impartial eyes as proof that the female sex is no less noble than our own.

What history says in women's favor.

On the subject of women, many people think that the opinion of lawyers carries great weight, since it is their specific business to make sure that everyone has his or her due. They place women under the tutelage of their husbands, like children vis-à-vis their fathers, and say that it is nature that has assigned them the basest occupations in society and has placed public positions out of their reach.

Against lawyers.

We think we are justified in mouthing these things after them, but, without wishing to detract from the respect certainly due to them, we might be allowed to disagree with them in this instance. They would be considerably embarrassed if they had to explain what they mean by

---

23. Name of the ancient council of nobles in Athens. The court remained the most venerated legal body in Athens until well after the Roman conquest.

nature in this context, and how it has created the distinctions they claim exist between the sexes.

We have to recognize that those who drew up the laws, being men, favored their own sex, as women might well have done if they had been in the same position; and since, from the very beginning of societies, laws were made as they are now with respect to women, the lawmakers, who had their own biases, attributed to nature a distinction that derives mainly from custom. In addition, there was no need to change the already established order to reach the goal they had in mind, which was to govern a state well through the administration of justice. If they persisted in maintaining that women are naturally dependent upon men, their own arguments could be used against them, since they realize themselves that dependence and servitude are contrary to the law of nature which makes all people equal.[24]

Since dependence is a purely corporal and civil state, it should be considered merely as a result of accident or of constraint or of habit—always excepting the dependence of children upon those who gave them life. Even in that case, dependence ceases at a certain age when people are thought to be old enough and experienced enough to govern themselves and to become legally independent of someone else's authority.

But between people of more or less the same age there should exist only a subordination based on reason, in which case those with less instruction would submit voluntarily to those with more. If we take away the civil authority that the law has given to men which makes them heads of families, we find between them and their wives only submission of experience and instruction. Each freely makes a commitment to the other at a time when women have as much good sense as—and often more than—their husbands. The promises and conventions of marriage are reciprocal, and power over the body equal. If the law gives greater control over possessions to the husband, then nature gives greater weight of authority over children to the wife. Since the will of the one is not the rule of the other, if a woman has to do what her husband wants her to, then no less must he in his turn do what she tells him to. In no way can a woman be forced to submit to her husband beyond reason simply because he is the stronger. That would be the behavior of out-and-out bullies and not of intelligent adults.[25]

24. Stuurman, "From Feminism to Biblical Criticism," 372: Poullain stressed that "the idea of justice can also be comprehended by unaided reason because it is founded on 'the order of nature which make all human beings equals.' This echoes [Hugo] Grotius's [1583–1645] position on the autonomous truth of natural law, but Grotius also recognizes the autonomous significance of Revelation in such matters as the Old Testament prophecies and the veridical power of miracles. Poulain does not."

25. Maclean, *Woman Triumphant,* 89: "The extent of the authority of the parents and husband, the laws concerning property in marriage, and above all else, the legal application of the double

It is not too hard to disagree with the scholars I mentioned above, since we realize that it is not their business to inquire into the exact nature of things in themselves. The aims of poets and orators may be satisfied by appearance and approximation, those of historians by the testimony of antiquity, those of lawmakers by custom. But we cannot dismiss so easily the views of philosophers who seem to be above all the previous considerations, as, indeed, they ought to be, since we think of them as making a closer study of things. Hence they enjoy public trust and their ideas are accepted beyond a doubt, especially when they reinforce our own opinions. *Against philosophers.*

Thus the general public sees confirmation of its belief in the inequality of the two sexes since it seems to be shared by those who serve as models for public opinion. What people do not realize, however, is that most philosophers have no other rule than public opinion, and their pronouncements are not based on scientific laws, especially on the subject under discussion. They took their prejudices with them into the Schools, and there learned nothing that would give them cause to reject them. On the contrary, all their learning is based on the opinions they formed in the cradle, and they consider it a crime or an error to cast doubt upon what they believed before the age of discretion. They are not taught to understand man through the body or the mind. What they normally teach could well serve to prove that between us and animals there is only a difference of degree. The sexes are not mentioned among them; they are thought to know enough about the subject. Even less do they examine their relative aptitudes and natural and legitimate differences, which is an extremely interesting subject, and could be the most important aspect of physics and moral philosophy. They spend entire years, and in some cases their whole lives, on trivialities and abstractions and in speculation about whether there are imaginary spaces beyond the world and whether the atoms or specks of dust we see in rays of sunlight are infinitely divisible. What trust can we place in the pronouncements of scholars of that sort when it comes to serious and important things? *A definition of scholastic philosophers.*

We might imagine, however, that although they are so badly taught, their principles might be sufficient to discover which of the two sexes has some natural advantage over the other; but this thought can occur only to people who either do not know them or are predisposed towards them. Knowledge of ourselves is absolutely essential for discus-

---

standard in cases concerning adultery all weighed heavily against what now would be considered as equitable treatment of the wife."

sion of this question, and particularly knowledge of the body, which is the organ of the sciences; we have to understand it just as we have to understand how binoculars work in order to understand how they magnify objects. Philosophers mention the body only cursorily, which is how they speak of the truth and of science, by which I mean the method for acquiring true and certain understanding without which it is impossible to examine whether women are as capable as we are. Rather than diverting myself with an account of their ideas on the subject, I will try to state in general what my own views are.

What science consists of.

All men being made alike, they have the same feelings and the same ideas of natural phenomena, for example of light, heat, hardness. Everything we try to discover about these phenomena reduces, in fact, to understanding what are the particular properties of each object which produce these ideas and feelings. All our teachers can do to bring us to this understanding is to direct our minds to what we observe, so that we can examine appearances and effects without haste or bias, and to show us how to impose some kind of order on our thoughts to find what we are seeking.

What liquidity consists of.

If, for example, someone without learning asked me to explain the nature of the liquidity of water, I would not give any definition, but I would rather ask him what observations he had made himself. For example, he may have observed that when water is not contained in a vessel it spreads, which is to say that all its parts separate and split from each other without the agency of a foreign body; that he can put his finger into it easily and without encountering the resistance offered by hard substances; and that if sugar or salt are added to it, he will perceive that both these substances diminish little by little, and that their particles are carried throughout the liquid.

Up to this point, I would have taught him nothing new. If I had made him understand in the same way what it means to be at rest or in motion, I would bring him to the recognition that the nature of liquids consists in their imperceptible parts being in constant motion, which makes it necessary to contain them in a vessel and makes them easily penetrable by hard substances. Further, since the particles of the water are small, smooth, and pointed, the water is forced into the pores of the sugar, the impact of which forces the sugar particles apart, and the water particles move in all directions, carrying the separated matter throughout the vessel.

This idea of liquids, which is a separate branch of physics, would seem much clearer if we could see it in its context; it contains nothing that perfectly ordinary women could not understand. If other areas of learning are taught in some kind of order, they are no more difficult. Indeed, if we pay attention, we find that all the rational sciences demand less time and intelligence than are needed to master needlepoint or tapestry.

Indeed, notions of natural objects are necessary and are always formed by us in the same way.[26] Adam's were the same as ours, children's are the same as old people's, women's as men's. And these notions are renewed, fortified, and maintained through constant use of the senses. The mind functions continuously, and anyone who understands how it functions in one area will easily discover how it functions in others. There is only a difference of degree between our perception of the sun and that of a tiny spark. To think clearly about either requires no special skill or physical exertion.

It takes no less intelligence to learn needlepoint and tapestry than to learn physics.

The same does not apply to the kind of work I have been speaking of. This takes greater application of the mind; ideas about it are arbitrary and therefore more difficult to absorb and retain. The reason it takes so much time to master a craft is that it requires long practice. It takes skill to keep the proportions on a canvas, to work the silk or wool evenly so that the color arrangement will be just right, to make sure the stitches are neither too tight nor too loose, to keep the rows even, to shade the colors into each other. In short, one has to have mastered countless different techniques of needlework to be competent at it, in contrast to the sciences, in which all one has to know is how to observe correctly works already accomplished and constantly uniform. The difficulty in practicing science properly springs less from the objects themselves and the disposition of the body than from insufficient aptitude in the masters.

We should not be so surprised, therefore, to see men and women without any kind of training discussing scientific matters, since the method by which these are learned is merely an adjustment of common sense which has become confused through over-hastiness, custom, and usage.

The view of science given above should be enough to persuade unbiased people that men and women have an equal aptitude for it, but

26. The paradoxical assertion of the marginal note must be read in relation to Descartes's notion of *good sense*. Poullain applies the principles of clear and distinct ideas to the understanding of scientific experimentation so as to demystify scholastic representations of science as being a privileged domain that learned men had made irremediably inaccessible to the woman's mind.

because the contrary opinion is deeply entrenched it has to be combated with principles in order to root it out completely. In doing so the combination of the outstanding qualities of the fair sex that we discussed in the first part and the physical reasons we are about to present will completely sway us in favor of women.

That women considered according to the principles of sound philosophy are as capable as men of all manner of studies.

The mind has no sex.

It is easy to see that the difference between the two sexes is limited to the body, since that is the only part used in the reproduction of humankind. Since the mind merely gives its consent, and does so in exactly the same way in everyone, we can conclude that it has no sex.[27]

It is equal in men and women.

Considered independently, the mind is found to be equal and of the same nature in all men, and capable of all kinds of thoughts. It is as much exercised by small concepts as by large; as much thought is required to conceive of a mite as an elephant. Anyone who understands the nature of the light and heat of a spark understands also the nature of the sun. When one becomes used to contemplating the things of the mind, one understands them as clearly as material things that are known through the senses. I find no greater difference between the mind of a vulgar, ignorant man and that of a refined, enlightened man than between the mind of the same man at ten years old and at forty years old. Since there seems not to be any greater difference between the minds of the two sexes, we can say that the difference does not lie

Whence comes the difference between people.

there. It is rather the constitution of the body, but particularly education, religious observance, and the effects of our environment which are the natural and perceptible causes of all the many differences between people.

The mind works the same way in women as in men.

A woman's mind is joined to her body, like a man's, by God himself, and according to the same laws. Feelings, passions, and the will maintain this union, and since the mind functions no differently in one sex than in the other, it is capable of the same things in both.[28]

27. In formulating this fundamental principle—the bedrock of modern feminist philosophy—Poullain owes as much to Descartes's physiological theory of the dualism of mind and body as to his notion of clear and distinct ideas.

28. See Descartes's *The Passions of the Soul* (para. 2), in *Phil. Essays*, 298: "Thus there is no better means of arriving at a knowledge of our passions than examining the difference between the soul and the body, in order to know to which of the two we should attribute one of the functions within us."

This is all the more obvious if we consider the head, which is the sole organ of knowledge and the place where the mind exercises its functions. A most minute anatomical study reveals no difference here between men and women; a woman's brain is exactly the same as ours. Sense perceptions are received and assembled there in the same way and are in no way differently stored for the imagination and the memory. Like us, women hear with their ears, see with their eyes, and taste with their tongues. There is nothing peculiar to one sex in the disposition of these organs, except that women's are usually more sensitive, which is an advantage. External objects affect them in the same way: light through the eyes and sound through the ears. Who, then, will prevent them from undertaking a study of themselves and examining the nature of the mind, from asking how many different kinds of thoughts there are and how these are stimulated by certain physical movements, from going on to examine the natural ideas they have of God and, starting with spiritual things, from putting some order into their thoughts and conceiving the science we call metaphysics?

It perceives things in the same way in both sexes.

Women are capable of metaphysics.

Since they also have eyes and hands, could they not perform a dissection of the human body themselves, or watch other people do so? In this way they could observe the symmetry and the structure of its parts, they could note their differences and relationship, their configurations, movements, and functions, and the changes to which they are susceptible. Such observation would enable them to find ways of keeping these parts in a healthy state and of bringing them back to health should they ever be altered. All they would need for this would be to learn the nature of the external bodies that interact with their own bodies, to discover their properties and everything that enables them to have a good or bad effect upon them. These things are learned by the use of one's senses and by the various experiences one derives from them, and as women are perfectly capable of both, they can learn physics and medicine as well as we can.

They are capable of physics and medicine.

Does it take such great intelligence to realize that breathing is absolutely essential to the conservation of life and that this is achieved by means of air which enters through the nostrils and the mouth, then passes to the lungs to refresh the blood circulating there and causes various different effects, depending on whether the mixture of vapors and exhalations it sometimes contains gives it thicker consistency?

Is it such a difficult thing to understand that the taste of foods depends, from the point of view of the body, on the different ways they are dissolved over the tongue by the saliva? There is no one who has

A definition of taste.

not realized that any food one puts into one's mouth immediately after a meal, because it is distributed quite differently from what was just eaten, has a much less pleasant taste. Whatever remains to be understood about the functions of the human body, if studied in a logical way, will present no greater difficulty.

Women can understand the passions.

The passions are surely the most intriguing aspect of this discussion.[29] There are two different things to be noted: the motions of the body and the thoughts and emotions of the soul associated with them. Women can understand this as easily as we can. As for the causes that quicken the passions, we can understand their workings as soon as we have studied physics sufficiently to understand how the things that surround us affect us and influence us, and through experience and use how we can yoke our will to them or dissociate it from them.

They can learn logic.

If a woman makes a regular study of the objects of the three sciences just mentioned, she will see that the order of her thoughts should follow that of nature and that they will be correct as long as they conform to this order. Over-hasty judgment is the only thing that will cause her to go wrong. If she observes the economy of thought that has brought her to this point, she can formulate a model that will serve as a future rule and establish her own logic.

If one persisted in maintaining that women are unable to acquire this learning by their own efforts—albeit a gratuitous claim—at least one could not deny that they can do it with the aid of mentors and books, as the most outstanding men have done throughout the centuries.

Mathematics.

We have but to invoke the talent for organization that we all recognize in women to realize that they can grasp mathematical proportions. It would be contradictory to doubt that if women were to apply themselves to constructing machines they would succeed as well as men, since we attribute to them greater dexterity and skill than we possess.

They are capable of astronomy.

A pair of eyes and a little concentration focused on natural phenomena are all we need to realize that the sun and all the luminous bodies in the heavens are really fires (since they give us warmth and light as do fires here below), and that they seem to align themselves

---

29. Descartes's theory of the passions was central to his theory of virtue. His treatise, *The Passions of the Soul*, developed the concept of a moral theory based on human free will to achieve happiness. To do so, one has to apply reason to do good, keeping in mind that by bringing the passions under the control of the will, humans will obtain all the goods that are in their power. See John Marshall, *Descartes's Moral Theory*, 97–98. In keeping with Poullain's feminist point of view, there is nothing in Descartes's theory that would preclude women from achieving the same goals.

regularly with different spots on earth, thus making it possible to plot their movements and their course. Anyone who can get a mental grasp of these vast models and of the machinery that sets them in motion can equally well grasp the mechanics of the whole world by correctly observing its many signs.

We have already found in women all the skills that make men apt for the sciences that deal with men as individuals, and if we go on with our examination we realize that they also possess the skills necessary for the sciences that deal with people in their relationship to others in civil society. *Distinctions between the sciences.*

It is the fault of popular philosophy to make such rigid distinctions between various disciplines that it is almost impossible, if we follow a specific methodology, to find a link between them. This means that we limit the scope of human imagination by thinking that one man can hardly ever master several sciences, that gifts for physics and medicine are incompatible with eloquence or theology, and that there have to be as many types of aptitude as there are types of science.

This idea stems, on the one hand, from the fact that we usually confuse nature with custom, taking certain people's competence in a particular field as the result of their natural constitution, instead of which it is an accidental inclination born of need, of education, or of habit; and on the other hand from our failure to realize that there exists but one science, namely, that of ourselves, and that all the others are merely specialized applications of it.

Indeed, today's difficulties in learning languages, moral philosophy, and so on arise from our inability to relate them to that one general science. It is possible, therefore, that even people who think women capable of physics or medicine will not necessarily think they are capable of the things we are about to discuss. There is, however, the same difficulty on both sides. All that is necessary is to think clearly. This we can do by applying our minds seriously to the objects before us to form clear and distinct ideas of them, to apprehend all aspects of them and their different relationships, and to pass judgment only on what is obviously verifiable. All we have to do in addition is to put our thoughts into some natural order to have a perfect science. None of this is beyond women's reach, and a woman who followed this path of instruction in physics or medicine would be capable of advancing in the same way in all the other sciences.

Why should women not realize that since the need to live in societies compels us to communicate our thoughts through external signs, *They are able to study grammar.*

the most convenient of these is speech, which consists in using the words people have agreed upon. Why should they not realize as well that there must be as many kinds of words as there are ideas, that there must be some kind of correspondence between the sound and meaning of these words in order for them to be learned and remembered easily and to avoid their infinite multiplication, that they must be arranged in the order that comes most naturally and that follows our thought most closely, and that no more should be used in speaking than are necessary for understanding.

These reflections should make it possible for women to take their place in the Academy to work towards the perfecting of their mother tongue, reforming or suppressing offensive words, introducing new ones, modeling usage upon reason and upon correct ideas of language. The method by which they learned their native language would serve them well in learning foreign languages, in mastering their subtleties, in reading their authors, and in becoming well versed in grammar and what we call the humanities.

Eloquence.   Women, like men, only speak to explain things as they understand them and to urge others to act as they would like them to, which is known as persuasion. They have a better natural talent for this than we do, and to do it with added art they would simply have to learn how to present things as they appear to them or as they would appear if they were in the place of those they are trying to persuade. Since all people are cast in a similar mold, they are always moved by things in a similar way. Whatever differences there are spring from their inclinations, their habits, or their status. This would become clear to a woman with a modicum of thought and practice, and if she could learn how to arrange her thoughts in the best possible order and how to express them in a polished, graceful way with the right gestures and facial and vocal expression, she would then possess true eloquence.

Moral philosophy.   It is scarcely believable that women should practice virtue to such a high degree without being able to fathom its basic fundamentals. Indeed, a woman with the kind of learning we have described would discover for herself the rules of her conduct as she discovers the three kinds of duty that comprise the whole of morality. The first relates to God, the second to ourselves, and the third to our neighbors. The clear and distinct ideas she would have formulated about her mind and the union of the mind with the body would lead her to the inevitable conclusion that there is another infinite mind, Author of the whole of nature, and to conceive for it the feelings on which religion is based.

After learning from physics what constitutes the pleasures of the senses, and how external factors contribute to the perfection of the mind and the preservation of the body, she would not fail to realize that one would have to be one's own worst enemy not to treat them with extreme moderation. If she then saw herself as a member of a community of people like herself, subject to the same passions and needs which require mutual assistance for their satisfaction, she would easily become persuaded of the philosophy upon which our whole justice system hangs, namely, that we should treat others as we wish to be treated and that we should therefore suppress our own desires, since their excess, which we know as greed, causes all life's upsets and woes.

Her conviction of the last of these duties would be confirmed if she were to push on with her study to discover the fundamentals of politics and jurisprudence. Since both disciplines are concerned uniquely with people's duties to each other, she would realize that in order to understand their obligations in society she would have to know how they came to create that society. She would therefore imagine them as separate from civil society, and she would find them completely free and equal, with the single instinct for self-preservation and an equal right to whatever is necessary for this end. But she would notice that since this equality involves them in wars or constant confrontations, which are contrary to their goal, natural intelligence would dictate that they cannot live together in peace unless each individual relinquishes his rights and draws up conventions and contracts, and that in order to give validity to these actions and to relieve their anxiety, a third party has to be called in who assumes authority and forces every man to keep his promises to others. She would also understand that since this third party is chosen entirely for the sake of his clients, he should have no other purpose, and that to achieve his goals he has to be master of people and possessions, of war and peace. *Law and politics.*

As she studies this question in depth, how could a woman not discover what is natural justice, what is a contract, authority, and obedience, what is the nature of the law, what is the purpose of punishment, what constitutes civil and criminal law, what are the duties of a prince and of his subjects. In short, she would understand through her own reflection and through books everything necessary to be a lawyer and a politician.

After acquiring complete knowledge of herself and a solid grounding in the general rules governing human behavior, she might wish to go on to discover how life is lived in foreign countries. As she would *Geography.*

have noticed that variations in time, season, place, age, food, company, and exercise provoke mood changes in herself, she would easily realize that they produce the same effect on entire peoples. She would see that their inclinations, customs, manners, and different laws are determined by their proximity to the ocean, to the north or the south, by the fact that their country has plains, mountains, rivers, and woods, by the greater or lesser degree of the fertility of the soil which produces specific crops, and by commerce and business with other peoples, near or far.[30] She could study all these things and learn the customs, the resources, the religion, the government, the interests of twenty or thirty different countries as easily as if they were individual families. For as far as the location of kingdoms is concerned or the geography of oceans and land masses, of islands and continents, learning from a map is no more difficult than knowing the streets and districts of one's own city or the roads of one's own province.

Origins of the diversity of customs among peoples.

Secular history.

Knowledge of the present might awaken in her a desire to study the past, and her knowledge of geography would be a great asset for this purpose, giving her the means to understand things like wars, voyages, and negotiations and to pinpoint the places where they took place, and the crossings, roads, and highways between states. But her knowledge of human behavior, based on her studies of herself, would give her insight into policy, interest, and passions and would help her to understand the impetus and mechanics of enterprises and the source of revolutions, and would allow her to fill out the account of grand schemes with the small details that led to their success but which have escaped the attention of historians. By using the correct ideas she has of virtue and vice she would pick up on the flattery, the passions, and the ignorance of authors and would therefore be proof against the corrupting effect of reading history which contains many examples of such faults. Since politics in ancient times were not as subtle as they are today, nor the interests of princes as complex nor commerce as widespread, it takes greater intelligence to understand and decipher our gazettes[31] than to read Livy and Quintus Curtius.[32]

30. Stock, "Poullain de la Barre," 201: Poullain is one "of those, who, before Montesquieu, had drawn attention to the influence of climate on social organization."

31. Publications giving general news, local and from foreign countries. Théophraste Renaudot (1586–1653) created the first modern newspaper in 1631 with (some) political, religious, and artistic information. In addition, his famous *Bureau d'adresses* organized public lectures on topics of general human interest open to a wide audience of both genders.

32. Titus Livius (59–17 B.C.E.), whose *History of Rome* is one of the classics of ancient Roman history. Quintus Curtius Rufus (1st c. C.E.), wrote a ten-book history of Alexander the Great.

Many people find ecclesiastical history more satisfying and more sound than secular or civil history, because it places greater demands on reason and virtue, and because passions and prejudices, when veiled by the pretext of religion, channel the mind into a very specific way of thinking. A woman's zeal in this area would be determined by her commitment to its importance. She would be convinced that the books of Scripture are no less authentic than the others we possess, that they contain true religion and all the maxims on which it is founded, that the New Testament, which is the actual source of the history of Christianity, is no more difficult to understand than Greek and Latin authors, and that those who read it with childlike simplicity, seeking only the Kingdom of God, will discover its truths and its meaning more easily and pleasurably than those of enigmas, emblems, and fables.[33] When she has ordered her mind according to the precepts of Jesus Christ, she will be able to lead others, to remove their doubts, and to solve problems of conscience more soundly than if she had filled her head with all the casuists in the world.

As she continues her studies, I can see nothing that would prevent her from observing as easily as a man would how the Scriptures have been passed from hand to hand, from kingdom to kingdom, from century to century right up to our own day, nor from acquiring from her reading of the church fathers a notion of true theology, and discovering that it consists merely in knowing Christian history and the individual views of those who have written about it. Thus will she become learned enough to write books about religion, to proclaim the truth, and to combat neologisms by pointing to what has always been believed throughout the whole church on controversial subjects.

If a woman can learn from history the nature of public societies, how they were formed and how they are maintained by a permanent, regulated authority exercised by a hierarchy of magistrates and officers, then she can also learn how this authority is applied through laws, ordinances, and regulations governing the conduct of those who are subject to it, both in respect to their relationships with other people according to their status, and to the possession and use of property. Is it so difficult to understand the relationship between husband and wife, father and children, master and servants, lord and vassal, members of an alliance, tutor and pupil? Is it so mysterious to understand possession through purchase, exchange, gift, inheritance, will, ordi-

Ecclesiastical history and theology.

Civil law.

---

33. Stuurman, "From Feminism to Biblical Criticism," 371: "It appears . . . that Poulain's observations on universal consent have to be understood ironically, and all that remains of his 'defense' of the authority of Scripture is the affirmation of its authenticity."

nance, usufruct, and to know what conditions are necessary to make these practices valid?

Canon law.   It would not seem to take more intelligence to grasp the spirit of Christian society than that of civil society, to get a correct notion of the particular kind of authority upon which its whole conduct is structured, and to distinguish precisely the authority which JESUS CHRIST bestowed on His church from that which is invested in temporal powers. When a woman has made this distinction vital to understanding canon law, she could study it and recognize how the church has adopted civil law and how secular jurisdiction has been confused with spiritual; how the hierarchy is organized, that is, what functions are fulfilled by prelates, what authority is vested in synods, popes, bishops, and pastors; what is the nature of discipline and its rules and changes; what are canons, privileges, and exemptions; how benefices were set up and their uses and possession controlled. In sum, she could recognize what are the customs and ordinances of the church and the duties of all its members. There is nothing here for which a woman is not eminently suitable, and she could thus become an authority on canon law.

These are a few general ideas of the highest kinds of knowledge that men have used to show how clever they are and to make their way in the world, and which they have taken over absolutely to the detriment of women. Although women have no less right to this knowledge than men, they are considered and treated by men in a completely unjust way, given that there is no counterpart to this treatment in any other area of material possession.

The institution of prescription[34] was deemed right for the peace and security of families. Prescription means that a man who has, in good faith and good order, enjoyed the use of something that belongs to someone else for a certain period of time, becomes the owner of it, and no one can lay subsequent claim to it. But no one has ever thought that those who forfeited their goods through negligence or something similar would be unable to retrieve them through some means or other, and their incapacity has always been regarded merely as a civil matter.

In the case of women, however, we have not been content to refuse them access to the sciences and the civil service after a long prescription against them, but we have gone even further and imagined

34. A legal term by which is implied the *de jure* possession of goods after a set time of *de facto* possession.

that their exclusion is based upon some natural feebleness. Nothing is more fanciful than this idea, for whether we look at the sciences themselves or at the faculties we use to apprehend them, we see that the two sexes have equal aptitude. There is one way and one way only to introduce into the mind the truth which is its nourishment, just as there is only one way to introduce foods into various kinds of stomachs for the sustenance of the body. As to the different aspects of the mind that make it more or less apt for the study of the sciences, we have to agree, if we look honestly at the facts, that the advantages are all on the side of women.

It is by no means because of natural inability that women are excluded from the sciences.

We cannot dispute that those men who are most coarse and heavy are usually stupid, and that, on the contrary, the more delicately built are always the cleverest. Experience is too widespread and uniform for me to have to appeal to reason to argue further. Therefore, since the fair sex is of a more delicate disposition than ourselves, women would be sure to be at least our equals if only they applied themselves to studying.

Who are those best suited for science.

I foresee that this idea will not be appreciated by many who will think that I am going too far. There is nothing I can do about that. We have taken it into our heads to think that the honor of our sex depends on our being first in everything, whereas it is my belief that justice demands that we give both sexes their due.

Indeed, all of us, men or women, have an equal right to truth since the minds of both are equally able to apprehend it, and since we both react in the same way to objects that make an impression upon our bodies. The right to the same knowledge which is given to us all by nature stems from the fact that we all have the same need of it. There is no one who does not seek his own happiness—the goal of all our actions. No one can achieve happiness without clear and distinct knowledge.[35] It is this, as JESUS CHRIST Himself and St. Paul give us to hope, that will constitute our happiness in the next life.

Both sexes have an equal right to the sciences.

A miser considers himself happy in the knowledge that he possesses great wealth, an ambitious man in the knowledge that he has risen above his peers. In short, men's whole happiness, real or imagined, is in knowledge, that is to say in the thought that they possess whatever thing they are seeking.

Happiness consists in knowledge.

35. See Maclean, *Woman Triumphant*, 36–37, who points out that amid the "imprecise generalizations about society, anatomy, and psychology, often facetious speculation on the relative importance of men and women, facile comparison with nature," Poullain's rational approach was rare in the feminist literature prior to the publication of his treatise in 1673.

All this leads me to believe that it is only the ideas of truth which we acquire through study, and which are invariable and independent of the possession or nonpossession of objects, that can bring true happiness in this life. For what brings it about that the miser cannot be happy in the simple knowledge that he has riches is that this knowledge must be linked to the desire or the vision of possessing them right now in order to make him happy, and when his imagination presents them as being removed from him and beyond his power he cannot think of them without anguish. Knowledge of oneself and all the other associated branches of science—especially those that affect our daily intercourse—is quite the opposite. Since both sexes are capable of the same happiness, they have the same right to all the means of achieving it.

That virtue consists in knowledge. When we say that happiness consists chiefly in the knowledge of truth, we do not exclude virtue. On the contrary, we believe that virtue is its most essential component. But virtue makes a man happy only to the extent that he knows he possesses it—or tries to possess it. In other words, although we need only see that a man practices virtue—however dimly he may understand it—in order to think him happy, and although its practice, albeit with his muddled and imprecise understanding, can help him achieve happiness in the life hereafter—yet he surely does not consider himself as being fundamentally happy without knowing that he is doing right, just as he would not consider himself rich if he did not know that he possessed riches.

Why so few people love virtue. This is why there are so few people who desire and love true virtue: they do not understand it, and since they pay so little attention to it when they practice it, they do not feel the satisfaction it produces which brings about the happiness we are speaking of. This satisfaction comes from the fact that virtue is not a simple speculation about the good we are obliged to seek but an effective desire that springs from our own conviction. We cannot practice virtue with willing hearts without feeling some emotion, for it is like those superb liqueurs that taste bitter or sour if the mind is occupied elsewhere and is not concentrating on the effect of the liqueur on the tongue.

That we need to be educated in order to be truly virtuous. Not only do both sexes need enlightenment to find their happiness in the practice of virtue, they need it even more to practice it well. It is conviction that impels us to act, and our conviction of our duty is strengthened in proportion to our understanding of it. What little we have said here about moral science is enough to make us realize that the science of ourselves is very important to reinforce our conviction about the duties to which we are committed, and it would not be hard to show how all the other sciences contribute to it, as well as to demonstrate that the reason so many people fall short in the practice of virtue or sink into profligacy is that they are ignorant of what they are.

The publicly held fallacy that one does not need to be learned to be virtuous springs from the fact that large numbers of so-called learned people are obviously corrupt, from which it is inferred that not only is learning unnecessary for virtue but that it is often positively injurious to it. To those of weak intelligence and little education, this error casts suspicion on most of the people who are thought to be more educated than others and at the same time incites contempt and aversion for higher learning.

Why some learned people are corrupt.

People overlook the fact that it is only false learning that leaves men in a dissolute state or leads them into one, because the muddled ideas that false philosophy gives of ourselves and of what forms the basis of our actions confuse our minds so completely that we do not know what the mind is. Neither do we know the nature of the elements surrounding it nor the relation between it and these elements. Since the mind cannot withstand the pressure of the difficulties lurking in this obscurity, it cannot help but succumb and abandon itself to its passions, reason being too weak to stop it.

The strange idea held by the common people that study would make women nastier and haughtier rests therefore upon panicky overreaction. Only false science could produce such an evil effect. True scientific study can only make one more humble and more convinced of one's own weakness, simply through contemplation of the workings of the [human] machine, the delicacy of its organs, the almost infinite number of changes and painful malfunctions to which it is subject. No meditation is more apt to inspire humility, moderation, and gentleness in any given man than the revelation, achieved through physics, of the link between his mind and his body, and the realization that he is subject to so many needs. He will understand that since his correct functioning depends on the most delicate parts of his body, he is constantly subject to countless upsets and unpleasant fluctuations, that whatever learning he may have acquired, the merest trifle will confound it, and that an attack of bile or an unusual heating or cooling of the blood will perhaps throw him off balance and into madness and rage and will provoke dreadful convulsions.

That study would not make women proud.

As these reflections would penetrate a woman's mind no less than a man's, they would banish pride rather than arouse it. If, after acquiring so much knowledge, she were to think back over her whole intel-

Very important advice for every scholar.

lectual past to see how she had reached the fortunate state in which she now found herself, rather than seeing cause for self-aggrandizement she would see reasons for further humility, for she would be certain to realize from this review that she had held many prejudices which she had cast off only after a fierce struggle against the effects of custom, example, and passion which conspired to keep her in a state of prejudice in spite of herself. She would also realize that all her efforts to discover the truth were almost worthless, that she came upon it by chance when she was least thinking about it, and in situations that occur scarcely once in a lifetime and then to only very few people. This realization would lead her to the inevitable conclusion that it is unfair and foolish to despise and scorn those who do not have our education or share our views, and that we should, rather, be more sympathetic and compassionate towards them. It is not necessarily their fault that they do not see the truth as we do, but rather that the truth did not appear to them when they sought it, and there is still some kind of veil before them or us that prevents it appearing to their mind's eye in all its clarity. Considering that she now accepts as true things that she previously thought false, she will realize that it might happen in future that she will make new discoveries that will lead her to think presently held truths erroneous and wrong.

If some women become arrogant as they acquire knowledge, there is no shortage of men who fall into the same vice. In women's case it should be seen not as a result of their learning but as a consequence of their having normally been kept in ignorance. Since, on the one hand, they usually have a very muddled education, and, on the other, those who *do* have an education think of themselves as having such a unique advantage, it is no wonder that they see it as a source of superiority. It follows almost inevitably, therefore, that the same thing happens as with those of lowly birth and few possessions who have made a dazzling fortune through their own efforts: when they find themselves raised to heights thought unattainable by people in their position, success turns them giddy so that they have a distorted view of things. At least it is likely that since any self-glorification attributed to learned women is nothing compared to that of those learned men who take the title of master or wise man, it would be even less prevalent among women if their sex had an equal share with men in the benefits that give rise to it.

That the sciences are necessary for things other than positions.   Thus it is a popular misconception that learning is pointless for women because they have no access to the positions which are the reason for taking up study. It is as necessary to women as happiness and virtue, because without it they can achieve neither. It is necessary for

precise thought and just deeds. It is necessary for knowledge of ourselves, of the things around us and our good use of them, and for the
reining in of our passions and the moderating of our desires. Preparation for civil and clerical positions is one of the applications of learning, and one's need of it is all the greater if one is to be a competent
judge or a bishop, since one cannot otherwise carry out these functions
satisfactorily. But to use one's learning simply to get these positions and
to exploit their benefits for one's own advantage is despicable and
sordid.

Thus it is only ignorance or secret, blind self-interest that can lead
to the assertion that women should remain excluded from the sciences
because they have never participated publicly in them. The riches of
the mind are not like those of the body; there is no prescription on *There is no*
them, and however long one has been deprived of them, one can al- *prescription*
ways reclaim them. In the case of tangible possessions, they cannot be *in matters of*
possessed at the same time by several people without each owner's *learning.*
share being diminished. For this reason, in the interests of the well-
being of families, it is right that the legitimate owners should be given
full possession of them at the expense of previous owners.

But it is completely different for the riches of the mind. Everyone
has equal claim to common sense. The scope of reason is boundless
and has the same influence over all people. We are all born judges of
things that affect us, and even if we do not all have the same power
over them, at least we can all have equal knowledge of them. Just as all
men are free to enjoy the light and the air without this interaction
harming anyone, so they are free to possess the truth without hurting
each other. Moreover, the better it becomes known the more attractive
and luminous it appears; the more people who seek it the sooner it is
found, and if the two sexes had joined forces it would have been discovered sooner. Truth and science, then, are unlimited blessings, and
those who have not acquired them can study them without in any way
undermining those who have already mastered them. Only those who
want to control other people's minds through credulity will find this
possibility unnerving, fearing that if the sciences become so widespread, then distinction will be too, and that the achievements to
which they aspire will become debased through wide currency.

The equal distribution of aptitude means that there is nothing *That women are*
wrong with women studying just as we do. They are perfectly capable *no less capable*
of making good use of it and of deriving from it two desired advan- *than men of state*
tages: one is to come to the clear and distinct understanding for which *positions.*
we have a natural desire—a desire, however, often smothered and over-

whelmed by the muddle of our thoughts and the needs and upheavals of our lives, and the other is to use their knowledge for their personal conduct and that of others in the various social levels of the community in which we live. This view is not the general opinion.[36] Many believe that women can indeed master what we know as physical or natural sciences but that they are not as well-suited as men for what we might call social sciences, like ethics, jurisprudence and politics. These people think that even if women could govern themselves by applying the maxims of the latter, they certainly couldn't govern others.

This idea stems from a failure to recognize that the mind needs only discernment and judgment in all its undertakings, and anyone who has these qualities in one discipline can easily apply them to another. Ethics and social science do not change the nature of our actions, which remain physical. For ethics is nothing more than an understanding of how men judge the actions of their peers as measured against whatever ideas they may have of good and evil, virtue and vice, justice and injustice. If the law of motion has been understood in physics and can be applied to all the changes and variations observable in nature, then by the same token once the true maxims of the social sciences have been understood they can easily be applied to new instances as these arise.

Those who occupy civil positions are not always more intelligent than others for all their good fortune, nor is there any reason why they should be, although one would hope that only the best qualified are admitted. Our behavior is the same and is governed by the same rules whatever our situation in life. The only difference is that our responsibilities and our vision are broadened as our position is more elevated, because more action is required of us. The changes experienced by those above us are like those experienced by someone who climbs a tower and sees further and discovers many more different objects than those people who remain on the ground. If, therefore, women can govern their own behavior as well as we can, they are equally able to govern others and to hold public and high state office.

They are able to teach. The easiest and most natural public use of what one has mastered thoroughly is to teach it to others, and if women had studied at a university with men, or at other universities set up exclusively for them, they could receive degrees and become Doctors or Masters of Theol-

36. Maclean, *Woman Triumphant*, 60: "The exclusion of women from public affairs is said by some to be a concession to the 'delicatesse de leur sexe' rather than a judgment of political abilities. It is rare to find pleas for a new dispensation in feminist work."

ogy or Medicine or both kinds of Law. Moreover, the natural gifts which make them so good at learning would also make them excellent teachers. They would find ingenious ways of enlivening their pedagogy, quickly discovering their students' strengths and weaknesses so that they could adjust to their needs. Their skills in communicating, which are the most precious gifts of good masters, would make them superlative mistresses.

The profession most closely resembling that of teacher is that of pastor or minister in the church, and the only thing that could exclude women from this is custom. They have a mind like ours, capable of knowing and loving God and hence of bringing others to know and love Him. They have faith in common with us, the Gospel and its promises speak no less to them. Charity includes them in its duties, and if they can practice its deeds can they not preach its maxims? Whoever can preach by example is even better qualified to do so with words. Any woman who could combine natural eloquence with the moral teachings of JESUS CHRIST would be as well qualified as anyone to exhort, to lead, to correct, to admit deserving souls into Christian society, and to weed out those who refuse to observe its rules after they had submitted themselves to it. If men were used to seeing women in the pulpit, they would think no more of it than women do at seeing men.

They are fitted for ecclesiastical positions.

The reason for our gathering in societies is to live in peace and to find in mutual aid everything necessary for the mind and body. We could not enjoy this state undisturbed if there were no authority; in other words, some people must have the power to make laws and to enforce them in cases of violation. People must understand what this authority entails and must believe that those who wield it have at heart the interest and well-being of their inferiors. Since women understand this equally well, why could not men submit to them and not only offer no resistance to their orders themselves but do their utmost to persuade their more recalcitrant fellows to obey them?

They are able to exercise authority.

There is, therefore, no reason why a woman should not occupy a throne, studying her subjects' natural disposition, their interests, laws, customs, and usages in order to rule them better, no reason why she would distribute patronage on any grounds but merit, or appoint to high office in the judiciary or the army any but deserving persons, or in the church any but enlightened and exemplary people. Is it too difficult for a woman to find out the strengths and weaknesses of her state and those surrounding it? To organize espionage missions to anticipate and undermine the intentions of foreign states? To keep spies and de-

They can be queens.

pendable emissaries in all suspicious countries in order to keep close watch on all relevant developments? Does governing a kingdom require greater effort and conscientiousness than women use in their families or nuns in their convents? Delicacy would be no less present in their public negotiations than in their private affairs, and since their sex is naturally the more pious and the more gentle, they would govern less harshly than have many princes. Their rule would inspire us to wish for what has been dreaded under most regimes, namely, that subjects would model themselves on their rulers.

It is easy to conclude that if women are capable of wielding supreme public power, then even more are they able to be its mere ministers, as well as its vice-regents, governors, secretaries, state counselors, finance ministers.

They can be generals in the army.

For my part, I would be no more surprised to see a woman with a helmet on her head than a crown, nor to see her presiding over a council of war rather than a council of state, drilling her soldiers herself, drawing up an army into battle lines, dividing it into various detachments with as much pleasure as if she were watching it done. Military art makes no higher demands than the other arts women are capable of except that it is tougher, noisier, and does more harm. A pair of eyes are enough to learn from a more or less accurate map all the principal roads of a country, the good and bad thoroughfares, the most suitable places for ambushes and encampments. There are few soldiers who do not know that you have to capture a pass before sending your troops into it and that you have to plan your campaign according to the reliable information of trusted spies, and even conceal your plans from your own army by means of ruses and counter-marches in order to keep your plans secret. A woman can do all of these things, as well as devising strategies for catching the enemy off guard: making sure he has the wind, the dust, or the sun in his face, attacking him on one flank in order to surround him on the other, giving him false alarms and drawing him into an ambush by pretending to flee, engaging in battle and being the first into the breach to urge on her soldiers. Persuasion and passion can accomplish anything, and when their honor is at stake women do not show any less ardor and resolution than it takes to attack and defend a stronghold.

They are capable of holding judiciary positions.

How could one reasonably object to seeing a sensible, well-educated woman presiding over a court of law or some other assembly? A good number of clever people would have less difficulty in learning the rules of state than the rules of gambling, which women understand perfectly well, and it is as easy to keep those in one's head as an entire novel. Can one not perceive the outcome of a legal case as easily as the denouement of the plot of a play? Can one not give a report of a trial as easily as an account of a comedy? All these things are equally easy to those who put equal effort into them.

As there are no important offices or positions that are not included in the above list, nor any others that require more learning or intelligence, we have to acknowledge that women are fitted for all of them.

Apart from natural physical capacity and attitudes towards the demands and duties of a position, there is an additional set of circumstances that determines ability to perform them in a satisfactory way: the conviction of one's obligations, religious and selfish considerations, rivalry between peers, the desire to achieve fame, to make, maintain, or increase one's fortune. Men will behave differently depending on how much they are influenced by these things, and since women are no less sensitive to them than men they are, insofar as positions are concerned, their equals in everything.

We can with some assurance exhort the ladies to concentrate on their study without paying any attention to the petty reasons of those who try to divert them from it. Since they have a mind like us, capable of understanding the truth, which is the only thing worthy of their attention, they should avoid putting themselves in the situation of being accused of hiding a talent they could put to good use, and of holding back the truth in idleness and luxury. There is no other way for them to insure themselves against the mistakes and surprises which lie in wait for those who learn nothing except through the gazettes, in other words, through hearsay; besides which there is no other way to find happiness in this life than through the conscious practice of virtue.

Women should apply themselves to their studies.

Whatever interests they may want to pursue apart from this, they will find in study. If their salons were transformed into academies, the conversations in them would be more substantial, more agreeable, and more wide-ranging. A woman can imagine the satisfaction she would derive from discussing the finer things of life from the pleasure she sometimes gets from hearing others speak of them. However trivial the topics of conversation might be, she would have the pleasure of discussing them more intelligently than usual; and the strengthening of women's characteristically refined manners by intellectual rigor would make them considerably more persuasive.

The value of study for women.

Women who seek only to please would find satisfaction in their studies. The radiance of their physical beauty would be enhanced a thousandfold when animated by that of their minds. Since less attractive women are always greeted with enthusiasm when they are intelligent, the advantages of a well-trained mind would amply make up for a lack of fortune and good looks. They would participate in the discussions among learned men and would doubly hold sway over them. They would go into business; husbands could hardly get out of leaving to them the running of the household and of following their advice. Moreover, if for some reason they could no longer occupy public office, then at least they would understand how it works and know whether it is being properly run. The difficulties in reaching this stage should not frighten women off. They have been greatly exaggerated. The reason for the belief that it is so arduous to acquire knowledge is that most people seeking it are forced to learn all kinds of useless things. Since learning up till now has been exclusively geared to transmitting the views of our predecessors, with people being overly given to relying on the traditions and beliefs of their masters, very few have been lucky enough to find the natural method. Such a method should be cultivated in order to show that people can become competent far more quickly and much more agreeably than they had imagined.[37]

That women have an advantageous disposition for the sciences, and that correct ideas of perfection, nobility, and honesty are as relevant to them as to men.

Up to this point we have only been concerned with women's heads, and we have seen that in general terms, a woman's head is in the same proportion as a man's with respect to all the learning of which it is the organ.[38] However, since even among men this organ is not completely similar and there are individual differences that make some men better suited for some things than others, we should now enter into specifics to see whether there is something in women that makes them less fitted for science than ourselves.[39]

We can see that they have a larger and more cheerful physiognomy than ours. They have high, lofty, wide foreheads, which is normally a sign of imagination and intelligence. Indeed, we find that women have a great deal of verve and imagination as well as good memories. All this means that their

37. Education being the key to their intellectual emancipation, Poullain has shown women of leisure and social standing how they could access knowledge with the natural method of self-discovery and the exercise of free will.

38. The following arguments, which appeal to psychology as well as physiology, are key in the debate over the equality of the sexes. See Alcover, *Poullain*, 65.

39. See his interpretation of the Holy Scriptures and patristic writings on that subject in his Preface to *Excellence*.

brain is constituted in such a way as to receive even faint and almost imperceptible impressions of objects that escape people of a different disposition, and it is easily able to retain these impressions and recall them to mind whenever they are needed.[40]

The warmth that accompanies this disposition brings it about that objects make a more lively impression on a woman's mind, which then takes them in and examines them more acutely and develops the images they leave as it pleases. From this it follows that those who have a great deal of imagination and can look at things more efficiently and from more vantage points are ingenious and inventive, and find out more after a single glance than others after long contemplation.[41] They are able to give an account of things in a pleasant and persuasive way, finding instantly the right turn of phrase and expression. Their speech is fluent and graceful and expresses their thoughts to best advantage.

That women are imaginative and intelligent.

All this can be seen in women, and I see nothing in their disposition that is inconsistent with a lively mind. Discernment and correct thinking are its natural attributes. To acquire these qualities one has to remain sedentary and spend some time thinking of a given thing so as to avoid the errors and mistakes to which one is susceptible if one flits from one thing to another. It is true that overly imaginative people sometimes get carried away by their superabundance of ideas, but it is also true that these can be concentrated through training. We have before us the example of the greatest men of our century who almost all possess a lively imagination.

It could be said that this kind of temperament is best fitted for social intercourse, and since man was not made to spend all his time shut away in his study, we should somehow have greater respect for those who have a superior talent for communicating their thoughts in an interesting and convincing way. Thus women who have a naturally attractive mind, thanks to their imagination, memory, and brilliance can, with some effort, acquire the qualities of a sound mind.

That is sufficient evidence to show that, as far as the head alone is

40. See Descartes's *Meditations*, VI, in *Phil. Essays*, 140–41: "My final observation is that . . . any given motion occurring in that part of the brain immediately affecting the mind produces but one sensation in it. . . . Moreover, experience shows that all the sensations bestowed on us by nature are like this."

41. See Maclean, *Woman Triumphant*, 50: "'Vivacité d'esprit,' which results from cold and moist humors, is another characteristic generally associated with women, although it is more often interpreted in an antifeminist way as 'légèrité' or 'caprice,' or as the faculty in women's minds which engenders deceit, intrigue, and dissimulation. Feminist writers associate the inventiveness of women with this mental attribute."

concerned, the two sexes are equal. There are some other extraordinary features of the body which need be mentioned only briefly. Men have always had the same tendency to, as it were, spill out their passions over all works of nature, and few ideas have escaped being associated with some expression of love or hate, honor or disdain. The ideas about the distinctions between the sexes are so gross and so embroiled with feelings of imperfection, baseness, incivility, and other absurdities, that since they cannot be touched upon without stirring up some passion and without setting the flesh against the mind, it is often prudent not to mention them at all.

Yet for all that, this weird mixture of muddled ideas, which is used by the small-minded to belittle them, is the basis for our unflattering notions of women. The happy medium between the necessity of explaining oneself and the difficulty of doing so with impunity is to indicate what we could reasonably understand by perfection and imperfection, nobility and baseness, civility and incivility.

Notions of perfection and imperfection.

Believing there is a God,[42] I readily believe that all things stem from Him, and after considering the natural interior state of things which consists, if we are dealing with bodies, in the relative disposition of their parts, and their exterior state, which is their capacity to influence or react with those around them, if, I repeat, I seek the reason for these two states, I can find none but the will of their Creator. I go on to observe that these bodies usually have a certain disposition that allows them to produce and receive certain effects, for example, that man can hear with his ears the thoughts of his peers, and can make them listen to his thoughts through the organs of his voice. I observe that bodies are incapable of these effects if they are differently disposed. From this I form two notions, one of which represents to me the first state of things with its necessary effects, which I call a state of perfection, and the other the contrary state that I call imperfection.

Thus in my view, a man is perfect if he possesses all the attributes he needs, according to divine law, for producing and receiving the effects for which he is destined. Similarly he is imperfect if he has more or fewer parts than he needs or some indisposition that keeps him from

42. Stuurman, "From Feminism to Biblical Criticism," 373: "Philosophically, the existence of God is demonstrated by the order of the world. The argument from design was of course a perfectly orthodox one, and it was probably one of the few ideas to which all schools and denominations subscribed. However . . . in these matters, his position is close to Deism and miles away from the preoccupations with the questions of providence and grace in the contemporary debate between Arnauld and Malebranche."

his goal. Since man was created needing food for his survival, I do not see this need as an imperfection, nor the fact that the consequence of the use of food is that the residue has to be expelled from the body. I find all things created equally perfect when they are in their ordinary, natural state.

We must be careful not to confuse perfection with nobility. The two things are quite different. Two creatures can be equal in perfection but unequal in nobility.

If I reflect upon myself, it seems to me that since my mind alone is capable of understanding, it should be preferred over my body and thought of as the more noble. But when I consider bodies independently of myself, that is to say, without wondering whether they can be useful or harmful, pleasant or unpleasant to me, I cannot bring myself to believe that some are more noble than others, since they are simply different configurations of matter. Whereas if I imagine the interaction between my and other bodies and consider whether they can do me good or harm, I have a different view of them. Even though my head, judged objectively, is no more important to me than the rest of myself, yet I prefer it to the other parts of myself when I think that it plays the bigger role in the union of my mind with my body.

This is why, even though all parts of one's body may be equally perfect, one sees them differently; those that are most strictly utilitarian are often viewed with some kind of distaste or aversion because their use is less pleasing. The same thing applies to everything that surrounds us and affects us, inasmuch as the reason for people's liking or disliking the same thing is that they are differently struck by it.

People's involvement in society [43] is what leads to their notion of correct behavior; so although there is no imperfection or baseness about relieving the body and although it is even a necessity and an indispensable consequence of one's natural disposition, and although all ways of doing it are equal, there are, nevertheless, some ways that are considered less correct because they shock the people in whose presence they are performed.

The idea of civility.

Since all creatures and all their actions considered per se and without reference to their use or their value are all equally perfect and equally noble, they are also equally correct, if we judge them in the same way. For this reason we can say that almost all views on correct

---

43. The word for "civility" in the margin is "honnesteté," meaning "decency," "correctness," and "respectability," as in the expression "honnête femme."

and incorrect behavior stem from men's imagination and whims. Proof of this is the fact that what is correct in one country is not in another, or is in the same country but at different times, or is at the same time. But among people of differing situation, rank, and outlook the same action can either conform to correct behavior or be contrary to it. This is why correct behavior is nothing more than a way of putting natural things to use according to the value we set upon them, and we would be well advised to respect this value.

This idea is so deeply held that everyone—whether they be our lady friends or the intelligent or the discerning—unthinkingly pays public lip-service, along with the general public, to the rules of civil behavior, whereas in private they shrug them off as being a burdensome inconvenience and an eccentricity.

It is similar with nobility. In certain provinces of the Indies ploughmen enjoy the same rank as our nobles have. In some countries the military have precedence over the judiciary, in others the opposite is true—each country behaves according to its views on these ranks or its assessment of their importance.

If we compare these ideas with those commonly held about women, we will easily recognize the error of the common people.

How the distinction between the sexes came about; how far-reaching it is; how no distinction is made between men and women as far as virtue and vice are concerned, and how temperament in general is neither good nor bad in itself.

How the differences between the sexes came about.

God desired to produce human beings dependent upon each other through the intercourse of two people. For this purpose he created two bodies different from each other. Each was perfect in its own way: both are presently constituted as they were ordained, and all those features that characterize their specificity should be seen as an integral part of their perfection. There is absolutely no reason to think that women are not as perfect as men, therefore, nor to see as a flaw what is an essential attribute of their sex without which it would be useless for the purpose for which it was intended, the beginning and end of which is fecundity. This is the highest purpose in the world, namely to bear us and nourish us in their womb.

Both sexes are necessary to produce together their offspring,[44]

44. Poullain's observations here must be placed in the context of his generation, when male and female anatomies were scarcely understood. By mid-century, the principal dispute was over the presence of a female seed in the process of generation. Poullain was

and if we understood the contribution of our sex, we would find it very
second-rate. It is hard to understand how those who maintain that men
are nobler than women justify their arguments as far as children are
concerned. It is, after all, women who conceive us, who form us, who
give us being, birth, and nurturing. Their effort is greater than ours, it
is true, but we should not use this against them to bring scorn upon
them rather than the respect they deserve. Who would want to say
that mothers and fathers toiling to bring up their children or good
princes working at governing their subjects or magistrates seeking to
mete out justice are less praiseworthy than those whose help and support they depend on to fulfil their duties?

Women contribute more than men to procreation.

Certain physicians have held forth at length—and to women's
disadvantage—about the temperaments of the two sexes and have dis-
coursed endlessly to show that women must have a completely different temperament from ours which makes them inferior in every way.[45]
But their reasonings are merely the frivolous conjectures that enter the
heads of those who judge only on the basis of prejudice and simple appearance.

On temperament

Since they observe that there are greater distinctions between the
sexes in the public than in the private sphere, they imagine that this is
how things ought to be; and as they cannot distinguish clearly between what comes from custom and education and what was given by
nature, they attribute everything they see in society to the same cause,
imagining that it was God who created men and women in such a way
as to produce all the distinctions we observe in them.

This is to put too great an emphasis on the differences between
the two sexes. These differences have to be limited to the design God
had in mind when he created human beings through the intercourse
between two people, and we should only take into account whatever is
necessary for this end. Thus we observe that men and women are almost identical internally and externally and that those natural functions necessary for our continued existence are the same in each. It is so
that they can give birth to a third that there are some organs in the one

---

not trained in the sciences that would have equipped him to meet the challenge of the
Faculty of Medicine, but his common sense nonetheless guided him sufficiently to point
out the obvious.

45. Maclean, *Woman Triumphant*, 47: "It is generally accepted at this time that woman is of
cold and moist humors, similar to children and criminals, a fact which does not escape
the notice of anti-feminist writers." Poullain will revisit the issue of temperaments in his
Remarks in *Excellence*.

that are not in the other. Women do not have to be less strong and vig-orous for this reason. Since only experience can make us good judges, can we not say that women are as varied as we are? There are strong and weak in both sexes. Men raised in idleness are worse than women and collapse at first when they have to work, but when they are hard-ened by necessity or some other factor they become as good as or even better than others.

It is the same with women. Those who have to do heavy work are hardier than those who merely ply the needle, which might lead us to think that if the two sexes had the same physical regime, they would be equally vigorous. This practice was actually adopted in the olden days in one republic where both sexes participated in wrestling and other sports;[46] and the same is said to be true of the Amazons of South America.

We should pay no attention to certain expres-sions unfavor-able to women. We should not therefore set too much store by those common ex-pressions deriving from the state of the two sexes today. If we want to make fun of a man for having too little courage, resolution, and firm-ness, we call him effeminate, as if we mean to say that he is as weak and feeble as a woman. On the other hand, if we mean to praise a woman who has extraordinary courage, strength, or intelligence, we say that she is manly. These expressions which are so flattering to them con-tribute in no small way to the high opinion we have of men, all because we do not acknowledge that they are a mere approximation of the truth, and that their so-called truth depends indiscriminately upon na-ture or custom, so that they are completely contingent and arbitrary. Virtue, gentleness, and honesty are so intimately associated with women that if their sex had not been held in such low esteem we would have praised a man who possesses these qualities to an extraordinary degree by saying "he is a woman" if men had been willing to accept that kind of language into their speech.

Be all this as it may, men should not have to depend upon physical strength for distinction, otherwise animals would have the advantage over them, as would the physically strongest among us. Experience shows us, however, that brute force makes men unfit for anything but manual labor, whereas those who have less physical strength usually have greater intelligence. The most competent philosophers and the greatest princes have traditionally been quite delicate, and perhaps the greatest captains would not have relished combat with the most

46. The reference is to ancient Sparta.

humble private. One has only to visit the courts of law to see whether the greatest judges necessarily rival the strength of the most insignificant ushers.

It makes no sense, then, to lay so much emphasis on the constitution of the body to justify the difference between the sexes when differences in mind are much more important.

Temperament does not consist of a single, indivisible point. Just as one cannot find two people who are identical, so one cannot identify exactly how they differ. Within the groups of bilious, sanguine, and melancholics[47] there are different individual variations, but all this diversity does not mean that they are not often as able as each other, nor that there are not excellent individuals of many different kinds of temperament. Even supposing that the difference between the two sexes is as great as is claimed, there are even greater individual differences between men who are thought, nonetheless, to be capable of the same things. The gap between the two extremes is so small that it is only a spirit of contentiousness that makes us pay attention to it.

It would seem that this exaggeration of the notion of distinction that we are speaking of occurs because we are not sufficiently precise in our observation of women. This error causes us to make the mistake of those whose minds are confused and do not distinguish correctly the property of each thing, attributing to one what can only be applied to another because they find the same elements in the same subject. The difference observed in women's manners and functions has therefore been transposed to the temperament since its true cause is unknown.

Be all that as it may, if we want to use the body as a point of comparison of the relative excellence of the two sexes, women can certainly claim the advantage—and this without even considering the internal make-up of the female body or the fact that this is where the most marvelous thing in the world takes place, namely, the formation of a human being, the finest and most amazing of all creatures. Who would deny their claim that their external appearance should give them first place, that grace and beauty are naturally and peculiarly their own and that all this produces an effect as visible as it is ordinary, and that if what goes on inside their heads makes them at least the equals of men, then the outside almost never fails to make them their superiors.

Women can claim the advantage as far as the body is concerned.

47. These terms refer to the medieval categories into which people were grouped, according, it was thought, to the constitution of their blood. See the series editors' introduction in this volume.

Since beauty is as real an advantage as strength and health, reason does not prevent it from being prized above the others. If we choose to judge its worth on the basis of the feelings and passions it arouses, then we find that nothing is more highly valued since nothing has greater impact, nothing arouses and stirs up more passions, confusing them and sharpening them in more varied ways, than the effect of beauty.

It would be unnecessary to say any more about women's temperament if a certain author, as famous as he is reputable, had not taken it upon himself to consider it as the source of the flaws generally attributed to them—which helps confirm people's belief that they are less worthwhile than we are.[48] Without repeating his opinions, I will say that in order to examine the temperament of the two sexes in relation to virtue and vice, we would have to consider it in a neutral state, where there is not yet either virtue or vice in nature. In this case we find that since what we call vice at one moment is called virtue at another, according to the use we make of it, all temperaments are equal in this respect.

All tempera-
ments are more
or less equal.

What is virtue.

In order to understand this idea better, we should notice that it is only our soul that is capable of virtue, which consists for the most part in the firm and steadfast resolve to do what one thinks best, depending on the different situations. The body is merely the organ and instrument of this resolve, like a sword held ready for attack and defense. All the different dispositions that make it more or less fit for this purpose should only be deemed good or bad insofar as their effects are more ordinary and more important for good and evil. For example, the instinct to run in order to flee the threat of evil is neutral, because there are some evils that cannot be avoided otherwise; in that case it is prudent to flee. On the other hand, it is despicable cravenness to take flight when the evil can be overcome by brave resistance that results in more good than bad.

Women are no
more prone to
vice than men.

Now a woman's spirit of steadfast resolve, which is the essence of virtue, is in no way inferior to a man's, any more than is her ability to recognize the situations in which it should be exercised. Women are as able as we are to control their passions, and they are no more prone to vice than to virtue. We could even tip the scales in their favor, since affection for children, incomparably stronger in women than in men, is naturally linked to compassion which we could call virtue and the bond of civil society, since the only reasonable objective imaginable

48. Cureau de la Chambre. See editor's introduction to this text, note 25.

for the establishment of society is to serve our mutual needs and wants. If we examine closely how passions are formed in us, we realize that, given the way women contribute to the formation and education of men, it follows naturally that they should treat them in their afflictions more or less like their children.

That the difference in behavior we observe between men and women springs from the education they receive.

It is even more important to note that the characteristics we possess at birth are neither good nor bad, for otherwise we will commit the commonplace error of attributing to nature what derives from habit.[49]

We rack our brains to find the reason why we have our faults and individual peculiarities; this is because we fail to observe the effects upon us of habit, exercise, education, and external condition, namely, the influence of sex, age, fortune, employment, position in society. It is incontestable that these different perspectives create an infinitely wide range of thought and emotion and thus give a different cast to our perception of truth. This variation is why the same maxim presented simultaneously to ordinary citizens, to soldiers, to judges, and to princes will strike each differently and cause each to react in such different ways. This is because people are so concerned with appearances that they take them as the yardstick of their feelings. Some pass off as trifling things that others take extremely seriously. The military establishment is shocked by things that delight the judiciary. People of similar temperament sometimes give a completely different interpretation to things that are viewed in the same way by people of a different temperament who share, however, similar fortune or background.

The effect of external surroundings.

We are by no means claiming that all men bring the same physical constitution into the world. Such a claim could be easily refuted. Some are quick and some slow, but this diversity seems in no way to prevent minds from receiving the same instruction. All it means is that some learn more quickly and less arduously than others. Therefore, what-

49. Maclean, *Woman Triumphant*, 21: "It is a common feature of feminist writings to demand the right of education. Whereas, however, most feminist writers are willing to concede that learning is appropriate and useful for woman's private morality, even the most enlightened deny that the fruits of such learning should be carried over into their marriage or social existence." Although Poullain did not advocate the active participation of women in civic life (saying only that they were capable of it), his insight on the power of tradition and custom sets his call for an egalitarian access to education apart from other "feminist" briefs.

Women's flaws are caused by their education.

ever temperament women may have, they are no less capable than ourselves of seeking truth and studying. If at present we find flaws or some defect in some of them, or even if we find that not all of them see basic things as men do (although experience shows the contrary), we should put this down solely to the condition of their sex and the education given them, which includes the ignorance to which we condemn them, the prejudices and errors we foster in them, the example set by other women, and the whole state to which they are reduced by etiquette, restraint, reserve, subjection, and timidity.

The education they receive.

Indeed, we go to any length to persuade them that the huge difference they see between their sex and ours is perfectly reasonable and divinely ordained. Differences in dress, education, and exercise could not be greater. A girl knows no security except under the wing of her mother or in the care of a nursemaid who never lets her out of her sight. She is made afraid of everything, told that ghosts lurk in any part of the house where she might be alone. In the streets and in the very churches themselves, there is something threatening if she is unescorted. The extreme care taken with her adornment becomes her exclusive concern. All the glances, all the comments about the importance of beauty absorb her mind completely, and the compliments she receives about it are her sole source of joy. As this is all that is spoken of, it becomes her one goal, and she has no higher ambition. Dancing, writing, and reading are the chief occupations of women. Their entire library consists of nothing but a few little devotional works, together with what is in their little book-box.

Their only learning is reduced to needlework. Their mirror is their master and the oracle they consult. Balls, plays, fashion are their only topic of conversation. They treat the salons like illustrious academies where they go to get all the latest news of their sex. If some of them happen to rise above the average by opening up their minds through the reading of books (which they acquire with great difficulty) they are often obliged to conceal this fact, since most of their friends, either from jealousy or other reasons, accuse them of trying to become bluestockings.[50]

As for the daughters of the lower classes who have to work for their living, intelligence is even more useless. Pains are taken to teach them

---

50. The term "précieuses" ("bluestockings") refers to a complex set of attitudes towards the women who gathered in the very sophisticated salons of seventeenth-century Paris and played elaborate word games with the men who also frequented these salons. On them, see especially Carolyn Lougee, *Le Paradis des Femmes.*

some trade appropriate to their sex as soon as they are able to learn one, and the necessity to keep at it prevents them from thinking of anything else. As soon as girls brought up in this way are old enough they are married off, or they are shut up in a nunnery where their life continues as it began.

In whatever is taught to women, is there anything at all that could be taken as solid instruction? It would seem on the contrary that there is a conspiracy to educate them in such a way as to dampen their courage, to cloud their intelligence and to fill it with nothing but idleness and folly, to stifle incipient virtue and truth, to invalidate any tendency they might have towards higher things, and to take away any desire to become accomplished like us by removing the means to it.

When I consider the way we treat what we consider to be their defects, I find that this conduct is unworthy of rational people. If both sexes are equally subject to fault, then the one that inveighs against the other sins against natural justice. If ours is the more flawed and we cannot recognize it, then we have no business talking of the faults of others. If we do see it and say nothing about it, it is unfair to blame the other which is less flawed. If there is greater good in women than in men, it is men who are guilty of ignorance or envy for not recognizing it. The greater virtue possessed by one person should be used to pardon another's vice, and if that same person's faults are insurmountable and the means to be rid of them or to be shielded against them are lacking, as in the case of women, then that person should be pitied rather than scorned. Further, if those faults are minor or merely superficial, then it is only lack of judgment or ill-will that can make us dwell on them. It is not difficult to show that this is how we normally behave in the case of women.

That the faults attributed to women are imaginary.

It is said that women are timid and incapable of defending themselves, that they are afraid of their own shadow, alarmed by a baby's cry, terrified by the sound of the wind. These reactions are not normally the case. Many women are as fearless as men, and we know that the most timid of them often make a virtue of necessity. Timidity is almost inseparable from virtue, and all worthwhile people have their share of it. Since they do not wish to harm anyone, and since they realize how much evil there is among men, it does not take much to arouse their fear. Fear is a natural emotion, and no one is free of it. Everyone fears death and life's misfortunes. The most powerful princes fear rebellion among their subjects and invasion by their enemies, and the most valiant captains are afraid of being attacked with their defenses down.

Timidity.

Our fear is proportionate to the strength we imagine we have to resist and is only reprehensible in those who are strong enough to repel the evil which threatens them. It would make as little sense to accuse of cowardice a judge or a man of letters, whose whole life has been devoted to study, if he refused to fight a duel, as to accuse a soldier, who has always borne arms, if he refused to enter into an argument with a learned philosopher.

Women are brought up in such a way that they have reason to be fearful of everything. They do not have any education that would prepare them to face intellectual challenges. They have never had access to the physical training that would equip them with skill and strength for attack and defense. They find themselves obliged to suffer without recourse the outrages of a sex so prone to excess, which despises them and often treats its own members with more rage and cruelty than wolves wreak on each other.

This is why timidity in women should not be treated as a fault but rather as a rational emotion which is the source of their characteristic modesty, and of the two most important attributes of life, namely, an inclination to virtue and an aversion to vice, which the majority of men cannot acquire despite all the training and education they are given.

Avarice.

The fear of becoming needy is the most usual cause of avarice. Men are no less subject to it than women, and if one were actually to take a count, I suspect that the former would be the more numerous and their avarice more reprehensible. As there is such a small margin between the two extremes of the vices and the virtue which represents the mean, the one is often taken for the other, and avarice is confused with laudable thrift.

Since the same action can be good in one person and bad in another, it often happens that what is bad in us is not at all so in women. They are denied all means of making their living through their intelligence. The doors into the sciences and the professions are barred to them, hence they are less well equipped to withstand life's adversities and misfortunes and are more vulnerable to them. We should not be surprised, therefore, that they take such care to conserve what little they have acquired with such great effort.

Credulity.

If they believe so readily what they are told, it is due to their disingenuousness which prevents them from thinking that the men in authority over them could be ignorant or self-interested. To accuse them of credulity would be a sin against justice, since it is even more prevalent among us. Even the most astute men are all too easily taken in by false appearances, and often their whole learning is nothing more than base credulity—though somewhat more extensive than women's. What I mean is that if they are thought to be more knowledgeable, it is only because of their unconsidered acceptance of a greater number of things which they have retained in their original form simply by going over them again and again.

What causes timidity in women is what produces the superstition *Superstition.* that even learned men attribute to them. In this case these men behave like people who are completely in the wrong, and who try to convince themselves they are right by shouting louder than others. They take themselves to be free of superstition because they observe it in a few uneducated women, whereas they themselves are most wretchedly buried in it up to their eyebrows.

Even if all men were true worshipers of God in spirit and in truth, and women only devoted a cult of superstition to Him, they would be excusable. They are not taught to seek knowledge of God for themselves; they know only what they are told about Him. Moreover, as men speak of Him with so little reverence and distinguish Him from His creation only insofar as He is Creator, it is not surprising that women, who only know Him through men's account of Him, worship Him through religion with the same feelings they have for the men whom they fear and revere.

There are some men who imagine they can humiliate women by *Chatter.* telling them that they are all nothing but chatterboxes. Women are right to be offended by such an insulting slur. Their bodies are formed by their distinctive temperament so that they preserve a clear impression of objects they have seen. They can recall them effortlessly and express themselves with wonderful facility, which means that as they are able to summon up their ideas at the slightest pretext, they can start up and carry on conversations at will. Since their insightful minds allow them to make connections easily, they go smoothly from one subject to another and can talk in this way for a long time without letting the conversation flag.

Verbal advantage is, naturally, accompanied by a desire to put it to use at the earliest opportunity. It is the only link that binds people together in society, and for many there is no greater pleasure nor any more rewarding use of the mind than to communicate one's thoughts to others. Therefore, since women can speak with ease and since they were raised with other women, there would be something wrong if they did not converse among themselves. They should not, then, be taken for chatterboxes unless they speak out of turn about things they know nothing about and have no wish to have them explained.

We should not imagine that chatter occurs only on the subject of clothes and fashion. Gossip writers' babbling is often more absurd. That mass of words piled up endlessly, which has absolutely no meaning in most of their output, is much sillier than the tittle-tattle of the most simple-minded women. At least what these women say is real and intelligible, and they are not vain enough, unlike most learned men, to fancy themselves cleverer than their neighbors because they utter more meaningless words. If men had such a ready tongue, it would be impossible to shut them up. Everyone talks about what he is familiar with: merchants talk about their business, philosophers about their studies, and women about whatever they have managed to pick up. They could well say that they would speak even better and more persuasively than us if as much care had been taken over their education.

Curiosity.

What some people find shocking in women's conversations is that they display a great desire to know everything. I cannot understand the attitude of people who find women's curiosity unappealing. For my part, I think it an excellent thing to be inquisitive; I would simply urge women to use moderation.

I see women's conversation much as I see philosophers', for in both cases one is allowed to speak of things one knows nothing about, and in both there can be misunderstandings.

It is commonplace among some people to treat the curious like beggars. If they feel in the mood to give, they do not become angry at being asked, and if they feel like showing off what they know, they are happy to be entreated—otherwise they make a point of saying that one is too curious. Because they have fabricated the idea that women should not study, they take umbrage when women want to know about what can be learned by studying. I admire this curiosity in women, and I pity them the lack of opportunity to satisfy it. Their only impediment is often a well-justified apprehension about approaching stupid, surly men who would just as soon mock as instruct them. It seems to me that

Curiosity is a sign of intelligence.

curiosity is a sure sign of a mind that is firm and receptive to discipline, signifying that learning has already begun and that we can proceed faster and farther along the path of truth. If two people are exposed to the same thing and one of them takes no interest in it while the other moves closer to it to get a better view, this is an indication that this person's eyes are more wide open. The mind is equally fitted for learning in both sexes, and the desire for it is no more to be sneered at in one than in the other. If the mind receives some impression that it perceives only indistinctly, it seems to be a natural law that it would want to understand more about it. Moreover, since ignorance is the most distressing servitude imaginable, it is as unreasonable to condemn a person for trying to escape it as to condemn a poor soul trying to get out of a jail where he is held prisoner.

Among all the charges laid against women, that of an inconstant and fickle temperament is the one that causes most grief. Men are no less susceptible to inconstancy, yet because they reckon themselves masters, they imagine that everything is allowed them and that once a woman is bound to them the bond should be indissoluble only on her side, although both are equal and entered the contract on an equal footing. *Inconstancy.*

We would be less inclined to accuse both of fickleness if we observed that it is part of human nature, for to say mortal is to say inconstant. This is a necessary state, deriving from the way we are created. We form an opinion of objects, we love them or hate them only on the basis of appearance over which we have no control. The same things can appear differently, sometimes because they have undergone some change, sometimes because we ourselves have changed. The same meat provokes different sensations, depending on whether it is more or less heavily seasoned, whether hot or cold; and even if it is unchanged, it affects us differently according to whether we are in good or bad health. Throughout childhood, we look with indifference upon things which move us to passion ten years later because our bodies have changed.

If one person loves us it is because we appear loveable to that person; if another hates us, it is because we seem detestable. We esteem at one moment those whom we despised formerly, either because they do not always appear the same or because they or we have changed. Someone who has found the door to our hearts open at one moment might have found it shut fifteen minutes earlier or later. *Why we should not accuse others of not liking us.*

The dilemma caused by opposing reactions to the same object convinces us, despite ourselves, that our emotions are not free, and that it is unjust to complain that we are being treated differently from the way we think we should be treated. Just as a tiny thing can spark love, so it can stamp it out, and we have as little control over the progress of this emotion as over its origin. Out of any ten people who yearn to be loved, it is usually the one who is inferior in achievement, breeding, and beauty who wins out over the others because that person seems livelier or more fashionable or better suited to the frame of mind we are in at that moment.

Artifice.

Far from making an accusation against women when we accuse them of using more artifice than men, we are actually speaking in their defense if we realize what we are saying because we are also acknowledging that they are equally intelligent and more prudent. Artifice offers a secret path to one's goal without causing one to be diverted from it. It takes intelligence to discover this path and skill to negotiate it. One could hardly hold it against women that they use artifice in order to avoid being deceived. Duplicity is far more pernicious and commonplace among men; it has been the traditional means of entering the civil service and public office, which offer plenty of opportunity for far greater wrong doing. Whereas men who are trying to deceive use their wealth, education, and power, which are usually overwhelming, women's only resources are caresses and eloquence, which are perfectly natural means and which can easily be resisted if we have legitimate objections.

Greater malice.

To add insult to injury, it is said that women are capable of more malice and mischief than men, and all the evil we lay at their door is contained in this view. I do not really believe that those who believe it claim that more women than men perpetrate evil. That would be an obvious falsehood. They are not employed in the civil service or public office where abuses are an open scandal. Moreover, women's virtue is too exemplary and men's waywardness too well known for us to entertain any doubts about them.

If we say of women that they are capable of greater malice, that can only mean that if they set themselves to do evil they are more adroit and extreme about it than men. So be it. This gives them a solid advantage. It is impossible to do great wrong without considerable intelligence and without, therefore, having the potential for great good. Hence women should not find this reproach more stinging than the one leveled at the rich and powerful for being more wicked than the poor because they have greater capacity to harm. Women might well reply that if they can do wrong they can also do good, and that if the ignorance to which they are condemned is the reason for their being more wicked than ourselves, then learning, by contrast, would make them much better.

This brief discussion of the most obvious faults thought to be natural and inherent in the fair sex reveals two things: first, that they are not as grave as public opinion makes out, and second, that they can be attributed to the pathetic education women are given. Whatever these faults may be, they can be corrected by education, for which women have no less aptitude than ourselves.

If the philosophers had followed this rule when they passed judgment on the subject of women, they would have spoken more sensibly about them and would not have uttered such ridiculous absurdities. But since most of the Ancients and Moderns have based their philosophy on popular prejudice, and since they were completely ignorant about themselves, it is no wonder that they were so badly informed about others. Setting aside the Ancients, we can say of the Moderns that the way they are taught, which makes them believe, albeit mistakenly, that they cannot possibly become wiser than their predecessors, makes them the slaves of antiquity. They are encouraged to accept blindly as eternal truth everything they find in ancient philosophy. Because everything they say against women is based mainly upon what they have read in the Ancients, it would be to the point to mention here some of the oddest ideas on the subject left to us by the illustrious dead whose ashes and even whose mortal remains are so venerated today.

Plato, the father of ancient philosophy, thanked the gods for three *Plato's view.* gifts they had bestowed upon him, but particularly that he had been born a man and not a woman.[51] If he was thinking of their present state, I would agree with him, but what suggests that he had something else in mind is the fact that he was reported as often wondering

51. Poullain is reflecting on variations of the saying sometimes attributed to Plato. Plutarch, in his life of Caius Marius (46.1) writes: "Plato . . . when he was now at the point of death, lauded his guardian genius and Fortune because, to begin with, he had been born a man and not an irrational animal; again, because he was a Greek and not a Barbarian; and still again, because his birth had fallen in the times of Socrates" (trans. Bernadotte Perrin [Cambridge, Mass., 1996], 9.595). Diogenes Laertius, in his life of Thales (1.33), presents a different version and through his source attributes the saying to Socrates rather than Plato: "Hermippus in his *Lives* refers to Thales the story which is told by some of Socrates, namely, that he used to say there were three blessings for which he was grateful to Fortune: 'first, that I was born a human being and not one of the brutes; next, that I was born a man and not a woman; thirdly, a Greek and not a barbarian'" (trans. R. D. Hicks [Cambridge, Mass., 1966], 1.35). Lactantius, a third-century church father, combines all the items included in the preceding writers cited and attributes them to Plato (*The Divine Institutes*, 3.19). Plutarch is Poullain's most likely source, assuming he received it directly from a classical writer as opposed to an anthology or a recollection from his school days. He clearly believes Plato identifies women with irrational beasts, though it is clear from the classical sources that this identification must have come later. When the elision occurred we have not attempted to trace.

Aristotle's view.

whether women should be placed in the category of beasts.[52] This reported belief should be enough for rational people to accuse him of beastly ignorance himself and to strip him of the title of Divine which only pedants now attribute to him.

His disciple Aristotle, who to this very day is known in the Schools by the glorious name of Genius of Nature because of the preconception that he understood it better than any other philosopher, claims that women are nothing but monsters.[53] Who would question this on the authority of such a celebrity? To treat it as an impertinence would be too overt a challenge for his stooges. If a woman, however learned, had written such things about men, she would have lost all credibility, and it would be considered sufficient refutation of such nonsense to answer that it must be either a woman or a fool who had spoken thus. Yet for all that, she would not be any less right than that philosopher. Women go back as far as men, they exist in as great numbers, and no one is surprised to meet them as he goes about his life. To be a monster, even in Aristotle's view, you have to have something singular and startling about you. Women have no such thing. They have always been the same, always beautiful and intelligent. If they are not made like Aristotle, they can say that neither is Aristotle made like them.

The disciples of this author who lived at the time of Philo had a no less grotesque opinion of women; on the basis of this historian's theory, they imagined that they are men or imperfect males.[54] This, no doubt, because their chins are not bearded; if not that, then I do not understand what they mean. The two sexes, to attain perfection, must be as we see them. If one resembled the other, it would be neither one nor the other. If men are the fathers of women, then women are the moth-

---

52. Erasmus comments in *Praise of Folly*: "When Plato shows himself in doubt whether to place woman in the class of rational creatures or in that of brutes, he only wishes to point out how flagrant is the folly of the sex" (trans. Hoyt Hudson [New York, 1941], 23). Hudson believes the text alluded to is *Republic* 5.451, where Plato discusses the role of female in relation to male guardians. Ian Maclean, on the other hand, believes the text alluded to is *Timaeus* 91a (actually b-c) (Ian Maclean, *The Renaissance Notion of Woman* [Cambridge, 1980], 40), though in both these texts, as Hudson and Maclean point out, Plato implicates men as well as women. In both, Plato is discussing the act of procreation which he regards as an animal act.

53. See the series editors' introduction, where the views of Aristotle are discussed and their sources cited. This particular assertion is from the *Generation of Animals* 2.3 737a27–28.

54. Philo of Alexandria (ca. 20 B.C.E.–50 C.E), a Jewish philosopher, whose view of women mirrored those of the Greek philosophers (especially Plato and Aristotle) who preceded him. See *Philo*, trans. F. H. Colson, 11 vols. (Cambridge, Mass., 1949), 1.131, 255–57.

ers of men, which makes them at least equal. We would have as much justification as these philosophers for saying that men are imperfect women.

Socrates, who was the oracle of antiquity on matters of ethics, when speaking of the beauty of the fair sex, used to compare it to a beautiful looking temple, but built on a latrine.   *Socrates' absurd view.*

We could only laugh at this idea, if it did not turn our stomachs. He seems to have judged others' bodies by his own or by his wife's, who was a she-devil who made him loathe her. He was said to have spoken this way about her sex in order to humiliate her, and to have harbored deep rage because he was as ugly as sin.

Diogenes, nicknamed the dog because all he could do was bite, saw two women go by one day deep in conversation; he remarked to his companions that they were two snakes, an asp and viper, who were passing their venom back and forth.[55] How worthy of a gentleman is such an apothegm.[56] I am not at all surprised that it ranks with the great philosophical sayings. If Tabarin, Verboquet, and Espiègle[57] had lived in his day, we would surely find their patter cleverer than his. Our man's nose was out of joint, and those who know him more or less realize that he had nothing else to say.   *Diogenes' view.*

As for the admirable Democritus, who was fond of a joke, we should not take too literally every word he uttered.[58] He was very tall and his wife very short. When he was asked one day the reason for this mismatch, he replied in his usual jesting manner that if you have to choose and there is nothing good to choose from, then the smallest is the best.[59] Had his wife been asked the same question, she could have made the equally valid rejoinder that since a big husband is no better than a small one, she took the luck of the draw, since she might have come off worse with a deliberate choice.   *Democritus.*

---

55. Diogenes of Sinope (412?–323 B.C.E.), Greek philosopher, reported in Plutarch's *Life of Antisthenes* 6.12.

56. In the margin Poullain writes that an apothegm is "the saying of a famous man."

57. Tabarin was the surname of Antoine Girard (1584–1626), a comedian famous in Paris for his bawdy monologues on current events. Verboquet le Genéreux was a pseudonymous author of crude comedies published ca. 1630. Espiègle was a fictional character bent on practical jokes.

58. A Greek philosopher (460–370 B.C.E.), who wrote on ethics, proposing happiness or "cheerfulness" as the highest good. He was known as the Laughing Philosopher in contrast to the more pessimistic Heraclitus, the Weeping Philosopher.

59. "Democritus," in *Fragmenta Philosophorum Graecorum*, ed. G. A. Mullachius (Paris, 1883), fr. 180 (p. 351). We are indebted to Marianne Pade, University of Copenhagen, for this reference.

Cato, that wise and severe critic, often prayed to the gods to forgive him if he were ever rash enough to confide the least secret to a woman.[60] The good man relished a famous incident of Roman history which antiquarians[61] use as a great argument to prove women's lack of discretion. A child of twelve, urged by his mother to tell her what resolution the Senate had passed while he had been present there, decided to trick her by making up the story that it had been decreed that every husband should be given several wives. She immediately went off to tell her neighbors in order to work out a strategy, and in half an hour the whole town knew about it. I would dearly love to know what a poor husband would do if, in a state governed by women, like that of the Amazons, he was told that it had been decided in council to add a second husband for each man. Doubtless he would say nothing.

These, then, are a few of the great and lofty thoughts that those whom scholars study as oracles have had on the subject of the fair sex. What is both comical and bizarre is that grave persons take seriously what these famous Ancients often meant as a joke, so true is it that prejudice and bias cause misunderstandings even among the very people who are thought to be the most rational, the most judicious, and the most wise.

POSTFACE

The most persuasive objections that could be brought against us are drawn from the authority of great men and from Holy Scripture.[62] For the former, suffice it to say that the only authority recognized here is that of reason and good sense.

---

60. Marcus Porcius Cato, called "Cato the Younger" (95–46 B.C.E.), a Roman statesman with a reputation for frugality and honesty. According to Maclean, *Woman Triumphant,* 22, "this is a commonplace taken from Plutarch's *Life of Cato* (viii), in which Cato comments on the insidious power exerted by women over their husbands."

61. In a marginal note Poullain says of antiquarians that they are "those interested in antiquity."

62. Stuurman, "From Feminism to Biblical Criticism," 369: "Cartesians frequently became involved in theological controversies, most notably about the Eucharist, but also about Scriptural interpretation. They were often suspected of heterodoxy, and the menace of censorship was never far away. Poulain was well aware of this: in an 'avertissement,' printed at the end of his first book, he asserted that his views were in no way contrary to Scripture, if only the latter was read correctly. In his third book [*Excellence*] . . . Scripture is discussed at length." The Fayard edition of *De l'Egalité des deux sexes* erred in placing Poullain's "Avertissement" (or Postface) before the Preface, for not only does this not conform to the 1673 and 1676 authentic editions, but its position alters the reader's understanding of the author's creative process.

As far as the Scriptures are concerned, they are in no way contrary to the aim of this work if we understand both correctly. Our claim is that if we set aside custom, which often places those of superior intellect and achievement at the mercy of others, there is complete equality between the sexes. The Bible makes no mention of inequality, and as its sole purpose is to provide us with a rule of conduct consistent with its ideas of justice, it leaves to individuals the freedom to judge as best they can the true and natural state of things. Upon close inspection, the objections found in it are but sophisms derived from prejudice. Sometimes these objections are applied to all women, when, in fact, they apply only to a specific few. Sometimes we attribute to nature what is, in fact, the result of education or custom and what sacred authors have said in the context of their own times.

ON THE EDUCATION OF LADIES

INTRODUCTION

Education (1674) is a sequel to *Equality* (1673). Two fundamental principles have emerged from Poullain's plea for gender equality: that the mind has no sex and that anatomy is not destiny. Thus the consideration of the historical legacy left by custom and tradition in light of Cartesian principles is necessary, and social values embedded in the patriarchal system need to be reexamined. Poullain has already concluded that the fundamental prejudice of women's inferiority had its origin in women's lack of intellectual exposure. But writing in the wake of the indictment of feminine scholarship in Molière's *Les Femmes savantes*, it is crucial for him to dispel women's fear of ridicule for transgressing their presumed role in life.[1] Poullain's goal is now to encourage ladies to overcome their own mental inertia by providing them in *Education* with an agenda to guide them. The text is divided into five conversations among a group of young adults and is preceded by a dedicatory letter and a preface. The dedicatory letter is addressed to the duchess of Orléans, cousin of King Louis XIV, who is lauded as a woman who embodies the kind of learning Poullain hopes to encourage other women to pursue. At its conclusion he openly seeks her patronage. Following the dedicatory letter is a preface, which Poullain opens with the convenient fiction that the conversations he has reproduced actually took place.[2] He also promises to write a book on the same subject, the education of children, though he never did so. Two ba-

---

1. See the editor's opening introduction for the cultural background and events that justified Poullain's treatises on women.

2. The preface sets the stage for the author's personalized mode of instruction, the literary "conversations" popular in the salons made of "honnêtes gens." The fictional character of the dialogues is signaled by Poullain's description, at the end of the preface, of persons who participated. They are described as "ideal types," that is, representatives of particular positions, rather than real human beings full of ambiguities shared by all members of their species.

sic premises govern his thesis. The first is the rule of free thinking. It makes
men judge things on the basis of reason rather than opinion, which he calls
prejudice after Descartes's principles.[3] Second, Poullain's modernist standpoint
in the Battle of the Ancients and the Moderns rejects outright the principle of
authority, which relies on models of the past for guidance and direction rather
than believing in the progress of civilization in a modern society.

The First Conversation begins with the arrival of Stasimachus—"the
teacher" in these dialogues—at the home of Sophia (wisdom), an intelligent
young woman who greets him with the comment that she has been arguing
for some time with a young man, Timander, over the equality of the sexes (using the recently published *Equality* to support her position) without success.
Stasimachus, it turns out, is the author of that book. In a telling exchange, Eulalia (a friend of Sophia's) says that women are more indebted to him than to
any other man in the world, and Timander adds that a statue should be
erected in his honor—a clue to the value Poullain placed on his earlier book
in the tradition of the *querelle des femmes*. Stasimachus/Poullain explains his concern for women's welfare, and he dreams of coming to their immediate relief
in two areas of masculine abuse of power: forced life in a convent for young
girls and marital authority in an ill-matched marriage. For these women, a
solid education could provide their mental salvation from societal ills. But in
1674, the very notion of supporting publicly women's access to a higher form
of learning was socially risky. The outcome of Molière's play was in everybody's mind. Timander describes with remarkable accuracy the précieuses's
affected mannerisms, for which they are faulted. But for Stasimachus there
are fundamental differences between these ladies with their insufferable arrogance and their misuse of knowledge and the true learned ladies who do
not have to compromise their femininity in order to assert their intelligence.
In any case, he would rather deal any day with the exaggerations of misguided précieuses than with the pedantic pretense of learned men. Timander
suggests that long study is not good for anyone, but would be less good for
women who have a more delicate constitution than men. But here the fault
lies with the Schools where boys are educated. Later in this conversation, the
question is raised of how learning might be made more pleasant and spread
abroad. Stasimachus suggests that the first goal could be accomplished by
confining instruction to French, and he adds that learning Greek and Latin is
unnecessary.[4] The second goal could be reached by hiring women to tutor
girls and nuns to train boarders and other nuns.

3. See the beginning of the "Second Conversation."

4. This shortcut was a concession to Poullain's ideal of equalizing women's chances to partake in
the dominant culture, as much as it was the confirmation of his ideological stand in the Battle of

The pursuit of truth is extolled as the most pleasurable of activities. Unlike sensuous pleasure, which never satisfies but keeps us in perpetual anguish, the quest for intellectual truth moves from joy to joy. And women can pursue truth as readily as men. Indeed, women who do so could, by inviting men into their salons, civilize their knowledge and teach them better social graces. In accomplishing these ends, women would also force men to change their view of women. However, the question of usefulness of scholarship for women remained a central issue in the antifeminist camp. The theory went that women did not need to be educated to the same level as men not only because they failed to grasp the concepts, but also because they were totally incapable of overcoming the defects of their irrational nature—a misogynistic logic that young Eulalia is quick to deflate. Poullain singles out the church's interdict on any form of feminine theology. Aside from lessons memorized from booklets on prescriptive devotion, the so-called feminine vocation prohibited women from seriously exploring the Scriptures. Here, the suggestion is made that in the New Testament women worked actively (publicly) in the church, a practice continued later in the early days of Christianity.[5] But in Poullain's time, people would judge suspiciously women theologians who violate their female condition; feminine pride and insubordination were automatically asserted to be women's real intent in exercising their independence in the realm of the Christian dogma. In fact, the most enlightened educators of the century were suspicious of any symptoms of feminine curiosity, a reality that undoubtedly explains why Eulalia has to read the New Testament surreptitiously (her mother tried to keep it from her). In reading it, she found to her surprise that it made no distinction between men and women regarding essential things (living by faith, being rewarded and punished for their behavior). By the end of their First Conversation, the young woman is ready to reject the social conditioning that has subdued her sex into an inferior state. Poullain understood that in order to demystify the prestige of masculine learning he had to neutralize first the fear of knowledge that often paralyzed a woman from considering the joy of intellectual pursuits.

In the Second Conversation, Stasimachus invites his friends to reflect on themselves under his guidance, in order to initiate them into Descartes's philosophy. Just as Descartes had come to cast an absolute doubt on any preconceived opinions before reaching for an objective understanding,

---

the Ancients and the Moderns. But the end result would be access by intelligent women to the realm of knowledge. See notes 7 and 8 below.

5. See translation, note 18 and related text. Stasimachus is quick to point out that he is not deferring to antiquity—as those who oppose the equality of women often do—but simply using it as an illustration.

Stasimachus undertakes to reexamine certain forms of knowledge acquisi-tion as he sets out to probe social conformism. A sharpening of Eulalia's crit-ical thinking skills will signal her first step toward the finding of truth. The second step will be her willingness to engage in an introspective evaluation. Setting the ground rules for a philosophical initiation, Stasimachus insists on the necessity of an unprejudiced mind to which truth could compel assent by virtue of its own rational clarity. Poullain's personal aversion to intellectual dogmatism was positively at work in his Socratic approach to the problem of authority. How one actually came to pre-judge people, things, and ideas was one of Descartes's early findings.[6]

Childhood represents consciousness as a clean slate most vulnerable to outside influences. A newborn baby (but also a child) has unchecked imagi-nation, and processes few external perceptions of the world that are not based on first impressions. Powerful sources of influence also affect the child's judgment, for example, parental nurturing of the child's character: the child's submission to the parents' power and prestige leads, by extension, to a lack of resistance to figures of authority at large. But in addition to early condition-ing, the most formidable obstacle to the development of independence of mind is tradition. Stasimachus distinguishes three types of intellectual de-ceitfulness practiced by people who cling to doctrines of the past.[7] The first category consists of a mixed bag of pseudo-learned men afflicted by a fatal lack of critical thinking skills. They understand acquisition of knowledge in terms of the collection, memorization, and imitation of ideas. They react in-discriminately to the suggestions of their senses, and inevitably succumb to custom. The custodians of false science, they exercise the power of words to obfuscate the weakness of their arguments.

The second area fraught with intellectual fraud is related to academic ideology. Stasimachus moves quickly from the prototypical savant of the Schools to the broader problem of universal consensus (or tradition). How-ever, both issues represent two sides of the same coin, i.e., principles of au-thority applied to (or rather obfuscating) the inquiry of truth. During the Renaissance, and continuing into Poullain's own day, humanists developed a veneration (exemplified in imitation) for the traditions of classical antiquity. Poullain criticized veneration of the Ancients taught in schools and universi-ties, not only because it encumbered individual free thinking with its heavy-

6. See in *Philosophical Essays, Discourse*, I, and *Meditations*, I: "Concerning Those Things that can be Called into Doubt."

7. There is nothing here that Poullain has not already addressed in the second part of *Equality*, but his essay on women's education is another forum to press his most forceful indictment of the Scholastics' legacy.

handed conformism to the past, but more importantly because it sought to prevent access to new ideas.[8]

Men reputed for their academic learning represent the third category of authority to distrust. Stasimachus deflates their self-importance, which is matched only by the vacuity of their discourse. He evokes the legendary disorderly conduct of their meetings, their cliques and cabals to impress their prejudices against each other, their querulous pig-headedness to win an argument, and generally their spirited confrontations at all costs but that of truth.[9] Furthermore, he deplores the fact that women are not allowed in these masculine assemblies of higher learning by reason of their gender, just as any reasonable person is shut out from their scholarly dialogues.[10] Finally, Stasimachus has succeeded in shaking the traditional apparatus of his friends' knowledge.

In Cartesian philosophy, methodic doubt eliminates prejudices and errors of judgment. But it is in the movement from this initial skeptical phase to seeking truth in a deliberate and absolute act of doubting that the certainty of the *cogito* emerges.[11] Likewise, in the Third Conversation and what follows Poullain sought to rebuild the foundations of knowledge on rational grounds. The first part of this conversation explains in general terms Cartesian rules of reasoning leading to the certainty of self-consciousness, and it presents Descartes's provisional moral code for use when seeking truth.[12] The second part provides a more reflective commentary on the (negative) behavioral consequences that adherence to social (and intellectual) conformism has on women.

8. According to Antoine Adam, *Grandeur and Illusion*, in the Battle of the Ancients and the Moderns the fundamental divide rests on the concept of what is called today "the march of history." Obviously, rationalists and modernists had both come to the conclusion that, in spite of the undeniable merits of antiquity, it was still "preferable to look for new forms of perfection rather than to stop" (148).

9. See Descartes, *Principles of Philosophy*, in *Phil. Essays*, 229: "The controversies of the Schools, by insensibly making those who learn them more argumentative and opinionated, are possibly the chief causes of heresies and dissensions that now plague the world."

10. Poullain must have experienced this type of intellectual oppression while attending such gatherings in the late 1660s. See the editor's opening introduction on the years preceding his initiation into Cartesianism..

11. It occurs in *Meditations*, II, in *Philosophical Essays*, 108 ("Therefore I suppose that everything I see is false") as well as in the first three paragraphs of *Discourse on Method*, IV, 60–61.

12. *Discourse*, III, in *Phil. Essays*, 56–57: "The first [maxim] was to obey the laws and customs of my country, . . . governing myself in everything else according to the most moderate opinions. . . . My second maxim was to be as firm and resolute in my actions as I could, and to follow the most preferable opinions, once I decided on them. . . . It is a very certain truth that, when it is not in our power to discern the truest opinions, we must follow the most preferable. . . . My third maxim was always to try to conquer myself rather than my fortune, and to change my desires rather than the order of the world."

From the start, Stasimachus, following Descartes's rules of evidence, proposes to apply hyperbolic doubt to undercut the pernicious effects of preconceived opinions.[13] It is one thing to doubt the physical world, another to doubt the moral (and practical) world. In the latter, it is necessary for us to act. Indeed, Poullain altered Descartes's *cogito*, "I think therefore I am," to "I exist, I who think, because I act."[14] This alteration brings him back to the world known through the senses. After raising the question of whether we can doubt even God's existence and affirming that this is possible within limits, he then goes on to caution that we cannot carry out radical doubt if we are to pay to nature and society the duties we owe them. Stasimachus cautiously acknowledges the superiority of Christian dogma without bothering to debate the point, which would have required ridding himself of ready-made beliefs in order to pass successfully the first rule of evidence.

Yet, matters of religion aside, his focus remains transfixed on the scourge of prejudice, against which a discreet but systematic doubt presents the ultimate defense. To accept an opinion based on its longevity and degree of popularity is to suppress the exercise of one's basic free will. Of course, Poullain's rejection of universal consensus permeated *Equality*, but this time Stasimachus weaves Descartes's notion of good sense into the very substance of his theory of education for women. He shows that a slave to conventional opinions will foolishly remain content in his servitude while suffering from its misery. He argues in favor of the privileges of the mind on the basis of its ontological origin. Since God is good, we must follow His example of becoming independent in our judgment, just as He enticed each person to judge the dispute between him and the synagogue when he performed miracles.[15] Thus, if reason is God's gift to men (and women of course) to use, societal obstacles to the full realization of one's intellectual potential must be removed. This line of reasoning ran contrary to every tenet of Scholastic philosophy, but, ignoring its anti-Christian implications, Poullain used Descartes's metaphysics to stress further his personal belief in a birthright to free thinking. This is a lesson not lost on young Eulalia, who concludes that she ought to cultivate her mind through serious studies, independently of external pres-

13. *Discourse*, III, in *Phi. Essays*, 54: "The first [rule] was never to accept anything as true that I did not plainly know to be such; that is to say, carefully to avoid hasty judgment and prejudice; and to include nothing more in my judgment than what presented itself to my mind so clearly and so distinctly that I had no occasion to doubt."

14. This turn appears more similar to the twentieth-century philosopher Edmund Husserl who, in his *Cartesian Meditations*, changed the Cartesian *cogito* to "I think something." See translation, note 38.

15. We find similar sentiments expressed by the author of Ecclesiasticus and by Jesus' apostles. See translation, notes 45 and 46 and related texts.

sures to the contrary. However, adverse stereotypes come to mind in the case of women's intellectual empowerment: the fear of neglecting their feminine charm in their pursuit of knowledge, and the unbecoming pride of learned ladies. Stasimachus invalidates both negative images as well as the social artifice of (false) humility, which is supposed to prevent this excess of feminine hubris. It is Timander, predisposed in favor of the scholastics, who enthusiastically acknowledges the merit of Cartesian rules on which Stasimachus has built his exposé, but not before admonishing his female friends to use their intelligence and reason as their guide.

The second part of the Third Conversation is intended to prepare women for serious study precisely when confronted with widespread cultural resistance. If knowledge based on authority has to be put aside, and if one has to assert one's free will to seek truth, how can one in practice live one's life comfortably while building this knowledge? Not out of nothingness and not in absolute opposition to the world. Stasimachus makes the distinction between the domain of theory (critical thinking in a period of abstract speculation) and the domain of practice (while going on with one's life). So, there are two kinds of truths, he says. He simply elaborates on Descartes's first maxim regarding the necessity to obey laws and customs in his country in order to conform externally in affairs of everyday life without renouncing his own set of moral beliefs. The basic notion that one can behave in public in a fashion that contradicts one's utmost private conviction was justified on the grounds of prudence and an awareness of the social constraints that impeded freedom of expression. In the larger context of Poullain's experience, it would have been a foolish suggestion to advocate the overthrow of social norms in order to assert his dissent, notwithstanding his reasons. To live well and happily was Descartes's prime motivation for hiding behind the covers of social conformism, and Stasimachus/Poullain embraces enthusiastically that intellectual dichotomy, which insures freedom of mind regardless of the politics of repression. The best illustration of Poullain's concern with the protection of his own peace of mind from the danger of intellectual transparency can be found in his metaphorical use of "two sets of clothes." However, it would be incorrect to assume his total disengagement from social activism. Like a typical moralist in the Counter-Reformation tradition of seventeenth-century France,[16] Poullain abhorred social upheaval that would create massive havoc for the benefit of a minority.

Obviously, Descartes's ethics could not circumscribe Poullain's defiant drive completely, because the issue of women's personal emancipation was at

16. See Toulmin, *Cosmopolis*, "What is the Problem with Modernity," 5–44.

stake after the publication of *Equality*. Eventually social transgression would have to take precedence, but in this conversation, which he modeled on Descartes's method for utilizing reason in search of truth, Poullain demonstrated enough political savvy to advocate a slow yet deliberate education of the masses. Stasimachus speaks of adding honey to the medicine to sweeten the pill of any radical idea rather than exposing ourselves pointlessly to public condemnation. At face value, Poullain's form of liberalism remained paternalistic and singularly elitist, although, of course, any judgment of this nature needs to be balanced against the magnitude of the task he contemplated.[17] Intuitively, he must have felt that mission daunting to the extreme, if the curious analogy he made with God's mysterious ways to express Himself through parables had any correlation with a Cartesian agenda. For now though, the advice is convincing enough for Eulalia—who objected to the doctrine of deceit—to yield to that line of logic.

Coming to the end of their conversation, of all the external obstacles thrown in the path of feminine intellectual pursuit, the stigma of curiosity continues to represent the major stumbling block for the intelligent woman. Apparently uninclined to consent to her teacher's ambivalent conformism, Eulalia rebels at the restrictions imposed on her gender's intelligence, and this is in fact where Stasimachus/Poullain draws the line on social conformity. He contrasts the kind of curiosity that seeks to perfect one's mind to the so-called feminine curiosity that is too often given to moral transgression. The latter he attributes to lack of purpose and direction—nothing that cannot be redressed. In defense of any inquisitive individual trained in logical thinking, Poullain underscored once more the freedom of the human mind to stretch as far as "sincerity and prudence" would allow. In concluding the discussion, Stasimachus recalls the progress made by his friends since the beginning of their conversations with a summary of their discoveries so far. They must ignore the crowd and its faulty wisdom and rely exclusively on reason. Having accepted the rationale behind Descartes's provisional code of ethics, they must now set it aside until their intellectual journey is completed. Stasimachus notes that they are more than halfway there, but it remains for them to learn how to achieve knowledge.

The Fourth Conversation (the longest of the five) turns its focus inward. All of us, Stasimachus insists, have the ability to reason, but most are caught in the throes of tradition and custom and make little of our ability to think. Eulalia recounts a dream she had after the previous conversation. The point of her dream is that what we receive from others by way of traditional au-

---

17. See Poullain's ambiguous remarks at the conclusion of *Education*.

thority or custom deludes us into thinking we are rich, while the real treasure is within ourselves.[18] To reinforce the dream she recalls the sterile conversations she heard in her mother's salon by supporters of scholastic philosophy; she describes how she rejected their views by claiming her own intellectual independence, of course scandalizing them, but also sending them into retreat. She has been "converted" by Stasimachus, but Eulalia's treasure remains to be cracked open. Naturally, Cartesian principles will provide the key. However, in matters of human nature Poullain's Socratic stance was diametrically opposed to his contemporaries' skeptical views on the power of introspection. Best analyzed by La Rochefoucauld (1613–80) in his *Maxims*,[19] it was believed that the study of one's self (in French "le Moi") resisted any honest investigation, because it always hid behind the multiple disguises of one's deceptive self-love ("Amour-propre"). For Poullain, however, his inner self presented no mystery to the natural light of reason. This particular threat of facing an opaque "Moi," which could so deviously promote self-delusion, epitomized for the worldly society of the 1670s another cultural impediment that had to be addressed and discarded before Stasimachus could commit in earnest to his investigation of the truth.

Since all the disciplines of knowledge from the theoretical through the practical sciences are contained in our knowledge of ourselves, we must begin with understanding the nature of body and mind, what they have in common and how they differ, how they are joined together, and what the consequences of their union are. The heart is the seat of the passions, and these give rise to varying (sometimes conflicting) movements in the mind.[20] The marvels that are within us—the way humans function through brain, blood, flesh, and bone—are greater than those of nature outside us. Nevertheless, we also need to know that we are connected to and interdependent with everything else in the world. We need the harmony of the entire universe in order to subsist, the best example being the perfect relationship between the elements (air, water, earth) and the sun. Thus by studying our-

18. His reference to the Socratic adage "know thyself" is commonplace in seventeenth-century epistemology. French classicism was imbued with the notion of psychological self-discovery as long as the inquiry recognized the principles of man's nature in a general, universal, and timeless fashion. See Toulmin, *Cosmopolis*, 32–34.

19. The *Maxims* were a product of salon culture. Madame de Lafayette (author of *The Princess of Clèves*) and Madame de Sévigné (famous for her letters) were his best friends. And the *Maxims* were undertaken as a joint venture with Madame de Sablé of the Port Royal circle and reflect a popular salon pastime. Following the publication of a pirated Dutch edition in 1664, authorized editions began to appear in 1665 and continued to do so with modifications until 1678.

20. Poullain misunderstood Descartes, who addressed that question in *The Passions of the Soul*, in *Phil. Essays*, par. 33, 308.

selves we become acquainted with everything in the universe. All the differences in the way humans see knowledge are based on the way each culture
views the relationship of mind to body. Those who see the two substances as
one speak differently from those who see them separate—thus Aristotelians
differ from Cartesians. For Cartesians, what we know about God depends on
what we know of our minds, as is true of all knowledge of things external to
us.[21]

After establishing that knowledge of the "external" (physical) world depends on the knowledge of ourselves, Stasimachus moves quickly from principles of sense perception of the world to the principles of sciences more
closely connected to our relationships with others. Poullain showed very
little interest in studying abstract sciences. He knew of Descartes's tree of
knowledge because he mentioned briefly, after logic and metaphysics, the
disciplines of physics and medicine.[22] Poullain's personal interest manifests a
degree of Socratic solipsism that Descartes had definitely avoided in his elab-
oration of his unified field of knowledge. For him, the fact that knowledge of
ourselves is the *most* necessary proves at the same time that it is the *only*
knowledge necessary, save for grammar, eloquence, and moral philosophy,
which can all improve the quality of our life. Here, Stasimachus continues to
build his case for self-consciousness by expounding on the Cartesian theory
of language. Whereas animals are seen as being pure machines, human language is evidence of the rational soul that distinguishes man from beast.[23]
Being specific to mankind, the use of language has to be understood and perfected. In a move that could be considered a vestige of his former scholastic
training in rhetoric, he places at the same level of importance what he calls
the art of self-knowledge with that of persuasion, or rather the art of thinking
with that of speaking—two sides of the same coin when we consider human
nature as unique. By the same token, his emphasis on moral philosophy is un-
surprising. His analysis of the nature of virtue provides a road map of conduct

21. Poullain's explanation follows closely Descartes's metaphysics with a fundamental exception. Although they both stress the interdependency of the body and mind, Poullain claims that
knowledge of the body precedes that of the mind. He clearly reverses Descartes's process, which
intuits knowledge solely on the basis of innate ideas, with no help from sensory experience. See
Principles of Philosophy, in *Phil. Essays,* par. 11, 233: "How our mind is better known than our body.
But in order to understand how the knowledge we have of our mind not only precedes that of
our body, but is also more evident." See also the translation, note 38.

22. In *Principles of Philosophy,* in *Phil. Essays,* 228.

23. See *Discourse,* V, in *Phil. Essays,* 72–73. In saying this, Poullain follows the Cartesian notion
that only humans have a soul (since only humans have self-consciousness). This idea has been
much debated. The recent notion of "animal rights" is based on evolutionary biology: there is no
difference in kind but only in degree (and that very small) between other animals and the human
animal.

for the quintessential Cartesian moralist. Stasimachus distinguishes between what we owe to God (to acknowledge ourselves His creatures), what we owe to the conservation of our lives (not to put ourselves in harm's way), and what we owe to each other (with the proviso that our own contribution to society must work to our mutual advantage). Poullain's defense of Cartesian theses provide an interesting twist to the Socratic "know-thyself." It was his contention that self-knowledge was sufficient to help women achieve virtue— another name for true happiness.

Poullain's confidence in the powers of the mind links with the Moderns' rejection of tradition. Only the knowledge of ourselves can rescue us from the basic error that has reigned throughout the history of the earth both in the sciences and in society, namely, to judge what ought to be done by what was done formerly or by what is done now, instead of judging everything with our own intelligence. Didn't self-consciousness direct Eulalia to find her buried treasure? Of particular importance in the final lines of this conversation is the distinction Poullain makes between his doctrine founded on self-knowledge and true knowledge received from God. He is careful to separate what constitutes divine inspiration from simple-minded perception of the external world. More to his point are superstitions that have portrayed women's nature in the worse possible ways as pawns of the Devil. Manifestly, in 1674 Poullain had total faith in the power of enlightened reason for guiding intelligent women towards their self-emancipation. Where should they start?

At the beginning of the Fifth Conversation, Stasimachus outlines a simple core curriculum that will enable his students to begin their self-instruction in accordance with the new principles they have adopted. The first list of required reading starts with a French translation of Euclid's elements of geometry and Port-Royal's principles of language and grammar, both of which provide an excellent training in methodical thinking. After an initiation to Arnauld and Nicole's logic, philosophy and physics constitute the main part of this program in which Descartes and the works of his French followers come in order of difficulty. Stasimachus leaves aside history and theology that require, according to him, very specific instructions from experts, only to suggest the private study of the New Testament in translation. His point is to encourage women (and men implicitly) to apply to their utmost capacities their introspective and analytic skills. In the Third Conversation, he enticed them judiciously to ignore the societal stigma attached to feminine curiosity. Here, at last, Poullain temporarily abandons all pretense of social conformism in a stance as incendiary as the spirit of the future encyclopedists. Building on our personal experience, learning directly from the great book of the world is another way to hone our critical minds.[24] This explains why Poullain's "must-read" list hardly contains a dozen books.[25] His distaste for any form of dogmatism is also present in the making of his secondary list of reading material. He suggests examining, following his master list and in addition to some optional Ancients' treatises on politics and rhetoric, the doctrines of a contemporary scholastic, Lesclache, and of longtime Cartesian foe Gassendi. All these books we should read at least three times: to get the general plan, to master the details, and to determine what is good and bad, useful and useless. A slave to no single doctrine, Poullain confirmed his independence of mind when he specifically noted that Descartes was not infallible, even while he disregarded the fact that he used so many of Descartes's accomplishments with very little compunction. For his part, by finding the truth and making it his own, notwithstanding its origins, he demonstrated as much intellectual autonomy as required to maintain what he called his "peaceful impartiality."[26]

Poullain remained true to himself when he acknowledged Descartes's genius in conjunction with his own "conversion" to the new philosophy. It came at a time in his life when he was already experiencing disappointment with the Old School. His initiation into Cartesian principles struck him as the answer to his personal quest, and thereafter guided him in his resolve to live by his own free will. He dropped out of the Sorbonne but was not unaware of the forces of repression, specifically the anti-Cartesianism of the official social order. He would have been quite foolhardy to declare his true colors—thus his precautions to avoid a straightforward confrontation with intellectual opponents. Seemingly taking his cue from Descartes's circumspect attitude towards the dissemination of his theories, Stasimachus advises genuine scholars, that is, independent thinkers, to be constantly on guard, especially watchful of the adversarial climate that permeates the public sphere. Simultaneously they must speak in code to identify themselves to other Cartesian soulmates. In that state of mind, Stasimachus proposes at last

---

24. This is a notion well shared with Descartes. See *Discourse*, I, in *Phil. Essays*, 50: "And resolving to search for no knowledge other than what could be found within myself, or else in the great book of the world, I spent the rest of my youth traveling."

25. He also mentions Descartes's letters to two women, Queen Christina of Sweden and Princess Elizabeth of Bohemia, the latter of whom contemporary feminist scholars believe influenced Descartes's thought. The letters of Elizabeth have never been translated in full, as have his letters to her. Lisa Shapiro is translating them for this series.

26. In this regard, Poullain's position toward the body of scholarship available to scrutiny rests on the principle of "innutrition" dear to Renaissance humanists. Although practicing a kind of silent imitation, he does not steal from anyone when he happens to agree with others' good sense.

to form a private association, comprising the four friends who would meet regularly, removed from distractions to continue their intellectual venture, but, more importantly, protected from the threats of the multitude. Here Poullain was entertaining the elitist idea of a happy few devotees to the truth, whereas until this moment his aim had been to establish the egalitarian principle of the mind across gender lines. Inasmuch as the notion of feminine scholarship was frowned upon in the salons of the leisure class, Poullain did not dare to proselytize further than through the publication of his book. What could Stasimachus and his friends do to further their knowledge? Their final withdrawal behind the walls of Sophia's hotel could be seen as a utopian attempt that regrettably diminishes the values of Poullain's liberating program.[27] It could also signify Poullain's optimism regarding the power of the mind that would eventually prevail in a new order.

Beyond the advancement of knowledge, Poullain was committed to matters of personal conscience that involved truth and error. His educational system rested on the argument of self-choice, which ineluctably affected choices to be made by both sexes. With the advent of reason (as Poullain perceived it), woman could no longer remain the slaves of a preordained destiny. The lessons contained in *On the Education of Ladies* were meant to serve as the blueprint for their personal struggle. The text certainly represented a subversive attempt to overcome the most insidious form of patriarchal domination. The feminine mind had to seek its own liberation. But Poullain's message went unheeded in 1674, and the last paragraph of his treatise, with its call for social disengagement, betrays an ambiguity of objective that may have contributed to the poor reception of its publication.

27. See Magné's introduction to Poullain's *De l'Education* (n.p.).

ON THE EDUCATION OF LADIES
FOR TRAINING THE MIND
IN THE SCIENCES
AND MORAL JUDGMENT

To Her Royal Highness
Mademoisclle

Having shown all women that there are no great achievements of which they are not just as capable as men,[1] I deemed it insufficient to show them how to reach the highest levels of learning like men, but felt that it was necessary, in addition, to reinforce with an outstanding example the reasoning that philosophy has furnished us, in order finally to establish the truth I have defended and to encourage the ladies in the glorious undertaking I propose. This example, Mademoiselle,[2] is found, most happily in Your Royal Highness, who, uniting in her person all that is noblest and most perfect in both sexes, has risen above both of them no less through the excellence of her mind and her learning than through the greatness of her birth and her courage. This is why everyone recognizes that it is the heroic qualities of Your Royal Highness as much as the rank and dignity owing her that attract the eyes and esteem of the whole of Europe and make men look upon her with admiration as the ornament of the kingdom, while women revere her as the glory of their sex. But at the same time, they must consider Your Royal Highness as an excellent model and should imitate her in a way that befits the

1. In *On the Equality of the Two Sexes*, 1673.
2. Duchesse d'Orléans, called "La Grande Demoiselle" (1627–93); she was first cousin to Louis XIV.

lofty reputation her virtue has won her by laboring mightily to overcome the inertia into which custom has reduced them and by employing part of the peace and leisure they enjoy in serious study, which would give them a solid understanding of what is necessary for the happiness and conduct of their lives. I would hope, Mademoiselle, they will realize that if Your Royal Highness brings such solid judgment to all things and speaks of them with such grace and accuracy, if she has such intelligence in business matters, such prudence in her conduct, and if she can make such a legitimate use of the possessions and honors with which she is surrounded, it is no less the effect of the affinity she has always had for fine things than of the greatness of mind so uniquely hers. It is, Mademoiselle, primarily with this in mind that I take the liberty of putting the illustrious name of Your Royal Highness at the head of this work, so that the ladies who read it for their instruction, recognizing at the outset the name of a Princess for whom they have such veneration, will be completely convinced, by remembering the example she has shown them, that they can succeed in the loftiest enterprise, and that when one has an upright heart and mind it is easy, as these conversations show, to find within oneself the precious treasure of knowledge and virtue. It is true, Mademoiselle, that my own self-interest as well as theirs moves me to act thus. As there is no one who does not know that Your Royal Highness has a most refined discernment for all works of intelligence, I promise myself that the approbation I trust she will bestow on this one will predispose the public in favor of him who is offering it to them, to discharge in his favor the gratitude due to her as first Illustrious Lady, whose merit is the most constant proof of the equality of the sexes, and to offer her this token of the profound respect with which he is,

MADEMOISELLE,
Your Royal Highness's most humble and obedient Servant,
POULAIN

PREFACE

These conversations did actually take place as they are recorded, at the instigation of a very intelligent young lady who was resolved to devote herself to study, and are published for the benefit of all ladies who find themselves with a similar ambition. This is why they have been given the title, *On the Education of Ladies*, although they are no less useful for men, just as books intended for men are also used by women, there being but one way of teaching both, since they are of the same species.

Lest the reader be surprised that we are speaking here only of women who have reached the age of discretion—although by the word "education" we normally mean the art of raising and instructing children—we should note that we can attribute to the word a broader meaning than we ordinarily do, and by showing what we should learn at a more advanced age, we show at the same time what can be taught us in childhood. And since education depends largely upon those who are responsible for it, and there are few who know what they should know in order to be able to teach well, we have thought it best to begin with what is useful for forming mistresses, before saying what we think of the method of forming the minds of the disciples according to the maxims we are proposing.

Now the most important principle of all is that we have to establish in men, insofar as is possible, a sovereign reason, that will enable them to judge all things sensibly and without prejudice. For although we have to accustom them at quite a young age to follow the basic practices of the society in which they live, nevertheless nothing is more pernicious for the perfection and the happiness of the mind than to subject them blindly to these practices, as we do ordinarily. This subjugation is the reason they become slaves to opinion and custom, and, taking each of these as an infallible rule in the sciences and in morals, they approve only what they think conforms with it and absolutely condemn what they see as contrary to it, which is the most frequent cause of bad reasoning and public and personal disorder and the reason why most people are governed by fantasy and caprice.

Thus we can look at these conversations as a first part, in which our pleasant task is to examine the taste of several people, before going on to the second, in which we will discuss in detail the education of children.[3]

Lest it should be unclear what we mean, we should say that by the words *prejudice, preoccupation,* etc., we mean judgments made rashly and without examination, or sentiments, opinions, maxims embraced without discernment. In all situations in which we speak against *opinion,* and in which some evil effect is attributed to it that we think must be got rid of, this word signifies a sentiment into which one has entered simply on hearsay and on the authority of one person or of several, without being able to understand the reason why it is good or bad, true or false, except that one has heard someone say it is thus. It is those people who judge things only by opinion and prejudice that we include in the words *the people, the vulgar, the multitude.* Those savants whose knowledge is based on opinion are those designated by the term *savant* in places where it has something base and despicable in its meaning.

3. Apparently, Poullain never wrote the second treatise.

It is to be hoped that people of intelligence, for whom this work is a kind of apology, namely, those people who judge by reason and not by opinion and who are the only people to whose judgments we should pay attention, will accept with approval and treat like a series of conversations one could have with ladies, what others might attribute to what they call vanity and self-satisfaction.

To satisfy the curiosity of the ladies who sometimes like to know the meaning of the names of the people who speak in these conversations, these names being usually taken from the Greek, they should know that

Sophia means a lady who is so accomplished and so wise that she can be called wisdom itself.

Eulalia, a lady who speaks well, with ease and grace.

Timander, a perfect gentleman who is persuaded by reason and good sense.

Stasimachus, the peacemaker, or the enemy of division, quarrels, and pedantry, this last word being understood as a vice of mind rather than of profession.[4]

FIRST CONVERSATION

When Stasimachus went to visit Sophia, an intelligent, well-bred lady, he found her in conversation with a relative of hers named Timander and a young lady named Eulalia.

He had scarcely arrived when Sophia, without giving him time to get out a greeting, blurted out: "You've come just at the right moment; this is exactly your kind of subject," and showing him the book *On the Equality of the Two Sexes* she added, "I've been arguing with Timander for ages and have this proof in my hand, but he isn't showing any sign of being converted."

Stasimachus, who realized from this greeting that he could speak with absolute freedom, replied: "Indeed, Timander must be extraordinarily stubborn not to yield—if only as a gesture to your great qualities, which are worth all the proofs in this book."

"Don't misunderstand me," replied Timander. "I have no doubts about Sophia's qualities. When I speak of women, and I claim that our sex is superior to theirs, I am speaking in general; I know perfectly well that if we examine them in particular, we will find any number like my cousin who are as clever and as thoughtful as men."

"Since you acknowledge that there are exceptions to your view, you

4. Alcover, *Poullain,* 51, presents Sophia as a Cartesian savant, Eulalia as a young girl with no learning, and Timander as a scholastic like "Stasimaque/Poullain" before his conversion to Cartesianism.

shouldn't generalize as much as people usually do," replied Stasimachus. "I am lucky enough to know several ladies who are in no way inferior to us, so I am in favor of the equality of the sexes."[5]

"You have probably read that recent book on the subject, since you are so firmly on our side," said Eulalia to Stasimachus.

"I have read and reread it," replied Stasimachus, "but I was already persuaded of its thesis long before it came out."

"If you hadn't been persuaded of it," said Sophia helpfully, "then the ladies would be under no obligation to you for defending them so well."

"You mean Stasimachus is the author of our book?" asked Eulalia.

"He is indeed," replied Sophia.

"Well then," said Eulalia to Stasimachus, "our entire sex is indebted to you more than to any other man in the world."

"True, true," said Timander. "If women knew the meaning of gratitude, they would erect a statue in your honor."

"It would be done right away if I had anything to do with it," declared Sophia.

"And I would be eager to make my contribution," added Eulalia.

"That wouldn't make me any happier," said Stasimachus. "I much prefer to possess the admiration of people like you than to see in the town square a lump of marble or stone bearing my face and my name. I'm very touched by your kind thoughts all the same; and to repay them in kind, let me say in all sincerity that I would love not only to erect statues to you but to give all ladies as intelligent as yourselves an opportunity to erect them to anyone they think worthy of one."

"Then yours would be one of the first," said Eulalia.

"I see now that I was mistaken in thinking that you just wanted to dazzle us with your wit when you wrote in praise of the fair sex," Timander said to Stasimachus. "You really do want to better their lot."

"I make no secret of the fact," replied the latter, "that my views on the subject are completely at variance with those of most men, and if I had my way I would grant women, especially the deserving ones, all the happiness they could desire."

"If I interpret Eulalia's expression correctly, she would dearly love to know what you would do to bring that about."

5. Fauré, *Democracy without Women*, 69: Poullain "directly addressed the effects of social differentiation between the sexes in order to affirm women's personal liberty. He refused to bring physiological determinism into his egalitarian argument. In this regard, Poullain differed from all those who tried to attribute a specific nature to women, whether to deprecate them (as the legal theorists had done), or to celebrate them (as the *Précieuses* had attempted to do)."

"Everything that prudence and my own instincts can suggest," replied Stasimachus. "Apart from a few exceptions in women's favor, I'd place an absolute ban on putting girls into religious orders against their will. I'd clamp down so hard on marital authority that not a single man would abuse it.[6] Nothing upsets me more than to see a woman condemned to live with a brutish or jealous husband who makes her life a misery. I'd set up an independent commission, half male and half female, to deal with matters relating to the fair sex. And as I think it absolutely essential to have an education, I would organize things in such a way that women could get one as easily as men."

"In that case," said Timander, "there's a good way to make them learned, and in very short order. They should take a marriage exam; the cleverest would go to the richest and handsomest husbands, as the prettiest do in China. But I'm afraid," he added, "that there would be strong opposition to such a ruling; learned ladies are in such bad odor that it would be severe punishment to an eligible man to give him one as a wife."

"You're confusing truly learned ladies with prudes and précieuses," said Sophia. "I hate those myself, although we're the same sex, and I'm not at all surprised that men can't abide them."

Idea of the
précieuse.

"It's so hard to draw the line between the learned lady and the précieuse, that one crosses it without noticing," said Timander. "I know several ladies who are learned, but not a single one of them isn't a précieuse too. I know they all have wit and good taste, but their wit takes such a precious turn and their good taste is so corrupted by their airs and graces that you would be completely put off by it. They behave as if they were goddesses, of a different race from their peers. When they are in company, they act as if they should be treated like queens; they don't deign to glance at anyone who dares to approach them, and think they are conferring an immense honor on a man if they occasionally turn their eyes in his direction. If they have a husband, either they ig-

6. Gibson, *Women in Seventeenth-Century France*, 68–69: "Legal discrimination, religious taboos, and social pressures, by undermining the status of women and debasing conjugal love, all contributed to put asunder those whom God had joined together. The seventeenth-century husband was conditioned to regard his nominal co-partner as an inferior whose physical and mental weakness justified his almost complete control over her property and person. She was the being from whom public opinion encouraged him to live remote, physically if possible, emotionally at least. Never must he show assiduity or passion for her lest he excite derisive comment, such demonstrations of interest and affection being more properly reserved for the mistress who compensated him for marital abstinence."

nore him altogether or they treat him like a servant; and if they don't, they talk about men as if there were not a single one who was worthy of living with them. Anyone who doesn't respond with signs of adoration to the maxims they pronounce as if they were the oracle is, according to them, completely lacking in intelligence. Their gestures are mannered, their speech affected. They listen to each other in raptures and to others with indifference. As if every word that proceeds from their mouths should be greeted with awe and adoration, they look around to make sure they are being admired, and when they finish speaking their vanity demands that they indulge in a little self-satisfied preening that is easier to imagine than to describe."

"You seem to be something of an expert on the subject," said Sophia wryly.

"Timander knows one kind of learned lady," replied Stasimachus, "whereas I know a different kind altogether whom I like very much. I find them natural, polite, and easy to be with.

"But," he went on, "even if they were as précieuse as the ones you *Idea of false* have just described with such feeling, we should be less put off by them *learning.* than by the regular savants and professionals we have at present. These are men whose learning has only served to turn their heads into a fortress against common sense, where reason can enter only through a breach. They fancy themselves as gifted as the Greeks and the Romans when all they have done is learn classical languages; they not only make oracular pronouncements but consider themselves to be infallible and expect the whole world to submit to their decisions and listen to them and respect them as if they were gods walking the earth. And far from spending any time with women and allowing themselves to be charmed by at least one or two, as is the case with your learned ladies—who, however fastidious they may be, do like the odd man— these men, I say, make it a virtue to put down the whole of the fair sex and avoid all contact with it, like wiverns and owls.[7] In short, they are savants to whom, for the most part, we could apply the words of the excellent poet:

> A pedant bloated with his knowledge vain
> His Greek spews forth with all his might and main;

7. Wiverns are vipers, serpents. In mythology they are two-legged creatures, but having the head of a dragon. The owl symbolized many things: Satan (since it hid in the dark like the Prince of Darkness), solitude, wisdom, an attribute of Christ who sacrificed Himself to save humankind. We have found no reference, however, to the males of either species avoiding contact with females.

And fizzing forth as from a shaken bottle,
Come rote-learned authors such as Aristotle.
For him the endless spouting is enough;
He'll never learn to understand the stuff.[8]

"Our learned ladies are at least as good as those pedantic men," said Eulalia.

"Of course they are," agreed Stasimachus, "and given the choice I'd take one beautiful précieuse over a dozen pedants."

"I'm sure you would," Timander interjected. "But be all that as it may, it would not do women much good to become as clever as men. On the contrary, according to your book it would be disastrous for them to be given the opportunity, since they would lose all the excellent qualities the first part ascribes to them in order to acquire the mind and manners of the scholar whom you describe in the same section.

"You know better than I what changes meditation and study can bring about in the student. His heart shrivels up, his imagination wears out, his eye sinks and clouds over; his face becomes wan and glum, his demeanor gloomy, melancholy, and tormented, his speech blunt, his manners gross and ill-bred. He becomes sullen and preoccupied, not to mention contentious, secretive, and quarrelsome.[9] Given that women's constitution is more delicate than men's, they would be more susceptible to these unfortunate effects. That's all they would need to finish them off for those whose opinion of them isn't great already. And if they lose the glow, the brilliance, the charm that make them so attractive and in exchange contract the opposite flaws, then they risk spending their time in vain."

"I don't agree that study has destroyed the learned ladies you know," said Sophia, "and far from its being true of male scholars, I know several who are sociable, well-mannered, and urbane, and you yourself are one of them."

"Out of politeness I'm not going to respond to that," replied Timander. "But if we are well-mannered, then according to Stasimachus we owe it to women, because we've learned our manners at the School for Women. Whereas if *you* had come to *our* School, goodness knows what would have happened, and I'm afraid that the world would become a country of barbarians and savages."

"Your fear would be justified," said Stasimachus, "if ladies were taught

---

8. We have not identified the author of this poem if, indeed, it was not Poullain himself.

9. See Montaigne, "Of the Education of Children," *Essays*, 1:26, in *The Complete Works*, 118–19. See also 121: "For all this education I do not want the boy to be made prisoner. I do not want him to be given to the surly humors of a choleric schoolmaster. I do not want to spoil his mind."

science in the way it's taught in our Schools, but if they follow the method laid out in the second part of the book you mentioned, they will get along fine. Science would provide them with a gentle and pleasant intellectual exercise which would challenge their minds without harming their bodies and would give them an opportunity to fulfil their potential."

"They're already doing that," retorted Timander, "and according to you, those who have never studied a thing in their lives are still able to express themselves well, to argue persuasively, and to live a good life."

"They would be able to do all those things even better," said Sophia.

"Yes, indeed they would," Stasimachus went on. "And if women who have the leisure and the means could only understand what advantages accrue from regular study, I'm sure that they would take time out of their usual activities to acquire the solid basis of knowledge which seems to be the basis for a truly happy life. If we are to find pleasure in our work and be assured of the joy of the afterlife through honorable behavior, then we must have a perfect understanding of the virtue of which it is the reward. As for happiness in this life, whether one finds it in absolute freedom of spirit or in the pursuit of pleasure, honors, and riches, it seems to me that we cannot achieve it without the enlightenment that truth gives us. This enlightenment serves to console us in our sorrows and to moderate us in our prosperity, raising us above the vicissitudes of fortune which tyrannize over those who remain blindly in its sway. Through it we understand our passions and our needs, and learn to temper the former and bear with patience the latter. It teaches us to know ourselves and the objects that surround us and to make natural, legitimate use of all things." *The usefulness of study.*

"What do you understand by this 'freedom of spirit' you just mentioned?" asked Eulalia.

"What I don't mean is some blind, rash permissiveness that we associate with libertines. I mean rather a judicious, enlightened freedom based on love of truth, not fettered or hampered by cowardice or error or ignorance or scruple."

"In that case," said Eulalia, "philosophy is more necessary than we realize."

"True," said Stasimachus, "and our need for it is too great for me to be able to go into it here. But even if it were not so necessary, the pleasure that it gives would attract more people to it if they better understood its rewards. I'm convinced that when the immediate needs of life *The pleasures of the mind are to be preferred to those of the senses.*

are satisfied in a reasonable way, nothing is more worthwhile than to seek the truth, and to study it either by oneself or with others."

"My greatest satisfaction comes from learning about things and communicating them to other people," said Sophia. "And when I make the comparison, I can't see how the satisfaction we get from the senses can possibly be called 'voluptuous.' Apart from the fact that we aren't naturally drawn towards sensuous voluptuousness but are rather pushed into it in spite of ourselves by the pain that torments us, this voluptuousness is nothing more than a lessening of pain which we appreciate either when we give our bodies whatever they desire for their preservation or when we take away whatever is causing pain. But, oh what grief and anguish to gain this pleasure! and how brief, unreliable, and impure is its duration! It starts to seep away as soon as we possess it. As soon as the ills to which it was the antidote pass, it becomes dull and insipid, and if we try to hang on to it after the pain that it was meant to heal is gone, it leaves its own pain, more acute and more irritating than before. In fact, the greatest pleasures are so short-lived that we call them 'fleeting joys'; we enjoy them in secret, as if they were something that didn't belong to us, and we say that stolen pleasures are the sweetest."

"Intellectual and spiritual pleasures are of quite another order, if I can put it that way," said Stasimachus. "As soon as a man starts his quest for truth, he finds a joy that engages him more and more, but a pure and complete joy which has nothing to do with his body, a joy quite exempt from confusion and envy, one that endures as long as we ourselves, that is owned independently of anyone else, that increases as it is spread around, that produces no bitter, searing pain, or danger of excess, but that, rather, eases life's sorrows and moderates the excesses which are their usual cause."

"As ladies are so fond of pleasure, and as knowledge of truth affords such great pleasure, I second you in persuading them to seek it," said Timander. "And they ought to be all the more keen to do this, since, according to you, they are as capable of it as men; besides, we always think of Truth as being female."

Allegorical idea of Truth.

"I don't know how it's normally represented," said Stasimachus. "I always imagine it as an accomplished lady deserving of the service and care of everyone; and I share the view of the Ancient who wrote the following poem in honor of this delightful mistress:

> Dear Truth, if those who worship thee through mist
> Could but thy glorious nakedness perceive,

Their much increased ardor thou'd receive
For none thy uncloth'd beauty can resist.[10]

"That reminds me of a painting done by a young gallant I happened to meet at a party recently," said Timander. "'On the subject of Truth or Knowledge' he said, 'I believe that she is the eldest daughter of Nature who has bestowed upon her all the beauty and charm that ought to make her irresistible to all men. She shines so brightly that she can be compared only with the sun in brilliance and clarity. She illuminates our souls and gives them strength and joy. But I can't help saying that I find her quite different from our own ladies in whom we cannot abide equality or rivalry. Truth is available in equal measure to all who seek her without causing any jealousy or disagreements, except among those who seek her through different methods. She is completely unlike those haughty, mettlesome beauties who are only happy if men are sighing and weeping over them, and who think a poor lover's services are adequately requited with a gracious glance. Truth wants no groveling and crawling among her friends; in her realm there is no talk of chains or slavery; she is gentle and accommodating; she always makes the first move, and the first sincere declarations that come from the depths of a man's heart are immediately rewarded by her most generous favors. She extends her hand to those who approach her, and if they are fortunate enough to welcome her, she pulls them up out of the commonplace and places them on heights of happiness that ordinary people never experience.'"

"If I were a man," said Eulalia, "I'd want that lady to be my paramount mistress and a model for the others."

"Although you're not a man, it doesn't mean that you can't seek her too," Stasimachus said to her. "She is a man for women and a woman for men, without having any of the disadvantages each sex has for the other. And I'd be delighted to have you as companion and rival in the quest for her. To spur you on, let me remind you that the interests of Truth are inseparable from yours, and that whereas you need her weapons to increase your influence, she needs your charm to help establish hers. You can't be unaware of the power of a fine thought when it comes from a mouth as beautiful as yours; just imagine how impressive Truth would be if you adorned her with the grace for which your sex is known.

"Even if you're not interested in Truth, think of us, and don't abandon us in a situation where your help is so necessary to us. Your example could give rise to a healthy spirit of emulation in the hearts of all men, who, fearing that

10. We have not identified the Ancient who is said to have written this poem.

women would beat them in an exercise at which they are vain enough to think nature has given them special advantages, would be goaded to apply themselves with greater zeal and disinterestedness to the acquisition of the knowledge they cultivate so carefully.

"What a great service you and women like you could perform for our scholars! If you admit them into your salons, you would provide the means for them to civilize their knowledge; if you let them take part in your conversations, you could communicate to them the social graces that you possess so abundantly and in which they are so singularly lacking. Little by little, the urbane and polished manners that are so becoming to you would rub off on them, eliminating their intransigence and coarseness, making them ready for contact with the social world.[11]

"You would get something out of this too; by bringing back to sensible behavior those uncultivated and rebarbative creatures who avoid you at the moment, you would force them to change their views and to admire a sex they have long despised. Take heart and show that you have the mind of a man in the body of a woman."

"Just a moment," Sophia said, smiling. "You're insulting us right after paying us compliments. Remember that our minds are as good as men's."

"I'm sorry," replied Stasimachus. "The prejudice is so well established that I was taken in by it without thinking. Let your true equality assert itself and show us that Truth is as much your characteristic as virtue and beauty. Overcome men's injustice and blindness, and bring about a reversal of vocabulary so that the term 'womanly,' which has a pejorative sense, becomes an expression of honor; and instead of flattering women, as we have in the past, by saying they have a male mind, we would praise men by saying they have a woman's mind.

"Isn't it enough that custom has made you the physical subjects of men, without your bowing to them in matters of the mind? Is it not shameful that that divine attribute should be vanquished by those who are vanquished by your faces? Come, come and score a double victory over us, and while you keep us in thrall through the gentle victory of your charm, ravish our minds with the beauty of your thoughts."

"There are several points in your gallant speech that I want to dispute," Eulalia said to him. "Although I don't have much experience, being still very

11. The notion that women's influence could civilize men's behavior was a commonplace in feminist literature. Maclean, *Woman Triumphant,* 151–52: "The debate about the 'conversation des dames' is undoubtedly won by the feminist faction, and after 1650 little is written to question the value and agreeableness of mixed social intercourse presided over by women."

young, I do have enough to realize that knowledge is a great source of strength to those who possess it. For if it makes men able to govern themselves and to govern others, it ought to be no less useful for us, if we could only be taught how to acquire it. Not only would we have help in bearing all the vexatious and unpleasant features of our sex, but also, if women were well educated, marriages would be better, families better organized, and children better brought up. We wouldn't have to be hanging about the ears of our director of conscience all the time, inventing petty sins to confess. Women could consult with other women in the same way that men consult with other men. A mother superior would lead her nuns, mothers would teach their daughters, and with each sex responsible for its own members we wouldn't perhaps be any worse off."[12]

The utility of the sciences for women.

"This is what I've thought for a long time," said Sophia, "but especially since the conversation Stasimachus and I had on the topic Eulalia just mentioned. I haven't forgotten your pointing out that there used to be deaconesses in the church, that St. Paul called Phoebe minister of the church of Cenchreae (Rom. 16:1), that he commanded Timothy to choose a widow not less than sixty years old (1 Tim. 5:9). Those are things that concern our sex, and it's written somewhere that deaconnesses were inducted with almost the same ceremonies as deacons (*Apostolic Constitutions*, I.8 and 19)."[13]

"I remember," said Stasimachus, "and I also told you that St. Clement of Alexandria testifies that the apostles took women along with them to minister to other women,[14] and to bring the Lord's doctrine to places where men do not enter. And as we are on the subject, I might as well tell you that it seems, according to the testimony of a Council and that of the great Origen, who ran a school for girls and women where he taught the most advanced areas of knowledge, that women took part in ecclesiastical ministry to other women."[15]

12. Gibson, *Women in Seventeenth-Century France*, 17, summarizes arguments of "churchmen and moralists who sought to prove that it was in the interest of both men and women that the latter should not be left in ignorance." Poullain's merit was less in advancing new ideas than in framing them in a logical system of thought.

13. See his Preface to *On the Excellence of Men*, for a discussion on women theologians in the ancient church.

14. A marginal note says this is from *Stromateis* 1.3, but that is incorrect. We have not located the passage.

15. A marginal note locates this passage in *Laodicia, ch. 11 on St. John*, but we have not located it. The tradition of Origen's directing a school for girls comes from Eusebius, *Church History*, bk. 6, chap. 8. Eusebius gives as a reason for Origen's supposed "castration"

"Are you suggesting that that discipline should be reestablished?" asked Timander.

"Not at all," replied Stasimachus. "I am not one of those blind worshipers of antiquity; nor do I believe that whatever happened in past centuries should be the rule in the present, except in essential things. I was just giving you some illustrations to show you that women were formerly more highly regarded by Christians than you would have thought, and if what Eulalia is hoping for should be established, there would be nothing novel about it. At the same time, I was also showing you that if someone has a sane, judicious mind, as she does, then one can come to the same conclusions as those whom one thinks of as very clever, without having had any contact with them.

"What I would like is for women to be taught with as much care as men, because that would be very sensible and would do no harm to anyone. It wouldn't be anything new, either, as it was done a long time ago. St. Gregory of Nyssa tells in the life of St. Macrina, his sister, that she was raised like a man in holy letters, and that she taught her brothers like Peter of Sebaste and the great St. Basil.[16] You know very well that St. Jerome rarely led women without having them study the Scriptures, and he even had several of them learn Hebrew so that they could read the Old Testament in the original.[17] If Priscilla and Aquila had known their religion no better than the women of to-day, they would never have been able to instruct the great Apollo.[18] And if the celebrated Marcella had been content with the orders of her director of conscience and the abridged catechism, then you can be quite sure that she would never have been able to confound the heretics, nor be consulted by the Pope and the clergy in Rome about the most problematic questions of the Scriptures."[19]

---

that he taught mixed audiences. Eusebius also mentions in 6.21 that Origen taught a queen and in 6.23 that girls trained in penmanship copied for him. See Eusebius, *The History of the Church from Christ to Constantine*, trans. G. A. Williamson (Baltimore, 1965), 247–48, 262–63.

16. Gregory of Nyssa's life of his sister, St. Macrina, had been translated into Latin in the sixteenth century. See our translation of *Excellence*, note 4.

17. Many of Jerome's letters to Marcella discuss points of the Hebrew Scripture, citing texts in Hebrew, for example, letters 25–26, 28–30, 34 (these are, however, untranslated). In Epistle 39.1 he says Paula's daughter Blesilla learned Hebrew well enough to speak it. In Epistle 108.27 Paula is said to have been able to chant the Psalms without an accent. See Jerome's letters in *A Select Library of Nicene and Post-Nicene Fathers of the Christian Church*, 2d ser., vol. 6 (Grand Rapids, Mich., n.d. but originally published in 1892), 49, 209–10.

18. See Acts 18:24–27.

19. St. Marcella (ca. 325–411) is known to us largely through a letter (*Ep.* 127) of Jerome, who referred to her as "the glory of the ladies of Rome." She was of a noble Roman family and devoted herself to an ascetic Christian life after the death of her husband of seven months. When the Goths sacked Rome in 410 she died after a few days, apparently from lack of food. Jerome relates

"You're fortunate in having St. Jerome on your side," said Timander, "because apart from what you've just said about him, he is thought to have spoken very favorably of the fair sex, which he sometimes preferred above our own."

Stasimachus continued: "Although what I've been saying about the ladies would be no less true even if the good church father had a completely contrary view, the fact remains that having a man of his reputation and influence on one's side is always a good thing. What makes me admire him even more is that he and I have some things in common: we have both been chastised for speaking up too openly in favor of women (always a contentious issue), and like him I couldn't care less what people think of my position."

"Unless I am very much mistaken, a man of your views is hardly the kind of person who is going to inspire in women a blind devotion that consumes their entire lives," Eulalia said to Stasimachus.

"I don't know what you understand by devotion," replied the latter. "There are several kinds. If you mean a disciplined, Christian zeal that leads us to perform immediately and joyfully God's commands, and to leave aside study and all other exercises in order to carry out with prudence the charitable works that Christ taught us, then I can assure you that I would urge this devotion, not only upon women, but also on men, as being the only thing really necessary; because knowledge tends mainly to virtue."

Idea of true devotion

"That's not what I mean by devotion," cried Eulalia. "I mean the kind of devotion that so obsesses a certain woman close to me that she would see it as criminal to talk about anything except domestic affairs,[20] a devotion which for her consists of certain arbitrary and inconsequential religious observances which other people—doctors, scholars, magistrates, almost all reasonable men and women who have something else to do—are all excused, without the priests, who are also excused, accusing them of being any the less Christian.

"I wouldn't reproach her for her conduct because of the respect I

---

that he was her teacher and that she became very learned, so that "after my departure from Rome, in case of a dispute arising as to the testimony of Scripture on any subject, recourse was had to her to settle it." Jerome also credits her with routing the heretics from Rome. There is, however, no mention in Jerome's letter of Marcella's being consulted by the pope. See Jerome's letters in edition cited, note 17 above, 253–58, as well as references to Marcella in the same note.

20. For the most enlightened educators of the century, views regarding how to free women from crass ignorance never considered an option outside women's traditional wifely duties.

owe her, and because everyone has a right to his own actions and fantasies, if she didn't impose hers on my sister and me, and if she hadn't told us endlessly, and made her confessor tell us (because we love reading) that girls shouldn't be curious, and that women ought to be satisfied with their prayer books and their needle. If I'd known what you have just told us and what is in your book, I would have used it against that confessor and made him realize that he can't see further than his breviary."

"People like that must be forgiven," said Stasimachus. "They say what they know, and they do what they can. They believe that women are inferior to men; they know nothing about learning, nor, therefore, whether you need it and are capable of it. And as they have heard that you aren't, you mustn't be surprised if they treat you according to their own limited understanding and preconceptions. If they were following their breviary or really paying attention when they are saying the office of certain great female saints, they would observe as much intelligence and generosity among women as among men; and if they realized that, for example, St. Catherine, St. Teresa, and St. Macrina must have been very brilliant to do what they did, they would judge that the highest learning is no more beyond your sex than beyond ours."[21]

"Our good priest should just come right here," said Eulalia. "I'd send him right back to his breviary. If he tells me again that women are fit only for the distaff, and that they have never studied, I'll tell him that the distaff is for people like him, that he probably isn't aware of what went on in the past, and that it's easy to mislead simple, ignorant people like ourselves."

"But how did you manage to escape the influence of the woman and man you mention?" asked Timander.

"Partly because they were trying to persuade me against my will. What really put me off was the following. A friend of mine, who is as unfortunate as I am, managed to get hold of some books without her mother's knowledge; she lent me the New Testament. I devoured it eagerly, especially as it was the only book I had, and I'd been forbidden to read it. The parts about Christian perfection did not impress me more than the rest. I couldn't for the life of me see that women are meant to live any differently from men in the faith: both will be punished or rewarded in the same way and for the same actions, and

21. The reference here could be either to St. Catherine of Sweden (1331–81) or St. Catherine of Siena (1347?–80). The former participated in the order founded by her mother, St. Bridget, and traveled to Rome in an unsuccessful attempt to gain her mother's canonization. The latter began by devoting herself to the poor, but achieved such renown that she became a mediator in conflicts between Florence and the Papacy. St. Teresa of Avila (1515–82) is famous for her writings, especially her *Life*, and for her founding of a number of reformed Discalced Carmelite monasteries for women. St. Macrina is mentioned above, note 16. All these women were very strong willed, the point Poullain is making.

learning isn't forbidden to anyone. I deduced, therefore, that those who try to turn us away from learning do so either for selfish reasons or from ignorance. It seems to me, therefore, that it would be better to follow the example of those scholars who only go to church when they have specific business there, and to spend one's time, as they do, in one's study, or with fellow scholars learning something good and sound rather than wasting it in frivolity."

"It would be a great pity not to cultivate your mind, which is so easily capable of serious thought," said Stasimachus.

"After all," said Timander to Sophia and Eulalia, "you both show such seriousness and good sense for women that I'm on the verge of conceding equality and believing that if, instead of amusing your sex with petty activities we gave them the same education as ourselves, I would go along with everything Stasimachus has been saying. I still don't see where we go from here, things being as they are. Not only does it take seven or eight years and immense effort to learn foreign languages, which women, perhaps, could not tolerate, but in addition, there isn't anywhere where they could learn them as we do."

"That's just what's been a source of grief to me for a long time," said Eulalia. "I've always had an intense desire to learn, but I'm terrified by the amount of work it would take, and I despair of ever being able to satisfy my curiosity."

"The effort it takes to go about it isn't as great as one imagines. I have thought about the wearisome part of my studies, and I think that shortcuts could be taken, especially for women. They aren't allowed into the civil service, for example, so they wouldn't have to learn foreign languages, as that is the only reason why people have to study them at the moment."

"You mean we could complete a course of study without learning either Greek or Latin?" asked Eulalia.

"You could do it using French books," replied Stasimachus. "Our language provides enough in verse and prose today in all the subjects one needs to improve the mind."

How women could be instructed.

"Indeed, I do have most Latin authors in French translation," said Sophia.

"And in addition, we have modern authors who are the equals of the Ancients in both language and content," added Stasimachus.[22]

22. By eliminating the old schools' mandatory knowledge of Latin, and to a lesser extent of Greek, the Moderns would gain women's support in the Battle between the Ancients and the Moderns at the end of the century.

"How can we get an education without going to college?" persisted Eulalia.

"The same way as most men, who never go there either," replied Stasimachus. "Whatever you want to learn can be taught by tutors, the way writing and dancing are."

"There's something else that could be done that would be much more convenient," interjected Timander. "Given that there are already mistresses perfectly versed in various subjects, they could teach girls, who in turn would be trained as teachers, just as our male teachers are trained in universities and other places."

"That gives me another idea," said Sophia. "We're put into convents at a very young age. Why could the nuns not be trained to teach the boarders and the other nuns, who would then become teachers in their turn?"

"It wouldn't be as hard to bring about as I had imagined," conceded Timander. "Two things would be necessary. The first is that two or three highly placed people should give their daughters an education, and for that a well-known convent and an individual teacher would have set an example. The other is that some man who believes in this should write two books: the first would be a guide for teachers, showing women who are of an age to study by themselves with the help of books how one should proceed expeditiously towards the kind of learning we need for our personal guidance; and the second would be the method for teaching children what they have learned."[23]

"I love that idea," cried Sophia.

"I'm sure it would work," added Eulalia.

"What about you?" Timander asked Stasimachus. "You are all in favor of women. Hadn't you thought of doing them that service? You look as if you could, and I remember that in your book you promised a new method."

"The person who wrote the Apology for Women should write the teaching manual too, so that they could acknowledge what an intelligent man can do for them. They would be all the more grateful to you for giving them the means to defend themselves and to promote, on their own, interests that formerly needed an outsider's pen."

"You would be sure to have their esteem, too," said Timander.

"I must confess that I'd thought about the project, and I haven't given up hope of bringing it off some day," said Stasimachus.

"This is too good an opportunity to miss," said Eulalia. "Since I've been

23. Poullain's idea, unusual for his time, was to create a teachers' college. In doing so he anticipates Mary Astell's call for a female academy of learning in England. See *A Serious Proposal to the Ladies*, 2 parts (1696, 1697), in Astell, *The First English Feminist: Reflections on Marriage and Other Writings*, ed. and intro. Bridget Hill (New York, 1986), 135–79.

meaning to start my studies for a long time, please tell me how to go about it. Sophia, you ask him, too."

"As Stasimachus is a civilized, helpful man who isn't coy about teaching what he knows, I'm sure he'll oblige me and my friends," replied Sophia.

"It's such a pleasure to talk to women like yourselves that you can be assured I'll do anything you want to please Eulalia. I'm all the happier to do it because you are not the sort of women who think you're not clever enough to understand sound arguments."[24]

"My view is that we're stronger than we think. People who don't know their own capacity refuse to embark on things they could well accomplish," said Sophia. "I'm quite sure that the greatest geniuses and those who have written most were like women once, not thinking during their childhood, before they had tried anything, that they could do the things they later accomplished."

"Stasimachus is so good at explaining things and at making what he's saying seem so alive that he could make himself understood by women with nothing like your intelligence," said Timander.

"Talk about *people* with intelligence, rather, because you're invited as well," added Sophia.

So Stasimachus invited him, too, and all four, delighted with their conversation, agreed to meet again in three days.

SECOND CONVERSATION

Stasimachus, who greatly enjoyed his conversations with Sophia, was delighted to have a legitimate reason for going back to her house and got there punctually on the afternoon she had indicated. Timander and Eulalia arrived shortly afterwards. As the latter was going to be the principal subject of conversation, and as Stasimachus much admired her looks and her intelligence, he opened the conversation with a few approving remarks about her course of study.

After some witty repartee she said, "If it's true that studying will make me a nicer person, do tell me how you think I should start."

"I'll be quite happy to keep my part of the bargain, but on two conditions.[25] The first is that you promise not to behave towards me with the blind deference that women usually show towards their teachers, because that's

---

24. This problem of feminine self-esteem is essential to Poullain's program. Stasimachus's remark alludes to Molière's character, Henriette, in *Les Femmes savantes.*

25. Stasimachus/Poullain's lesson builds on the double concept of error and falsehood following Descartes's example and method. See, in *Phil. Essays, Discourse,* I, and also *Méditations,* I, 104: "Concerning Those Things that can be Called into Doubt": "And thus I realized that once in my life I had to raze everything to the ground and begin again from the original foundations, if I wanted to establish anything firm and lasting in the sciences."

The state of
mind necessary
to teach and to
be well-taught.

something I hate. On the contrary, you should keep your wits sharpened to contradict me; only agree with what you're quite sure is right; think of what I say not as a hard and fast rule I'm laying down but as a model of what I would do if I were starting my studies all over again. In short, be as wary of me as if I were setting an ambush. And I promise that I'll be equally pleased to find myself going with you along the right path as I will to learn from the warnings of our friends here that I've taken the wrong path."

"I wouldn't dare to tell you everything that's in my head, for fear of compliments," Eulalia answered slyly. "I promise to follow your first condition to the letter. Now tell me, what's the second?"

"That you'll allow me to ask you three things about your request before I give you a direct answer: (1) Whether you know what you are, and what is the state of your soul; (2) Whether you know what you're doing when you ask about acquiring knowledge; and (3) Whether you think you're ready for the greatest resolution a person can make."

"You've changed to a completely different tone," replied Eulalia. "I can't help feeling you want to embarrass me by asking me things you can see I obviously don't know, and that no-one but yourself has ever thought to ask me."

"Don't be surprised," Sophia said to her, "that's typical of Stasimachus; don't be put off by it."

"Now don't get the idea that I'm spying on you in secret and keeping track of your virtues and vices," said Stasimachus, turning back to Eulalia. "All I'm asking for is an honest and reasonable confession of ordinary weaknesses that should be no cause for you to blush, since none of us is free of them, and from which I myself am probably not completely exempt."

"Just how important is this confession?" asked Eulalia.

"Let's put it this way. You must realize that it's impossible for someone of your age to acquire the knowledge you desire and to put it to good use unless we know at the outset where your intellectual interests lie. You must know that anyone who is trying to bring his land under the plough starts by finding out what its good and bad points are, and he plants the seeds only when he has made the necessary preparations. You probably realize, too, that physicians are most successful when their patients themselves understand the nature of their illness. So you can think of knowledge, either as a second crop that makes the mind fertile, or as therapeutic medicine that brings it back to health, all of which should make it clear why you should be aware of any indisposition you may have, so that we can decide together which is the most suitable and effective remedy. You can't imagine how useful it will be for us to work together, since bad communication between pupils and teachers often produces insurmountable difficulty and resistance."

"I'll do whatever you think is necessary to avoid that," said Eulalia.

"Let's get back to our discussion, then," said Stasimachus. "To begin at the beginning: is it not true that you are quite convinced of the truth of many, many things? You take it as absolute truth that the world is a great globe with a limited surface area beyond which there is a vast space with nothing in it, known as the void; that the sky is a vault overarching everything, that with constant motion around the earth, which you think of as the center of the world, the sky carries along with it the heavenly bodies that you imagine are attached to it like great golden nails; and that by some secret means which you do not understand, these imaginary nails exert an influence on us which causes most of the general and specific upheavals that occur here below.[26] Don't deny it. Wouldn't you snigger, at least to yourself, at someone who told you that the moon is perhaps an earth like ours, inhabited by animals?"

"Absolutely," replied Eulalia, "and speaking of animals, although I don't talk to them myself, nor have I ever seen anyone have a conversation with them, yet when I see every day what dogs can do, I'm tempted to wonder if they aren't as intelligent as we are."[27]

"You could continue with what you know about the tides, about magnetism and attraction and repulsion," went on Stasimachus. "But to come closer to home: you are convinced that the affection we feel towards our parents is innate, that the soul is distinct from the body, that the soul is our reason for whatever we do in life. And however much you visualize the soul as something without matter, you nevertheless divide it into two parts, the superior and inferior, and the latter position is given to whatever within you is at odds with the rules and laws you have been taught. You love truth and virtue, you try to avoid vice and error, and you can distinguish between them. You are enlightened about your sex, knowing that it is the equal of ours. But though that fact is incontrovertible, at least insofar as women who are fortunate enough to resemble you are concerned, I have no doubt that if your guardians came along and said that the book on equality is bad and contradicts the Scripture, you would give up all the positive thoughts you had had about it, and would be as repelled by it as you are were attracted to it earlier.

26. He is describing the premodern cosmology of Aristotle and Ptolemy.

27. About animals' lack of intelligence, see Descartes, *Discourse on Method*, V, in *Phil. Essays*, 72: "And we should not confuse words with the natural movements that attest to the passions and can be imitated by machines as well as by animals." See also Alcover, *Poullain*, 61.

"If I add to your opinions the deference and submission you bear towards custom and public opinion, then I think I will have put my finger on the principal articles by which I can judge the state of your conscience. I say the principal articles because they include, one way or another, many things you take as certain, for instance, ideas of truth and falsehood, vice and virtue, and the stories you learned in your childhood about the return of spirits and the miraculous effects of magic told you by the women in your household, or read in books thought to be the truth by certain members of your sex because they are in print."

"I realize," said Eulalia, "that even without having commerce with the Devil, it isn't completely impossible to know in part what is going on in people's souls."

"No, indeed," replied Stasimachus, "and I'll go even further. I could tell you about the passions and desires you think you are keeping secret."

"How can you do that?" asked Timander.

The basis for most people's certitude.

"By means of secret insights I have into Eulalia's soul, which reveal to me things that she didn't know about herself. I hope you'll forgive me," he added to Eulalia, "if I give you a sample, so that you can see what is the basis of your convictions and the source of the notions that govern your conduct. Remember that big things have small beginnings. Kingdoms started with a simple family consisting of two people, great conflagrations with a mere spark, and the biggest animals with something as small as the smallest. I don't need to tell you what was happening to you when you were in your mother's womb; it isn't hard to imagine that at that time you had only confused thoughts which normally had as their sole object the internal changes that food can produce in the body.

"Thus to assess what happens to us during childhood, we have to go back to our emergence from the place where we received life and see ourselves at that moment as young strangers washed up by the ocean on the shore of a new world where we know neither the things in it nor the people who dwell there nor the language they speak nor the laws they are subject to.[28]

We judge on the basis of prejudice and error during childhood.

"Doesn't it seem to you that the needs and difficulties to which a newborn baby is exposed because of the change of environment are so troubling and distressing to him that he is incapable of thinking about

28. See Descartes, *Principles of Philosophy*, para. 71, in *Phil. Essays*, 251: "The principal cause of error is found in the prejudices of childhood."

who he is; that the woes that assail him are so unremitting that they make him incapable of attention; and that having as yet no knowledge of how dangerous it is to make hasty judgments, he is carried along un-resisting by passions and by the needs to which he is subject? And you can well imagine that if nothing intervenes to prevent it, his imagina-tion will gradually make its way down the slope it is obliged to follow.

"Indeed, a child's eyes are no sooner open than the objects sur-rounding him crowd into his mind; and since they are all so unusual and so astonishing, they keep him constantly in a state of such won-derment that it shows on his face until they all become perfectly famil-iar to him. Since this mass of things allows him no time for balanced judgment, he has to absorb them willy-nilly. If you take into account the fact that the close association between mind and body makes them interdependent and highly interactive and that the movements and impressions of the body are immediately followed by the perceptions and judgments of the soul, you will easily realize that it's inevitable that we be taken in by the most superficial appearances during childhood. We should note that at that tender age the mind is concerned only with the immediate sensations of pleasure and pain that affect the body, and receives impressions only of corporeal objects that fill the imagination, with the result that it is only capable of conceiving coarse, physical ideas."

Timander offered a summary: "So then, the relationships that we establish when we open our eyes, which on the one hand are so essen-tial to us, become, on the other hand, more pernicious as they make us rasher in our judgments and more incarnate, as it were, in our thinking."

Stasimachus went on: "Our condition isn't improved when we make new associations as our hearing is sensitized and we start to un-derstand meaning with our ears. Since people are not merely showing us new things when they speak to us but are also indicating whether those things are good or bad, the impression of the things we see is for-tified by that which we receive through our ears, and the weight and speed of our imagination become so frantic that we are hardly able to resist that impression.

"But the way we see those who care for us as children is reinforced by additional considerations. As we are unable to obtain the most nec-essary things without their help, the idea of those things becomes so intimately associated with the people as to be inseparable from them. The need for food, for example, doesn't evoke in a child the image of the breasts which provide it without also bringing to mind that of the woman to whom they belong."

The authority of our parents, of our masters, and of our peers is the main basis for our certainty.

"What you say is quite true," said Eulalia. "I've very often noticed that babies always prefer their nurse's arms to those of other women, and even refuse those who are trying to suckle them."

"It's true even to the extent that mothers and fathers are treated as such only on the authority of the nurse; and I've also seen children look at their nurse when they are offered something as if to ask whether it's good or bad, and whether they should accept it or not," added Sophia.

"I have no difficulty now in understanding that this growing necessity is the source of the love we bear to our mothers and fathers or those who stand in their stead," conceded Timander.

"This is a basic fact," Stasimachus went on, "but what we should be considering further is that our need of those who are raising us gives them absolute authority over our minds and that authority is subsequently increased by various specific incidents. Apart from the many marks of affection we receive from them as we are growing up, we notice that not only do we depend on them to indicate to us what is useful or pleasant and to keep us away from what is harmful or disagreeable, but they actually anticipate our needs through their advice and their attention. We, of course, are unable to detect when they are dishonest with themselves, but we do realize that if they are dishonest with us, it is on purpose and for our own good. It follows that since we don't know what we want, and in any case could only get it through their intervention, we become more and more inclined to submit to their authority and their wisdom. We want what they want, we like what they like, we condemn what they condemn, and we approve only what they tell us to; in short, their passions and their judgments are taken on as our own. Further, our submission to them is reinforced partly because of our awareness of our weakness and our ignorance together with the credulity of childhood, partly because of the threats and promises made by them and the rewards and punishments they dangle before us to make us believe and obey them, and finally because of the good or bad things that befall us according to whether we follow their advice or not.

"Since our deference towards our fathers and mothers is the most complete and all-encompassing we can imagine, our deference to others during our childhood is an extension of it. We know and worship God in the way they tell us and show us by their own example. We respect and believe our masters because our parents tell us to. Since the authority of our superiors is a transference from that of our parents, we attribute the same infallibility to them and accept their precepts and maxims as absolute truths.

"Whatever manner of life we take up, whatever people we obey, whatever opinions we espouse, whatever fashion we follow, our main motivation is the authority and example of our parents and those they have told us to imitate and heed.

"We must acknowledge, therefore, that the first principle of everything you know and believe and do is the trust you placed in your parents and your masters; and the second principle, which follows from the first, is the blind trust you place in the customs and example of your peers. Those are the sources of all our ideas of truth, knowledge, virtue, justice, and civility."

"Since we're being honest here," said Eulalia, "I have to confess that I have no argument with anything you've said, and up to now it's always been a matter of pride to me to think, speak, and act like other people and to follow the instructions and example of my mother."

"If what you've just said is as honest an assessment as it seems, then you're further along the path you want to follow than you realize," said Stasimachus. "You've already taken the first and most important step, which is to recognize the state you are in at the moment, or rather the basis of your belief. Let me show you that state in its true colors.

"Supposing that what you've just heard is not a figment of my imagination, you shouldn't take it amiss if I say—setting aside your desire to seek the truth—that those people who think as you have always done are in the most pitiable state. They imagine they know a lot, and they know nothing. Their condition is worse than if they were in complete ignorance of everything, in which case, having no idea of the truth, they would be less distant from it. And we can say, without exaggeration, that they seem like insensate or stunned people who imagine themselves immensely rich because a trick of their imagination convinces them that everything they see is theirs.

Notion of a person who knows nothing that is not based on prejudice.

"Indeed, since these people have indiscriminately accepted everything they have observed, doesn't it necessarily follow that far from being precise, discerning, and meticulous, they should be full of confusion and shadows that darken and blind them? Since they have always followed their first inclination without ever stopping to examine things seriously, they make rash, ill-advised judgments; and because they are too easily carried away by appearances or custom or some other gushing stream, they have mistaken false light for true enlightenment and are thus filled with error and misconception. They latch on to any faddish position and defend it stubbornly and with all kinds of fantastic arguments; any opposition throws them into a rage, and since they are completely absorbed by their own fantasies, they either refuse to listen to what is said to them or they pervert it, so that it becomes impossible to correct them by pointing out their errors and showing them the truth.

"Since these people act using their memory rather than their judgment," he went on, "and don't even understand the language they are using, they are more enamored of words than of reason, wanting nothing but what is hidden and mysterious, never happier than when using elaborate and hallowed terms that fill the mouth and the ear, leaving the mind in a void and in endless inanition. They base their judgments on tone of voice, manner, social class, age, possessions, and the clothes people wear, and they take account of these instead of weighing words.

"To assess the worth of their virtue, remember that they pride themselves on being ready to change inside and out if they get the signal from those who govern them. You can conclude quite correctly that if these people had been born in another century or in a country whose doctrine and customs are quite different from those they profess, then their views and conduct would be altered accordingly. You can also guess that their virtue is a faddish virtue, a virtue of imitation, like that of monkeys or play actors, in short, an empty specter possessing only appearance, so that it vanishes away as the curtain falls and the audience disperses. They are the puppets of popular fantasy; they condemn today what they will approve tomorrow; they are like weathervanes or mobiles. And since they don't have claws to hang on to what they know, nor strength in their resolution apart from what comes from the outside, they could well be compared to a vessel which has neither anchor nor tiller and is tossed hither and thither by the wind and the waves.[29]

"This is still a flattering portrait, and a few extra lines and shades could make it more true to life. But don't imitate me, I beg you; and without flattering yourselves, see if you don't recognize yourself in that picture and the lessons you could learn from it."

"I find myself so deformed," replied Eulalia, "that I could hardly confess it without your assurance that the confession could make me more beautiful than I am."

"You have all the more reason to be hopeful, since you have not only a good mind but also the desire and the means to get out of such a deplorable state, which most people lack," said Timander. "I don't mean only women, but also men who are unaware of what Stasimachus has just pointed out, and what it is absolutely essential to know."

29. Poullain's train of thought leading to this conclusion follows Descartes's first famous sentences in his *Discourse*, in *Phil. Essays*, 46: "Good sense is the best distributed thing in the world. . . . The power of judging well and of distinguishing the true from the false . . . is naturally equal to all men."

"But," he continued, turning to Stasimachus, "it seems to me that Eulalia could draw from your lecture the opposite conclusions from what you have in mind, namely, to persuade her to let go of custom and human authority as she seeks the truth. We seem to have a natural tendency to fall into error and prejudice. Doesn't it seem as if the most efficient means out of our difficulties are the following: we should have recourse to the public voice; we should take as most surely certain what is decreed by general consensus; that rather than someone risking error by relying upon his own judgment, he has nothing to fear if he relies on the opinion of a large number of people, particularly smart, bright people who know what they are doing and wouldn't have made their opinions public if they hadn't been the best; that it's unlikely that so many people would be wrong or would connive at wrong-doing; that the best path is the well-trodden one; that one should hang on to the thickest part of the tree; and that there is less danger of getting lost with a crowd than going straight ahead with a single person?"[30]

"Ah, there we have all the clichés that leap straight to people's minds, and particularly women's minds," said Stasimachus. "They have been raised to be more submissive and more timid than men, clinging more easily to opinion and custom, which they find harder to give up. But I would like to ask an intelligent woman how she knows that the main highway is the path of truth or that the thickest part of the tree she is clinging to isn't a figment of her imagination, that the self-styled savants are truly learned and as infallible as she would like to imagine. But since this point about public authority is of prime importance for the ordering of the mind, let us try to examine it properly to Sophia and Eulalia's satisfaction, leaving questions of history for another conversation.

"Let's get back to the question of principle: do you not agree that between one man and another, there is no subordination? One is naturally the equal of the other and both are equally prone to error, so it would be imprudent to give our consent to what one man says to us simply because he says it. In that state of equality, we might as well be-

Public opinion or the voice of the majority gives us no certainty.

30. As a Modern in the Battle against the Ancients' dominance, Poullain here argues against the principle of universal acceptance for judging the quality of a work or the soundness of an idea. Historically Poullain was never directly involved in the public events that began "The Quarrel between the Ancients and the Moderns" in 1686. In fact, many Cartesians joined the Ancients' camp. But one can value Poullain's modernity as a precursor in the cultural wars that mark the "fin-de-siècle." See above and below, notes 22, 33, 43, and related texts for further insight into his judgment.

lieve ourselves as other people; and if we submit to someone, he ought, by the same token, to submit to us; and each individual should do this equally with all the others and take on the feelings and thoughts of all his peers, as there is no reason to prefer one over the other."

"That's obvious," said Timander, "and if we accept as true some external thought or opinion, we have to have some motive for doing so; and the most natural and frequent motive is the title and position of scholar."

"But how are we to know that a man has the necessary skills?" asked Eulalia.

"Either through our own intelligence or through the testimony of others. We can tell for ourselves when we are acquainted with a subject whether someone speaking about it knows it as well as we do."

"In that situation," interrupted Sophia, "our opinion of the capacity of a person isn't based on the good opinion we have of that person but on our own capacity."

"And if we are unacquainted with the subject," Stasimachus continued, "and a man who is thought to be an expert speaks about it and brings clear and distinct ideas into our minds, so that we can tell, if we pay attention, whether things are indeed the way he represents them."

"It's also obvious that our approval of him is based on the truth he has imparted to us, not on our belief in his expertise," said Sophia.

"But what are we to think of people who don't make themselves understood?" asked Eulalia.

"When that happens," said Stasimachus, "because of lack of intelligence among listeners, they are responsible for taking the measure of themselves, and it's like talking to the blind about colors."

"Eulalia means intelligent people," said Timander.

"As far as they are concerned," replied Stasimachus, "when the subjects in question can be understood by intelligent people who are listening carefully, and the words they hear give them no illumination, then I think they can conclude that the people who are speaking to them have nothing but words in their heads, or chimerical imaginings that cannot get out of the head that conceived them, and all one can do with such talk is to acquiesce civilly or selfishly. For I fail to see how a reasonable man can agree, in the depth of his soul, to things that are at variance with his true feelings or to words devoid of ideas that the mind can get a grip on.[31] Thoughts are for ourselves and words are to make us intelligible to others. To stop at pure

---

31. This was a doctrine equally shared by the seventeenth-century classicists, best expressed in Boileau's *Art poétique*, 1674. See Adam, *Grandeur and Illusion*, 157, 196–97.

sounds is to smother our desire for knowledge and to go against nature and the perfection of the mind. Even if we are sure that a man has the keenest intellect on earth, that he has examined things without impediment or error, that he has followed all the behavior and the rules necessary for understanding the truth, that he has anticipated all the difficulties that could be raised about his views, if he can't make himself understood on a given subject we should take no more notice of him than if he had said nothing at all, and all we can conclude from his speechifying is that he has told us things we haven't understood, unless we want to say that he hasn't understood them himself."[32]

"I think the most positive proof that a man is learned is when he knows how to make others understand what he knows, and in this respect there are people who are deadly and people who are lively," said Eulalia. "And I must tell you that you can't accuse me of what Stasimachus was just accusing women of—taking as true anything they see in print."

"You have the best possible attitude," replied Stasimachus. "We are no more bound to believe what someone has written than what he has declared orally, even though we are sure that the writing is indisputably by the author whose name it carries, that it hasn't been altered by those who have copied, translated, commented on, or argued with it, and that books by the adversaries are not better and have not been suppressed or corrupted. If we're allowed to contradict an author when we speak to him, even more can we find fault with his works, as there is no fear of shocking him, even if they were written five hundred years ago and if there were as many millions of men who had given their approval."

"That's exactly my problem," said Timander, "because, on the one hand, when someone tries to tell me something I don't understand, I can't agree with it blindly, as most people do, but I feel I must agree when I learn that the idea has been embraced by a large number of learned men during the course of many centuries."

"That doesn't surprise me," replied Stasimachus. "It's a very common difficulty arising from a confusion between our knowledge and the method by which we acquired it, so that we don't pay proper attention to the weight that the testimony of several centuries ought to carry. There are some things that we can understand for ourselves, by our reason, by our own intelligence, things that are the object of philosophy and grammar and other sciences. There are others that we can understand only through the intervention and

32. Molière satirized such "philosophers" in *Le Bourgeois-Gentilhomme*. See the introduction to this text, note 9.

report of others, such as things that have happened in places and times in which we have not lived. In these cases, men's testimony is absolutely necessary, and when we find a general, uniform consensus among many intelligent people with different interests who agree on the same fact, then I don't see how we can refuse to accept it; otherwise we would have to give up on everything we call history and believe only what we see."

"I understand all that," replied Timander, "but what about things related to the mind?"

"You say yourself what you should believe," replied Stasimachus, "and your problem contains its own solution, because the workings of reason ought to be understood by the reason. To understand nature, we have to understand it ourselves. We can use the help that the authors have left us, but we should show them no greater deference—although their opinions may have been followed for several centuries and by a large number of people thought to be learned—than if we were their contemporaries. The truth or falsity of an idea is not founded upon its antiquity nor on the multitude of people who have approved or condemned it."[33]

"I still had a few doubts about this," said Sophia, "but I no longer have them. I see now that there is no standard procedure regarding opinions, as there exists none in favor of error nor against the truth."

"So that you can better understand the deference you should have for scholars' consensus about the same author," Stasimachus continued, "I should tell you how they normally espouse the opinions they defend. With respect to their prophets—in this conversation let me call the great men by this name—they are just like a flock of sheep following the first one they come across, trying to follow the leader everywhere. When, by chance or otherwise, they find themselves walking in someone else's footsteps, they think only of following him, and imitating him like slaves, merely copying one another, so it's hardly surprising that throughout two thousand years there would be such uniformity of opinions, or, rather, of language."

What credence we should give to the assent of savants.

"The philosopher Aristotle can serve as a better example than any other, as he had greater credit than any other in our country. Although he didn't say too much in favor of women" and he glanced at Sophia and Eulalia, "and even called them monsters, he should still be considered, nevertheless, as one of the greatest men of his time. His reputa-

33. This last sentence describes well what the Moderns held against the Ancients.

tion drew disciples to him, as happens today to those of his champions who are in fashion. You can judge the stability and the progress of his doctrine and his following by what is happening at the moment. To tell you something else at the same time, you should know that when we go to the state schools for instruction, at an age when we accept as true those tales of Richard Sans Peur and the lovely Maguelone,[34] and all the other tales our grandmothers or nursemaids have taught us, the first thing we are taught is the Scholastic Creed, the first article of which has us believe that Cicero, Virgil, Aristotle are the inimitable originals who created the finest works we possess, and there is no hope in the arts or in the sciences if we do not take them as our models. Our masters are assiduous in maintaining this veneration through the eulogies they offer on behalf of these authors from time to time, and as they make us learn with respect their works, they make us venerate them all the more through a system of punishments and rewards they impose in order to get us to succeed. With this preparation, we move up into the philosophy class, where everything resounds with the discourses that are pronounced in praise of the Genius of Nature. But since our teachers talk no more of prejudice than if we had just been born, they confirm ours by leaving us in it. They fill us with aversion for any philosophers who are not of their opinion, and, reinforcing that aversion with considerations about religion, they inspire us with hatred for the poor unknowns by quite brazenly turning us off reading them, just as they have not read even the table of contents of their works because of the same scruple that they try to communicate to us.

"Nevertheless, we treat them like the oracle. We tell ourselves, tacitly— as do women—that there is no way they are not very clever people, since they have been invested with the necessary titles and authority to teach in the state system. Thus, while our judgment is in a state of suspension, we are exercising our memories by learning various things that can only be said in Latin. And after we have burdened ourselves sufficiently with the classical language and know how to speak it, we become Masters with honors, as did our own; we form disciples in our turn, and Masters who resemble ourselves. In this way our doctrine is perpetuated from year to year and from century to century, and taken up in the provinces. Since each of us is measured for what

---

34. These are folktale characters related to the myth of "the youth who wanted to learn what fear is." In most European versions, the young farmer boy (also known as "Jean-sans-Peur" and "Guillaume-sans-Peur") bravely tricks the Devil several times. Eventually, he is able to marry the Princess. See Paul Delarue, *Le Conte populaire français* (Paris, 1976), 1:293–305. In Poullain's time, Mother Goose tales belonged strictly to the oral tradition of the countryside, until the academician Charles Perrault (leader of the Moderns' cause at the end of the century) published in 1697 an altered version of *Contes de ma Mère l'Oie* for his aristocratic audience.

he thinks he knows according to the good faith of those who have taught it, we have as much assurance today as did those who lived in Aristotle's day. The same situation prevails in all the sciences."

"You remind me of the way I used to study," said Timander. "And I conclude that it is not normally through reason that one rejects a doctrine, since it's more usually through chance and custom than by reason that one espouses it. As the consensus of several people on a subject indicates merely that it has their approval, not that it is true, we should judge of their opposition to an idea only that it has been contested, not that it is erroneous; that it has been unfortunate in being the weakest, not the worst."

"What you say is so true," added Stasimachus, "that when what is thought to be a new sect or opinion appears, it is seen as a monster that should be strangled at birth; there is such fear it will grow that it is suppressed without being seen. And if this behavior is questioned, those who reply think they are giving a satisfactory answer when they say that this opinion is contrary to usage and to what the Ancients believed."[35]

"That's amusing, as if the Ancients were wiser and less human than their descendants," said Eulalia. Then turning to Stasimachus: "But what I would really like to know is whether you would defer to the opinion of several people who were actually or reputedly very intelligent who had examined a question together."

"If they really were intelligent people who could make me understand the question, I would readily defer to them, as I would defer to a single one who could teach me the truth," replied Stasimachus. "But if they were intelligent only by reputation and I were in their presence, I would have to stretch the limits of politeness, since I wouldn't want to pick a fight with them."

The extent of the authority of an assembly of learned men.

"I absolutely agree with you," said Sophia. "When there are so many people together, I think that one has to be on one's guard against mass confusion. There are always almost as many different interests and opinions as there are people in those big gatherings. The desire to show off or the shame of giving in means that everyone sticks to his own opinion ever more stubbornly. The need to manipulate people,

35. See Adam, *Grandeur and Illusion,* 130: "Both the Church and the government tried to halt the progress of the new philosophy. In 1671 the faculty of theology recalled that only the teaching of Aristotle had been authorized. The royal government repeatedly issued strict orders with the same message. In 1680 it cancelled lectures that were to be given by the Cartesian Régis."

the fear of not upholding one's views or of shocking those with an opposite opinion, and the deference we are accustomed to have in a
crowd mean that most people go over to the side of the biggest, that
the strongest wins, that people are all swayed the same way, and that
the majority opinion carries the day. And for every one who is impartial, twenty are not. Even if they all were, there would not be more than
two, perhaps, who would be of the same opinion. Does everyone not
have his principles and his own method? One is prejudiced in one area,
another in another. One is fiery, hasty, opinionated, and enthusiastic;
another is cool, slow, and shy. Some are well informed about things,
others only partially, or not at all. Some pussy-foot around the topic,
others come to grips with it; sometimes words occupy the conversation too much, sometimes not enough; and this motley crowd never
produces anything worthwhile.[36] I also know," she added, "that the old
dyed-in-the-wool establishmentarians are firmly stuck in their prejudices and defend them tooth and nail, and since they often have usage
and public authority on their side—not to mention the cliques and cabals—they force young people to yield."

"You give such an accurate picture of what goes on in the majority
of learned meetings that if women were allowed in them I would swear
you had taken part in the most prestigious ones," said Stasimachus.

"That's because I've read a few accounts, and I'm also visited sometimes by clever people who tell me what's been going on in the meetings they go to," replied Sophia. "I remember one of my friends who is
very well informed about past and present history telling me about the
weirdness of opinions and customs; he said that people with the best
intentions had very often been forced, for reasons of state and for public well-being, to go along with the most obvious errors and quite irrational practices."

The considera-
tion given to
custom.

"That doesn't surprise me," said Timander. "People are in such great
awe of their opinions and customs that it sometimes makes political
sense to maintain them as they are. People tend to look on them as a
heritage or a vine left by their fathers. They are always ready to rise
and take up arms, to sacrifice everything and destroy themselves to
preserve chimeras. Wise politicians are right in seeing the people as a
mettlesome horse that becomes runaway if it is not carefully re-
strained, as well as stroked and cajoled to stop it rearing up and to keep

The genius of the
people.

36. Stasimachus is echoing Descartes, *Discourse*, VI, in *Phil. Essays*, 77: "Nor have I ever
observed that, through the method of disputations practices in the schools, any truth has
been discovered that had until then been unknown."

it between the traces. In short, it has always been said of the people that they want to be deceived and left in their misapprehensions and that it is dangerous to try to shift them out of them."

"Such pig-headedness isn't limited to uncouth, ignorant people," said Stasimachus. "Scholars are guilty of it too, and among them there are longer and more frequent convulsions and uprisings than among the people you have been talking about. Whereas a neatly expressed doubt, a sympathetic description, a well-turned speech can make the dregs of society lay down the arms that an opposing doubt made them take up, and whereas a popular uprising fizzles out when there is no leader, among professional scholars, once the brand of contention is lit, it causes a more deadly blaze as it inflames the mind. Everyone becomes a leader; one is no sooner overthrown than another arises; once they are unleashed on a campaign, they are like gadflies that can't be rounded up.

"They think they are more rational than the ordinary people, so it is harder to persuade them. That's why the colleges have had to forbid altogether public discussion of certain topics that make people too heated and to allow only affirmative discussion of others, because they conform to public opinion, although those who hold the negative view are not condemned. In the last resort, scholars are reduced to the level of grade school children when they are in revolt and have to be calmed down with the cane. In all centuries there has had to be appeal to sovereigns to exert absolute power and royal prerogative to quell the uproar that opinions have aroused."

"But it's only third-rate scholars who are convulsed in that way," said Sophia. "I know others who are quite the opposite and who so hate arguments and rows that they avoid places where they think they could occur. But one of the things I most admire them for is their love of truth. Their disinterestedness is so great that even though they possess the most honorable titles they never make use of them with well-meaning people and would not like someone who deferred to their opinion simply because of their rank of Doctor, as they don't think that rank makes a man more credible."

"They're right," said Stasimachus. "Their rank is only the sign that they have been found able to uphold the opinions of the country and of the group that examined them. If it were a proof that one possesses the truth, then we would have to accept that all the English, Turkish, and Chinese doctors possess it too. And certainly not everyone would agree with that."

"I am not trying to be the champion of everyone who has the title of Master," said Timander. "We don't have to believe that they are all orthodox, as we can see that they do not always agree among themselves and that they sometimes make accusations against one another."

"So what is the purpose of the approbations of those Doctors that I see at the ends of most books?" asked Eulalia.

"To act as their own testimonial," replied Stasimachus. "If you have ever read one of them, you will have noticed that they give assurance that the books they are given to don't contain anything contrary to religion or to certain popularly held views that one must not offend against. Not all kinds of truths can be told, and since a person who gives his approbation is a public figure, he cannot allow truths—even though he himself might be persuaded of them—to be printed in a book if they are going to be controversial."[37]

"So the approbation of a book isn't necessarily an infallible mark of truth?" said Eulalia.

"Not at all," replied Stasimachus. "Apart from the fact that things are approved in this century that were condemned in others, or that we reject in France things that are accepted in Spain, many philosophic and controversial opinions that depend on the discretion of the reader can slip into books— even books on religion."

Sophia turned to Eulalia and said: "Since these gentlemen have been speaking largely to you, then you have to draw the conclusions from what they have been saying."

"I can see quite clearly," replied Eulalia, "that we must not take as law the voice of public opinion in matters we can judge for ourselves, that opinions are like fashions: we don't always receive the most appropriate or the best, but simply the first that occur."

"You are right," said Timander. "Customs are like great rivers that begin as a little trickle of water and are fortunate enough not to get lost at their source, as it were, but are swollen by all the streams that run into them as they flow."

"I also believe," he went on, "that we can conclude from this conversation that if the consensus of a whole kingdom and a few centuries were a guarantee of truth, then the most conflicting opinions would be equally true or false, since there is hardly a single opinion held today the opposite of which was not maintained at some time, or was championed not only by those thought to be clever, but by whole nations."

"With these reflections we can clarify the first thing I asked you about the state of your soul and the knowledge you possess. I'm really pleased that you are convinced you know nothing with certainty, except that you have a firm, constant will to understand things to the best of your ability. What you

37. In the later 1660s the atmosphere in Paris was less than favorable to freedom of speech in the press. Poullain alludes to the paradoxical position of the Royal Censors who, as public servants, could not hold to "truths" even though they might be personally persuaded of them.

are looking for is a way, an assured rule, that will give you discernment and justice in all things and will teach you to distinguish, by their proper characteristics, truth and falsity, vice and virtue, good and ill fortune. What you want is an effective remedy for prejudice and error that will bring you back to perfect health and act as a guard against the ills and relapses you fear. You are hoping for a light that will chase away darkness, confusion, and the clouding of the mind to bring back clarity and calm and restore to your thoughts the good order that should be there. In desiring to become learned, you are seeking a natural position, and once you are in it you will be able to see yourselves and everything surrounding you according to the dependence and relationship in which nature has put you."

As the conversation had begun early, and it was during the long summer days, and as the four people involved had decided to spend the whole afternoon and evening together, Sophia invited the three others to relax by walking in her garden. They walked down into it, Stasimachus offering Sophia his hand, and Eulalia taking Timander's.

THIRD CONVERSATION

After walking for a while, sometimes all four together, sometimes two by two, depending on the place and their whim, Sophia and Stasimachus, Eulalia and Timander were forced by a sudden rain shower to take shelter in a summer house in a corner of the garden.

When they were seated, Timander began the conversation by saying to Stasimachus: "Wasn't I right when I said recently that science spoiled beautiful women and made them bluestockings or melancholics? You yourself have observed it, and I noticed Sophia nudging you three or four times to draw your attention to Eulalia's reveries which she had already noticed. If the mere desire to become learned and what she has heard you say on the subject bring about these fits of absent-mindedness that I witnessed during the walk, then I don't know what will happen to her when she really gets down to her studies."

Eulalia, who was perfectly happy that Timander should provide the opportunity to return to the conversation that had been interrupted only to avoid tiring her with a long discussion on a topic that is not often raised with ladies, replied with a smile: "If you had been with Sophia and I with Stasimachus, you would have had no reason to complain of either him or me.

"I have these fits you accuse me of when someone talks to me of boring things just after talking about serious and important things. What made me so absent-minded with you was that I couldn't help thinking about the resolution Stasimachus asked me if I was capable of. I was tempted several times to question him in order to find out as we were walking along."

"You are so kind about my interventions that I must, out of gratitude, satisfy your curiosity any time you like," said Stasimachus.

"I would be delighted to have you do it right now, as long as Sophia and Timander have no objection," said Eulalia.

"It was my intention to come back to the subject," replied Timander.

"As far as I am concerned, Stasimachus knows perfectly well that there is nothing I like better," said Sophia. "I'm sure he hasn't forgotten all those afternoons we spent together talking about all kinds of strange things."

"I remember them with pleasure," said Stasimachus, "and since you are all in agreement, and we are trapped here by the rain." He addressed Eulalia: "You realized that the ignorance and rashness we are born with make us so prone to prejudice and error that no man in his extreme youth can protect himself against the infiltration of all of those faults found in the people who raise him. You also realized that you have never examined anything, that you doubt that those who taught you examined anything either, and you have seen that even if they know things, as far as you are concerned they might as well not know them if you yourself don't know them.

"So you should make up your mind to examine seriously what is in your mind, and in order to succeed, you should imagine that you have never been spoken to about it, indeed, that you have never even thought about it."

To understand things properly, one must make up one's mind to examine them without prejudice.

"So you are claiming that one should try to attain a state of general doubt," said Timander.

"You can call it what you like," replied Stasimachus. "But it is a constant that in Eulalia's frame of mind she is right to consider everything in general as she considers in particular the cases where she thinks she has made an error, after taking them as certainties. I call this doubt, this frame of mind, a state of impartiality or of objectivity in which we lean neither to one side nor the other, suspending our judgment until doubt has been allayed."

"It seems to me that a single person who is aware of his own fickleness and inclination to error should not be more diffident about reviewing his thoughts than a whole group of experienced people about revising theirs when they fear that unexpected errors may have crept into them," said Sophia.

"I agree that there are lots of things that need to be examined," said Timander. "But if we think that everything has to be examined we are presupposing that someone is mistaken about everything, which is hardly likely."

Everything must be examined.

"I take it that a man is not mistaken about everything and that most of his opinions are reasonable," said Stasimachus. "How could he tell those that are from those that aren't and give reasons for his opinions, if we suppose that he originally accepted them without discernment and without examination? This is why he can't be any more certain of the truth than of error, both having entered his mind by the same route and under the same guise; therefore all his judgments should be considered prejudices he should reject, and if he wants to try to know things, then he should act as if he is mistaken about everything."

How we can doubt our own and God's existence, etc.

"Do you think that we can and should doubt everything?" asked Eulalia. "For example, whether we exist, whether we have a body, whether the sun exists, whether God does, and whether Christianity is the true religion."

"What a lot of problems all at the same time, and of such different kinds!" answered Stasimachus. "To give you an ordered, intelligent response, let me ask you to consider that some of our knowledge depends on ourselves and some on our relationship with others. Some is easily acquired, some [acquired only] with difficulty, since what is near us is more easily observable than what is far away.

"There are two things to know about each object, its existence and its nature; the first is easier to understand than the second. Thus all our doubts do not have the same force; some must be weaker than others. There is no one who has not realized from his own experience that if we have no interest in something, uncertainties about it are all the more troublesome, as it is more difficult to resolve them.

"We can also distinguish two kinds of doubt. The first is based on physics and pure speculation: when we try to find out how things are in nature, and it is indifferent for our conduct and our peace of mind how they are. To know whether the earth turns around the sun or the sun around the earth, for example.

"Others are of a practical or moral nature, like wondering whether we may kill a murderer who is attacking us.

"There are also useful doubts, as, for example, to examine whether we should put our happiness in pleasure, and other pernicious ones that lead to our disadvantage and our ruin, for example, if we try to cease acknowledging our superiors until we have sufficiently considered whether submission is their due.

"Now it is prudence that should be our guide in the sciences as well as in moral behavior and that should indicate the things we should doubt, and how and when we should do so.

"You are aware that to understand things is to know them with enough certainty and insight to trust them until one arrives at a notion so clear that it would be absurd to doubt it.

"You are also aware that order is necessary in the search for the true, as in other things in this world, and you will easily judge that the order based on the dependence of our thoughts consists particularly in starting with the simplest and clearest and surest so that we can use them as steps to go on up to those that are less so. As it is easier to assure ourselves that a thing exists rather than to know what or how it is, the first doubts we can raise and the easiest to dispel are those that concern the existence of things; and the reasons that enlighten us about the first doubts should be the first and most general, and should serve as a basis for all the certainty we can hope for.

"This presupposes, I grant you, that if we are to be certain of the existence of something, then it is of our own existence, and whatever doubt we have on that score brings with it its own illumination, because since it is a true action which cannot stem from nothingness, it seems that an attentive mind cannot seriously doubt that it exists. However, if someone asked us to justify our belief in our own existence, then in order to reply other than as an ignorant man would, we have to make of ourselves the same demands that others might make of us, and conclude that we exist because whatever doubts acts, and whatever acts exists.

"Apart from the fact that the pattern of our learning means that we form that first doubt, what convinces me even more of the necessity of forming it is that it seems to me that upon this clarification depends that of all the other doubts concerning the existence of things and even concerning essence, as it is completely useless and often chimerical to speak of things that do not exist.

"The mind is more justified in doubting that it is connected with a body than in doubting whether it itself exists. For seeing this body as a thing separate from itself, and with imagination making it believe, often by means of illusion, that it had things that it did not actually possess and which even could not exist at all, it seems that the mind might mistrust the imagination in this instance, and question whether it might not be playing tricks in claiming that it has a body. We, at least, should reason our way to assurance, whereas other men know it only through custom. Here is how I go about it.

"I concluded just now that I exist, I who think, because I act.[38] There being a thing from which I cannot be separated which brings me pleasure and pain without any contribution on my part, and sometimes even despite myself, then this thing that I call my body must really exist."

"When I raised objections," said Eulalia, "I had given no thought to the pattern and the interplay between the various things we know, nor to the nature or the diversity of our doubts; nor had I thought that that doubt or that impartiality encourages us to find clear reasons for what otherwise we know only confusedly."

"That indeed is all I claim," replied Stasimachus, "and allow me to further elucidate by saying that it is all the more urgent to doubt the existence of our bodies in this way, since, being only able to apprehend others through its agency, reason, which proves to us that it exists, proves in the same way that others exist as well. Thus, just as we conclude that we have a body because our senses make us aware of it, we also conclude that there are others around it, because we are made aware of them, and they strike us by the impressions they make upon us."

"I think I understand that quite well," said Eulalia. "What about the existence of God? Can we doubt that?"

"We can doubt that," replied Stasimachus, "as do the theologians, who, when they speak of God in their treatises, ask first if there is one, and after proving that there is, offer several objections to show that there is no such thing, and each replies according to his principles. The least we can do is to examine the proofs that are commonly given for the existence of God so that we can see their strengths and weaknesses and can select the ones that seem the most persuasive, or look for better ones.

"As far as the Christian religion is concerned, although it is among those things I said I would not discuss here, I will just say that since it has all the marks of a true religion, and since those who transmit it are uniform in their testimony, we should remain steadfast in it, since we were fortunate enough to be brought up in it.[39]

38. Poullain emphasizes the notion of existence over Descartes's deduction of essence. For both philosophers, the mind's essence consists in the act of thinking, but Poullain *proves* the existence of the body (and the physical world) *before* establishing the existence of a non-deceiving God (cf. *Principles*, par. 13, in *Phil. Essays*, 234). But in the early days of Cartesianism, he was not alone in struggling with Descartes's metaphysics. See Alcover, *Poullain*, 52–53.

39. Poullain here contradicted his own premises, arguing that we should accept the religion (Christianity) in which we have been brought up because the testimony of those who transmit it is uniform. According to the Second Conversation, the fact that the testimony of those who have transmitted Christianity to us is uniform has nothing to do with its truth or falsity. Poullain

"This does not, however, rob us of our freedom to study it in a methodical way like the theologians, to strive to clarify the difficulties we may have, and to seek rules and principles that would enable us to distinguish popular opinion from the true beliefs of Jesus Christ and the church, so that we can argue for the truths we should know."

"Common sense should make us realize that it would be absurd to doubt positively if we are to pay to nature and society the dues that we cannot avoid paying them."

"Indeed," said Timander, "the necessity of paying one's dues to these inexorable taskmasters, and the danger that would result from failing to do so, resolve more decisively than all the reasoning in the world the doubts we could have in this respect. In my view, what we ought to do, according to your principles, is to try to understand why we are obliged to submit to their laws and when we can dispense with them."

"In short," said Stasimachus, "almost all our doubts tend towards an examination of whether we consider things and act as individuals as most people do. This is why the suspension of opinion we were talking about should not be followed by inaction, or, if you prefer, by a general suspension of the actions of life; and it should not prevent, on the occasions we have for decision-making, our being satisfied with the most ordinary and obvious motives and reasons, in order not to lose in deliberation, through over-zealousness, the auspicious moments that occur. Prudence demands that until we are in a position to take up the cudgels after a judicious inquiry, we should follow the most moderate opinions and the practices accepted by the wisest of those among whom we live."[40]

"In order to do what you say," said Sophia, "we should hang on to some of our views about our conduct, which is at variance with the idea you just stated that we have to rid ourselves of all the opinions we hold without having put them to the test."

"One doesn't necessarily obviate the other," replied Stasimachus, "because the opinions we keep only concern the external part of our actions, and the need to conform with others; but these should not be the basis of our views. So we need take no notice of them when we examine things for ourselves. We say that it is normal to speak or act or think in a certain way, and

---

hedges here. In the following paragraph he says we can study Christianity in order to clarify difficulties (he does not say: to determine its truth or falsity).

40. Poullain proceeds to explain Descartes's moral code of conduct, as he is plotting his lesson directly from *Discourse*, III.

that we have to go along with it, but even so we do not necessarily believe that such and such a custom is reasonable if we have not examined it."

"So then," said Eulalia with a smile, "we have to give up the world,
since that's what you want."

"I beg your pardon," replied Stasimachus, "it is not I who believe
that, it's reason. If you have cause to be suspicious of your imagination's
capacity for deceit, as you have assured me you have, then you must
also have cause to be suspicious of other people's, since you know them
to be capable of error, and since they have told you that that is the
case."

*There is no
disadvantage
in giving up
everything to
examine
everything.*

"But," queried Eulalia, "is there not a disadvantage about such a
general renunciation?"

"I don't know of any," replied Stasimachus, "and be assured that if
you can do it with some things, as you have no doubt you can, then
you can do it with everything, since reason which pushes you in some
directions is no less powerful in pushing you in any other. For having at
present nothing but the opinion of men to support you, either you
have to submit completely or you can withdraw completely. You have
nothing to fear from such rational behavior which leads you for once in
your life to arm yourself against falsity and error. You have everything
to win and nothing to lose.[41] For if what you think you know is other
than you imagine it, should you not make an effort to grasp it correctly; and if it turns out to be as you had believed it to be, it would
bring you enormous satisfaction to realize that you were not mistaken
and a considerable advantage to proceed henceforward on the basis of
reason, where hitherto you had been guided by chance and custom."

"Perhaps Eulalia is afraid of doing a disservice to charity by putting
society to the test," said Sophia to Stasimachus.

*To put people to
the test is no
disservice to
charity.*

"Eulalia is too intelligent to be worried on that score," replied
Stasimachus. "She knows perfectly well that one does not sin against
charity as long as one does not sin against reason, and if reason commands us to be wary of our neighbor, then charity will not intervene. It
is one thing to look upon men as capable of deceiving both themselves
and others, which is a reasonable precaution, but another to say posi-

41. The formulation recalls Blaise Pascal's wager on the existence of God: "Let us weigh
up the gain and the loss involved in calling heads that God exists. Let us assess the two
cases: if you win you win everything, if you lose you lose nothing. Do not hesitate then;
wager that he does exist" (Pascal, *Pensées*, trans. A. J. Krailsheimer [Baltimore, 1966],
151). Poullain's bet is definitely on the power of reason.

tively that they are deceivers. In short, since the charity we owe ourselves warns us to be watchful, the charity we owe others does not censure the fear we might have of being caught off guard. This fear does
not give us dispensation from the offices of respect or aid which are
their due."

"Given the difference you make between fact and right, then," said
Timander, "we have to yield up opinion completely."

"That has to be done sooner or later," replied Stasimachus. "I am
convinced that the successful outcome to our studies depends on this
yielding. Since I did not learn this from my teachers, I had to begin
from scratch, following the example of some wise people I know, who
often confessed that hanging on to a simple prejudice had held them
up for a long time on their way towards truth. The maneuvers our
minds engage in to reconcile themselves with public opinion spring
back on themselves in a most devious way—if these opinions have not
been completely destroyed."

"You agree, then, with those people who think that the relationship between our errors and our prejudices is pretty much the same as
that between our clear and distinct ideas," said Sophia.

"That's exactly what I think," replied Stasimachus. "I have noticed
that many people who have sloughed off prejudice in some areas are
only half-hearted in others and completely unprepared in yet others.
So that this holding on to prejudices is the most frequent reason why
people within the same sect can hold views as different as if they had a
quite different belief. Prejudice and error are, in this respect, similar to
leaven which spoils the whole dough it is mixed with.[42] In order to receive the truth into the lovely soul Heaven has given you," he said,
turning to Eulalia, "imitate wise people who, when they are going to
preserve a precious cordial in some rich vessel, first clean the vessel
carefully, lest some putrid dregs spoil the rest.

"It is not simply because of what we have just said that you should
follow the advice I give you. There is another more urgent reason for
freeing yourself from the tyranny of opinion. I must warn you that you
will know no peace or happiness in this life as long as you insist on remaining under such a tyrannical regime. The longer you remain there,
the more you will be exposed to the uncertainty, disquiet, and agitation you have already experienced. You will be constantly buffeted by

*What is
tyranny of
opinion.*

42. See 1 Corinthians 5:6–7: "Your glorying is not good. Know ye not that a little
leaven leaveneth the whole lump? Purge out therefore the old leaven, that ye may be a
new lump, as ye are unleavened" (KJV).

the strange, ever increasing torrent of emotions provoked by differences in temperament, inclination, habit, age, sex, and social situation which spreads and maintains itself by means of conversations, actions, and intercourse in which society engages us. And you will languish your whole life long in slavery more miserable and harsh than the most miserable captives suffer in Tunis or Bizerta.

"A slave in Tunis is a slave in body alone and has only one master he must obey. A man who is a slave to custom is a slave in spirit and has as many masters and tyrants as there are people whose example he tries to follow. The former got his chains by right of conquest and by the law of the strongest. The latter is himself responsible for his chains and submits of his own free will to the weakest and basest segment of society. The former tries to break his bonds and to escape, the second seeks only to bind them tighter, and to remain more firmly attached to them. A slave of Algiers, while overtly doing the bidding of a master, can still keep his internal freedom intact, bemoan his misfortune, accuse his master of cruelty, and think about his escape. But a person who is the slave of opinion is a prisoner inside and outside; he is content in his servitude while suffering its misery; he adores the hand that keeps him down; he makes a virtue of proclaiming its innocence and asserting its justice, and would think it reprehensible even to harbor the thought of seeking freedom. To cap this blindness and misfortune, he is tormented in private as well as in public; not only does he rage against those who are not as blind as he is, but he is cruel and foolish enough to accuse and excoriate those who, bound by the same captivity, show signs of wanting to escape."

"You are forgetting one thing," said Timander, "which is that when we turn our backs on the world, we enter a terrifying solitude; and if we distrust people, we have to make up our minds to walk alone and to seek truth as if we were the only people in the world, with no possibility of ever talking about it to anyone. That must be very difficult, because there is always some reason to doubt one's strength and to fear falling into even greater error if one gives oneself over completely to reason."

"Excessive panic," responded Stasimachus. "You are scaring yourself with ghosts in broad daylight. You are piling up several prejudices and turning them into a monster to frighten yourselves with. Is it not true that if you had been raised in seclusion and had seen only ten or twenty people in your life, it would be no hardship for you to give up their views? So our present reluctance comes only from the fact that we have been raised among a large number of people who uphold an opinion and who have told us that it is upheld by a great number of other people we don't know. Who can assure us that all those who give external witness to an opinion are really convinced of it in their hearts, and that it is not merely from self-interest and politics that they defend what they first espoused out of caprice and prejudice? In every century there have been great men who have mocked popular fantasies. There have been many others who have not revealed themselves, although they were equally skeptical. How many people do we see caught up in the study of opinions who recognize that the world is full of folly, but that it is a strange folly to run counter to what is commonly held? It is sufficient to come across one who is undeceived to realize that there are many others in the same situation. As you are confounded only by numbers, remember that ten men apprehend and learn things the same way as ten million, and that the latter are no more to be feared than the former as far as thought is concerned. The ones who speak to us should be considered as mere warning bells, set up to put us on our guard, and whose large numbers merely confuse us. There is no difference in message between a single person waking us up in the morning to tell us that it is daylight and a large army firing a salvo to tell us the same thing."

"After what we have just been saying about large numbers of people who might examine things," said Sophia, "it seems to me that we would be less well off to trust them than to trust one single man who is concentrated and dedicated and who understands what it is to think. He is better able to consider things. He is not distracted by anyone or dazzled by the passions aroused by the presence of people. And if he consults Nature honestly, I am quite sure she answers him clearly, whereas he would be in danger of confusing her voice with that of men if he turned towards them to listen to what they have to say about the objects he is considering."

"That seems absolutely right to me," said Stasimachus. "A man who applies himself in the way you just mentioned seems to me like a wise and inquisitive stranger who talks to people in all the lands he passes through, and who, being informed of all the rarest things these lands contain, goes to see them for himself to check whether what he has been told is true. Those, on the other hand, who seek only to conform to others' opinions are like people who seek no further than the accounts of others, believing implicitly those who have written them.

"I don't understand," he said, turning to Timander, "why you think we should distrust our reason more than that of others, as if we are not capable of making as good use of ours as other men are of theirs. What use would be our capacity for distinguishing the true from the false, the good from the bad, if we did not use it? Since every man possesses his

We should follow our reason.

own reason and his own understanding, he should use them to govern himself independently of others when he reaches the age of discernment. Since we no longer need nursemaids or reins to keep us on our feet as soon as our legs are firm enough for us to walk by ourselves, so the help and authority of men should no longer be necessary as soon as we can think for ourselves.

"How do you imagine that disciples can be taught by their teachers, can equal and surpass them, as happens every day in the mechanical arts—and would happen even in the sciences if we were not so foolishly intimidated by the authority of great men—except by our recognizing at the same time that we should use our reason to be in a position to judge what we are taught, to discover any errors in it, to correct them, in short to perfect things by adding our own contribution to what has been handed down to us.[43]

"The entire conduct of our lives is based upon this use of reason and our own intelligence, although we don't realize this, blinded as we are by our prejudices. Don't we all claim to have reason on our side? Does not each one of us have his individual ways and means of reaching his goals? Do all those who govern us have the same policies? If we are asked in any given situation why we do this rather than that, and why we do it this way rather than that, do we not have the right to reply either that it's no one's business but our own or that that's the way we think it ought to be? And whether we seek to justify our conduct or correct that of others through our advice, do we not ordinarily invoke our experiences and our reasons? Whether you accept or resist what I say, you use your own reason and intelligence, not someone else's. For in order to judge whether I am right or wrong in what I say, you have to pit my reasons against the ones I argue against, myself against my opponents. You appoint yourself judge between us, and to decide between us you have to place yourself above us."

"I would have thought," said Sophia, "that everyone behaves that way in their public or private lives; they either choose a way of life, a condition, a custom, a sentiment, a religion, or they act like beasts or idiots."

"This way of acting according to reason," continued Stasimachus, "is the rule we should follow in all things, and which God Himself desires us to follow in things relating to Him.

"Since it is He who has given us the capacity for discernment, He wants us to use it and to judge things according to truth and justice. We cannot hope to resemble Him in perfection, holiness, and understanding except in-

---

43. See Adam, *Grandeur and Illusion*, 148: "The Moderns, taking reason as their starting point, believed in the progress of the human mind. They held that there was no point in fighting against what is now called the march of history."

sofar as we follow His example of becoming independent in our judgments, paying no heed to numbers or conditions of people, but thinking sensibly and without prejudice. As proof that He does not want us to wear out the eyes He has given us nor to obey Him like blind men, remember that He often takes the name of Truth, Splendor, and Sun to help us in our understanding, and He illuminates our efforts by the light of truth which He sends out just as the sun illuminates the physical eyes with its splendor, and that truth, goodness, and justice are as manifest in the way He behaves towards us as the sun and light at high noon."

"I have never thought otherwise on this matter," said Sophia, "from having often read, without prejudice, the goals and considerations that God offers us in the Scriptures to encourage us, by means of a gentleness worthy of His divine majesty, to live in the way He has set forth. Sometimes He shows us that the whole universe is His, that He has no need of the things He has given us, and that in setting forth His law He is thinking only of our own good. And sometimes to strengthen our obedience, which is so salutary for us, He tells us He is our God, our Sovereign, and our Father, omniscient, omnipotent, and of infinite goodness. If He asked nothing of us but blind obedience, would He give us such overwhelming intimations of our duty? Would He not act in a sovereign way? And if He wanted our reason to wither away before Him, would He not have prescribed an absolute science, divinely authorized and ordained?"[44]

"That reminds me of one thing," said Timander. "It is this: God pits His own glory against that of idols, so to speak, and His truths against the errors of false prophets, all the while giving us guidance about how we recognize them, which makes me absolutely convinced that He knows that each of us has enough strength and intelligence not to let ourselves be led astray."

"Whatever you may think," said Eulalia to Timander, "it is my opinion that we are better off examining things together rather than by ourselves. Conversation opens the mind: one person sees things from one angle, another from a different perspective, and if each person puts forward what he knows, as you have just done, then we all benefit from each other's views. We each encourage the others to notice important truths that we would pass by without a second thought in the privacy of our own studies. What you have just said reminds me that the Scriptures seem to have been written with the sole purpose of accusing sinners of abandoning virtue in order to pursue vice. Now if we were not incontrovertibly obliged to use our own intelligence to

---

44. He expresses here a very dangerous thought on free thinking, well in advance of the eighteenth-century philosophes.

recognize both, then the reproaches and threats leveled at us would make no sense. All we would have to say as we pursue vice is that we are simply doing what most people do.

"Could it not be said that when Jesus Christ performed miracles in the presence of the people to give authority to His mission and doctrine, He charged each of those present to judge the dispute between Him and the Synagogue? It was as if He had said, 'Decide whether it is I or the Doctors of the Law who teach the way you should follow.' And when the Divine Master saw that the Jews were so enslaved by custom and so stubbornly attached to current prejudices that neither the purity of His doctrine nor the power of His miracles could prize them away from them, He upbraided them for not using their own discernment to distinguish the true from the false."

Luke 12.
"Your remark is quite correct," said Stasimachus to Eulalia, "But do be aware that when I say that you have to walk alone in the path of truth, which is as narrow as the path of virtue, all I mean is that you have to consider it as if you were alone, whether you are in fact alone or with other people. And when I speak of companies, I mean vast numbers of people, among whom passion always plays a role. For I by no means wish to banish conversations or arguments, but they should always be between three or four people who love unadorned truth, who seek it in all sincerity and without scruple, who apply their minds to it, and are pleased to hear it from each other without being compromised. By proceeding thus, we will certainly make better progress than if we were alone. I confess that I have read the Scriptures several times, but I had never made the same observations as we have just made. I was so blinded by prejudice that had Eulalia not mentioned the words 'public prejudice,' I would never have noticed that the Scriptures are so opposed to prejudice and credulity that they accuse of inconsistency and frivolity those who agree straight away with whatever is suggested to them, without taking care to examine it first.[45] In the same spirit the Apostles exhorted the faithful to be discerning about men for fear of being seduced by them and carried off willy-nilly in all directions, and to prepare to receive the religion they profess.[46] For how are we to persuade an idolater or a Mohammedan of the falsity of their religion and the truth of our own if we do not reason with them to show them that one is contrary to reason and the other in conformity with it. The idol-

45. See Ecclesiasticus 19.
46. See 1 John 4:1.

ater must also possess sovereign reason, which, when it is awakened by the preachings of a Christian, places itself between the two religions, so to speak, and decides which of the two merits his adherence."

"Since all these truths are apparent and incontestable, what do people mean when they talk about reason being blind?" asked Eulalia.

"Although I cannot answer for what other people say," replied Stasimachus, "and I can only speak for myself, I'll tell you that I think it's true in several ways: (1) because since ordinary people let themselves be led like the blind, without recourse to their reason, we can indeed say that their reason is blind; (2) since most people do not have the leisure nor the means to cultivate their reason, they have no option in most situations but to let themselves be led by the hand; and (3) reason is blind in all men who allow it to be obscured by prejudice, by error, or by their passions. But it is not so blinded that there is not sufficient light remaining for the gleam of truth to shine through. When we understand how to accept reason and cultivate it through serious study, then our blindness dissipates, and reason shines through with the brightness that you already know so well."

What it means to say that reason is blind.

"I gather from what you say," said Eulalia, "that in order to keep going to the very end, I have to be convinced that I have sufficient reason and intelligence to do so, and I have to keep telling myself that I have."

"Yes indeed," said Stasimachus, "and you should have done that a long time ago."

One has to be convinced that one has sufficient reason to continue.

"But is there not some danger in telling oneself that?" protested Eulalia, "and does it not constitute criminal presumption?"

"If that were not the case," replied Stasimachus, "and you felt within you neither intelligence nor reason, there would be no point in telling you. When you stand in front of your mirror and it tells you in all honesty that you are fair and lovely, do you tell it that it's wrong?"

"And how would I do that if it were true?" asked Eulalia.

"Since God has also given you reason and intelligence," continued Stasimachus, "and since He desires you to use them—inasmuch as it is mainly for these gifts that we have to give some account and for these blessings that we owe Him the greatest thanks—we must be able to tell ourselves that we possess them."

"Indeed," said Sophia, "how would we make proper use of them and make tribute of them to God, their source and origin, if we did not acknowledge them in ourselves? I believe," this wise young woman continued, "that the qualities of the mind are no less delicate and no less estimable than those of the body; and if we are allowed to recognize that we possess strength, beauty, and friends, then we are surely allowed to believe that we possess reason and good sense."

"You have too great an interest in this question," interrupted Timander, "not to pronounce in its favor."

"You would be your own worst enemy if you did not declare the same interest," riposted Sophia. "But," she continued, "it seems to me that we are presumptuous and overbearing when we make haughty claims to attributes we don't possess, or when we use those that we do possess to sneer at our peers. Nothing seems to me more pernicious than false humility; it makes a bastard of our intelligence, saps our courage and strength, snuffs out our enthusiasm, and by keeping us in a state of inertia and lethargy makes us incapable of carrying out any of our plans. It can only prepare people to accept, in blind submission, whatever anyone wants to make them believe, and to allow themselves to be manipulated without resistance."

"Well then," said Timander, "we seem to have found the formula for discovering the truth: refuse to accept anything that isn't true, reject any opinion arrived at without examination and on the basis of hearsay, work as though you were alone in the conviction that you have intelligence and reason and with the intention of cultivating them and using them as your guide."[47]

"What I would like to know," said Eulalia, "is what is this truth we keep hearing about and which is the subject of these conversations and the end of the quest I want to embark upon."

"If we haven't yet given a precise definition of it," said Stasimachus, "that's because it hasn't yet been necessary. This is the right place to discuss it."

"What you are about to teach us will, perhaps, clear any doubts that remain about what we have been saying," said Sophia.

"To formulate a clear idea of the truth," began Stasimachus, "you should know that there are two aspects that have to be taken into consideration: first the state of things in nature and outside our minds, and second their state within the imagination of those considering them. If we do not consider them in the first way, and rely upon what others tell us, then we learn only what pertains to the second state, and we learn nothing except that there are people who opine thus, but nothing of the way in which they make their judgments. Clearly we are still in the situation of those who know only by hearsay what there is in a country they have not visited. It would be erro-

---

47. From this point the general discussion shifts from the Cartesian rules that led to the *cogito* (with a provisional code of conduct to follow while seeking truth) to a social commentary on the risks to women who demonstrate their intellectual nonconformity.

neous to mistake the state of things in people's minds for their state in nature, because the one does not always give us an idea of the other. Thus the common people, who confuse the two by relying on popular opinion, in fact do nothing but echo a jumbled version of the voices they have heard, so that those who dominate people's thoughts by means of the credence we give them can say that they have as many mouths and organs as there are repeating the views they are spreading. Those who submit to them in this way are no different from talking birds, except that they are quicker to learn the words taught, words that make them act in several different ways.

"The other way of looking at things—and this is the way of intelligent people—is when, without regard for men's imagination, we turn our eyes to these things and consult the images which allow our minds to picture them. When, after a general renewal and a complete stripping away, we apply ourselves seriously, sincerely, and rigorously to this study, the idea we then have is the true notion we can have of it. Thus the truth is, properly speaking, the correspondence between our thoughts and their objects, and that is what is sought in the sciences. Now this correspondence consists in knowing things as they are. Since truth is the opposite of prejudice and error—which of necessity lead to obscurity and confusion—it should have the opposite qualities, namely, discernment and evidence. Thus, when we are resolved to admit nothing but what is true, we must admit into this category only what has its essential characteristics, for it is only acute and clear thought and interior and luminous penetration that can be the purpose of our persuasion and the prop of our consent. This is why the discourse of those who do not transmit any idea into the mind of those who listen to them carefully must be considered as nothing but empty and pointless noise."

"What I find troublesome about this study of truth," said Timander, "is that it is not up to us to discover it; otherwise all men would know it, since there are few people who do not love it. But although we love it, we rarely know what it is. When we think about it and desire to find the way towards it, it is up to us to seek the path, but it is not up to us to find it. Chance has to play a role. When we discover the path and try to take it, we have it in our power to apply ourselves to one object or another, to stop for as long or as short a time as we please; but it is not within our power to see these objects in one way rather than another. When we have no subject for doubt, our mind is naturally inclined to judge things according to the ideas presented.

What is up to us in the search for truth.

"When we look at the sun, therefore, by necessity it seems to us brilliant and round, and we judge it to be so if we have no reason which forces us to suspend our judgment."

"If that is the case," said Eulalia, "we would have no certainty in our understanding because it is not up to us to make it as perfect as it can be."

"I beg your pardon," said Stasimachus, "we can assert that our understanding is certain, and that we know things perfectly when we have studied them, because we know them with all the certainty that we have been able to acquire, and because the state of our nature can tolerate it.

That we should
always be
ready to change
our minds
according to
reason.

"We should remain firm in the beliefs we have adopted after reasonable examination. But this certainty must not be obstinate, as is that of those people and false scholars who are so stubbornly attached to what they think they know that they regard everything that contradicts them as absolutely wrong and refuse to listen to anything except what coincides with their own views."

"It seems to me," said Sophia, "that since it is not our will but our reason that attaches our intelligence to a viewpoint, the intelligence should always be ready to detach itself when reason dictates it."

"I would have thought, on the contrary, " objected Eulalia, "that the inclination to pass from one opinion to another is a sign of superficiality and inconstancy."

"No, I don't think so," replied Sophia. "It is superficial to change one's mind on a whim and without reason, but it is wise to change it when one has good reason to. Do we not change our plans and our behavior every day according to our situation and experience? Constancy does not mean remaining firm and unshakable in the same opinion or in the same resolve, but rather in remaining firm in the resolve to do nothing but what is good, and to admit nothing but what is true. Far from being disadvantageous, the move from one opinion to another, provided it is accomplished according to reason, should be extremely useful to us, since it puts us on the path where we should be.

"If we sincerely love the truth, we should not fear the change which will put us into contact with it."

What consti-
tutes true
wisdom.

"I agree," said Stasimachus, "for whatever our age and our situation, we remain subject to error. I believe that we should always take precautions against making mistakes, though without letting these precautions force us into uncertainty or irresolution or confusion. Since it is a fault common to all men that we all fall into error during childhood, that most of us remain in it throughout our lives, and that there are few people who make a useful effort to get out of it, we can say that true wisdom does not so much consist in not falling into error as in doing what one can to get out of it. In the same way, true prudence consists in being on our guard rather than in avoiding the misfortunes that come our way. As in practice, where the success of an enterprise does not depend completely on those who undertake it, one should be self-sufficient and act with absolute assurance when one has taken necessary measures, insofar as occasion, experience, and capacity allow. During the period of speculation, one should hold firm and be assured of having found the truth when one has done everything possible to discover it."

"I wish, for the sake of honor and for the peace of everyone, and especially those who pass themselves off as scholars, that they all shared your views," said Sophia. "They would see that if we happen to hold views that are opposed to theirs, we should not be castigated; and instead of flying into a rage against their opponents and trying to tyrannize them into acknowledging their own views, they would allow them freedom of thought and would be satisfied to explain quietly that they believe them to be wrong."

"In order to make a correct judgment on how to behave in situations where one is in disagreement with the largest number, and to avoid argument," Stasimachus went on, "it is important to remember two things. One is that even if we are not complete masters of our thoughts, we are of our speech and actions; and the other is that custom dictates things in such a way that they do not always turn out as we imagine they should, or as we would like them to.

"This is why we can identify two kinds of truth, one internal or physical and stemming from nature, the other external or moral and coming from society. *There are two kinds of truth.*

"The first is the knowledge that we can acquire by means of philosophy, of the true state of things, and the way they should unfold according to that state, without reference to opinion or custom. The second is when we know the way things actually do take place and are recounted in the country or the society in which one finds oneself. Physical truth concerns individuals who seek it through study, and moral truth concerns the public and intercourse between people. The first is called internal because it relates to the feelings and thoughts we keep to ourselves and do not reveal to anybody; and the second is called external because its sole object is our outward actions.

One should
speak and act
like the common
people when one
acts in public,
but think like
the wise.

"These two kinds of truth are very different, but they are not at odds, for although there is a prescribed way of acting and speaking, it is nonetheless not false that one should act and speak according to the manner established by custom."

"How is it possible," Eulalia inquired, "to speak and act other than as one thinks?"

"One should often do so," replied Stasimachus. "There are many occasions when one should speak folly to the fool and sacrifice the individual good to the public good, unless we want to act contrary to the useful maxim that we should think like the wise man and speak like the common man, and so destroy the main purpose of society by adopting an affected individualism to prevent giving to others or receiving from them the help necessary in life."[48]

"We have to make up our minds," said Timander, "to conform with men to avoid becoming victims of the almost brutal rage of which they have always been capable, not only in forcing themselves to imitate each other in all things, but—and this is cruel—in wanting to be imitated and in allowing themselves to be shocked by words and actions in which they have no interest whatsoever and which have no effect on their person, their reputation, or their possessions."

"You are speaking only of the exterior," said Stasimachus, "which we should view as a fashion, liable to change at any time. As for the interior, if you believe that we do not have control over it, then you must also believe that we cannot make it correspond completely with the exterior, except through confusion and prejudice."

"Indeed," said Sophia, "if we were always obliged to adjust to public opinion, the ignorant populace would have the advantage, both because it forms a majority of the public voice and conforms most closely to it and also because it would lay down the law for people of intelligence and enlightenment, which would be absurd. It would serve no purpose to work to acquire skills, since the ignorant would always have, through caprice and chance, what we take enormous pains to acquire. The sciences might as well be abolished as pernicious if we don't try to use them to try to gain an understanding of things that is different from the understanding of the vulgar multitude, who are no better than beasts."

48. Poullain seems to subscribe to French classical morality, which fosters in an individual the greatest conformism for the benefit of the "outside world" (in French "le dehors") while it promotes the concealment of emotions for fear of revealing one's "inside thoughts" ("le dedans") out of fear of betraying the secret depths of one's self ("le Moi"). But for him the fear derives from public censorship. See below, notes 58 and 86.

"If mob opinion is sound, we can always return to it," said Stasimachus, "and if it is unsound, then we cannot flee far enough away from it.

"That is why," he continued, speaking to Eulalia, "we should avoid the mistake of most great men who corrupt the talents they receive from Heaven by internalizing the need to conform externally to custom, and who have been thwarted in their attempts to reform, without public authority, the imagined errors of both the learned and the vulgar, without considering that truth and falsity are indifferent to the majority of men, who accept and reject them in the same way, through caprice and obstinacy, and who, when they change masters and climate, do not change conduct but rather carry on as before, remaining slaves to usage and opinion. Remember that it is the same for the things of the mind as for those of the body. Both should contribute to our conservation, not to our ruin. We are not in this world to establish our imagination at our own expense, but, on the contrary, to see to it that everything we put into our heads, everything we know, everything we possess, should be for us and for our advantage.

"Remember that the learned in whatever field have always disagreed with one another and still do, that each side claims to lay down the law for the others and to have public opinion on its side. Thus neither of them agrees with that public opinion. Notice that all states differ from one another, all provinces have different customs and views from every other province, in every town each group and each society has its practices and its sayings. Without mentioning fashion, special interest, possessions, business, and specific aims, do you not see that each individual has his goal? That several who seek the same goal take different paths to reach it? We all want to be happy, none of us wants to be duped, and we each choose the means to this end that we think fit. You want to find the truth, so you follow the way that seems to you the shortest and the most certain. You do not pose as someone of singular views, you do not avoid meetings with others out of a spirit of individualism or snobbery, but you take the path that seems to you the most certain, without trying to prevent others from entering it. If you do not take the common path, it is not because you want one all to yourself, but because you are right in thinking that that is not the best one; and you chose that one in the conviction that everyone ought to be following it. If you concentrate on working mainly for your own perfection, you should be concerned only with yourself and with what seems to you the most convenient and the most useful as far as your internal life is concerned. Since, however, you have to live among other people, you should imitate those who are rich and wise, who have two sets of clothes, a comfortable one for the house, where they are at their ease, and a fashionable one for company and for the city. In other words, you only half understand things if you only understand them for yourself; you also have to know the art of expressing them, not only to adapt to the weakness and reach of the common people, but also to be able to communicate convincingly to them the truths you have discovered. Inasmuch as they pay attention only to words and act on memory rather than on judgment, it is sometimes possible, by using the right manner, to instill correct thinking into their minds."

"I still have some misgivings about what you say about being able to speak other than the way one thinks," said Eulalia. "It still seems to me that it involves counterfeit and dissimulation, which, as you well know, is condemned by most people."

"Your misgivings are those of opinion, not of reason," replied Stasimachus. "I know perfectly well that we condemn dissimulation, but I also know that we condemn it in general because it is wrong in certain situations, as when it is mixed with artifice and the aim of deceiving, in short, when it is contrary to the charity we owe our neighbor. But when we disguise our feelings for others' benefit in order not to be useless to them out of contrariety, or for our own interests (when we do not harm those of others), no one could reasonably object, and we would in no way call that lying.

"Do you believe that you would not be your own murderer if you were to expose yourself pointlessly to the fury of a mutinous crowd, or that you would not be guilty of arousing sedition and civil war by refusing to uphold some opinion that you did not believe to be true? And would you not think it a crime if you did not chase away the would-be assassins of some poor wretch who had taken refuge with you?

"No, no," he continued, "there is no reason not to moderate the dose, to add honey to the medicine, to sweeten the pill. Men are made in such a way that their sicknesses should be concealed from them so as not to depress them and their problems minimized so as not to discourage them. One's aims should be made to appear anodyne by means of varnish and pretexts. Society would fall apart if we tried to prevent politicians from putting us off the scent and setting us barking up the wrong tree.[49]

"The company will not be displeased," he went on, "to have a few rational, authoritative examples to which we cannot but yield. It appears throughout the Scriptures that God always treated men with great consideration and that to accommodate Himself to the weakness of their minds which can

---

49. In spite of the fact that Poullain seems to adhere to Descartes's first maxim, his personal life and work consistently contradict his call for public conformity. Here, in the context of his treatise for women, he accepts Descartes's provisional morality reluctantly for lack of better protection against freedom of expression. See below, note 86.

understand almost nothing except in crude and bodily images, He showed Himself to them solely by figures, by emblems and enigmas; and He allowed Himself to be given hands, ears, and even passions in order to make His conduct more understandable to people. Although it seems, as some scholars believe, that the creation of the world took place in an instant, in order for it to be understood by people it had to be made into a story of several days."

"Since you have read the Gospel, you will surely have noticed that the Savior of the world warns you by word and example not to profane His doctrine by speaking it abroad to all sorts of people,[50] and there are some situations in which telling what you know is casting pearls before swine,[51] giving people the opportunity to become enraged and turn their wrath against you and treat you most cruelly. How many occasions were there when, finding it inappropriate to reveal His sayings unadorned, He covered them with the veil of a parable? Were there not times when He considered that the Apostles themselves were not entirely capable of bearing the great truths He had to teach them, and revealed them only in part?[52] Although He knew that God is everywhere at the same time, He nevertheless brought people to associate Him with a dwelling in Heaven, because since people judge the excellence of things by their situation, they imagine that as the heavens are the highest and most glorious part of the world, they are also the worthiest to be the throne and the courts of Divine Majesty. In order to give the wicked greater fear for the state of woe that endures for eternity after this life, He represents it sometimes by the word Hell, whose meaning is opposed to that of Heaven, sometimes by terrifying fires, sometimes by fearful darkness, sometimes by gnashing of teeth, in other words, by all that we can conceive of that inspires us with horror. It was in the same spirit that St. Paul at first fed nothing but milk to those he was instructing in the Christian religion, reserving solid food for when they had stronger stomachs."[53]

"After so many very convincing proofs," said Eulalia, "so many reliable testimonies and such excellent examples, I can no longer doubt that I should hold the views you have suggested to me in order to have a good understanding of things."

"I don't think I need remind you that we need take no notice of what people commonly say about scholars," continued Stasimachus.

We need pay no heed to what people say.

50. See Mark 4:10–11.

51. See Matthew 7:6.

52. John 16:12.

53. 1 Corinthians 3:2.

"For you must be aware that it is through caprice and prejudice that they say that scholars are dangerous and that great minds are the most susceptible to error. You need not fear the accusation of 'nonconformist'[54] that is hurled at those who do not think they should bow blindly to the opinion of the common herd and refuse to admit of any opinion without reason."

"For the time being," Eulalia continued, "I treat those comments like comedy routines that satisfy and console idiots. By idiots I mean those who have no intelligence whatsoever or who spoil such intelligence as Heaven has given them by accepting all kinds of opinions without examining them.

"There is only one thing I still fear," she added, "which is to be unable to use my reason fully. As far as the people are concerned, it seems to me that since they show exaggerated sympathy for those they take to be in error because they do not follow public whims, scholars and those who try to be scholars should not give them any more thought than they would a maniac who is riding his own hobby-horse.

"In fact, does one not have to be mad to maintain that the greater reason someone has, the more dangerous and deplorable a state he is in? For to be a scholar is to have greater reason. It is worse than saying that the healthier and stronger one is, the more miserable one is."

"Intelligence can be as pernicious as other faculties," said Timander, "when those who possess them abuse them, and we should only condemn those who misuse this talent."

"That's all well and good," replied Eulalia, "but I'd like to know how a woman who can't even recite 'Our Father' knows how to make rational use of her mind, indeed, who does not even know what a mind is? How can she be on the path toward truth or falsehood when she cannot tell one from the other? I myself am convinced that we cannot make a better use of our intelligence than to gain a deeper understanding of things, nor a worse one than to leave it unused, as do the common people, blinding and stifling it by following the interests and whims of others. I am even tempted to say that one should rejoice instead of being embarrassed to see oneself condemned by an ignorant multitude, for that is an infallible sign that one is thinking and speaking differently from the crowd, a sign that intelligent people should seek, since the thoughts of the multitude are confused, unsure, false, and unpredictable. I am no longer surprised that those whose opinions are very different from those of the common people should always be rejected by them as well as by those popular scholars who base their doctrine on childhood prejudices. I realize also that it is of this knowledge that the Scriptures speak

54. The French is "esprit fort."

when they call it a source of vanity and pride, inasmuch as it is impossible that such a wicked effect could be correctly attributed to the knowledge we are seeking, which has as its only aim rational thinking and as its basis a pure and honest love of truth."

"I have a suspicion," said Timander, laughing, "that this so-called love is rather curiosity in your case."

"And if it were," Eulalia interjected swiftly, "what would be wrong with that? If you are still under the misapprehension that curiosity is a defect and accuse our sex of it, talk to Stasimachus, or consult his book, and you will see how he justifies us and shows that curiosity is a great advantage.[55] What convinces me that criticism is motivated only by caprice and prejudice is that when I asked several people—among them that good gentleman who is not happy that women should show any curiosity—if they knew what curiosity was, he was at pains to point out that I was myself curious, and that therefore I was hardly in a position to speak of others who are curious. One day when I insisted that he enlighten me on the subject of why curiosity is so reprehensible, all I could get out of him by way of an answer (to this and to many other questions) was an 'I don't know what to tell you, but I know very well that one should not be so curious; everyone knows that.'"

On curiosity.

"Indeed," said Stasimachus, "curiosity can be bad like the rest of our inclinations. But to understand how that happens, you should be aware that we have two dominant desires corresponding to the principal needs of the mind and the body. The first desire has as its object the possession of all things necessary for the preservation of the body, while the second is concerned with the knowledge that can contribute to the perfecting of the spirit. The first is called concupiscence and the second curiosity. Considering them in general, without reference to the actual situation or to social institutions, there is nothing reprehensible about either one or the other, and it is equally legitimate to want to possess everything and to know everything.

"There are also similar differences among the insights of the mind as among the possessions of the body: some are for necessity, others for convenience, and others for pure pleasure and a superfluous satisfaction. The result is that it is primarily the way we react to things that makes our desires good or bad. Our curiosity, therefore, is ruinous, indiscreet, and overhasty if it ruins our health and our wealth, makes us

55. Feminine intellectualism, often confused with malicious curiosity, was at the crux of the Querelle des Femmes, revived in 1672 with Molière's *Les Femmes savantes.* See Timmermans, *L'Accès des femmes à la culture,* 318–86.

importunate and antisocial, causes us to apply ourselves in an inappropriate way to certain studies, or leads us to prefer the less useful to the more necessary things, to abandon our duties, to take on too many things at once, to pass too hastily over the things we value, and thus to fail to observe in our thoughts the order that ought to reign there if we are to find the truth.

"Curiosity is also rash when we try to understand things which exceed our intelligence. Thus we cannot criticize enough the curiosity of those who try to discern the extent of Divine omnipotence: whether it could create a world different from this one, annihilate a creature, or make a stone capable of seeing God. Many try to fathom the secrets, designs, and conduct of Providence and hundreds of other such things which are clearly beyond our grasp. We become a laughing stock when we try to penetrate such deep abysses without even knowing ourselves.

"Curiosity, therefore, is contrary neither to prudence nor to justice, and we can try to satisfy it completely, provided we do so in a methodical and orderly way. Black magic, for instance, is a black and wicked art only when it transgresses against the law, and when it is studied with the intention of abusing it and of creating the profanations its practice demands. Otherwise it is no more criminal than astronomy. It is no less permissible to inquire whether there are demons, whether one can communicate with them, how one can have commerce with them, than to ask the same questions about the antipodes."

"One of the most pressing reasons for speaking so much against curiosity," said Timander, "is the fear that if men let themselves be led along they will go farther than they should."

"I have been wondering for some time," said Sophia, "what it means to go too far."

"I have the same difficulty as you," said Stasimachus, "and I have never found anyone to resolve it. Whatever happens, we should be comfortable and confident when we seek the truth with sincerity and prudence, since that is what we ought to do."

"According to some people," said Timander, "it is going too far to depart from commonly held opinions and to accept new ideas, which is another effect of curiosity."

"Is it just that?" retorted Eulalia. "You aren't paying attention. Remember that you just told us that the choice in matters of opinion does not depend on an attentive and reasonable mind; rather, the mind is carried by a natural proclivity to accept those opinions it thinks best, ancient or modern. My view is that if one truly loves the truth, one is ready to accept it from whatever hand, whatever country, and whatever age it comes."

"How are we to know," asked Sophia, "the age of an opinion? One *On views we* person may think it is new because he heard that it has not been fash- *call new.* ionable for very long, but it could have had currency in another coun- try and in another century of which one knows nothing. How many authors are there whose works are lost or unknown, or clever people who do not say what they think? For since the common people cannot stand to have people speak differently from them, I am almost sure that the most learned remain silent and that those who cause the greatest furor are most often those who have the good luck or the talent to turn public fashion to their own advantage."

"As the antiquity of ideas is no indication of their truth," added Stasimachus, "their newness is likewise no proof of their falsity, and if consideration of their newness were a sufficient reason for rejecting them, we would not have to accept any of them, since even the most ancient were new when they were formulated, and every one of them is new to us when it is first presented to our minds."

"People must really be stubborn about this," said Sophia. "Do we at the moment have the same laws, the same customs, the same policies, and the same discipline that people had formerly? Are not all men sus- ceptible to changes of thought, language, conduct, and ambitions as they are to fashions, according to situation and experience? Since the mind is given the freedom to expand as much as possible in the arts, why is it constrained and repressed in the sciences? Pilots who discover new lands are rewarded and privileges are even given to artisans who have found something new. Thinkers should therefore be allowed to develop their studies as best they can."

"They should simply wrest permission without saying anything to anyone," said Stasimachus, "and if they make an interesting discovery they should keep it for themselves and their friends without allowing their indiscreet and immoderate zeal to lead people to see them as headstrong reformers who insist on trying to revolutionize the public against the will of those who govern.[56]

"Here, then," he continued, turning to Eulalia, "are the most im- portant things we can say to clarify the three requests I made a while ago. I imagine you see better now how necessary it was, before giving a direct answer to your question, to show you that at your age one is

---

56. Noteworthy and totally in character with Poullain's convictions is the fact that he ignores Descartes's third maxim to change his desires rather than the order of the world.

usually full of prejudices and errors, that it is impossible to remove these without a sincere and full-scale rejection, and that in order to acquire certain understanding we have to begin to examine all things afresh in the light of reason alone—as if we had never heard them spoken of or were alone in the world. But even though you began by a method quite different from the one popularly followed, namely, by forgetting everything you thought you knew—unlike the others, who begin by learning what they believe they did not know—you must nevertheless be convinced that you have traveled more than halfway to reach the great truths of which men are capable."

"You have shown us," said Sophia, rising, "that popular science and wisdom are vanity and folly. I hope that the first time we are fortunate enough to have you to ourselves again, we will learn in what you place the wisdom you profess."

"You will learn," replied Stasimachus, "as soon as you let me know you are ready." After which the four people took leave of each other.

FOURTH CONVERSATION

A few days after this meeting, Stasimachus received a note from Sophia telling him that Timander was to dine with her that day, and as Eulalia was to be there too, she was asking him to come and complete the conquest that seemed to her well under way.

Stasimachus replied that although he interpreted her message as the signal for a meeting in which he would be defeated, he would obey nonetheless.

He arrived at the appointed time. Greetings were exchanged and Eulalia teased him playfully: "You're a strange man; you enjoy making people think. I am not surprised that you are a supporter of women; you have in common with them the thing that everybody finds fault with: when you get an idea in your head, you make it a point of honor to see it through."

"I don't know whether I have been lucky enough to succeed in your case," Stasimachus replied, "but I have to tell you that until now I have been so careful about what I undertake that, if I am dealing with reasonable people, either I have always managed to persuade them or they me."

"As you are always guided by reason," said Timander, "I am not surprised that you are swayed by other people's, or that others are persuaded by yours. On that point, however, I have to say that women don't resemble you."

"You always generalize so much that you always have to add some restriction," commented Eulalia. "There are more reasonable women around than you think, and you should, at least for the time being, count me among them. It's not that I claim to be more reasonable than the others, but if it can be considered reasonable to make an effort to become so, then you should certainly think of me in that way."

"I am afraid that you are much more reasonable and better-informed than you would have us believe," said Stasimachus, "because without an extraordinary mind it is very hard to come to grips with great men, as you do, without having studied them."

"I am also lucky enough to have come to grips with you and to have studied you," riposted Eulalia, smiling.

"I am not joking," said Stasimachus. "I am talking about the great men of antiquity, who defined wisdom as love of wisdom or the desire to acquire it. This is what bears the name philosophy, which we have from them, as we have that of philosopher, which means lover of wisdom and of reason."

"And do remember, Stasimachus, what you said recently," said Sophia, "that wisdom consists in the *desire* not to be mistaken rather than in not *being* mistaken at all, and that is probably the model Eulalia took for the definition of reasonable she just applied to you."

"Whatever the model, one obviously needs a lively intelligence, in the marketplace of thought as well as that of goods, to realize a lot from a little and to profit from everything," said Stasimachus.

"According to your principles—and you have been so convincing that I can say they are also mine—we can recognize that we don't lack intelligence, and we should either thank God for it or prepare to take advantage of a talent He has given us," said Eulalia. "That's why, I confess, I think I have sufficient intelligence both to encourage you to give me further means of cultivating it and to thank you personally for inspiring me to become aware of vast numbers of things I had never considered before and to interpret dreams and reduce people to silence."

"What a lot of paradoxes and mysteries all at once," Sophia said to her. "I can't wait for you to explain them."

"That's just what I plan to do," said Eulalia, "and I hope to show Stasimachus, as I would my master, what I have learned from the two lessons he has given me."

"Oh, for goodness sake don't use those words here," cried Stasimachus. "We are all here as equals. I hate the word 'master' for a variety of reasons, and I am certainly not going to use it of a beautiful young person who will soon be my mistress."

"After our last meeting," said Eulalia to Stasimachus, "I went to bed earlier than usual, and as I am fortunate enough to have a good memory, I tried to go over in my mind most of what you had said. After a while, I felt as if a blindfold had been taken from my eyes, and I could suddenly see many things that had seemed utterly obscure before. Among other things, I ran through my mind—albeit in my limited way—everything I know of how society works—how we talk about things and how we act upon what we have said—and as I was comparing men as a group and men as individuals, I noticed something odd that terrified me, as it seemed of greater consequence than you had given me to understand [in our preceding conversation].[57]

"It seemed to me that during childhood everyone learns things the same way, and they remain attached to their beliefs for the same reasons that persuaded them in the first place. Since their knowledge is usually based on prejudice and error, their science, conviction, and belief can be very limited—a blind and stubborn attachment that flies in the face of reason and good sense.

"Almost all the different peoples of the world have views peculiar to themselves, and although they have arrived at them with an equal lack of discernment, every one of them claims to have the most rational and gives the lie to his neighbors, but with such conviction on both sides that it is impossible to judge which is right and which wrong, unless one is equally dispassionate about all their views and can rise above them to consider them impartially.

"Although people's learning is based on the authority of their teachers, who are the sole source of their information, and although they accept as the truth the first thing they have learned, yet if these same people should later change their views and reject as erroneous what their teachers had taught them were constant truths, they would be the first to turn against those same teachers and accuse them of not conforming to public opinion. Further, this public opinion must, naturally, be that of the country in which we were raised, for although common people judge the truth of opinions by the number of people who hold them, they pay little attention to them if they are not of their own nation. In fact they will blithely accuse of error three quarters of the people in the world if they are told that those people speak and live differently from people in the province, town, or community where they are, or even differently from a single man who governs them.

"For most people, all it takes is for someone of an opposing sect to say something for it to be false, and if it is said by those they admire then it must be true and absolute. Those who could legitimately be suspected of sacrificing truth to fortune are adored by the people who, on the other hand, persecute most cruelly those who, with complete disinterestedness, have been seen to sacrifice fortune to the truth they seek.

57. In the first pages of the chapter, Eulalia is reviewing the lessons learned in the previous conversation.

"Finally, I have observed that men don't agree among themselves. Even in really important things they depend on hearsay, as if they had neither reason nor intelligence. By a staggering contradiction, although all individuals—even those whose task is to lead others—make it a cardinal virtue to believe or to say that they are not wise enough to govern themselves, to profess to be blind, to recognize that they are subject to errors into which they have fallen incessantly in the past and still fall every day, in spite of all this they either depend on the instincts and advice of others or they follow only their own instincts and whims. What is even more absurd, the majority of them expect people to defer to them without question, as if they were oracles who cannot make a mistake. The ones who have less intelligence and understanding take it upon themselves to lord it over their peers, to give them advice, and to condemn their behavior when it doesn't conform to their own.

"But I found an even greater contradiction when I tried to reconcile men's words with their actions. I saw that they practice the opposite of what they preach, that they almost never follow the rules they lay down for others, that in their inmost being they prize and covet what they condemn in public, that they fear less the contagion of manners than of doctrine, and that they consider it worse to not speak as they do—even though they live quite differently   than to speak differently and to live a life quite the contrary of the one they approve. I found myself, therefore, in a dilemma about whether I should follow their words or their actions, whether the words follow the actions or the actions the words, or whether there were specific rules for different people, and whether there are any maxims that I might use to reconcile such an obvious contradiction. I then realized how right you were in recommending me not to depend on anyone else in matters that are governed by my reason, and to wait for the time when you would be good enough to tell me what I should do now."

"I came here today on Sophia's orders to tell you what I did when I was in a similar state to the one you are in now," said Stasimachus, "but I won't do that until you have finished."

"I went to sleep with all these thoughts running through my head," Eulalia continued. "I dreamed that I had gone to live in a great commercial city where each citizen had a right to a share—though an unequal share—in all the goods that were brought in. Although the goods were extremely fine when they came off the ships, they became worn and tattered as they went from hand to hand until they became unrecognizable. Nonetheless, those who got them last and in the smallest quantity were deluded enough to think themselves as fortunate and as rich as those whose hands they had already passed through.

"I was one of the unfortunates, and as I was about to receive my share, I met on a street corner a distinguished looking lady who took me by the hand with a majestic but gentle air and asked me where I was going. She told me I was most foolish to go to so much effort to get such pathetic, paltry things, and to set such store by them, when I left unused in my own house an inestimable treasure legitimately mine that would make me happier and richer than if I possessed all the goods of all the inhabitants.

"I allowed myself to be led by her along a little path that no one had noticed, although it was perfectly visible, into a garden that belonged to us. She ordered the man who was with her to dig, whereupon she showed me treasure which filled me with such delight that I woke up immediately.

"As I am not a melancholy person, I often have pleasant dreams that I remember when I wake up and which beguile me while I lie in bed. I was particularly happy with this one for reasons I won't go in to now, and as I still felt the effects of it—as one often does when a dream has stirred up one's emotions—I was even happier to keep going over it as it seemed to me to be connected with the subject of my meditations of the previous evening.

"After thinking about it for a while, I interpreted the merchandise as human opinions that come from a single source and are degraded as they pass from hand to hand. The last people to receive them are the simple and common people, who, through overweening foolishness, try to keep up with the scholars and even go so far as to condemn those they think are opposed to their views, making up their minds more decisively than those who have spent their whole lives in the contemplation of these things.

"The lady, strongly resembling the one you described a while ago, is Truth itself which is accessible to all men. Those who open up the path that leads to it are represented by the men who were doing the digging, and the treasure is the store of reason that we have within ourselves.

"As for the rest, I have to tell you that yesterday we received the visit of two men who are thought to be scholars because they have the right manner and wear the right robes. But they are scholars of the ilk that Stasimachus was mentioning. We talked of this and that and in particular of the conduct of certain persons about whom much ill was spoken. These gentlemen got completely carried away on the subject and were soon imitated, as usual, by everyone there. I was prevailed upon to say what I thought, and there was some surprise that I did not make the fiery response that my previous enthusiasm had led them to expect. I simply answered that if the people we were talking about were in error, then we should excuse them. My mother said acerbically that I seemed to have my doubts, to which I replied that I had no doubt that it was the custom to condemn people who behaved in this way.

"'But what about you?' asked one of the gentlemen severely. 'Do you not condemn them too?' 'I condemn them too, if you condemn them,' I replied, 'and I believe that they are wrong to flout custom like that.' 'There is more than custom involved,' replied the gentleman. 'The thing is wrong in itself,' and to persuade us, he cited the authority of five or six men whose views are in print. I told him that I could see from these proofs that people in the past had spoken like him, or rather that he spoke as people in the past had spoken, but that I was not convinced that that was necessarily the way to speak because I had not studied the question.

"Finally, after a long argument, I was obliged to tell him that I was sorry he had spent so much time and money learning how people had spoken in previous centuries, and that having seen very few books I knew as well as he did that that's how people spoke and acted, and if we really want to know what people are saying about something we have only to go from shop to shop and ask the shopkeepers or stand at the entrance of town squares and ask the opinion of everyone who comes along. In this way one could canvas more opinions in one day than in a whole lifetime in all the libraries in the world.

"The result of this was that the gentlemen cut short their visit and left with obvious signs that they were displeased that I had dared to reason in their presence. My mother, who realized what was going on, would have spoken to me severely if she had not feared making me lose the desire she thinks I have to take the veil, because she saw that I was more withdrawn than usual.

"This conversation reminded me of an argument the same people had had one day with a rival group who happened to be at our house. As the feelings between them aroused quite a lot of controversy, I had always imagined, as do all who make hasty judgments on various opinions, that theirs was very important, and I was delighted to have the opportunity to hear it discussed in detail.

"When the argument began, the adversaries seemed as opposed as they could be, one affirming vehemently what the other denied equally vehemently.

"As all those present, myself included, had been schooled in the opinions of the gowned scholars, we were at pains to applaud them, although we did not understand all they were saying any more than they did themselves, and although their antagonists, or adversaries, spoke reasonably and sensibly. I have thought it over subsequently. I even looked upon the antagonists as perverse people who were the sworn enemies of the truth, simply because I had heard them referred to as such, and because they are, indeed, seen as the enemies of our fantasies and our opinions. The harsh words they were exchanging confirmed me in this view.

"The more heated the discussion became, the more completely they seemed opposed. Finally, having gone over a lot of ground without discovering anything, they tried to arrive at a clear and precise explanation. I must confess that I was greatly surprised to discover that people I thought were as far from each other as heaven and earth were so close in their views that apart from a quibble over language they were the best friends imaginable.

"I forgot to mention that they argue with a completely different attitude and in a completely different way from us. We talk here in order to learn, we are prepared to change our minds if someone suggests better arguments than our own, and we use our reason exclusively, without worrying about what other people say. They, on the contrary, swear that they will die with the same opinions they have clung to from the cradle, whatever anybody says. Their sole purpose is to convince others, and their only resource is the authority of examples and books, with no reference to reason at all. The result is that the one who speaks loudest is victor, as if he were the cleverest.

"As they are less concerned with explaining their own thoughts than with explaining those of classical authors, you would have got the impression that the important thing in this big argument was not how to think reasonably about the subject under discussion but what was thought about it several centuries ago. What I found funny was that a contrary proof of one single author left them speechless. I came to the conclusion that popular science is a science of words that consists entirely in a way of speaking. When a yes and a no come into opposition in the discourse of professional practitioners, they believe that they are in opposition also in their minds. They can be opposed in sentiment without knowing it, as long as the opposition is not formalized in the sentences they use, just as they imagine they are opposed in their minds—although in fact they are not opposed at all—if their words carry some kind of opposition, real or imagined. More often than not, it is self-interest or passion that reconciles or divides them. They make it a point of honor not to retract what they have already asserted, especially in public, and throwing themselves into their studies only to confirm what they learned from nursemaids, parents, and masters, they provoke aversions and disputes, not because of the different ways they understand things, but from prejudice, custom, self-interest, example. In a word, there is reason to suspect that the greatest wars between them are a lot of hot air.

"We women, on the other hand, who have no insight into these arguments—either because there is none to be had or because we have not been given any or because we have been told that we don't have any—still let ourselves be persuaded that they are important. We become involved in them (the extent of our involvement depending on chance or enthusiasm), and are indeed as stirred up by them as the people who start them. We take on the emotions they inspire in us and often become the victim of the idol of the scholars who wax fat and wage war at our expense.

"Since we have such numerous and powerful reasons to distrust the imagination of others, since centuries and kingdoms are divided in their opinions, since in the same state those who are thought of as knowledgeable—philosophers, spiritual directors, casuists, doctors—are of such opposing views, since there are not only many different sects but even in the same sect the same opinion is diversified in as many ways as there are people to uphold them, since, in fact, in all areas there are as many opinions as heads and mouths, then I conclude that one would have to be an enemy of truth and devoid of reason not to use the latter to seek the former in a way that Stasimachus will advise me."

"Certainly your thoughts and your account will not discourage him," said Sophia. "But I would like to know how he interprets your dream."

"Although I don't believe in dreams," replied Stasimachus, "because I see them as the natural effects of our imagination, even so I still think that they are sometimes connected, not only with people's temperament, circumstances, and the countless details of their lives, but also with the future and its bearing on the past. That is why there is a close relationship between what we talked about in our earlier conversations and what is to be the topic of this one. I am not at all surprised that Eulalia dreamed about what is going to happen to her today."

"Am I going to find a treasure today?" asked Eulalia.

"Yes," he replied, "you are—one without which all others are useless or pernicious."

"Then it will be through your intervention," said Eulalia. "It comes back to me that you look like the person who was digging at the request of the beautiful lady."

"If that's the case," said Timander, "then I imagine that the beautiful lady is my cousin who invited Stasimachus and that her house is the place where the fortunate discovery is to take place."

"Sophia is such a rare and accomplished person, and she's so fond of me, that I could quite easily believe she came to me in a dream," said Eulalia.

"As far as the treasure is concerned," said Stasimachus, "it is everywhere Sophia is, but we can say that Eulalia too is a treasure and that she contains one within herself, as do all humans.

"This treasure is a portable library that we all have within us, containing only goodness and truth for those who have the key and know how to use it. It is the treasure of science and wisdom which consists in the knowledge of oneself."

Sophia realized that this conversation would be fairly long and absolutely crucial, so she ordered her servants to admit no one, and to make sure they would not be disturbed she led the company into the pavilion in the garden where they had spent the better part of the day on the previous occasion.

When everyone was seated, she said to Stasimachus: "Eulalia has satisfied you, or rather, you have satisfied yourselves on the three questions you put to her, and it is only fair that you should grant the request she has made of you."

"Since that is what you want," replied Stasimachus, "and since I have already started, let me tell you how I see Eulalia's situation at the moment. I see her as an opulent princess who has an immense treasure with a vast quantity of medals and coins. She takes out the ones of inferior alloy and tries to sort the others into matching groups.

"That is exactly what you should be doing," he said to Eulalia, "and what you are really asking me is how to put your thoughts in order. You should know that at your age you are not going to learn very much new, since you already have all the main elements of the sciences you are studying. You have the notion of a God upon whom theology is founded. You have the notion of yourselves, of your thoughts, words, and actions which are the object of metaphysics and physics, medicine, and grammar and eloquence. If you add to all that the information you have about civil society, you will find the basis of moral philosophy, jurisprudence, and history.

"Now in order to constitute a body of science, our thoughts should be disposed in a specific arrangement so that sciences can be distinguished from the usual mass of jumbled thoughts on a single object. But we have to remember that there is a necessary relationship and dependence between all the sciences, similar to those between the different parts of the human body. Understanding this relationship in order to guide the mind through the course of our studies is so crucial that all progress depends on it, and it is failure to observe this relationship that renders the popular method so defective and so sterile, making the knowledge that it leads to not only pointless but positively pernicious as a way of perfecting the mind and finding happiness in life.

"You will find it easy to understand this encyclopedia—that is to say the connections between the sciences—if you think that every time you have been on a mountain or in the middle of a plain and looked about you, it appeared that everything you could see in nature formed a kind of circle and hemisphere, the center of which was precisely the spot where you were standing."

"That has happened to me quite often," said Eulalia.

"Imagine that we do indeed have a similar relationship with every-thing that surrounds us," Stasimachus continued. "Everything forms different sized circles around us, the closer ones smaller and the farther ones larger. The actions of the objects upon us, therefore, are like lines going from the circumference to the center, and all our actions upon the objects are like other lines that leave from the center and make their way towards the circumference.

All sciences are included in that of ourselves.

"You must understand also that the objects will have made some impression upon us before we can think of understanding them and grasp their significance."

"That's obvious," interrupted Timander. "A deaf person could never imagine sound nor a person born blind light."

"So," Stasimachus went on, "this impression is like a signal that the things themselves give us, which draw us outside ourselves. What we are trying to achieve is perfect knowledge, which consists in knowing what it is outside ourselves that corresponds to what we see within us. But since we are unable to penetrate things through a real and interior presence, all we can hope to acquire through our research is to know whence come thoughts, images, and ideas and how they enter our minds, with the emotions that accompany them.

"You must be aware that no interaction between our mind and what surrounds us takes place without some involvement of our bod-ies. They are the like a ventriloquist that makes possible communica-tion between us and nature, the channel and the instrument of all our understanding and all our actions."

"That is obvious enough for there to be no difficulty," said Sophia.

"Think, further, that the role of the various sciences is to guide in different ways our thoughts and actions vis-à-vis the same objects," Stasimachus went on. "Logic, for example, which is the art of thinking, teaches us to guide our minds to understand any object whatsoever. Metaphysics indicates the general ideas we have of all manner of things, and physics indicates all specific ideas, considering things indepen-dently of the institutions of men. Theology (the science of religion), jurisprudence, and moral philosophy prescribe the use we should make of them according to divine and human laws. Finally, grammar and elo-quence give us precepts, the one to declare simply what we think of things and the other to declare the same in a more elaborate way in order to persuade.

We must begin our studies by understanding ourselves.

"Let's take as a basis what I have just suggested and see what conclusions follow for our purpose. Where should we begin our studies? Is it with moral philosophy, with eloquence, or with history? Obviously, these would be a bad beginning. Since all the sciences can be reduced to thinking, acting, and speaking well, there is no doubt that we should begin with the one that teaches us how to think, how to speak, and how to act, in other words, with the one that teaches us how to know ourselves."

"Indeed, it does seem as if that science includes all the others," said Sophia. "We can't know how we think if we don't first know what we are, and we can't know what we are until we know at the same time how we act, and how we ought to act."

"Stasimachus's view seems all the more valid in that it conforms entirely to the notion of the ancient philosophers who recommended to their disciples only that they study and know themselves," added Timander. "This is the origin of the famous maxim 'Know thyself' that was inscribed on the facade of the most famous temple in the world, that of Diana of Ephesus, as though they were trying to make it known through this inscription that mankind could ask for nothing more important."

"That maxim is still current and is still in everyone's mouth, since it is perfectly commonplace to say of those who err through presumption or laziness that they do not know themselves," said Eulalia. "Since the world is eternally subject to these faults, it seems to me that the precept intended to correct them will also be eternal. But what absolutely convinces me it is true, apart from the approval of the philosophers, is that I can't refuse to accept it. For if there is one thing we have to know it is ourselves, and it is clear that our knowledge is organized in such a way that if what is within us is closer to us, then that must take precedence over what is farther away."

What deters us from the study of ourselves.

"What ought to engage us in that knowledge, however, is what drives us away from it," Stasimachus went on. "As you know, we usually neglect the things we possess or think we possess, and we desperately try to get hold of what we don't possess, believing that it is better and superior."

"It's true," said Timander. "We imagine we know our own family and genealogy naturally, and we neglect them to study the genealogy of others. It's the same with history. We study the history of the an-

cients and of our neighbors, and we never think of our own. We are more curious about what is going on in distant provinces than what is going on where
we are."

"Often men leave their country to go off to the ends of the earth," added
Sophia, "and when they come back they are more foreign in their own country than foreigners who are visiting for the first time."

"Can't we find some reason for this aberration?" asked Eulalia.

"There are several," replied Stasimachus, "and I thought I had pointed
out the principal one when I spoke of the origin of our errors."

"I remember," said Timander. "You pointed out that the contact the mind
keeps with external things draws it so much outside itself that it has neither
the leisure nor the inclination to reenter itself, and its constant preoccupation with the same external things for the conservation of the body keeps it
bound to them, so that in its preoccupation it even forgets what it is."

"The difficulty about shutting ourselves up within ourselves," Stasimachus continued, "is that it requires us to withdraw into a solitude that
seems all the more terrifying since we only see and feel ourselves, speak of
ourselves and by ourselves. Our ideas are cold and lifeless, our hopes are not
aroused, and the soul does not experience the excitement and pleasure
brought by consideration of other things that are the objects of its passions."

"Couldn't we also say that example plays an important role, and that if
the men we live among and learn from speak and think about external things,
we are inclined to imitate them in this respect as in everything else?" asked
Eulalia.

"That's quite true," answered Stasimachus. "But my view is that one of the
most frequent causes of this distancing from ourselves is the conformity between ourselves and our peers. We think we know them because we know
their faces and their appearance, and we also imagine that we know ourselves
even better. Yet by one of those contradictions Eulalia was just talking about,
when we come down to the individual and speak of the necessity of knowing
oneself, then we protest that it's like moving mountains and that we will
never get to the end of it, that man is hidden from himself, that there are
countless hidden recesses of the heart he can never uncover; and by piling up
these and countless other figures of speech widespread among the people, we
create a monster which frightens us needlessly."[58]

58. Poullain rejects the seventeenth-century moralists' pessimistic views of self-knowledge and,
in particular, La Rochefoucauld's theory of amour-propre. See Marcelle Maistre Welch, *"De l'Education des dames pour la conduite de l'esprit dans les sciences et les moeurs (1674) ou le rêve cartésien de Poullain de la Barre,"* in *L'Education des Femmes en Europe et en Amérique du Nord de la Renaissance à 1848*, ed.
Guyonne Leduc (Paris, 1997), 142–43. See notes 18 and 86.

"Isn't there an element of prejudice in that?" asked Eulalia.

"Absolutely," replied Stasimachus. "We are prejudiced about nearly everything that exists, and most of all about ourselves. We are not only the authors of the prejudice but also its theater and its victims. As far as the things that touch us most closely are concerned, we immolate ourselves to our ghosts, so to speak. Considering all the weird and grotesque ideas we have about ourselves, we are merely chimeras, phantoms, and ghosts, attributing to ourselves characteristics we do not possess. We cut ourselves off from what is most basic to us and disfigure to such a hideous extent the marvelous creation we are that we become horrible in our own eyes and are afraid to look at ourselves. Although we are made in a certain way, and nature makes us realize that and protests constantly against our own imagination, we still try to be the way people tell us we are. If anyone asks us why we are saying that that's how we are, we simply reply that it's because such and such people have told us so."

"Which makes me think," said Sophia, "that there is a warning in this: it's simply not feasible that a man who knows other men and everything in nature should be incapable of knowing himself. As an undeniable proof that we can, we talk only about ourselves. Not only do we bring everything around to ourselves, taking ourselves to be the end and center of everything, but we are also the subject of all our conversations. We talk about the body and the soul, about sickness and health, about happiness and unhappiness, about virtue and vice, about temperaments, habits, pleasures, about what used to be done formerly and what is done at the moment and what will be done in the future. Now it seems to me that if we knew nothing about ourselves, we would not be able to talk about ourselves so continuously, and if we can say so much with the help of natural intuition, we should be able to say a lot more with the intuition of philosophy.

"But I believe," she added, "that we will be able to speak with greater certainty when Stasimachus has told us how he conceives that knowledge."

What self-knowledge consists in and how easy it is.

"We can be sure," said Stasimachus, "that we know ourselves sufficiently well to be guided, either in the sciences or in moral conduct, when we understand the nature and variety of the principles of which we are constituted: what are mind and body, what are their distinguishing and common features, whether they really make a whole or are really distinct, how they are joined together and what are the laws, effects, and results of that union.

"But as all the actions of the mind, limited though their number is, depend on the participation of the body, it is essential to understand the contribution of the latter. One does not need a precise knowledge of anatomy, nor of the number, appearance, situation, and use of the many parts of the body, and even less of all the variations to which they are susceptible. It is sufficient to have an overall idea of the constitution and the normal functions of the principal parts, for example the eyes, ears, nose, mouth, stomach, intestines, lungs, heart, veins, arteries, brain, nerves, and muscles.

"One should understand the mechanics of breathing, the digestion of food, and its transformation into blood; how blood is transformed into vital spirit, flesh, and bones, or rather, how the blood forms, changes, and mutates for nourishment, growth, generation, feeling, and movement; and what wakefulness, sleep, dream, sickness, health, life, death are.

"We should also understand how the external senses like sight, hearing, smell, taste, and touch are stimulated in us and the same for external feelings like hunger, thirst, natural appetites, and the passions. In a word, it is enough to know, in respect of the body, how it contributes to movement and feeling to maintain its union with the mind."

"It is most unlikely that this science which, according to you, includes all the others, should be compressed into so few things. It must be that those you have enumerated contain an infinity of others, which are very difficult to understand," said Timander.

"Pardon me," said Stasimachus, "if I say that your astonishment reminds me of a man who has not yet learned the alphabet, and who, when he looks at the quantity of words, books, and different languages in the world, cannot grasp that twenty-two or twenty-three characters are enough to produce such a prodigious variety. Furthermore, since the construction of words is arbitrary, one can know the letters of which they are composed without knowing either the words or the languages. But the fundamental ideas of the learning we are speaking of are not subject to men's whims, nor are other ideas based on them. A man who knows what I have just been pointing out may say, therefore, that although he does not understand all the details of our actions, he understands them sufficiently in the specific, and may judge everything that concerns us and see whether others are mistaken."

"What makes it easy for me to agree with you," said Sophia, "is that I remember that those who understand things best are the ones who speak least about them; they are succinct and decisive, and they are able to put more meaning in four words than others can in twenty."

"That's the case in all the sciences," Stasimachus went on, "where the clever people who go straight to the point take the shortest route, whereas those who don't know merely beat about the bush."

214 On the Education of Ladies

"You will notice in passing the origin of the long discourses and huge tomes whose number terrifies those who believe that reading them is necessary to become learned," said Timander.

"There are a few books that are absolutely necessary," replied Stasimachus, "but there are still more that are useless.[59] There would, however, be more if men could resolve to withdraw into themselves and use the key to the library they carry within themselves. This key is their reason, its principal use being to help us consider once and for all in our lives what we perceive and to admit nothing that is not clear and of which one does not have some idea."

"If you wanted to begin this study all over again or guide someone else who wants to start, how would you go about it?" asked Eulalia.

The program to be followed in studying oneself.

"I'll tell you," replied Stasimachus, "and you will see how easy it is to achieve. In my studies of the most important sciences, like theology and moral philosophy, I have noticed that the source of difficulty and error in areas that are not purely historic and factual derives from the fact that we do not understand how the mind is affected by things, how it perceives and interprets them, in a word, how it suffers and reacts. This ignorance stems mainly from the fact that we do not understand exactly how the body acts as its organ, whence it follows that we do not understand the use of speech, which is the channel of the sciences and the facilitator between minds, nor do we understand the use we can make of everything around us. To remedy this disadvantage, I would first take up the study of the human body as being the most obvious and the most simple."

"I would have thought, on the contrary," said Timander, "that it would be easier to begin with the study of the mind. For if it is easier for man to know himself and what immediately surrounds him than what is remote from him, by the same token it seems that the mind would know itself better than it would know the body."

"That's true," replied Stasimachus, "provided one can separate the mind from the body. But if we consider them as a single, interdependent entity—which will help us to extricate ourselves from the difficulty into which prejudice places us—I am convinced that knowledge of the body should precede that of the mind. Now to understand the structure of the body and of the organs, together with their functions, we simply have to observe them in a methodical and dispassionate way, accepting nothing but what the senses tell us, and supposing in

59. See below, the beginning pages of the "Fifth Conversation."

this as in all things pertaining to the body only the five principles of first understanding which are known to everybody, namely, matter or what is extended, shape, situation, movement, and rest of each part.

"There is only one thing in the human body that cannot be perceived by the senses, a subtle matter called animal spirits, which are highly mobile blood particles, and which, carried to the brain and from there transported to the muscles by the nerves, give feeling and movement to our bodies.[60]

"But we have no trouble understanding that there can exist matter of this kind, although it is not perceptible by the senses, if we accept that otherwise we cannot explain the movements it gives rise to, and also that bodies can be reduced by division to such extreme smallness that they become imperceptible to our senses, which, having a predetermined size, cannot be disturbed by all kinds of objects."

"We cannot doubt," said Eulalia, "that there exists something sufficiently small to make no impression upon us when we remember that if we look in the direction where the sun casts its rays we see specks of dust of different sizes, which otherwise we would never have believed could be scattered through the air when the weather is overcast."

"After considering the attributes of the human body, we pass on to the mind which, it seems to me, is easier to apprehend since the senses play no role. On the contrary, we have to shut our eyes and ears to anything that could distract us. If we do so, it is obvious that as we consult ourselves our mind can tell whether it actually is the body it has studied or whether it is distinct from it, and whether it is capable of something other than thought, namely, of getting understanding by various means, of defining itself according to its understanding, and of provoking the body to react in different ways.

"Without wishing to influence you in a matter you have to examine for yourself," he added, turning to Eulalia, "I have to tell you that every time I compare my mind with my body, it seems to me that there is nothing that happens within us that does not serve to demonstrate the distinction between them. Whether the mind apprehends something by means of the senses, or uses the body for some movement, it realizes that it is as different from them as from the external instruments it uses for the same ends, except that it uses the body directly and is inseparable from it, whereas it can separate itself from those other things, and it cannot activate them except by the intermediary of its own body."

---

60. Poullain is following Descartes, *Passions of the Soul*, par. 10 ("How the animal spirits are produced in the brain"), in *Phil. Essays*, 300–301, and following.

"I think you can add another reflection to these," said Timander. "It is this: we understand perfectly well how to use a pen, for example, to produce its effects; whereas we know simply that we use our bodies without knowing how it happens."

"We could add many reflections of this nature," replied Stasimachus, "to prove something I mention only in passing to give Eulalia the chance to think about it, because she has to take pains to investigate all these truths herself in order to experience the pleasure of possessing them completely.

"As far as the operations of the mind are concerned," he continued. "they are less numerous and simpler than those of the body, therefore easier to understand, because, since they can all take place with respect to almost all the objects that touch the mind, there is almost nothing that cannot serve to reveal them. To better achieve this discovery, it should be preceded by another, to which the constant experience of life leads us, namely, that the mind is indifferent to many kinds of thoughts and that it passes from one to the other as it determines. Thus when an object is apprehended through the intermediary of the senses that is called sensation; if it is perceived through the eyes we call it sight, if by the ears, hearing.

"When we picture to ourselves an object in the guise of a corporeal image—a lion, for example, or a palace—this is to imagine. When the object presents itself to the mind a second time and the mind realizes that it has already thought it, this is to remember. Judgment, which is the second operation of the mind presupposing the first, is an action by means of which we attribute to a thing what we recognize as relevant to it, or we separate from it what we recognize as not relevant to it. Reasoning is when we form a third judgment on the other two. Is all that so mysterious?"

"Not at all," replied Eulalia. "All we have to do, as you say, is to reflect on what we do in order to understand it. I can see perfectly well now that all I have to do is pay attention in order to know, for example, what it is to doubt, resolve, be hungry or thirsty, feel pain and pleasure. And all this convinces me of what you prove in the book on equality, that it is no more difficult to become a philosopher than a carpet-maker."

"When you really get down to your studies," Stasimachus went on, "you will see even more clearly. To return to the point, you believe, perhaps, that it is very difficult to understand how we feel. There is no difficulty in doing so, however, for those who have understood once and for all that the brain is related to other parts of the body through the nerves, which are like little strings running from the extremities to a specific point in the head where the impetus and impression they receive from objects are registered. But what you will scarcely believe is that, knowing how one of the senses works, that of sight, for example, you will pretty well know how the others work, since they all function in the same way; you will also know that any differences derive from the greater or lesser sensitivity, either of the organs or of the objects that strike them, bringing to them diversity of figures and movements. Since there are objects which make themselves known through several senses, we have the advantage, by knowing how we perceive them with our eyes, of being half way towards understanding how we perceive them through the other organs. As an indication of the simplicity of this study, it is enough to have examined one organ—that of sight, for example, which is the most extraordinary of them all—to assess the disposition of the others and their differences."

"Don't you find," asked Sophia, "that it is not so easy to understand the passions?"[61]

"I find the opposite," replied Stasimachus. "All we have to do is to observe, on the one hand, what our interest is in the objects that excite our passions and what is the basis of this interest, both on the part of the mind and of the body, and, on the other hand, what are the specific movements of each passion. This poses no difficulty for those who remember that the mind is attached to the body by such close ties that it is necessarily interested in everything associated with it, and that the body is like a machine made in such a way that it interacts with everything that surrounds it, so that most things can help or harm its well-being. One is brought quite naturally from this observation to the conclusion that the body must be capable, within and without, of different movements, either towards what is good for it or away from what is bad for it."

"Experience teaches us that," interrupted Eulalia.

"But," Stasimachus continued, "since all these movements depend on the heart, which is the mainspring of the machine, and on the blood, which maintains communication between all the parts of which is it composed, it is easy to recognize (provided one pays sufficient attention) what the movement of each of them should be in relationship to the interest we take in everything that affects us, and to notice the internal and external character of each passion of the soul."

"That is perfectly intelligible," said Sophia, "but you will allow that the bizarreness we observe in the effects of the passions has something incomprehensible about it."

61. Descartes, *Passions of the Soul*, par. 7 ("A brief explanation of the parts of the body and of some of its functions"), in *Phil. Essays*, 299.

"I couldn't agree more," replied Stasimachus, "that this is not comprehensible at the first attempt. But we can penetrate this mystery with a little reflection and method."

"We observe that our passions never exist by themselves but are always mixed, that the most powerful is the most evident, and that the mixture is the effect of the blending of the considerations that accompany the one that excites the dominant passion, so that the diverse and sometimes opposing passions that come together at the same time in the same person weaken or strengthen each other, and fighting or following each other, give rise within us to a myriad of thoughts, goals, concerns, movements, and different effects. This is why, once we have formed an idea of the simple passions like admiration, love and hate, sadness and joy, and desire, as well as some mixed or complex emotions, like hope and anger, then in order to understand the confusion and the intermingling, either in ourselves or in others, we have only to examine all the circumstances, like the time, place, object, disposition which precede them, the age, temperament, sex, condition, religion, and host of other considerations that make up our main thoughts. All of which demonstrates clearly that the science of ourselves is easier than we had imagined a while ago, and what should confirm us in this belief is that we carry within ourselves, or rather we actually *are* the book in which we must study this belief. What we should know, therefore, is not what is happening elsewhere in some remote provinces, but what is happening within ourselves hundreds of times a day, for there is not one of those occasions when the mind and the body do not perform almost all their communal and individual operations, which we can recognize without difficulty, this knowledge being really nothing but the history of what we feel."

"Even if it were more difficult than it appears to acquire this science," said Sophia, "it seems to me that it would be even less difficult to hold on to it. For apart from the fact that it is based on very simple principles not subject to change, which have the same beginning, duration, and end as ourselves, it seems to me that as all our actions are performed on the same principles, they can all serve to confirm what we learned first of all."

"As all these actions have a necessary connection and sequence," added Stasimachus, "we cannot think of one of them to get some understanding of it, without also thinking at the same time of all the others and their organs.

"Take, for example, the first action taken to preserve life, which is to give food its preliminary preparation to make it acceptable to the mouth, so that it can be changed into our substance. We can't think about it without also remembering at the same time all the animal functions. For the movement of the teeth and nearby parts depends on that of the muscles and nerves which are filled with the spirits that flow to them from the brain, where they were carried by an agitation that served to separate them from the grosser parts of the blood. It should be remembered at the same time that the blood is a warm, red liquid, that it circulates in the arteries and the veins, that it is composed of the subtlest and most delicate of the foods that have been digested in the stomach where they have descended after being prepared in the mouth. I won't mention the saliva whose function is to dissolve meats and to arouse the taste by means of the tongue, nor the solvent which is found in the stomach to process what we have swallowed, nor the movements and the functions of the places through which the food and the blood pass, each one dependent on all the others. As the same things apply to the actions of the mind as to those of the body, we can imagine whether whatever involves both of them is difficult to learn and remember."[62]

"There are many people," said Timander, "who would despise this science if it were made so simple for them, since most people judge the value of things according to the effort they put into them."

"If I had to speak to less discerning people," said Stasimachus, "I would have had to approach it differently. This knowledge, however, for all its simplicity, remains the most amazing and the most beautiful."

"You're piling one paradox on another," said Eulalia.

"Nonetheless," continued Stasimachus, "the fact remains that we contain within us miracles greatly surpassing what the common people prize most, miracles so astonishing and extraordinary that there remains nothing new to be discovered for those who have understood them to their full extent. Indeed, is it not a subject for wonderment that a creature who can possess the whole earth and hold sway not only over the other animals but over his peers, reproduces in the same way as trees and plants, and has as precarious and lowly a beginning as the meanest of beasts? That a tiny quantity of matter animated according to the laws of movement can be distributed in such a precise way and transformed so miraculously that out of it comes blood, veins, nerves, flesh, bones, a heart, a lung, a head, a stomach, arms and legs? In short, countless organs and parts to form the human body, capable of an even greater number of movements, functions, alterations and changes? That these parts, distanced from each other as they are, and diverse in their form and situation, should be so intimately bound up with each other

The science of ourselves is the most amazing.

62. By paraphrasing Descartes's physiology from *The Passions of the Soul* in easy prose, Poullain pursues the support by the salon society of "mondains," those unschooled in modern science either by choice or by neglect.

that they all contribute mutually to their preservation? That they all participate in the good or bad that befalls them? That they come together in one
single part, the brain, to receive movement, whereas the heart gives them
life? That they take their nourishment and their increase all at the same time?
That food having been transformed into blood by an amazing metamorphosis, this same blood is distributed everywhere and supplies to the bones,
flesh, feet, hands, and to all parts of the body as much as each needs, or to say
it more clearly, that the blood, through yet another metamorphosis, passes
into the substance of all our parts?"

"That alone," said Timander, "contains more marvels than there are in
the rest of nature. It is obvious that the beasts of the air, earth, or sea possess
nothing like the perfection we possess, at least not to the same degree, and
that there is less reason to marvel at the production of trees, fruits, stones, or
metals than at our own.

"We look with wonder at the streams that spring from the mountains,
the rivers that flow over the surface of the earth, and the ocean that girds the
globe. Yet these three things have nothing that can compare with the blood
that flows in our veins, either from the point of view of the way in which it
was formed or that of the changes it undergoes or that of the uses it is intended for."

"What, then, do you think is the nature of the heavenly bodies that shine
in the sky and the sun that illuminates us? Do you not place them above
man?" asked Eulalia.

"I do indeed," replied Stasimachus, "but only from the point of view of
their situation. Because they are basically nothing more than a mass of subtle,
agitated matter like the light of a torch, which does not deserve, as you will
realize one day, to be put on a par even with the eyes with which we see
them. If you allow, I shall give you a brief summary of my view of this: to
place a greater value on the earth, the sky, and the stars than on man, for
whom they were created, is to measure beauty and the excellence of things
by the pound and the yard."

"Is there not good reason," asked Sophia, "for us to be astonished at the
sight of a piece of magnet attracted towards or repelled by another magnet,
depending on which side is presented? Or that certain trees have a natural
antipathy for some trees and a sympathy for others? Or that a small fire can
consume so much matter which leaves only a few ashes?"

"I agree that all that should astonish us until we have had time to investigate the cause," replied Stasimachus. "What is much more astonishing, however, is that the sight of something of little consequence can set our whole
machine in motion and arouse our passions and concerns, and that without

any light or fire being visible in us we consume ourselves when there is no food and so little remains of the large quantities we consume."

"You haven't mentioned the connection or the interdependence between us and everything in the world," said Timander. "In order to subsist we need the harmony of the entire universe, the destruction of which would be followed by our own. The contest of the elements is necessary for maintaining life, the light of the sun for illumination, the air for breathing, the earth for support, water for moisturizing, fruits for nourishment, animals for various uses, man to be created and to flourish. It seems to me," he added, "that we cannot but marvel that although we are a mere atom in comparison with the vast expanses that surround us, yet the whole of nature can enter us through two apertures as small as the eyes and can be preserved in a capacity large enough, despite its tiny size, to contain hundreds of worlds if they existed."

"All these marvels," Stasimachus continued, "surprise me less than to see in one creature two substances as completely diverse as the mind and the body, joined, however, in an indissoluble bond that begins and ends with life itself. Their union is so perfect that it never fails and so complete that nothing happens to the body without the participation of the mind."

"What I find amazing in this union," said Sophia, "is that although the mind is enveloped by the body, so to speak, there is nothing that it cannot understand through its intermediary. Without having to be transported into the objects that strike it, it can make distinctions in the confusion that is presented to it, consider all their aspects, judge their size, movement, and all their qualities. It can rise to the heights the imagination can reach, descend to the depths of the abyss, penetrate even to the center of the earth. Without stirring it can go from one end of the earth to the other, recall the past, examine the present, and foretell the future."

"To crown both my wonderment and the miracles that are within us," continued Stasimachus, "is the fact that when the mind joins its thoughts to the impressions of the body it is as if a double world were created, one spiritual and ideal and the other gross and corporeal. The mind disposes of the universe as though it were master of it, extending and diminishing it, changing and restoring it at will. By some kind of omnipotence it forms new ones, and by some artifice that we would never be able to imagine if we did not see its results we use the air to communicate to each other everything we have in our minds."

"Since man is the finest thing in the world," said Sophia, "we do not need to rehearse his excellence and compare him with works of art, since art strives to imitate nature. Besides which, since art is one of the perquisites of

man, it is easy to see that it cannot make us sufficiently skillful to produce an effect whose beauty approaches what is specific to us."

"That is why," continued Stasimachus, "however we look at ourselves, whether we consider what we have received from nature, what
we are capable of, what can happen to us according to differences in
sex, temperament, age, exercises, and climate, we have to conclude
that we are right to say man is a world in miniature and that if he is a
small world in size he is a great one in marvels."

"I have to add my conclusion, too," said Eulalia. "The more you
speak of knowledge of ourselves, the more I am convinced that that
should be the first task of a mind that wishes to apprehend fine things."

Knowledge of
ourselves is the
most extensive
and most impor-
tant of all.

"You will be still more convinced when you realize that it is the
most important and the most extensive knowledge of all those we can
acquire. You have no doubt that the goal of all our actions is to make us
happy. Some try to find happiness through study, others through use
of their physical strength. But I myself hold that it is absolutely impossible to find pure and complete happiness unless we withdraw into ourselves to discover the principles and rules we should follow. As we
are conversing together," Stasimachus added, "not simply to entertain
each other or to kill time but to learn to use this knowledge in solid reflection and through reasonable and enlightened conduct, let us examine methodically what I have just suggested.

"To labor to become learned, according to what we have said in
our previous conversations, means to use reason to discover the truth
and to free oneself by this means and to safeguard oneself against prejudice and error.

"I confess that I do not see, not only how one can achieve this aim,
but how one can form a clear and distinct idea of *reason, truth, error,* and
prejudice if the study of ourselves does not furnish this idea. *Reason* is the
power of the mind to distinguish the true from the false, the good from
the bad. *Truth* is the shortest, surest, and most natural way to study
things. *Prejudice* and *error* are false and bad ways to study them. You know
that reason has always been persecuted, that there are some people
foolish enough to believe they do not possess any, and some people
tyrannical enough to want to take from others the reason they do have.
Each one claims to have truth on his side and accuses of error those
who do not think as he does. Who, then, will give us these four basic
ideas? How will we learn whether we possess reason, what it is, what its
limits and uses are? How shall we know what is the correct way of
studying things if we do not know what we are, how our minds are af-

fected by objects, how and in how many different ways it can apprehend them?

"To understand things," he went on, "is to have clear and distinct ideas of them. Is it possible to form these ideas except by distinguishing them one from the other, or to make this distinction without withdrawing into one-self?"

"Absolutely not," replied Eulalia. "The reason I believe that is so is that we are accustomed to say that in order to judge things correctly we have to consult ourselves and see what is in our minds."

"We have to go further," said Stasimachus. "The discernment I was speaking of should begin with ourselves, not only because in the order of our understanding the first rank is occupied by the understanding of ourselves (since that is the easiest), but also because without it the others would remain forever confused and obscure. You are not unaware that when several things that are related often occur together, it is easy to mistake one for the other. Hence most people confuse the soul with the body, both because of their proximity and because of the relationship between them, which means that one almost never acts without the other. This is why I have no doubt that the objects that assail the mind pell-mell are often confused, there even being some that could be confused with ourselves. Also, experience teaches us that the things to which we are attached by some particular interest never present themselves to the mind without awakening at the same time the emotions they have caused. Thus a baby is joyful every time its nurse presents her breast, and many people speak of gold, jewels, and other things of that kind as if they had intrinsic value, simply because they have not realized that their price is the effect of our will and often our whim; thus they transfer to things what exists only in their imagination."

"That makes me realize," interrupted Eulalia, "that having now the basic ideas of things, I should first sort out those which are mine, in the same way that if I were a wealthy princess, to use your analogy, and I had in my treasury several kinds of foreign coins mixed up with my own, I would want to sepa-rate them according to their stamp and their imprint, prudence dictating that I should begin with those which bore my own."

"The importance of proceeding thus," continued Stasimachus, "will seem even greater if you remember that we have already said we are only seeking to be certain of two things relating to objects: their existence and their essence. You remember also what we said in our third conversation, that the order we must observe to be intelligently certain of the existence of things demands that we should first be certain of what is within us. This is how it is with the essence or nature of things, which is nothing but the way in which

they exist. The essence of fire, for example, which we are trying to understand, consists in knowing the disposition of its parts which enable it to produce the effects of which we have the idea. Thus, the same method that
makes us certain a thing exists also assures us that it exists in such and such a
way and is of such and such a nature.

"In order to discern each thing correctly we must have clear and distinct
ideas of *being, substance, accident, mind, attribute, quality.*[63] Now as these ideas,
which are the first and the most general, are the purview of the mind, it is easier for the mind to conceive them by considering them in relation to itself,
just as it has an idea of a thing that exists."

"All that makes us realize," said Timander, "that in order to think correctly about any subject whatsoever, we first have to know how to think and
in how many ways we do think, which means understanding man's mind and
the body which is its organ. Indeed," he continued, "it now seems to me that
all the different philosophical sects have arisen as a result of their not having
followed Stasimachus's precepts, because it seems to me that their differences spring from their different beliefs about the way we understand things,
and their different attitudes depend on the way they see the mind and the
body. The ones who think that the two substances are in reality one and the
same talk quite differently from those who claim the contrary. Those who
believe that the mind has no ideas that it has not received from the senses
have different opinions from those who believe that the senses simply provide the occasion. Some are convinced that our concepts are merely words,
and their adversaries accuse them of not sufficiently studying man and of not
knowing the nature of speech. Finally, the Cartesians who follow a method
similar to that of Stasimachus speak of God, themselves, beasts, stars and
other things differently from the Peripatetics [Aristotelians], namely, the
philosophers of the Schools, who behave in a completely different way."

"So then," said Eulalia, "in order to judge these sects and to decide which
is the best—a decision which has to be made in very difficult circumstances—we have to know ourselves."

"That is necessary not only in philosophy but also in theology, areas not
purely historical or factual but in which reason plays a role, as in scholasticism, where everyone uses whichever philosophical principles he espouses,"
continued Stasimachus. "For example, can we judge of the corruption of nature if we do not know nature in ourselves, or rather, what we have from nature and what from education, example, and custom. Perhaps we could speak
with more authority about the different states of man, like the one we call the

---

63. See Descartes, *Principles of Philosophy,* pars. 54–61, in *Phil. Essays,* 245–47.

state of innocence, and that of pure nature, if we were better informed about the state into which we are born. Perhaps, too, in order to say something reasonable and clear about our future happiness, we should first concentrate on discovering what we are, how happy and how adaptable we can be, and how we can know God here below."

"So you believe that knowing ourselves helps us to know God?" asked Eulalia.

Knowledge of God is based on knowledge of ourselves.

"It helps wonderfully," replied Stasimachus, "to have rational assurance that God is a real, existing Being, and that His Being is thus. Indeed, if there is a piece of work in this world that makes us acknowledge an all-powerful hand, then it must be man, who, as you well know, embodies greater beauty and skill than everything we know. I cannot imagine that someone who is convinced of the distinction between the mind and the body, given their union, could refuse to acknowledge a superior cause which joined them together, since it is inconceivable that this union is the result either of the will of the soul or the disposition of the body or a chance encounter."

"Could we not follow your first principle and say that the reason for our existence is also the proof of the existence of God?" asked Sophia.

"Yes indeed," replied Stasimachus. "And that is the first reason I wanted to discuss. If we consider the ideas in our minds we can remove any doubts we may have about ourselves and come to the idea of a sovereign Being, which always occurs to a thoughtful man. We then have good reason to conclude that the infinite mind this idea represents does indeed exist.[64] And as we can only know God by contemplating His creation, we can easily understand that it is the creature which most resembles His essence that teaches us what we should know about Him."

"Indeed," interjected Timander, "what philosophers say about divine nature is based on what they know about the nature of the mind. For we can see that those who think the mind is simply a body more subtle than the others also believe that the Divinity is an extremely subtle and mobile body spread throughout all matter to give it motion. And those who believe, on the contrary, that our soul is incorporeal,

---

64. This "conclusion" is from the ontological argument for God's existence that Descartes develops in the third of his *Meditations*, in *Phil. Essays*, p. 118: "For although the idea of substance is in me by virtue of the fact that I am a substance, that fact is not sufficient to explain my having the idea of an infinite substance, since I am finite, unless the idea proceeded from some substance which really was infinite."

also claim that God is of the same nature. But both agree on judging God's behavior against themselves, subtracting what they think of as their imperfection."

"As nothing is more important than to know God," said Eulalia, "you make me even more eager to know myself so that I don't attribute to Him anything unworthy of Him."

"What should make you even more eager," Stasimachus went on, "is that you would be in a position to know an extremely important truth, either for your own satisfaction or for that of those people you plan to tell about it. This truth is that the Christian religion in its purest form bears the two internal precepts of a true religion: one teaches us a pure, spiritual cult worthy of the God we worship, and the other prescribes for our conduct the maxims that best conform to reason and to our need to live in society.

"This knowledge of yourself teaches you the value of material, perishable things so that you will not seek them with too much zeal. But by teaching you how they can contribute to holiness and perfection of the mind it will enable you to avoid the superstition into which unenlightened people fall so easily."

"I can already see," Eulalia said to Stasimachus, "that you were right when you said to Timander that science taught in the way you conceive it would be a gentle, easy exercise for ladies. With a basic first principle and moderate application, you have already led us a long way in a short time by offering us an infallible rule to assure us of the existence and the truth of all things, namely, to have clear and distinct ideas about them. That seems to me so obvious that I think I am ready to show through reason that there is a God, that we have a mind and a body, and that there are other bodies besides our own. I also believe that what proves these things exist proves also that they are different. For since we can conclude that they exist because we have an idea of them when we concentrate, we should also be able to conclude, by the same reasoning, that they exist differently, the idea of one being different from that of the other. It also seems to me," the young lady continued, "that since objects do not make an immediate impact on the mind, but strike the extremities first, order demands that we know the body in order to know how it serves as intermediary."

Knowledge of external things presupposes knowledge of ourselves.

"What Eulalia is saying seems absolutely right to me," said Sophia. "In my view, the body is to the mind as binoculars are to the eye. We can look through the binoculars, we can see that with one end objects seem nearer and with the other they seem farther away, but we will never make sense of these two effects until we understand how lenses are made. It's the same with the body. We can say, without knowing how it is constituted, that it is used to feel, the eyes to see, the other organs for their specific functions, but so long as we fail to understand its workings, I don't believe we can give a clear explanation of feeling in general, nor feeling in specific cases. What, for example, is sight, hearing, smell, or rather taste, color, odor."[65]

"Indeed," said Stasimachus, "since sensation of things rests on a perception, a signal received by the mind through an impression made on some part of the body, it serves no purpose to try to explain how an object has caused this perception if we do not understand the change in the body that precedes it."

"It appears," said Timander, "that what you are saying about sensation in general and external sensation in particular could also be applied to internal sensations like hunger, thirst, and passion; and I am no longer astonished that I have understood none of this up till now.

"I realize, furthermore," he added, "that without this knowledge it is impossible to explain clearly how we remember things, how we imagine them, how they come to our minds when we are asleep, and a thousand other things we carry on about."

"What I would like to know," said Sophia, "is why the philosophers want us to consider animals when they wish us to study ourselves."

How knowledge of animals can contribute to our knowledge of ourselves.

"Not all philosophers do that," replied Stasimachus, "and those who do have their usual reason for it. They have heard that that is the direction we should take. For us it doesn't matter whether we look to philosophers or animals; one teaches us as much as the other. If we want to look outside ourselves, then it seems to me that the most efficient thing to do is to speak to our peers whose actions have more in common with our own than those of dogs and cats. Besides, there is practically nothing that happens to animals that does not happen to people. All that we can say if we study animals both internally and externally is that they have a body similar to our own, capable of the same functions. But the examination of a human body will teach us at least as much about our own bodies."

"Those kinds of philosophers have recourse to animals in order to show that consciousness is necessary for the actions they perform," said Timander.

"We are better off to consult ourselves since we perform those actions as often as the animals and have performed them since birth,"

65. See Descartes, *Meditation*, VI, 133, and *Principles of Philosophy*, pars. 191–95, in *Phil. Essays*, 265–66.

Stasimachus continued. "Moreover, we have seen other men perform them, and we have talked many times to our peers about them, which we have never done with animals. Are we any better informed? In order to know whether the functions of the body require consciousness, we have to have examined ourselves and seen what role our mind plays."[66]

"The mind is so far from being the cause of most bodily and necessary actions," said Eulalia, "that not only does it not know how they take place nor how the body is made, but how they happen despite ourselves. We often experience pain and passion that we would be happy to do without."

"So far are animals from teaching us what we are talking about," said Stasimachus, "that the arguments of philosophers on the subject only help us to the extent that they make us think about what is happening within ourselves. This is so much the case that if we examine the question we are convinced by what we tell ourselves, and by telling it to others we encourage them to notice it in themselves."

"We're overlooking one thing," said Timander, "namely, that what proves knowledge of ourselves is the *most* necessary also shows that it is the *only* kind necessary, and that it encompasses all the others which are merely specific applications of the principles it offers us. Logic or the art of thinking, which consists of the reflections made by the mind in its search for the truth, and metaphysics, whose object is general ideas about the mind and the body, both presuppose this knowledge.

"Not only is man the finest object of physics, which is the science of nature, but he is also its premier object, since, as we have been saying, it is impossible to know the disposition of objects which are perceived by the body if we do not understand how the body is constituted to interpret this knowledge.

"As for medicine, it is easy to see that what we have noted about knowledge of ourselves is its basis. For apart from the fact that we cannot understand illnesses without understanding the motion and changes of the blood, we can have scientific knowledge of remedies only through their color, flavor, hardness or softness, which demands a perfect understanding of sensation.

"Thus the sciences which concern us as individuals, and which we need in solitude, are based on knowledge of ourselves. And there can be no doubt that the social sciences are also based on it."

Eulalia asked what is meant by the social sciences and Stasimachus answered: "They are the ones we need to sustain the society in which we live.

---

66. See Descartes, *Principles of Philosophy,* Preface, in *Phil. Essays,* 222ff.

You can well imagine that if we did not know how to communicate our thoughts, and if we had no rules for keeping the peace among us, society could not survive. We need, therefore, to know how to speak (which grammar can teach us) and to understand how to live well (the subject of moral philosophy), together with jurisprudence and politics. Now in order to speak and act well, we have to be able to think well."[67]

"You must be aware," said Eulalia, "that there are many people who speak well and live well without ever having studied."

"That's true," replied Stasimachus, "but there are few of them who know how to live and speak. There are two ways of living well and speaking well: either through luck and habit, which is the case for most people, or through knowledge and understanding, which is limited to very few. Having knowledge or understanding means being able to give an explanation for one's conduct, not through the rules of whim and custom, which are used as a pretext by everybody, but through the rules of good sense, which cannot be arrived at without study of the self."

Grammar is based on knowledge of ourselves.

"You mean that when we understand things well, we can speak well," interrupted Eulalia.

"What I mean first and foremost," replied Stasimachus, "is that in order to know a language competently, we should have compared our thoughts with our words or our way of thinking with our way of explaining our thoughts. Such comparison demands very specific reflection that most people are incapable of, which explains why there are so few people who know their own language and who read books with any profit."

"Since we will soon be studying the book on the origins of the French language, I won't ask you to elaborate on this right now," said Sophia.[68]

"I have no difficulty with the question of language," said Timander. "Since it is specific to man, man is almost always its subject, it is always addressed to him, and its aim is to influence his mind and to bend him in the direction it desires through its persuasion. In order that language can have intimate and certain information, it must have precise and complete knowledge of man. To be eloquent, therefore, we have to understand everything within a man: his passions and his interests, what

Eloquence is based upon knowledge of ourselves.

67. See Descartes, *Discourse*, V, in *Phil. Essays*, 72–73.
68. Poullain had already demonstrated his linguistic inclinations in *Les Rapports de la langue latine avec la françoise pour traduire élégamment et sans peine*, 1672; and would do so later in *Essai des remarques particulières sur la langue françoise pour la ville de Genève*, 1691.

he received from nature, what from society. We need to know what produces the variety of temperaments, examples, customs, and exercises,
and everything that makes men's minds as different as their faces."

"You're forgetting," said Stasimachus, "the item that is most important and least commented upon, because it is the least well understood,
namely, that we have to have complete understanding of the origin of
the prejudices and errors we are subject to, whether they are those of
nature or of society, age, sex, condition, usage or religion, those being
the elements that most frequently govern our conduct and also the
ones most likely to mobilize the common people. From all this, we can
say that the art of self-knowledge and that of persuasion are one and
the same, the former being the art of thinking and the latter that of
speaking. The former provides thought and the latter the trappings
that allow us to exhibit it."

*All of moral
philosophy is
based on self-
knowledge.*

"It seems to me," said Sophia, "that the art we are discussing could
also be called the art of living happily, since it is impossible, without
knowing what we are, to arrive at the state for which we are best fitted,
which is what Stasimachus calls happiness, or to achieve in an informed way the inner freedom which is the main component of our felicity."

"What prevents us from reaching that state," said Stasimachus,
"are our uncontrolled desires, which derive from our ignorance and our
poor education. For either we try only ineffectually to achieve a knowledge of truth because we do not understand how necessary it is to us
and how accessible it is, or we imagine that there are other things more
urgent for us to acquire and we seek them with greater zeal, without
considering that the possession of things like pleasure, honors, and
riches is not entirely up to us, and that a man does not acquire them
without harming others. And when he does possess them, he normally
makes bad use of them, because he does not understand their worth,
nor their relationship to ourselves.

*What
constitutes
virtue.*

"As virtue consists of the way we consider the good and bad that
befall us and of the way we should deal with them (by moderating our
desires), we should delve within ourselves to find maxims based on the
reasons that can further instill into us what religion teaches us, for the
world being full of prejudice and error is scarcely fit to illuminate us.

"If we are to consider moral philosophy from a different point of
view, then we should consult ourselves to get a solid understanding of
the three essential duties of life. The first is our obligation to the Author of all things, the second is what we owe ourselves, namely, what

the mind owes the body for its conservation and how it can use it for its own perfection, and the third indicates what we owe to each other, given that we must all contribute to our conservation for our mutual advantage."[69]

"Since the best part of life and moral philosophy is taken up with intercourse between people," said Sophia, "the art of conducting ourselves properly towards them presupposes, of necessity, the need to understand them for ourselves, because this intercourse is all the more successful if we can govern minds by means of the passions, knowledge of which is the most important aspect of our discussions."

"If individuals are unable to live together without knowing each other," said Timander, "then public figures who regulate the conduct of others are no less obligated in the same way. It seems to me that the talents which make people eloquent are the same ones that make them politicians, and that to govern men we also have to know them, if for nothing else than to persuade them."

"That's perfectly true," Stasimachus continued, "and concerns no less the jurists than the politicians and orators. I maintain that all of them, in order to be skilled in their profession, should not only have a thorough knowledge of men as individuals, according to their natural, physical state, but also in general, according to their civil and moral state. In short, after learning everything that concerns the first society, namely, the mind and the body, the nature of the two substances of which it is composed, the conditions and laws of their union, and what is capable of destroying it, they should learn everything about civil society."

"Can you believe," asked Eulalia, "that it is so essential to know ourselves in order to understand others and to learn whatever concerns the first society in order to understand what concerns the second?"

"Certainly," replied Stasimachus, "knowledge of ourselves has to precede that of others, since we can only judge others by what we feel ourselves, whether we speak of natural needs, of pleasure and pain, of virtue and vice. As you well know, true ideas of these things cannot come from the outside. To relieve you of any concerns you may have about these, I would urge you to consider that the philosophers all have their particular moral view, depending on the specific ideas they have about nature. Moral science is based on nature, inasmuch as it is a science consisting merely of the reflections we make on the natural state of things as opposed to what can be established by men. Now as behavior is usually governed by custom rather than reason, we have to go back to nature to rise above custom and usage to see what is good

69. This paragraph can be considered to be Poullain's personal and private code of ethics.

and what bad and in what circumstances and to what degree one should follow them. This return to nature is even more urgent for politicians, since civil
society has as its goal the conservation of the society of mind and body. Thus
it is of supreme importance to understand this society in order to know what
the Author of nature has put in us to pursue this conservation and how we
would react if, immediately after birth or having never lived in society, we
were inclined to form one better adapted to our conservation. It is, in my
view, absolutely impossible to conceive without prejudice what natural law,
civil law, and the law of people are, or the nature of authority, law, punishment, equity, and justice, or the duties of subjects and princes, superiors and
inferiors, or the reasonable duties of each person in his state and in the conditions in which he finds himself, if we do not see distinctly what has given
rise to all these things."

"What you say seems even more important to me," said Timander, "since it
was commented upon recently at a gathering of people skilled in all kinds of
domains—philosophers, theologians, canonists, politicians, and lawyers—
who were all divided over a question of great consequence. After a lot of discussion back and forth, a man of good sense pointed out that they were all in a
state of prejudice, some confusing nature with custom, others giving too much
weight to the authority of custom and law, others sticking too closely to the
letter. Those sticking too closely to the letter, he said, did not understand the
meaning of equity, while those giving too much credence to custom and law
were ignorant of the natural use of chastisement and punishment. The same
man pointed out, on the subject of the conversation, the necessity of knowing
what would make men unite in the way they do today, and the reasons on
which they would establish the order that would be necessary to them."

"To sum up," concluded Stasimachus, "it is only knowledge of ourselves
that can rescue us from a basic error which has reigned throughout the whole
earth since the beginning of the world and is found in the sciences as well as
in society, namely, to judge what ought to be done by what was done formerly or by what is being done right now, instead of judging everything with
our own intelligence, which shows us what we should do."

"Oh, there's my dream come true," exclaimed Eulalia, "and I am indebted
to Stasimachus for having found a treasure infinitely more valuable than the
one I dreamed of last night."

"Don't flatter yourself that you made this discovery alone," said Timander. "Sophia and I have a share in it too. But we are indebted to you, for it is
because of you that Stasimachus has shown us that we are richer than we
imagine. These riches are not in danger from rust or thieves, they cannot be
taken from us except by the taking of our lives, and they are of such a nature

that all the efforts of anyone who tried to strip us of them would serve only to secure our possession of them."

"Try to make the most of your gifts," said Sophia to Timander. "Do you realize," she went on, speaking to Stasimachus, "that everything you have just said about the need to know oneself confirms my faith in what you said previously. For since the road that you point out is the first and only one we need take, and since so few savants follow it, we should be all the more suspicious of their kind and should take the strange habits of speech and behavior displayed by them as an obvious sign of their delusion. And that's not all. Even if they were all on the right path, which we can't know unless we are in their company, it is pointless to take them as guides in the belief that they know the path. Sooner or later we have to abandon them to retreat into ourselves. Indeed, what they teach us cannot but encourage us to withdraw into this state."

"It also seems to me," said Eulalia, "that I am still more completely convinced of what Stasimachus claimed the other day, that the truth is revealed no less to a single person than to thousands and that those who claim that women are less apt for this than men don't know what they themselves are capable of, since we all have the same principles and therefore we know things in the same way. What finally determines me to study is that it seems that the sciences are absolutely necessary, whatever kind of life one takes up, since it is impossible otherwise to think and speak and live well, or, in a word, to achieve happiness or true virtue."

"Following your principles," Sophia asked Stasimachus, "could we not say that the human mind, considered in isolation, is universal and capable of all kinds of knowledge?"

The human mind is universal.

"We could indeed say so," replied Stasimachus, "and it is all the more true that the human mind, considered in isolation, has these qualities since it has them in the same way in its union with the body. For the knowledge we are speaking of is universal knowledge, so that anyone who possesses it could be said to have universal intelligence. Not only does it have general notions which can be adapted to everything we can imagine, such as being, substance, accident, body, mind, figure, rest, and movement, etc., but there are also ideas that are specific to all the sciences. This universality makes me think that, as there are fewer differences between the sciences than we usually imagine, there is no need to create such a wide discrepancy between men as far as their minds are concerned and to understand how one is better adapted for one science than the others."

"There are some, however," said Timander, "which demand better memory than others."

"That's true," replied Stasimachus, "but they all demand an equal amount of penetration and judgment. Apart from the fact that the mind should follow the same procedures for discovering the truth in all these instances, they are merely different ways of getting to the same goal, since, as we have already said, they are no more than different methods of understanding the same object. It is also certain that we are not skilled in one science alone, not so much because of the similarity that exists between their principles but because of the connections between the objects they study. To be truly learned, one has to understand the harmony of natural law as well as of divine and human law, which can only take place within ourselves. This universal knowledge can rightly be called the point of view of everything, either because we observe what is above us, like God, or what is beside us, like other men, or what is below us, like purely corporeal creatures."

In what way the mind is limited.

"You know," said Eulalia, "that people usually say that the human mind is limited, which hardly sits well with the universal quality that you attribute to it."

"One doesn't preclude the other," replied Stasimachus, "provided we know how to handle them. The one certain thing is that our mind is limited by the brevity of life, which does not give us time to examine the infinite number of things, manners, circumstances, and incidents that exist in nature and in society. It is also limited by the constant requirement we have of satisfying the needs of our lives, which takes up our best moments and too often intrudes on the attention we should be devoting to the complete understanding of something. What limits us even further is the prejudice that grips us, sapping and smothering our strength and inhibiting its growth."

"I believe," said Timander, "that what makes us so limited in our knowledge is the way it is acquired and stored. Our mind is so taken up with matter and so dependent on our body that it cannot understand anything much without its intervention. Now as there are many situations where the body cannot be present, it is almost impossible for the mind to know what they are. Thus, although we can have a notion of all things, we cannot always conserve them, since the impressions of the bodies to which the notions are attached are erased imperceptibly through the alterations and frequent weaknesses from which the body cannot protect us."

"Some other thoughts come to my mind," said Stasimachus, "about the science of ourselves. Not only is it the basis of all the others, it is also the norm used to separate the good from the bad and to distinguish the useful from the useless—the soundly based from the vain and pernicious—in each particular. There are some people who believe that men are governed by the stars and that their influence produces diverse inclinations, temperaments, and revolutions in this world. Others treat this view as an aberration. How do we decide between two such contrary opinions without a perfect knowledge of men and their behavior, such that it enables us to perceive how this relates to what happens to them? How do we know whether dreams contain mysteries and whether we can reasonably see in them omens for the future, when we have no idea how they are formed during sleep?

The science of ourselves is the rule for all other sciences.

"We can say the same for divinatory and conjectural sciences like geomancy, necromancy, augury, and ancient haruspices,[70] which we cannot judge accurately unless we understand the link between us and the external things which are the object of these sciences.

"There are countless things we attribute to magicians and sorcerers which the common people think can happen through words. It is obvious that if we are to speak of them with any certainty, we have to know not only what impressions we are susceptible to and how they occur naturally but also what constitutes speech and what it is capable of.

"There are many popular opinions and prejudices that the scholars themselves fall headlong into because they do not understand our inner disposition, nor how external objects are perceived by the mind through the intermediary of the body, nor what is the natural order and progress of our affairs in civil society. Thus simple-minded people often attribute to God's very specific providence hundreds of fortunate or unfortunate events that in fact occur because of a general order that God has established in the world. Many people see the Devil everywhere and imagine, for example, that an encounter with a woman is a trap he has set for them and that the arousal and thoughts the en-

---

70. Geomancy is the art of divination through the interpretation of designs created at random by throwing a handful of dirt or stones on a flat surface. Necromancy is the occult science that claims to communicate with the dead in an effort to learn about future events. Augury is the skill to interpret omens from natural elements such as lightning and thunder, or to foretell significant events from the flight and songs of birds. Haruspices were in Ancient Rome prophetic observations derived from examining the entrails of animals. Rationalists such as Pierre Bayle and Bernard de Fontenelle attacked such superstitions at the end of the seventeenth century. See Hazard, *The European Mind*, 155–79.

counter stirs up in their sick imaginations is an illusion he has created. They also imagine this scenario as though there were within men and women reciprocal Devils who consort together in order to lure them into their snares.

"Nothing is more commonplace than to attribute to grace things that are caused by nature, since we do not understand the extent of nature's sway. How many people are there who imagine that they are Heaven's darlings and have been blessed by particular favor. They may, for example, have abstained for a few days from behavior they condemn in others out of helplessness or out of human considerations they are unable to perceive, or they may, after intense examination of their past life, feel depressed and discouraged as one usually does after deep reflection about earthly things, or they may have chanced upon a moving speech at a moment when their passions were appeased after satisfaction and subsequently spent a few weeks without feeling any emotional impact.

"Thus we can conclude that so long as we do not know what we are, we do not know anything, and that we will know everything when we know ourselves."

FIFTH CONVERSATION

After talking about self-knowledge for a while, they came upon one or two difficulties which were easily solved, since they arose not from the sciences themselves but from the way they are usually taught, whereas they were actually talking about the way they should be taught. After that, Eulalia declared that she wanted to have the books that would help her acquire the knowledge they had been talking about and asked in what order they should be read.

Books one should have.   "It would be a good idea to start with geometry," said Stasimachus, "not to make a prolonged study of it, but rather to sharpen your wits on it, since the figures and proportions it deals with are not things that you can have any prejudices about. It is therefore quite natural to look at them for themselves, for in doing so you get into the habit of divorcing yourself from human authority as you seek the truth.

"Besides, geometers make a particular profession of admitting nothing but what is true, and of using a most natural method in order to do so. A careful reading of their works, therefore, can contribute significantly to the formation of a clear idea of the truth and to the acquisition of the geometric mind, which is fair, exact, and methodical—and much admired by clever people. You can take as your model the works of Henrion.[71]

"If the book about the basics of the French language that Sophia was talking about were in print, it would certainly be the book to start with to understand the true principles of grammar with the meaning of almost every French word in use. In the meantime, you can use the *Methodical Grammar*.[72] Then you can go on to:

"*The Logic of Port Royal*.[73]

"*The Method* and *The Meditations* of Descartes.

"*The Discourses on the Distinction and the Union of the Soul and the Body* of Monsieur de Cordemoy.[74]

"The fourth part of *The Physics* of Monsieur Rohaut which deals with the animated body.[75]

"*The Discourse on Man* of Descartes, together with the Remarks of de la Forge.

"*The Treatise on the Mind of Man* by the same de la Forge.[76]

"*The Treatise on the Passions* by Descartes, and it would be a good idea to add Monsieur de la Chambre's treatise." It's a well-written work in which there are some wonderful things about the details of the internal and external nature of the passions.

"After that you can read the first three parts of *The Physics* by Monsieur Rohaut.

"If you wish to read Descartes' principles and the first volume of his letters to the Queen of Sweden and to the Princess of Bohemia, that's even bet-

71. Denis Henrion, mathematician (d. 1640), translated Euclid, *Les Quinze Livres des éléments d'Euclid*, 1632.

72. Antoine Arnauld (1612–94), known as the "Grand Arnauld," Jansenist theologian, published the *Grammaire générale et raisonnée* (1660), so-called *de Port-Royal* in collaboration with the grammarian Claude Lancelot (1615–95).

73. Published in 1662 by Antoine Arnauld and the Jansenist moralist Pierre Nicole (1625–95).

74. Géraud de Cordemoy (1626–84) historian and philosopher, published *Le Discernement du corps et de l'âme en six discours, pour servir à l'éclaircissment de la physique* in 1668, 2d ed. 1671.

75. Jacques Rohault (1620–75), physicist and mathematician, wrote *Traité de physique*, 1671 (which remained a classic through the eighteenth century). With Sylvain Régis, he "expounded Descartes's system with the main emphasis on the mechanistic account of nature. In their case, the Cartesian doctrine tended to link up with the philosophy of experience" (Adam, *Grandeur and Illusion*, 131–32). Rohault's lectures drew large crowds of salonnières and mondains, who became acquainted with scientific experiments, such as the rainbow's and the magnet's natures. See Gustave Reynier, *La Femme au XVIIe siècle: Ses ennemis et ses défenseurs* (Paris, 1933), 162–63.

76. Louis de La Forge, or Delaforge, physician, wrote *Traité de l'esprit de l'homme, de ses facultez et fonctions, et de son union avec le corps, suivant le principe de René Descartes*, 1666.

77. Cureau de la Chambre (1594–1669) wrote *Les Charactères des passions*, 5 vols., 1640–62.

ter. You will realize from these letters that he didn't consider women incapable of the highest sciences.[78]

"I haven't mentioned history and theology books, because those are subjects that require explication. I would simply say that since theology is basically founded on the New Testament, it is never too soon to start reading that in the proper frame of mind. It has been translated by several authors, the choice of which I leave up to you.

"There is too much to say about the authors and the way to read them intelligently for me to talk about it today. Apart from the fact that everything I would tell you about them is founded on the enlightenment that philosophy can give us, it would be as pointless of me to talk about them as it would be for you to read them without having made the all-important study of yourselves on which everything else depends.

"In order to make your studies more useful and to add to the pleasure brought by the reading of a large number of books, get into the habit of relating to your reading everything that comes into your mind. As all books of reasoning should be based on experience, you can best acquire this intelligently and efficiently—more so than many people will have done after years and years of labor—by trying to let nothing happen in yourselves or in those around you without making some reflection upon it. Observe everything, look at everything, and listen to everything without scruple. Examine everything, judge everything, reason about everything—about what has been done, what is being done, and what you foresee will be done. But in all cases, don't let yourself be influenced by mere words nor by hearsay. You possess the power of reasoning: use it, and don't sacrifice it blindly to anyone. You know very well how many people restrict the jurisdiction of common sense and claim that there are many things not part of its domain; examine carefully whether it's not popular opinion that imposes such strict limits.

"It is a maxim of good sense, and acknowledged by all learned people, that it is a proof of ignorance to have recourse to the first cause and to extraordinary and supernatural means when second causes and ordinary means will do. If you take the trouble to examine things closely, you will find that it's the learned who are the most likely to offend against this maxim and to invent mysteries for want of a proper understanding of Nature.

"Apply yourselves first to discovering the cause and source of popular

78. Princess Elizabeth of Bohemia (1618–80) became one of Descartes's principal correspondents in the 1640s. He dedicated both the *Principles of Philosophy* and *Passions of the Soul* to her. His *Letters* (containing also his correspondence with Christina of Sweden) were published in three volumes, in 1657, 1659, and 1667. The first volume addressed questions of moral philosophy. See Alcover, *Poullain*, 135.

prejudices by seeking within yourselves the way they entered your minds. All men without exception are susceptible to prejudice during their childhood, so try and find out what maintains, fortifies, and increases these prejudices, taking into account age, sex, condition, interests, education, custom, and religion.[79]

"Remember that chance plays a greater role in our happiness and instruction than care and prudence, and it is no more up to us to encounter good masters and good books than it is to have all the thoughts necessary to become thoroughly learned. They come into the mind when we least think about them. This is why you should be attentive and circumspect to let nothing escape you that can serve for your instruction. It just takes one well grounded, relevant, sustained thought to lead you well on your way, and don't be afraid you will go astray as you advance.

"Be careful of one thing: you will often find stopping places on your road. You will believe that they are eternal verities, when, in fact, they are perhaps major errors and prejudices. Think them over carefully.

"I should warn you that the way to not learn at all or to learn badly the most important things is to be put off by the masses of small thoughts that frighten the simple-minded who look upon them with terror as subjects of temptation. They are often no more than little ghouls and ghosts.

"The best way to get rid of them is to meet them head-on, to stare them down, and to not let on that you are intimidated by them. After all, we can't remain children forever, afraid of our shadows or of big, bad wolves.

"Whatever thought enters your mind, have no fear; stop it at the door without dismissing it. If it's a friend it will be of use to you; if it's an enemy, you will have to look at it in order to know it. Since your peace of mind and your happiness depend on it, don't be influenced by any except reliable people in this matter, because things that would not be good for those with depraved tastes will be excellent for you if you have a discerning taste. And rest assured that a little reading with a lot of experience will bring you in a short time to the highest point of human wisdom."

"That's right," said Timander. "Another thing is to observe men in their natural state, and not to limit yourself to looking at them from the perspective of a library. Familiarity with the world must finish off what good books have begun, and one is much better informed when one sees things enlarged on the world stage than when one sees them in miniature in a book.[80] Given men's outlandish behavior—and Eulalia gave us an illustration of it in her

79. See Descartes, *Principles of Philosophy*, par. 71, in *Phil. Essays*, 251.
80. Descartes, *Discourses*, I, in *Phil. Essays*, 50.

story a while ago—which comes out in the way they speak and act, and the way they criticize what they personally dislike and praise what they like, someone with a crafty mind could take it into his head, without ever setting foot outside his own country, to make as weighty and convincing pronouncements about the diversity of humors, customs, opinions, and religions of all the peoples of the world as if he had traveled round the entire globe."

"My view," said Eulalia, "is that the way to become a visionary and a misanthrope[81] and to let authors go to one's head is to have them constantly in one's hands and to shut oneself up in one's study. The reason why certain people want the earth to become a cloister and a place of solitude and for men to become like bears in their behavior towards each other and like torturers towards themselves is perhaps because they have blanched at various works or over the story of a wounded melancholic, whose headache they have caught, and have built themselves castles in Spain where they want us all to live with them."

"Whatever we say about moral science," said Stasimachus, "which, in my view, is the most important of all the sciences, should also be extended to the others, and in particular to physics. We have to observe and listen to nature in order to understand it properly. In short, in all subjects, we should do little reading—though good reading—and a lot of experiments, reflections, and reasoning."

"It's not the quantity of books but their quality that makes one accomplished," said Sophia, "and I have always heard it said that a man who has only one book, but is really committed to it, is more redoubtable than if he had several, to which he was equally attached."

"There is no doubt that that's the case with basic and standard books, like the ones I have pointed out to Eulalia," said Stasimachus. "It is better to read them ten times in order to master them than to skim through thirty others. One should also concentrate on them more than on superficial ones, and one should not be put off if one encounters a few difficulties that give one pause. For apart from the subjects dealt with in them which are completely different from normal topics of conversation and sometimes even the opposite of usual opinions, some people find it difficult to get into a book straight away. It can also happen that some of the things in a book presuppose knowledge of another. The first reading of a book, therefore, should make clear the plan and the general idea, the second should indicate the detail, and the third should make clearer to us what is good and what bad about it, what useful and what useless, and the connection between the principles and the specific consequences that derive from them."

81. In a marginal note, Poullain defines misanthrope as "an enemy of humans."

"It seems to me," said Timander, "that it wouldn't be a bad idea, when we study such books, to distinguish between what is important and what is less so, because although it's a good thing to study and understand everything, it still seems to me that there are some things that could be called minor, either because they are little discussed and have little currency, or because they don't lead to great truths, and therefore it matters little whether they are one way or another."

"What you say is a fact," Stasimachus replied. "For example, although the rainbow is one of the most amazing natural phenomena, nevertheless, because it is very difficult to understand thanks to a large number of features that have to be observed, and because the time one would have to devote to it would be better employed at something leading to knowledge of ourselves, I wouldn't advise Eulalia to make a long study of it at first. I would advise, rather, that one should make an effort to understand oneself and to examine whatever is relevant to oneself.

"Don't insist upon understanding a book at first," he said to Eulalia, "and do not give up on it until you have understood it. You should read attentively and thoughtfully once or twice the ones I have indicated and in the order in which I have mentioned them. Then afterwards you can study them in any way you like. It might also be a good idea to glance at Justinian's *Institutes* to understand the principles of the law. They have been translated into French and Monsieur de Pelisson has paraphrased part of them.[82]

"As far as eloquence is concerned, it consists in thinking and speaking properly. Philosophy, experience, and usage contribute to both, and books on rhetoric, such as they are at the moment, are not of much use. However, if you want to know what it is, you can read the *Rhetoric* of Aristotle or the *Orator* of Cicero or Quintilian; we have them in French.

"As far as politics is concerned, this consists in knowing not only the specific interests of those who govern but also what should be the attitudes of all those who form a society, superiors as well as inferiors. It isn't such a difficult science, since it is founded on what ought to be our notion of the equality of men according to nature and upon the obligation they have to work to safeguard each other through mutual assistance.

"If you want to know something about popular philosophy and to find

82. Justinian, eastern Roman emperor, 527–65, codified Roman law in three parts: The *Codex* was a codification of all imperial constitutions from the emperor Hadrian (117–38) to the present and was promulgated in 529; the *Digest* (or *Pandects* or *Institutions*), opinions of classical jurists (particularly Ulpian and Paulus), was published in 533; and the *Novels*, covering legislation during the century preceding Justinian, was compiled during the same period. These three compilations together make up the *Corpus Juris civilis* (*Corpus of Roman Law*) associated with Justinian's name. Paul Pellisson (1624–93), historiographer of Louis XIV, published a French paraphrase of Justinian's *Corpus Juris civilis* in 1653.

242 On the Education of Ladies

titles that will make you think, after you have read the works of Descartes you can try those of Monsieur de l'Esclache.[83] They seem to be a summary of the philosophy of Monsieur Gassendi."[84]

"Since you want us to be able to justify our behavior," said Eulalia, "please tell me what I should answer if someone asks me why I prefer the Cartesian to other philosophies."

"I am proposing it," replied Stasimachus, "because I am trying to spare you the time and effort necessary to learn Latin and Greek, which you need in order to study Aristotle, Plato, or Epicurus. I thought, therefore, that I should suggest a French philosopher. Now among those we have, I can't think of a better one than Descartes. And to prove that it's not merely because I am partisan that I regard him more highly than the others, I should tell you that his work has all the qualities and conditions you could expect in a sound philosophy. You remember that in our conversations we have seen that the greatest enemy of truth is prejudice and that we must rid ourselves of it to be happy and learned. We have also seen that almost all of us have enough reason and good sense to seek the truth, that we have to begin our search within ourselves, and that we consider that we have found it if, when we consider things carefully, we have formed clear and distinct ideas about them. From all this we should conclude that the best philosophy is the one whose methods and principles conform most closely to these maxims. I know of no one who does so better than Descartes. None has better discussed prejudice nor countered it more convincingly. His philosophy presupposes common sense and enough reason in the majority of men to lead their lives; it gives clear and distinct ideas of truth, reason, the mind, and the body; and instead of simply wishing, as did the Ancients, for the consummate understanding, which we have been discussing, Descartes undertook to discover it, and achieved this with such outstanding success that the only task he seems to have left his successors is that of studying him. What is particularly impressive in the execution of such a grand project is that it was conducted with those few principles I enumerated when we were discussing how easy it is to know ourselves. If this is so," he continued, "you can well imagine that I would want to sing endless praises to our philosopher to justify your choice

83. Louis de Lesclache, *Abrégé de la philosophie en tables*, 1652, and *Première Partie de philosophie*, 9 vols., 1656–66.

84. Abbot Pierre Gassendi (1592–1655) was a philosopher and an astronomer who opposed Descartes's mechanistic philosophy in favor of Epicurus's atomist doctrine. In fact, the first part of *Abrégé de la philosohphie de Monsieur Gassendi* appeared in 1675, but it was only a French translation of Gassendi's lectures, first published in 1658, *Syntagma Philosophicum*. Alcover, *Poullain*, 135 n. 10, concludes that Poullain was ill informed on Gassendi's work.

and mine, and to prove that I was right not to recommend any of the scholastics, inasmuch as those of them that I have read no more speak of error and self-knowledge than if the words were not yet in use and what they signify were not among the things that enter the human mind.

"But please note that I am not claiming Descartes is infallible or that everything he proposed is true and unproblematic, or that one has to follow him blindly, or that others couldn't find something as good or even better than he has left us. All I am saying is that I believe him to be one of the most reasonable philosophers we have, whose method is the most universal and the most natural, the one that most closely conforms to good sense and the nature of the human mind, and the one most likely to distinguish the true from the false even in the works of the one who is their author."

"I gather," said Timander, "that you studied scholastic philosophy and that you still know it."

"It was the first philosophy I studied," replied Stasimachus, "but as it has already been seven or eight years since I read it and as it takes as much time and effort to retain it as to learn it, I don't know it as well now as I used to."

"Have you ever been asked to justify giving it up?" asked Eulalia.

"It happens all too often," replied Stasimachus.

"And what is your answer when you are asked the reason?" persisted Eulalia.

"I tell some people that it wasn't I who left the philosophy of the Schools but the philosophy that left me, because I stopped cultivating her, because she is a coquettish bluestocking that cannot be kept unless she is constantly pampered. As for others, they are usually quarrelsome people who are trying to pick a fight. Instead of giving them a straight answer, I ask the same question they asked me, to tell me why they first studied Aristotle rather than Epicurus in their school books."

"That's a great way to embarrass people," said Timander. "I, at least, who have studied that stuff, would be terrifically embarrassed if you asked me why I took up the scholastic position. I would be afraid of lying if I replied that it was due to discernment, because I had no more discernment than others when I took it up. I went to the Schools because I was sent there, and because I saw my peers going there. I followed the opinions they attributed to Aristotle because our masters, who called themselves disciples of his, presented them as the most reasonable of all. They taught us to look upon Epicurus and Descartes, whose very names they were ignorant of, as the mortal enemies of the general under whose banners they had conscripted us. I can tell you quite honestly that if I had fallen into the hands of masters who had a completely different position, I would have gone along with it like the others, and I would have looked upon the Peripatetics as godless riffraff if I had been told to."

"That's in part the answer I give to certain people," said Stasimachus, "and I add that if I had given up their doctrine for the same reason that I had taken it up, and if I now stick to Descartes's doctrine for the same reason that makes them stick to theirs, namely, caprice and habit, then they would have no right to scold me nor to condemn my conduct, which would be as reasonable as theirs."

"But," objected Timander, "haven't those gentlemen ever pointed out that all the universities in France are Peripatetic, and that the Cartesians are in such bad odor that people won't even listen to them?"

"As it is the most convincing proof that they have of the rightness of their opinions, they never fail to point it out. My answer to them is that not only are there large numbers of people of worth and intellect around today who are quite as good as the Peripatetics and who hold Descartes's views, but there are whole universities in England, Holland, and Poland from which Aristotle has been ousted in favor of Descartes. The stranglehold of the former in our universities is simply a sign that he has more partisans there because he is the older and the stronger, and the latter is not allowed in because he is weaker and younger."

"I seem to have heard somewhere," interjected Sophia, "that Aristotle's philosophy has had a checkered career and that he was rejected at some times and accepted in others."

"That's true," Stasimachus said. "One of the greatest men of this century has written a fine work on the fortunes of Aristotelian philosophy in which he records the testimony of a large number of the most influential of the church fathers who claim that it should be driven from Christianity as a pernicious doctrine and even that it was formerly banned from the University of Paris by an act of Parliament.[85]

"If that's the case," said Eulalia, "then those who uphold it can't be seen as very good Catholics or very good Frenchmen."

"That's not what I'm saying," riposted Stasimachus. "I'm sure that it would be quite possible for a man who had a very good understanding of religion to give an apologia for Aristotle.

"As for the nation, I would have thought one would be better off following a Frenchman and a Catholic like Descartes or Gassendi than a pagan and a Greek, because people embrace the latter's ideas not because of reason but because of habit and because they are older."

---

85. Presumably Gassendi's *Exercitationes paradoxicae adversus Aristotleos* (Genoble, 1624).

"I would really like to know one thing," Eulalia said to him. "What were the real reasons for your conversion?"

"I was motivated pretty much by reason," replied Stasimachus. *Opinion of* "Here's what I can tell you for the time being. As far as my age allowed, *scholastic* I rose to the highest scientific degree our classics-dominated system *philosophy.* awards to those who have studied the opinions it teaches. Then I started to think about what I had learned. I was appalled to realize that I had been wasting my time and that my only qualifications were on parchment and in titles."

"What made you think that?" asked Sophia.

"I realized that everything I knew was of no use in the world except to make my way along a path I had no intention of taking," replied Stasimachus. "I could see that right-thinking people couldn't bear the way we argued, and I could only do it in Latin anyway. I was completely at a loss if anyone tried to get me to explain myself intelligibly without using certain words and catch-phrases I claimed were sacred, and when my mind went blank I was left with nothing to say. To cap it all, I could not find a satisfactory solution to problems about things that formerly I had taken to be perfectly clear and certain. You can well imagine that it brought me no little anguish to think that after studying from nine to twenty with great zeal and considerable success for a student, I was little better off than if I had never done anything, and I had to start all over again, according to certain people I talked to."

"What was your view of women during that time?" asked Eulalia.

"Do you have to ask?" Stasimachus replied. "You can guess that as long as I was a scholastic I considered them scholastically, namely, as monsters, and as very much inferior to men, because that's how Aristotle and some of the theologians I had read considered them. To come back to my story," he added, "when, one day, I found all the sciences of the Schools particularly distasteful, by a great stroke of luck I allowed myself to be taken off by a friend to hear a Cartesian lecturing on a subject concerning the human body. As I had lost a lot of the argumentativeness and contrariety common among my fellow students, I listened calmly to a man who would not have fared so well at my hands in former times, and whose doctrine I had mocked endlessly, though all I had ever seen of the book was the cover. I confess that I was astonished to hear nothing but what was clear and intelligible, to realize that he was reasoning on the basis of principles that were so simple and so true that I could not fail to agree with them, and to hear him draw conclusions from them that clarified in a few words certain mysteries that had completely baffled me. The more he spoke the more I became convinced that he possessed reason and good sense. Do you know what I thought after I had left him? That the Cartesians were quite different from the way they had been represented to me, that their crime was to not pass themselves off as brilliant and to make things too concrete and down-to-earth for their enemies who enjoy obscurity. I began to be disillusioned by my masters and to think that, like me, they had been the dupes of opinion and habit. The scorn and aversion I had been taught for Descartes were transformed into admiration. I resolved to study him, allowing my memory to forget everything I had learned, and the change suited me so well that in six months of following the method I have told you about I made more progress than in [the preceding] six years of following the popular method. And I can assure you that although I haven't read any philosophy for three years now, nevertheless, when I reflect upon myself in the way I have told you, I have made more progress than if I had been glued to my books."

"As I see it, you have no fear of being libelously called a Cartesian since you declare yourself to be one quite openly," Timander said.

"I have no fear of being called thus by reasonable people like yourselves," rejoined Stasimachus, "when you are seeking only the truth and couldn't care less from which camp it comes. If I have declared my true colors to you, it's because I could not do otherwise, since I had to point out to Eulalia the books she needed. Without that, you would have had to rely on conjecture. I firmly believe that right-thinking people shouldn't take sides and shouldn't opt for anything specific. You should simply make it a policy to follow reason and good sense. And if you meet people who ask you whose side you are on, the best and briefest reply is that you aren't on anybody's side, that you are a friend of Aristotle, Plato, and Descartes but that you are an even greater friend of the truth, and that the way we think about a thing is our own way, not someone else's, although we may agree with him."

"What Stasimachus is saying certainly strikes a chord with me," said Sophia. "If, after meditation, we accept certain principles, even though we got them from some learned man, they are no longer his but ours. The effort we have put into getting them is the price for our ownership of them, and they are no less ours than the physical possessions we have acquired through legitimate means.

"One is even tempted to say that the possessions of the mind are more legitimate than those of the body because, apart from the fact that we can hide them, that we can't lose them except when we lose our life, and that everyone can enjoy them equally without inconvenience to anyone else, it is a fact that the application and time they took us are incomparably more precious than gold and silver. And as we are under no obligation to identify the people from whom our riches come, and as we keep and show our titles only to maintain a possession we could lose, there is no need to tell nor even to remember from whom we learned what we know, since we are indebted only to ourselves."

"Someone could make us a gift without our knowing about it," said Eulalia, "or without our contributing more than the consent demanded of us. But as far as sciences are concerned, however anxious other people may be to pass on to us their ideas, we have to make our own contribution and accept through our own efforts the gift that they want to give us."

"I must confess that passing on what little insight I have achieved is one of my greatest pleasures," said Stasimachus. "But the pleasure would be increased a thousandfold if I could do it in a quarter of an hour. Eulalia is the person above all in the world to whom I would like to make a gift of every thing I have in my head and to give her in an afternoon what has taken me years and years. But to my sorrow, all I can do is to give her some advice to save her a bit of time and effort."

"Since authors can only teach us what takes great effort on our part, I am surprised that people are so interested in the reputation of those whose works they have read," said Sophia.

"It is a mania that people have always had," remarked Timander. "The reputation of a famous philosopher or theologian affects people as if they were his nearest relatives or his heirs, as if on publication they had not abandoned ownership and censure of their works to those who buy and read them. When I meet people who make it their business to defend the reputation of a scholar whose works they have studied, who are forever quoting him and are more concerned with him as a person than with the truth he preaches, who are less upset by criticism of his doctrine than by criticism of the reputation they think he deserves, and who try to get everybody to follow him, I imagine them as servants who dare not say that the uniform they are wearing is their own, or as agents whose sole purpose is to attract clients and to peddle merchandise that doesn't belong to them."

"Those who have a pure and sincere love of the truth stick to it alone. They seek it everywhere and they find it everywhere, in Aristotle as well as in Descartes. As they come from all sects, without allegiance to any one in particular, they maximize the good in all of them. In some they appreciate the content, in others the form, in others the intent, and as they understand people's strengths and weaknesses they are easily adaptable and are liked by everyone without being disliked by anyone. People do not distrust them, and their ideas are accepted without suspicion. Since they are free of the animosity everyone has against sects other than his own, they enjoy the advantages of them all without the disadvantages."

"This peaceful impartiality is a long way from the intrusive enthusiasm of people who want to convert others to their point of view and do not rest until everyone gives in to them," interrupted Sophia.

"Nothing is more pernicious than an unwelcome zeal to impose one's opinions," Stasimachus went on. "Besides taking away the freedom we ought to leave each other, disturbing our peace, and being contrary to the spirit of truth which is the enemy of force and violence, it further produces divisions, hatreds, tumults, and civil wars which are much more deadly than wars fought out of self-interest or glory."

"It seems to me that one of the surest signs of mistake and error is not to want to be contradicted and to use curses and threats, fire and the sword, to force others to speak as we do," said Timander.

"When we are with those kinds of people, the best thing is to say nothing," said Stasimachus.[86] "If they have the gauge of the wind and they ask you to salute, then you had better surrender. They do not want to be undeceived, and it's foolish to try. They are determined to stick blindly to the opinions they have held since childhood; they make it a virtue to hang on to them, whatever truths are suggested to them. We should leave them in peace as we want them to leave us. All we can do in conversations with them is to make suggestions as if they were problems, without showing too much enthusiasm for the solution, because most of the semi-learned, and in particular the scholastics, have, among other annoying faults, that of attributing to an interlocutor the objections he has made to them as if they were his own views, when they can't answer them. This is why the charity we should have for them and for ourselves doesn't always allow us to push them to the limits, unless it's perfectly obvious that we could convert them or temper the overbearing insolence of their character. We must, in fact, handle with great care people who are slaves to opinion, as if they were capable of insulting a wealthy man and causing his decline and ruin—something that has happened all too often.

"We have to study for ourselves alone and as if we were alone in the

---

86. Poullain sympathized with Descartes's self-imposed censure. See *Meditations*, VI, in *Phil. Essays*, 80: "All these considerations taken together were the reason, why, three years ago, I did not want at all to divulge the treatise I had in hand, and why I had made a resolution not to make public during my lifetime any other treatise which was so general or so basic of which one could understand the foundations of my physics." In 1633 he was about to publish *The World* (finally published in 1664, fourteen years after his death) when he heard of the church's condemnation of Galileo Galilei's support of the Copernican theory. See also above, notes 48 and 58.

world, think to the best of our ability because we do not think as well as we would like to. We have to remain in society because we can't divorce ourselves from people completely, but we shouldn't show off our intelligence too blatantly or reason constantly in their presence, because they will find us trying. Make a note of the prejudices, errors, and follies of others, look impartially upon scholars' quarrels and internecine rages, observe the contradictions they get into, the absurdities they maintain, and the chimeras that preoccupy them, and, without taking sides in their squabbles, try to be indulgent rather than harsh with them, and seek the truth in tranquility, as Eulalia declares she wants to."

"That seems like excellent advice to me," said Sophia. "The impartiality you urge us to bring to all opinions makes us calm and adaptable and allows us to discern the good in everyone, but it also means that true scholars who recognize our desire for the truth have no difficulty in telling us about their amazing discoveries, which they would never speak of to people they find intransigent. Thus intelligent people can easily profit from other people's work and learn in the course of a conversation what has taken years of research and what the majority of people will never discover otherwise. For not only are there a lot of worthwhile things that are not published, either because the author doesn't dare to, or because it doesn't occur to him, but it's very hard to get hold of them even when they are public, either because the books that contain them are extremely rare, or we do not know of their existence, or because they are usually in Latin."

"Since the world is such a strange place," said Eulalia, "how are we to make people realize that we are eager to find the truth and to find out whether they are keen on it too?"

"It's not so hard," replied Stasimachus. "If one isn't biased oneself, then one soon discovers whether others are. It's all the easier if you have been in the habit of observing other people's intelligence and of reflecting upon yourself and others in the way we have spoken of, because this study teaches us the way people usually understand things and their motivation for their persuasion. It also teaches us their strengths and weaknesses and makes us capable of dealing with them. I must say, however, that we have to take chances in this business and drop words into conversations in order to judge people's minds by the way they react to them. Depending on whether they follow, oppose, or reject what they hear, we proceed according to what we think best. But to be on the safe side and not to take any chances, we should get into the habit of phrasing our thoughts so subtly that they always have several sides, so that we always have a way out in case someone takes them the wrong way."

"In conversation groups," said Timander, "women always have an advantage that we men don't have. Apart from the deference we have for whatever they say, the prejudice that makes us think they are less intelligent and less sound than men plays in their favor as far as science is concerned. Not only do we go along with them and support them when we think they are wrong, but even if we think they are quite intelligent in spite of that, we merely tell them that they haven't expressed themselves quite correctly and that they are only women. You know perfectly well what we understand by that word: *frivolous, stubborn, and unfit for the great verities.* In the case of men, as they are taken to be more reliable, we are more shocked to find them disagreeing with us and push them harder."

"It seems to me that those prejudices may be advantageous to us on the one hand, but disadvantageous on the other," said Eulalia. "As we are supposed to be indiscreet, prone to babbling and superstition, and easily carried away by our enthusiasms, I don't imagine that the learned would be very ready to disclose their secrets to us."

"Certainly any of them who have any prudence at all would be inclined to hide from people who have such bad qualities. But when they talk to sensible and judicious people who don't sacrifice their good sense to popular opinion and who want to be put straight, in a word, who have all of Eulalia's good qualities, then they always speak perfectly openly."

"No doubt you list beauty among Eulalia's qualities," said Timander. "I have noticed that when that advantage is accompanied by intelligence, it gives women such an absolute ascendancy over the hearts of scholars that they can get anything out of them. I know one," he added, "who disagrees with popular opinion in many ways, who told me recently that when he is conversing with very intelligent women—and he named them—who have all the blessings we have just mentioned, he is perfectly open with them, and far from being as reserved with them as he is with men, he feels the urge to tell them all he knows."

"It is in such encounters that we could say that there is in both men and women not a demon but a corresponding genie," Eulalia said, smiling.

"Call it what you like," Stasimachus intervened. "Call it a demon if you like, a genie, an inclination, an instinct, whatever you please. As long as the word doesn't frighten you, I can assure you that I will always have one in me that will be so partial to you that you will be able to make it tell whatever it knows."

"I wish I could persuade Eulalia of the same thing," said Timander.

"I have no reason to doubt your good faith," replied Eulalia, "any more than that of Stasimachus. I think I have been very lucky to have met you, and

I hope that when I meet intelligent, admirable people like you I'll be allowed to share their insights, as you have been kind enough to share yours with me."

Thereupon the four of them rose and went outside. After expressing their mutual admiration, they resolved to form a little society, to meet as often as possible and to follow the guidelines they had established, to cele-brate together the freedom of the mind that is one of life's joys and which dis-tinguishes those who value it from the vulgar, self-preoccupied multitude.[87]

87. Stock, "Poullain de la Barre," 34, reports that in the second edition of 1679 "this pleasant op-timism has given way to a more serious attitude. They carry on their discussion, 'afin de pénétrer de plus en plus dans la nature des choses, ce qu'elles sont en elles mêmes & a nostre egard, & quel usage nous devons faire de chacune' (in order to penetrate further and further into the nature of things, what they are in themselves and for us, and the use we ought to make of each [kind of knowledge])." The final sentence of this edition states that "these four people continued their meetings with much satisfaction and profit." To the end Poullain had to balance his natural right to free speech with his assertion of personal freedom against the politics of oppression carried on by the French monarchy. Thus his utopian circle of friends meet in clandestine surroundings.

ON THE EXCELLENCE OF MEN:
PREFACE AND REMARKS

INTRODUCTION

On the Equality of the Two Sexes (1673) did not generate a critical conversation as Poullain had hoped and anticipated. He therefore decided to fill that lacuna himself. The result was *On the Excellence of Men Against the Equality of the Sexes* (1675). His aim was the same as that in his earlier two treatises, to defend the equality in mental capacity of men and women, which he did in a long Preface at the beginning and briefer Remarks at the end, sandwiched between a tract *On the Excellence of Men* in which he put forth a compilation of misogynistic arguments advanced to support the cause of tradition (not translated here). At the end of his Preface he explained that the following treatise "should be read as if it came from an unknown hand, zealous for the glory of our sex, in order to see whether the author has been biased in his favor in diminishing the proofs of his adversaries and whether he has said against women all the ill that can be publicly said of them."

The Preface adds a new dimension to his earlier defenses of women, a consideration of Scripture and the church fathers, designed "to provide women with powerful arguments to defend themselves against those who use Scripture to humiliate them." The Remarks offer four pointed comments on the culture of his time and a rebuttal to that culture put into the mouth of a woman, which concludes the treatise and Poullain's defense of women.

The Preface attempts something new in Poullain's defense: to invoke tradition against tradition. In *Equality* and in *Education* he attempted to replace tradition and custom with Descartes's version of reason, that is, a reason that determines the truth through its apprehension of clear and distinct ideas, bracketing out all received notions from the past. But in *Excellence* he recognizes the power of tradition and attempts to defuse it by offering an alternative interpretation of Scripture and the church fathers in which (1) women and men are equal, (2) neither has dominion in marriage, (3) dominion over the animals belongs to both equally, and (4) passages of Scripture interpreted as subordinating women to men and speaking negatively about women in general are rethought.

He begins by quoting from three eminent church fathers—Clement of Alexandria (ca. 150–ca. 215), Basil of Caesarea (ca. 330–79), and Ambrose (ca. 339–97)—and invoking the names of two others—Jerome (ca. 345–420) and Origen (ca. 185–ca. 254)—in support of the equality of men and women. All say that men and women have the same nature and the same advantages that belong to that nature. These fathers also put forth misogynistic views, particularly Jerome, whose *Against Jovinian* was one of the foundations of medieval misogyny expressed in writing. Even so, the real authority for traditional misogyny was certain passages of Scripture. Poullain confronts these head on.

Is woman created in the image of God, according to Scripture? Augustine established the view that became the orthodox one, repeated by Thomas Aquinas: woman was created in the image of God as an intelligent nature, but inasmuch as man, not woman, is like God and is the beginning and end of woman, woman is not in God's image but in man's; it is therefore by grace rather than nature that woman is the image of God.[1] Poullain rejects the orthodox interpretation. The issue is settled by Genesis 1:27, which proclaims that God made man (humans)[2] in his own image, male and female. Nothing, says Poullain, could be more categorical than this. At the same time, other passages have been used against women and Poullain proceeds to discuss these.

Does not St. Paul say that man is the image and glory of God and woman the glory of man (1 Cor. 11:7)? Poullain points out first that Paul did not say woman is the image of man, only that she is his glory, and being his glory does not make her his image. He adds that if the first woman, who came from man (Gen. 2:22–23), is not in the image of God, then only Adam is the image of God, because all other humans have come from women. Further, if the woman is less noble by virtue of having come from the man, then all men since Adam, inasmuch as they have been born of women, are less noble than women. All this is not to say that women are more noble than men, but rather that the essence of the image of God does not consist in the manner in which it was made but in the characteristics that make it resemble the thing it represents. And these characteristics belong to women as much as to men.

1. Ian Maclean, *The Renaissance Notion of Woman: A Study of the Fortunes of Scholasticism and Medical Science in European Intellectual Life* (Cambridge, 1980), 13 (par. 2.5.1), and sources cited.

2. Poullain makes explicit that the use of "man" throughout Scripture embraces all human beings.

What of God's pronouncement in Genesis 1:28: "Have dominion over the earth, I give you all that the earth produces, to you it shall be as meat." Was this dominion given only to Adam or to Adam and Eve together? To both, since women are as much the image of God as men, as the passage itself makes clear, and God gave dominion to those created in his image over every other created thing. In Genesis 2:15, 18, 21–23, which recounts the creation of woman from man's rib, no mention is made of dependence. Moreover, the fact that Adam was created first (traditionally used to promote male superiority) is counterbalanced by the fact that Eve was created in Paradise while Adam was created outside it—not to mention the fact that man was created of mud while woman was created of something more noble (man's rib).[3] That she was created his helpmeet does not imply dependence or inequality, for they are helpmeets to each other. Men are as much for women as women are for men.

Poullain next cites Genesis 3:1–6, 16, the serpent tempting the woman and God pronouncing that the woman's sorrow would be multiplied and that she would be ruled by her husband. Many have used these words to prove that women should be submissive to and ruled by their husbands. However, when Paul exhorted women to remain submissive to their husbands, he did not invoke this passage, which would have been a much stronger reason for their submission than those he gave. But even if we accept the interpretation of this passage that women are to be submissive, does that prove women are dependent? No, because we are all dependent on one another. Dependence does not prove inferiority. Moreover, the passage applies only to married women, not all women. Neither does it carry the weight of a divine imperative, accompanied by threats against those who do not obey. On the contrary, many women have ruled over kingdoms or empires and so exercised an authority much greater than that of husbands over wives.

Eve's subjection to her husband was not punishment for her sin. First, she was weaker than Adam, and so more excusable.[4] Second, it was Adam, not Eve, who received the prohibition from God. Third, she resisted the devil and Adam did not. It is difficult to believe that God would have rewarded Adam (with dominion over Eve) after he committed an egregious sin. Nor

3. The ideas that Eve was as (or more) noble than Adam because created in Paradise and of a more noble substance (Adam's rib rather than mud) is traceable at least as far back as the early thirteenth century. See Henricus Cornelius Agrippa, *Declamation on the Nobility and Preeminence of the Female Sex*, trans. Albert Rabil Jr. (Chicago, 1996), 14–15 and n. 32.

4. The first woman known to us to engage in a debate over the relative guilt of Adam and Eve argued similarly. See Isotta Nogarola, "On the Equal or Unequal Sin of Adam and Eve," in *Her Immaculate Hand*, ed. and trans. Margaret King and Albert Rabil Jr. (Binghamton, N.Y., rev. ed., 1992), 57–69. A volume of the works of Isotta Nogarola (1420–66) will appear in this series.

does Scripture anywhere say that Eve fell further than Adam from the power God had given them jointly over all the goods of the earth. "Dominion" implies authority equal to that of God over creatures, humans over animals, princes over subjects, masters over slaves; husbands have no such dominion over wives. The only two kinds of authority that exist are the authority of force and that of reason. Husbands do not have the authority of force over their wives—all well-regulated states forbid it. Authority, then, is reduced to the authority of reason, which both sexes share equally (because they share equally the image of God). When we obey, we obey our own reason rather than the person who commands that we obey. Setting custom aside, men and women have equal power over each other.

If men and women share dominion over all other things equally, they are equal, so that men cannot claim dominion in marriage. Here again, Poullain appeals first to the church fathers and then examines Scripture. Among the church fathers, in addition to those mentioned earlier, he cites the eastern theologians Gregory of Nazianzus (329/30–389/90) and Gregory of Nyssa (ca. 330–ca. 395); and the western theologians Gregory the Great (ca. 540–604) and Augustine (354–430). Poullain calls these fathers to witness that there is a double standard[5] which gives husbands (and fathers) control over wives and children, whereas God had said "honor your father and your mother," establishing their equality in law—so Gregory of Nazianzus; and that the man who attributes to himself a power that belongs only to God elevates himself above God to whom he should be subject—so Gregory of Nyssa. These two fathers are supported by Poullain's citation of Gregory the Great. He calls Jerome as witness as well, invoking his citation of Genesis 12:1, in which God tells Abraham "harken unto thy wife Sarah and do as she would have thee do," to show that husbands are obliged to submit to their wives when they are right. Augustine's assertion that only God should be placed above humans is interpreted to support mutuality in marriage. As Poullain says at this point, one mate is obliged to obey the other only when the one commanded recognizes the command as one given by reason as well.

Where did subordination in marriage come from? Poullain believes it came from a false analogy between the state and the family. Social organization (requiring three or more persons) is based on fear. Subordination, dependence, and the right to command are necessary. But marriage is composed

---

5. Gibson, *Women in Seventeenth-Century France*, 63: "Marriage, everyone knows, was a 'religieuse et dévote liaison' instituted for the production of heirs, not the gratification of sensual desires. The healthy male, however, could hardly be expected to contain himself within such narrow limits," but "the same tolerance was not accorded to the opposite sex," because it could result in a "pollution of the race."

of only two persons and is based on love, not fear. Husband and wife are not constrained to live together, but do so voluntarily. Hence their power is equal, or rather, it should be equal, but often is not because of custom. Indeed, when God told Eve that she would be under the sway of her husband, he was warning her that Adam, being so upset about the sin in which she had a part, would make laws to his own advantage and subject her to his rule. This, says Poullain, "is actually the only reasonable interpretation—and one worthy of the Scriptures—that we can give the passage if taken literally." It is a prediction of misfortune, not an authority given to husbands.

What, then, of the passages in St. Paul that preach submission of wives to husbands (Col. 3:18; 1 Cor. 11:3; Eph. 5:22–24)? Poullain suggests an analogy: slaves are also told to remain where they are, which does not mean that slavery is based on divine law; neither should the exhortation of wives to be submissive. Moreover, Paul also says that in Christ there is neither slave nor free, male nor female, as if he meant that these differences exist only in people's minds. Still further, in saying husband and wife should relate as Christ to the church, he is providing them with the most perfect model available, urging wives to submit to their husbands to the same degree as the church submits to Christ. But Christ does not wish to wield worldly power and declared his kingdom to be not of this world. Hence subordination to him is not a subordination based on power but on truth, reason, and love.

In his own time Poullain's argument was radical, in two respects. First, by interpreting the Scriptures in a historical sense, he applied to them the same criteria as would be applied to the interpretation of any other book, a practice that was only in its infancy during his lifetime and for more than a hundred years after his death. Second, his view of marriage as egalitarian and democratic rather than hierarchical and patriarchal was much at variance with the mores of seventeenth-century France (and indeed, all of Europe).[6] But he was less so in the consequences he drew from his ideal of equality for female participation in social life.

He argues as follows. Men have assumed the principal positions in society and attributed great status to them. But such status is based only on opinion and has nothing to do with human nature. The fact that Scripture adopts the language of male prerogative only means that it adopted the usage of all languages in doing so. Applying this observation to Paul's language in 1 Corinthians 14:34–35 and 1 Timothy 2:11–14, the fact that women are told to learn in silence, be subject, and not teach in public does not mean that they are less capable than men of teaching and governing; the issue is per-

6. See *Education*, note 6.

mission, not capacity. For women do in fact teach their children, not to speak of servants, husbands, and even communities—but they do not do so in public. One, however, is no more difficult than the other.

Paul recognized that sin entered the world through the first man (Romans 5:19). It does not affect the equality of Adam and Eve that Eve was deceived by the Devil and Adam through Eve. Adam could just as well have been created after Eve as before her and been led immediately astray, and if at that time men had been under the power of their wives they might have been told that they should not rule over others but should obey their wives.

Therefore, the equality of men and women means that either could have been entrusted with the tasks of civic life. But he adds that although both men and women *could* govern, there is no injustice in men not sharing with women the power they have, and no reason why civic positions should be divided between men and women. Rather, he argues, it makes no difference who holds these positions "provided that whoever it is does not abuse them." Therefore, he concludes, religion does not condemn our social institutions but approves and sanctifies them, preserving a true equality, which is based on the law of love, while supporting an apparent inequality. In the same way, the apostles and prophets did not speak against the inequality of wealth but only against abuses arising from it; thus did they establish the law of Christian charity.

Poullain arrives at the same position by considering the numerous passages in Proverbs and Ecclesiasticus[7] where many disparaging remarks about women are to be found. He points out that Scripture speaks more about the defects of women than those of men in imitation of the way women were commonly spoken of in all cultures. Their defects are so emphasized that we might be led to think they are responsible for all the dissoluteness in the world. But note, says Poullain, that these books were written by men. If men had written about themselves, they might have been forced to change their behavior, which they did not wish to do.[8] Moreover, the books were also written for men, constituting the kind of advice a father might give his son in his relations with women. If women had written these books, the defects of men would certainly have been emphasized. In any case, what is said in these passages about women could just as well be said about men. To prove his point, Poullain offers a counterexample of what a mother might say to her

7. Ecclesiasticus is, for Roman Catholics, a canonical book, but for Protestants an apocryphal (i.e., not canonical or authoritative) one. Poullain was still a Roman Catholic at the time he wrote this text and treated the book as Scripture. In any case, the book had been used to support many misogynist treatises.

8. Poullain is saying here that men lived in what we would today call a state of denial.

daughter about her relations with men. If we were honest, Poullain concludes, we would admit that almost all the evil is on the side of men. Although women have as much need of men as men of women, it is men who seek, solicit, and pressure women. And when sin is committed, as in the case of David and Bathsheba, it is the man who is blamed by Scripture, not the woman. Women can make a strong case that it is men who corrupt them. Poullain could have drawn from this analysis the conclusion that because men had botched things so badly, women should take over positions of public authority; instead, he concludes that since men have caused the evils of society, it is only right that they should stay in positions of power in order to make amends.

Thus Poullain's discourse never crosses the line to engage in open subversion. From our own contemporary point of view, we can see that Poullain did not recognize that inequality in power meant inequality in life and that no assertion of equality of capacity would actually *change* anything; or perhaps he did recognize that he could be as radical as he liked in supporting equality of mind, since that would be no threat to the social order as he knew it. The reason may very well have been a perception on his part (albeit largely unconscious) that equality in marriage could be effected without a social revolution, whereas equality in the social sphere could not. He was therefore willing to advocate equality in mind and marriage without being willing to open the question of social reorganization.[9] Still, in his own time, even the advocacy of female equality in marriage went beyond what earlier writers in favor of women had been willing to support. Moreover, in his Remarks, to which we now turn, he opens the possibility of a different basis of social organization, especially in the concluding speech put into the mouth of a female protagonist.

The Remarks seek to add to or reinforce the arguments presented in *Equality.* Poullain feels it pertinent to say four things.

First, women's equal *capability* with men is the central question, not whether women should do what men do. Women bear children, which men cannot do, and that is a vital service to society. Equality does not require doing the same things; it is enough that men and women do equivalent things.[10]

Second, the fact that something has been believed for a long time and by many people is nothing to the point. The Muslim religion is false, but it has

---

9. Poullain's opinion remains consistent with his expressed moral code of conduct. See *Education,* note 69. See also Welch, "Les Limites du libéralisme patriarchal de Poullain de la Barre," 41–52.

10. Angenot, *Les Champions des femmes,* 64, appropriately stresses the modernity of Poullain's foresight in dealing with the question of "equivalence" in the debate over gender equality.

been around for a thousand years and has converted half the world. It is not surprising that women have accepted their lot, since they are taught by men.[11]

Third, the analogy between humans and animals does not hold, since other animals do not have our intelligence. Our preference for one animal over another has to do only with our own whims. Nor does the greater contribution of men to procreation any longer hold. There is nothing in human sexual intercourse that suggests males are active and females passive in that process, as common opinion has it. It is pointless even to bring this up.[12]

Fourth, the principal arguments used to depict men and women as having contrary natures actually are based on custom, not nature. The argument that men and women are composed of opposite humors (warm/cold, wet/dry) is one of these. Women are said to be colder than men, but the heat needed to produce a creature in their wombs belies this. Nor can it be claimed that women are fundamentally coquettish by nature and more prone to love than men; moral attributes cannot be drawn from biology.[13] Another argument based on custom but masquerading as based on nature is women's greater enthusiasm for marriage. Custom has imposed on them greater modesty and restraint in matters of love. But modesty is nothing more than the fear of being blamed. Men promote this feminine virtue as the most effective antidote to the presumed lustful and changeable nature of women, and thus this "virtue" belongs not to nature but to social teaching and practice. Sexual subjection is therefore another masculine enclosure erected around the female body at the expense of the woman's natural rights. Poullain's conclusion is that love in both sexes has social advantages for the human race; this is the redeeming feminism that emerges from the last pages of the Remarks.

Poullain concludes his remarks by putting into the mouth of a female a reply to a friend of hers who said she could not abide people who think women are more tenderly constituted than men. His female protagonist's

11. Simone de Beauvoir understood the seriousness of the force of historical conditioning on a young girl's mind. See *The Second Sex,* 625.

12. Poullain may have been aware of (though he does not mention) the work of Reinier de Graaf, *De mulierum organis generatione inservientibus tractatus novus* (Leiden, 1672); French translation *Nouveau Traité des parties génitales de la femme* (Lyon, 1672), 51–53. De Graaf, a Dutch biologist, had observed that female ovaries produced eggs prior to the intervention of male semen in the female uterus. His theory challenged previous hypotheses of the cold womb.

13. In contrast, Dr. Nicolas Venette, ten years later, wove a network of necessary concordances between female sexual anatomy and female psychology. In a particularly colorful instance, Venette found a parallel between the "good condition" of a woman's uterus and her complexion, bright eyes, pleasant voice, and engaging conversation—so much so that he concluded that love lies at the core of female sensual nature and leads to the arousal of her sense of tenderness and kindness. See Yvonne Knibielher and Catherine Fouquet, *Histoire des mères du Moyen Age à nos jours* (Paris, 1977), 41.

point is that it is not insulting to a woman to be told that she has a greater penchant for love than does a man, inasmuch as it is only love that gives us spirit and pleasure. Look at the transformation that comes over people when they fall in love. If love can do that for someone lately struck by it, imagine its effect on those who have more of it as part of their nature than others. Yet, men disdain us for this and exalt their own willingness to expose their lives to danger out of a desire for glory—which can only come to them if they lose their lives! But we are put into this world to do good and to love, not to do evil and to hate. Thus those who have a greater facility for love are more excellent than others. God has shown that love is what he desires for all creatures, which is why he has inspired all his creatures with the desire for union (and love is the desire for union). What is true for God is true also for humans, in two respects. First, each human is united only through the fusion of body and spirit, and seeks to preserve himself by keeping this union intact. Second, each human seeks to unite with a person of the opposite sex to produce another like ourselves. It is in this act of creation that we are actually the images of God. In this process we cease to act for ourselves and act for others, making us more like God who also creates, as in a vast womb, a work different from himself. This process of creation involves a woman much more lastingly than a man, who only deposits his seed in an instant. Thus, men should be for women inasmuch as nature has made them serve women.[14] It is comical that men have transformed their submission into their elevation and domination, just as we see the most useless men (the nobility) dominating the craftsmen, farmers, and merchants who actually do the work and produce the wealth.

There has been a long history of the development of civilization, but out of it has come nothing as certain as love. At the beginning of the human enterprise all were equal. Justice and sincerity ruled; men were untroubled by enemies. But men took advantage of their strength to subjugate others, moving further and further from the age of gold through their greed, ambition, and vanity. Truth and justice were hidden, and love had to appear to be blind. Such a history inspires mockery and pity. And when we add to all this the way men have treated women, we can say that they do not deserve to wear any of the signs of their so-called excellence.

14. Poullain defends the notion of the rehabilitation of the woman's body on moral grounds with incalculable consequences for the future of feminism. See Monique Rémy, *Histoire des mouvements de femmes: De l'utopie à l'intégration* (Paris, 1990), 69. See also Welch, "Le Corps feminin dans la pensée de Poullain de la Barre," 73–74.

ON THE EXCELLENCE OF MEN

Against the Equality of the Sexes

PREFACE

If women, because of the beauty which is their particular attribute, deserve to be called "the fair sex" par excellence, then the question whether they are equal to men should also be called "the fair question," since there is perhaps none more important nor more widely discussed nor more complex in all human knowledge. It concerns all the attitudes and behavior of men toward women, of women toward men, and of women among themselves. It cannot be properly discussed without recourse to the most fundamental elements of knowledge, and it will serve as a basis for settling many other complex questions, mainly those of ethics, jurisprudence, theology, and politics, which cannot be discussed freely in a book.

I will refrain from saying that it is also the basis of salon society, since I do not wish to disparage it in the minds of those who use their wisdom to condemn what they do not understand and their virtue to prove their aversion to the things they dearly cherish in their innermost hearts. This subject, then, should be to everyone's taste, for there is no one who does not take *some* interest in it. I am astonished that after so many threats to write against the *Equality of the Two Sexes*, no one has yet done so, at the very least to respond to the expectation that these threats had raised. This is what has moved me to take up my pen again to write this *Treatise on the Excellence of Men*, not to prove that they are more excellent than women—being more than ever persuaded of the contrary—but simply to provide a way of comparing the two opposite 265

views and to judge better which is more correct, by means of studying sever-
ally and in all their clarity the reasons on which they are based. In order to
give a fuller account of this comparison, I have decided to put into this Preface the summary of a more complete response to the authority of Holy Scripture that is set out in the second part of this *Treatise.* I have judged this addition,
moreover, to be necessary, not to duplicate books but to make a more balanced volume and to provide women with powerful arguments to defend
themselves against those who use the Scripture to humiliate them.

The view of the equality of the sexes is easier to establish through the
rules of Scripture than through those of philosophy, provided that in both
cases we do not rely on childhood prejudices but rather use our own eyes to
discover the truth we seek—being certain that those who read Holy Scripture precisely and without prejudice will find there nothing to give them reason to believe that God has made men more perfect and more capable than
women nor, as a consequence, that the former are, in His eyes, more noble
and estimable than the latter.

This is no doubt how the church fathers proceeded, and it will be useful
to invoke their writings in support of our opinion, to show that it is not contrary to sacred theology, since it is confirmed by the great theologians.

St. Clement of Alexandria[1] is one of those who has given the clearest explication. He writes:

> One thing incontestable among us is that men and women are of the
> same nature and that they have, therefore, the same power of acting
> and of practicing virtue. If they seem to be of different natures this can
> only be an appearance, for their nature is at bottom the same.[2]

Elsewhere Clement adds:

> They have the same God, the same master who is Jesus Christ, the
> same church, the same hopes, the same graces, the same things to learn
> and to do for their salvation; in addition their actions in life, both of
> body and of mind, are common and similar. Their sex is different only
> in that women marry men and men marry women. But it will not be

1. St. Clement of Alexandria (ca. 150–ca. 215) succeeded Pantaenus, the earliest recorded director of the Christian school in Alexandria, in ca. 190. Three of his works survive: *Stromateis*
(Miscellanies), where we find one of more positive treatments of marriage (bk. 3) penned by a
church father; *Protrepticus* (Exhortation to the Greeks); and *Paedagogus* (On Christian life). When
Clement fled Alexandria during a persecution in 202, he was succeeded as head of the catechetical school there by the much more famous Origen.

2. Poullain cites this passage as coming from the *Stromateis* 1.1, but the passage is not there. We
have not located it.

thus in the next world whose reward is not promised here below either to the male or the female in particular but to both in general under the name of mankind, which is equally common to both.[3]

Basil[4] uses the same reasons and nearly the same words:

The advantages of nature are entirely equal in men and women, without any difference, and they have an equal power to do good. Women should not, therefore, say that they do not possess any strength and that they are of an inferior condition to men's. If they are weak it is only in the body and not at all in the soul which is the seat of strength, constancy, and virtue in which often there is not a man capable of equaling them.

And some lines later this great man adds that we should in no way dwell on the body, which is only a cover, so to speak, or clothing of the soul, and which, although a little less robust in women than in men, does not prevent the soul from having the same power to act and to practice virtue. It should be remarked that, for virtue to be perfect, intelligence of understanding and strength of will are required in order to use the body as an organ. Both sexes possess this to the same degree.

St. Ambrose,[5] after remarking that the actions of men and women cannot be different because they have the same nature, the same power, and the same prerogatives, declares that we should not dwell on the differences in the sexes where there is no question of comparing the advantages of the body but only the advantages of the soul which does not at all admit of sex.[6]

---

3. Poullain cites the source as *Paedagogus* 1.r, so that it appears he was using a manuscript. We have not located the passage.

4. St. Basil the Great (ca. 330–79) was one of three Cappadocian fathers (along with Gregory of Nazianzus, his friend, and Gregory of Nyssa, his brother) who worked out the language that led to the adoption of the doctrine of the Trinity at the Council of Constantinople, 380. His sister, Macrina (ca. 327–80), was responsible for turning him from a promising secular career to the Christian priesthood. He composed a number of theological tracts and a great many letters, including an important one on education that later became important to Italian humanists in encouraging the study of pagan classical literature. The citation is said by Poullain to be from Homily 10, presumably of the Psalms, since Basil published two groups of homilies, one of which ends at 9.

5. St. Ambrose (ca. 339–97), educated in part by his mother and his sister, Marcellina (ca. 330–ca. 398), he became bishop of Milan after having held high administrative office as a Roman official, and eventually one of the four "doctors" of the Western church (together with Gregory the Great, Jerome, and Augustine). He was partly responsible for the conversion of Augustine to Christianity. He was best known as a preacher; he dedicated three sermons to his sister Marcellina, *De virginibus*. His other well-known work is a treatise on ethics.

6. See Maclean, *Woman Triumphant*, 2–3 for a summary of traditional responses to these questions.

I will not mention St. Jerome[7] nor Origen,[8] since there is hardly anyone who does not know of the high regard they had for women. Let us pass on to Scripture.

The first place where the two sexes are spoken of is the end of the first chapter of Genesis in these words: "So God created man in his own image . . . male and female created he them . . . and said unto them: Be fruitful and multiply, and replenish the earth, and subdue it, and have dominion over the fish of the sea, and over the fowl of the air, and over every living thing" (1:27–28).[9]

Had this passage been composed expressly to prove equality, it could hardly have been more explicit or more categorical. The word "man" applies equally to male and female as it does in almost all the rest of Scripture, and there is no evidence that would make us apply it to one with an idea of greater excellence than to the other. On the occasions when it designates the male in particular, it is merely following the usage that gives to the male the name of the entire species.

Indeed, whether we define man as an animal capable of reason, or as a creature made in the image of God, either definition applies to the two sexes indiscriminately, since both are capable of the same functions of body and mind included in the general idea of man, and the principle of knowledge, will, and action, through which we resemble God, is no less perfect in women than in men.

This is the thought of St. Basil when he explains the words: *God made them in his own image:*

---

7. St. Jerome (ca. 345–ca. 420), the most learned man of his age, best known for translating the Bible from Hebrew and Greek into Latin. His version became standard in the Western church for over one thousand years. He was also well known for championing virginity over marriage, especially in his treatise *Against Jovinian.* The wealthy Paula and her daughter Eustochium (see Jerome's letter to her, in his collected letters, no. 22) followed him to Palestine and paid for the construction of monasteries, living under Jerome's direction.

8. Origen of Alexandria (ca. 185–ca. 245) was the most important theologian of the early Greek Church. He was catechetical teacher in the school at Alexandria, 202–30, then in Palestine from 231 until his death. He was a prolific writer, and the most important and complete of his surviving works is *On First Principles*, a statement of his theology. He was long famous for compiling a biblical text based on many languages placed in parallel columns (known as the *Hextapla*), which, not surprisingly, did not survive. Of all the fathers mentioned by Poullain, he is the only one who was not sainted, though his influence continued to be great nonetheless.

9. This and subsequent quotations from the Bible are given in the King James Version (KJV), published in English in 1611. Although Poullain was still a Roman Catholic at the time he wrote his three feminist treatises, it is not known whether he adhered to the Vulgate translation (attributed to Jerome). But at least the KJV belongs to his century. In a number of biblical citations, Poullain conflates passages without alerting the reader to the gaps. We have represented the gaps in his citations by ellipses and cited at the end of each passage the verses he actually printed—which he does not always correctly (or fully) identify in the margins of his text.

The writer of the story of Genesis feared that ignorance would lead us to believe that by the word "man" he was referring only to the male when he said that "God created man in his image"; he added, therefore, "God made them male and female," which allows us to understand that a creature was made in the image of God and is to be found no less in the woman than in the man.[10]

St. Gregory of Nyssa writes:[11]

I believe that these words, "God made man in his image," include all men in general, since in Jesus Christ, according to the Apostle, there is neither male nor female. There are necessarily two parts in us, one of which is meant to represent the image of God and the other the subject of the difference of the sexes. And when the Scripture tells us that God made man in his image, we should understand this as the divine part in us which is capable of intelligence and reason and which does not participate in sexual difference, not as the part devoid of reason which is differentiated by sex. And this God-given grace was bestowed upon the entire species in general and equally, because the Spirit is in all in the same way.

This shows the error of some modern theologians who, in order to repress women, have claimed that they are not images of God as men are and that this was the opinion of St. Paul. Here are his own words: "Man is the image and glory of God and woman is the glory of man. For the man is not of the woman but the woman of the man" (1 Cor. 11:7). Does that mean that woman is not the image of God? If she is of the man, because she comes from him, she is, therefore, of God, as are children although they come from their fathers. The Apostle does not say that woman is the image of man, but only his glory, which is very different. For she would not be his image for that reason, in the same way that all creatures are not the image of God, even though they are His glory and His handiwork.

If women are not the image of God because the first woman came from a man, then only Adam is the image of God, because all other men come from women. And if the woman is the image of man and less noble than he is because she comes from him, all men are, by the same reasoning, the images of women and less noble than they.

10. Again, Homily 10, presumably of the Psalms—from the same source as the first citation of Basil. See above, note 4 and related text.

11. St. Gregory of Nyssa (ca. 330–ca. 95). Younger brother of St. Basil (see above). He was a theologian of considerable originality who did much to help develop the doctrine of the Trinity in its orthodox form. *De Opisi*, chap. 15, cited in the margins of Poullain's text, we have not identified.

The reason for all this is that the essence of the image does not consist in the manner in which it was made, but in the traits and characteristics which make it resemble the thing it represents. Now the characteristics of divinity are found in women as well as in men, since like men they can attain the resemblance of action which is the glory of Christianity and which makes Christians images of God par excellence above the rest of mankind; for Christians imitate the holiness and perfection of God Himself; that is to say, they perfect their intelligence and their minds and they regulate their passions and actions according to maxims offered by the Gospel and according to the model of God's conduct which He gives as an example for them to follow.

In the opinion of those who maintain that it is through the dominion God has given us over all the things of the world that we are His images, women are still as perfectly His Image as we are. God gave this dominion to them as completely and as absolutely as to us when He said to the male and the female: "Have dominion over the earth, I give you all that the earth produces, to you it shall be as meat" (Gen. 1:28).[12] In fact, since the empire and dominion we have been given is nothing but the right and power to use all the things the earth yields to fulfill our need of them, and since this need exists equally in both sexes, the right to use them belongs no more to one than to the other. So much for the first chapter of Genesis. Let us move on to the second.

The Scripture says:

The Lord God took the man and put him into the garden of Eden to dress it and keep it . . . and said, it is not good that the man should be alone, and resolved to make him a helpmeet for him which should be in his likeness [or, in other words, a companion of the same nature in order to help him]. And the Lord God caused a deep sleep to fall upon Adam and he slept: and he took one of his ribs . . . and [of] the rib . . . made he a woman. . . . And Adam said, This is now bone of my bones and flesh of my flesh: she shall be called a name that shall mark her origin for she was taken out of Man
(Gen. 2:15, 18, 21–23)[13]

12. Poullain's citation of the text was incorrect, as occurs in a number of instances. We have corrected them silently.

13. In the Vulgate, Jerome used *virago* to translate the Hebrew *ishshah*, "woman," in an attempt to reflect the (etymologically false) idea that the word for "woman" (*ishshah*) in Hebrew derived from the word for "man" (*ish*); thus in the Vulgate translation of Genesis 2, the first woman (*virago*) is formed from the rib of the first man (*vir*). There was therefore primacy of the male subject both in the story of Creation and in the language that described it. The Latin reads: Hoc nunc, os ex ossibus meis, et caro de carne mea, quae vocabit Virago, quoniam de viro sumpta est.

There is no mention of inequality or of dependence in this pas- *Virago.*
sage. It is true that Adam was created first; but if this is an advantage it
does not pertain to him alone, and it is counterbalanced by the honor
God bestowed upon Eve in creating her in an earthy paradise, the time
and place being purely external factors which neither confer on things
nor suppose in them any particular excellence; otherwise the beasts
would have been more noble than Adam, their creation having preceded his; the elders would be more excellent than their juniors, the fathers and mothers more excellent than their children, in a word, all
those who are older than others.

What makes us believe that God began with males as if He placed
greater value on them than on females is that we judge His conduct
and attitudes according to those of men who generally love and favor
the eldest over the youngest and boys over girls, although this preference often arises only from whim and custom.

If we ask therefore why God began with men rather than with
women we must answer simply that He willed it thus, since He gave us
no reason for it in the Scriptures. For in this situation as in myriad others, we must avoid the hubris of those who, trying to give authority to
their fantasies, attribute them to God, saying that He wished to do
things for reasons which they make up themselves when they do not
find any in the Scriptures, whether He had any or not.

Thus, since the Scriptures give no indication why God acted thus,
and tell us that both man and woman are the images of God, without
making any distinction between them, let us not say that God esteems
one more highly than the other.

But, it will be objected, not only did Eve come after Adam, she
also came from him, having been formed from one of his ribs. That is
true. But I would continue: Adam was created after the mud; he emerged
from the mud and the slime of the earth; thus the earth and the mud are
more noble than he is. And if I were to argue hypothetically, that is to
say, by giving imaginary reasons, I would state my view that God created the first woman in a place more remarkable than Adam and
formed her body from a tougher and stronger—even more noble—
matter, since it was from a man's rib, instead of being made only from
slime as Adam was, to teach us that women are more excellent than
men. What would be the reply of those who rely on hypotheses?

Would they say, as they tend to, that God did not wish to make
woman from the head of man for fear that she would be his equal, nor
from his feet for fear that he would hold her too much in contempt, but

from his side to show her that she should consider him to be her head and her master? A woman would stop them immediately and would ask them where they had learned such fine arguments. And she would be able to add that God drew Eve from the side of Adam in order to teach them that they should go about as equals, side by side. Is that not much more natural? Apart from the single case of Eve, other women owe nothing to their husbands for their birth and do not claim to be of a more perfect substance than their children, although they contribute to their generation in a way completely different from Adam's generation of his wife.

In addition, Eve, in her actual form, could just as well have been created first to furnish a rib for her husband, and the latter could have been given to her as a helpmeet in her likeness, without it being possible to conclude on that account that he was of a less excellent nature or that he and his descendants should be dependent upon women.

The situation of helpmeet does not imply either dependence or inequality. Princes are the helpers of their subjects, and subjects of their princes, as are we all to one another in society. God Himself is often called our succor and our help. Adam was helpmeet to his wife as she was to him and as women and men are reciprocally, being of the same nature and equally necessary to each other. For neither a man alone nor a woman alone can produce an offspring, as this passage says: "It is not good that man should be alone," or "man should not be alone, let us give him a person in his likeness," or "of the same nature as himself to help him." Thus it is unreasonable and pointless for anyone to generalize in saying to women that they are for men, since men are equally for them, since it is only of Eve that it could be said that she was made for her husband in the common meaning of the term; apart from which it is more normal to have a more favorable impression of the person who helps than of the one who is helped, because the latter needs the former and depends upon her for the help he receives.

> The serpent said unto the woman, Yea hath God said, Ye shall not eat of every tree of the garden? And the woman said unto the serpent, We may eat of the fruit of the trees of the garden: but of the fruit of the tree which is in the midst of the garden, God hath said, Ye shall not eat of it, neither shall ye touch it, lest ye die. And the serpent said unto the woman, Ye shall not surely die: For God doth know that in the day ye eat thereof, then your eyes shall be opened, and ye shall be as gods, knowing good and evil. And when the woman saw that the tree was good for food, and that it was pleasant to the eyes . . . she took of the fruit thereof, and did eat, and gave also unto her husband with her and

he did eat. . . . Unto the woman he said, I will greatly multiply thy sorrow . . . and thy desire shall be to thy husband and he shall rule over thee.

(Gen. 3:1b–6; 16)

Those who use these last words in order to show that women are inferior to men and that they have all been subjugated because of the sin of the first woman do not perhaps know that these words "thy desire shall be to thy husband, and he shall rule over thee" are found only in the Vulgate, in place of which the versions translated from the Hebrew like the Vatable[14] and the Polyglot,[15] accepted by all the learned, read thus: "In sorrow shalt thy bring forth children yet thy desire shall be to thy husband."

It is of the utmost importance to observe that the Apostle did not use this passage in his most spirited exhortation to women to remain submissive to their husbands, which would be much stronger than the reasons he does offer them and which we shall examine elsewhere.

Although these two observations are substantial enough to destroy our adversaries' position, I am willing to go along with them in their interpretation of this passage. But I ask them what is their intention. To show that women are less perfect than we are? The Scriptures do not say a word about perfection at this point. That they are inferior and dependent? We admit that they are [dependent]. But children depend on their fathers and mothers, subjects on their princes, all of us on one another. Are we less perfect? Not at all.

This passage refers only to married women. What shall we say of those who are not married? And whatever meaning we give to it, how could we prove that it does not include any other than the first, to whom it is exclusively addressed? It is true that it seems that after Adam males have always enjoyed preeminence. But all it requires for that is that Adam should have set the example for it, however he acquired it. And men have kept it until the present day, just as we see that the same family keeps the scepter in a kingdom as long as there is no revolution to force it to change hands.

Let us examine the basis of this. If the words "thy husband shall rule over thee," etc., means that women have been made dependent on men, that goes

14. François Vatable (d. 1547) was a self-taught linguist appointed by François I to the chair of Hebrew at the Collège de France. He did not actually translate the Bible but wrote notes to accompany Estienne's translation of 1545. The notes represented such a valuable philological and clearly reasoned exegesis that they were retained in the revised edition of Estienne's translation published in Salamanca in 1584–86.

15. Probably a reference to the edition of the Bible with the text in several languages published in Paris by Antoine Vitre between 1629 and 1657.

for us as well. For it follows that earlier and before this condemnation one sex did not depend on the other, that it would not depend upon the other without Eve's sin, and that it depends on the other to this day only because God has ordained it in this way. [This is so] not because of any inequality that exists between them but as punishment for a sin committed by a woman, in which a man also participated, denoting an equal weakness. According to the legal maxim, "the exception confirms the rule," that is to say, if women have become dependent by a particular decree pronounced against them, we must conclude that they are not dependent because of some general rule, since they become dependent only by accident and by an alleged law.[16]

I say an alleged law, because it is not a real law. The passage, "thy husband shall rule over thee," etc., was not conceived at all in the usual form of divine laws, which are imperatives and accompanied by threats against those who do not obey them. Women who are not married are exempt, although they are the same race and sex as Eve no less than the others. Just think how many women there are who have taken husbands below them in social class without becoming in the least subservient to them. How many princesses who, far from being ruled by men have, on the contrary, ruled over kingdoms or whole empires and have exercised over men an authority incomparably greater than that which husbands have over their wives. Wives are not all equally dependent on their husbands—some more, others less, according to climate and custom, in Europe very many fewer than in Africa and Asia. All this makes it quite obvious that only custom and the laws of men have put women under their authority, and that if, as we have seen, they have the authority to extend or limit this power, they also have the authority to abolish it altogether without contravening the orders of God.

Those who maintain that the first woman was made subject to her husband as punishment for her sin overlook the fact that their opinion is still flawed by arguments which are directly at variance with the idea that the Scriptures give us of God's justice, teaching us that He punishes people according to the evil they commit so that the most wicked always receive the harshest chastisement.

It cannot be denied that Eve was less guilty than Adam. She was a woman, and therefore weaker according to common opinion, and thus more excus-

---

16. The distinction being made here is between "natural law" (given by nature or God) and "positive law" (actual laws promulgated by a king or passed by a legislature). Poullain argues that women's dependence is based on positive law which, in his view, is arbitrary (hence he calls it here "alleged law"), not on natural law (which he designates here by "some general rule"). Theories of natural law had been revived and developed during the seventeenth century by Hugo Grotius (1583–1645) and Samuel Pufendorf (1632–94). See Alcover, *Poullain*, 84.

able. It was not she, but Adam, who had received the prohibition from God. She resisted the devil and Adam did not. This is the reason why the first sin is imputed to Adam by the theologians. It was to him that God first spoke after the Fall. It was he who was so roundly mocked by God when, after clothing him in an animal skin, He said to him: "Behold, Adam is become as one of us" (Gen. 3:22). And it seems it was purely due to him that his companion was driven from the earthly paradise, since the Scriptures named only him in this exodus: "Lest Adam eat also of the Tree of life and live for ever God sent him forth from the Garden of Eden."

Yet Eve was the most unfortunate, for in addition to the necessity of dying which she shared with Adam, she also lost her liberty in becoming subservient to him. It is thus that the common people conceive dependence. Adam, on the other hand, seems to have been rewarded for his disobedience and to have had reason to rejoice in it, seeing that he thus gained dominion over a person who had been his equal hitherto. But it is hardly likely that God would have given him a privilege whose exercise demanded much wisdom and reason at a time when he had just sinned so disgracefully against both. This shows yet again that it is a childish illusion to say that the Devil first spoke to Eve as being the weaker. That would be to attribute to him our own prejudice, in the same way as we attribute it to God when we imagine His purposes.

Yet another thing. What is the nature of this dominion that was given to the first man and his descendants? Dominion is properly the power and the right that we have to make a thing serve all manner of uses. How could it be shown that Adam had God-given mastery over his wife to a greater degree than she had over him? We are masters only of two things: ourselves and the external things that are necessary for the preservation of our lives, because that is all we possess. All the sages have recognized with St. Paul that the husband and wife have a reciprocal power over the person of the other. And the Scripture does not say that Eve fell further than her husband from the power that God had given them jointly over all the goods of the earth, nor that she was obliged to depend on him for the use of these goods. The women among us do not depend on their husbands in this respect either, but only on the dispensation of the property held in common, again according to specific conventions and to a greater or lesser degree according to different countries and customs. The word "dominion" implies an authority equal (1) to that which God possesses over creatures, as when Scripture says that He is the Lord (*Dominus*), that is to say, He has an absolute dominion over them; (2) to that which humans have over animals which is noted in the words: "Let them have dominion over the fish of the sea," etc.; (3) to that which princes of the earth exercise over their subjects and which Jesus Christ meant when He forbade His Apostles to try to rule as princes; (4) to that which masters have over their slaves, valets, and vassals, when they are called lords (*domini*). For since on the one hand it cannot be shown to what God has reduced this alleged dominion of husbands, and on the other hand it would be ridiculous to wish that it were similar to that of God over His creatures, of princes over their subjects, of masters over their slaves, of fathers and mothers over their children, so there is reason to conclude that men's only authority is what they choose to attribute to themselves.

In order to clarify some of the difficulties that might arise, we should note that there are two kinds of superiority, one of will and power when one can force others to do what one wishes, the other of mind and learning when one has enough to guide the conduct of others. For the first, it is only God who possesses it, because He is the only sovereign, on whom all of us without exception depend. The reason that one person is not naturally subject to the will of another is that since their wills are equal in extent, self-interest, and blindness, everyone having an equal right to all things, there is no reason why one should be more dependent than another. Thus women are as much exempt as we are from this domination of the will, since they share in it equally with us, unless, by abandoning reason in favor of the use of force— an attribute in which we surpass them—we want to subdue them, as we subdue the beasts.

As to the superiority of learning and mind, nature has not put it in one sex more than the other, since a disposition for knowledge does not belong to men when they come into the world any more than it does to women.

Far from believing that God has given to males superiority of power and rule, we conceive it in God Himself only because in Him it is allied with sovereign wisdom, so that we necessarily believe that He can will nothing but what is wise, but it is never found alone in men without excesses and injustice. Even the authority of princes is reasonable and legitimate only when it is accompanied by wisdom and prudence and when they use force solely to lead back to reason those who have strayed from it.

Inasmuch as men are not permitted to employ force in their relations with their wives—and almost all well-regulated states forbid such behavior— all our natural authority is reduced to the power of reason and belongs equally to the two sexes. This is perfectly easy to understand if we realize that public and private authority has as its sole end to indicate to those who are subject to it what reason requires them to do; in no way does it seek to subject them to the will of those who publish it, for these people are merely the instruments of reason. Thus, when we are capable of reason and when our laws conform to it, it is not the person who commands that we obey, but rather our own reason which is aware of its obligations; and in these situations we should act as though, while pondering our obligations, our own meditation had led us to what we are duty bound to do. The wise recognize only the authority of reason. When they do what they are ordered to do, if there is reason in it, then it is reason they obey; and if there is no reason in it, then in obeying it they still follow reason—reason which makes them understand the necessity of yielding to custom and the law of the strongest and of adjusting to the weakness of others.

According to this principle, setting custom aside, men and women have equal power over each other, a woman being able to govern her husband, a husband his wife. If the latter is obliged to submit to reason when her husband suggests it to her, then the husband is no less honor bound to listen to reason when reason speaks through the mouth of his wife. All other authority between them is tyrannical and usurpatory, exceeding what is sanctioned by equitable, comprehensible human laws.

These reflections can be supported by the writings of several church fathers on the subject of domination. St. Gregory of Nyssa writes:

Testimony of the church fathers on the subject of domination in marriage.

The man who attributes to himself what belongs only to God alone and who imagines that our sex has the right and power to dominate over women is a man who wishes to elevate himself through pride above nature and thinks of himself as possessing a different nature from those who are subject to him. You condemn man to servitude and subjection, whom nature has made free and master of himself. You bring in a law contrary to the purpose of God when you destroy the natural law which God has Himself established, and in this way you oppose the commandment He has given when you seek to put under the yoke those that He has created to be lords of the earth. Have you forgotten the limits that God has put on your power, and do you no longer remember that your domination is confined to mastery over the beasts? Scripture says "Let them command birds, fish, and four-footed beasts." You do not think, therefore, that you are setting yourselves above people who are free by nature, unmindful of what has been subjected to you? You reduce to the level of beasts and even insects those who are of the same nature as yourselves.

When Scripture cries through the mouth of the Prophets, "Thou hast subjected everything to man," it means what is beneath reason, like cattle. Only beasts, therefore, who are not endowed with reason, ought to be in servitude to humans. When a thing comes under your power, it is merely a new name that comes; power adds nothing to nature, neither duration nor privilege. You who are the lord and master of others, and those of whom you are master come into the world and live in it in the same manner, and you are equally subject to passions of the soul and alterations of the body. Tell me, therefore, you who remain always a man, and who are equal to others in everything, in what way do you claim to have sufficient advantage to want to be the master and absolute lord of them?[17]

St. Gregory of Nazianzus,[18] in accusing men of injustice for having made a law which is favorable to them and not at all to women, testifies often that he does not approve the law of dominion that they attribute to themselves, and on which is based the conduct that he condemns. He says:

I see that most men are ill disposed towards women and that the law they have made is unjust and should not be upheld. For why keep women in shackles, while husbands are favored and left in liberty. . . . I cannot approve this custom or this law, and I am not surprised that it is disadvantageous to women. It is men who have made it. They have placed children in the power of their fathers, but God has done otherwise. Honor, he says, your father and your mother if you wish to be happy, and let him who has spoken out against them be put to death. You see the equality that the law itself establishes. In fact man and woman have the same Creator. They are both but the same image of God, they have the same law, the same death, the same resurrection. As we get our birth equally from the man and the woman, we have the same duties toward our fathers and our mothers. Since, therefore, they have the same privileges and the same honors in marriage, why should the law that you make not be equally advantageous to both?

The same conclusion can be drawn from the principles of St. Gregory the Great,[19] who says:

17. See above, note 4 or 11.

18. St. Gregory of Nazianzus (ca. 330–90) was one of the Cappadocian fathers (see above, note 4). He was an eloquent preacher. Poullain identifies the quotation as from *Orations*, 31. We have not identified the source.

19. Pope Gregory I, the Great (ca. 540–604), was the fourth and last of the "doctors" of the Western church. As Pope he took many initiatives for the civil administration and military de-

There is a natural equality between men and we read in the Scripture that God said to Noah after the flood that he should make himself feared by the animals. He did not say that man should be feared by man, but by animals, for it would be to presume in pride—which is contrary to nature—to try to make oneself dreaded by one's equals. It is, however, necessary that those who command should be feared by those who obey them (he is speaking of princes and magistrates). But it is only when they do not fear God, so that those who are not deterred from sin through fear of the judgment of God should at least be deterred from it through fear of men. When those who command are feared by the wicked, it can be said according to the first order of God that they do not so much rule over men as over animals, since they become dreaded only by those who, by the dissoluteness of their lives, sink from the nature and condition of men to that of beasts.

According to these principles domination is contrary to nature; the power of making oneself feared and obeyed, which is what is meant by domination, is based only on lawlessness and simply adds a new name to the one who assumes it.[20] Women, being no more prone to lawlessness than men, have as much right as men to dominate, except that laws and custom prevent them. And in order to show husbands that they are obliged to submit to their wives when they are right, we could cite the passage that St. Jerome uses to prove equality. "Harken unto thy wife Sarah," said the Lord to Abraham, "and do as she would have thee do" (Gen. 12:1).

This equality of dominion, or rather this mutual interdependence in marriage, is also very easy to establish in the writings of St. Augustine,[21] who claims that man should place nothing above himself save God alone, who is

---

fense of Italy. He upheld the primacy of the Roman See and refused to recognize the title "Ecumenical Patriarch" adopted by the Patriarch of Constantinople. Sending missionaries to England (597) turned out to be one of the great accomplishments of his papacy. He was a fertile author, his *Pastoral Rules* being among his best-known works. Poullain cites it here as *Pastoria*, 2.6, but we have not identified the passage.

20. Here again (see note 16 above) Poullain is calling actual laws that govern his own country "lawlessness." See Gibson, *Women in Seventeenth-Century France*, 59–60, 61: "Wifely subordination which tradition recommended was underlined by certain aspects of the complex legal system governing marriage." Particularly in regions under customary law [which coincide with the northern part of France where Poullain lived], "the authority which the husband possessed over his wife's property and legal actions was extended to her person."

21. St. Augustine (354–430) was the most famous of the Latin Fathers, one of the four doctors of the Western church. He was a prolific writer, best known for his *Confessions* (creating a new genre in Western literature) and the *City of God*, his theological philosophy of history, in 22 volumes, written to defend Christianity against the charge that Christians were responsible for the fall of the Roman Empire.

truth itself, and the sovereign reason by which he should be guided. Accordingly, women are obliged to submit themselves to men only when they recognize in them this sovereign reason, or when this same reason makes them realize that they should humor an unreasonable husband and yield to him through the law of the stronger.

Subordination, dependence, command are not the necessary consequences of marriage.

Those who weigh human society only by its mass have difficulty conceiving this equality of power in marriage. Because they consider this little society on a par with those composed of a great number of persons, they imagine that subordination, dependence, and the right to command are equally necessary here, for they have failed to consider carefully why these things exist in large societies.

It is easy to understand that if men wished to take full advantage of the power nature gives them over all things, they would be constantly at war. This is why they have to submit to laws and to sovereigns who have the power to control rights and the use of goods in order to maintain peace, and who delegate to subordinates the authority they cannot wield alone.

Thus fear of dispute over what can be possessed is the principal motive for civil society. Subordination and dependence are based on the number of persons linked together, on the multiplicity of their duties, on the fact that those who are employed do not always know what they are supposed to do, and on the strong possibility of confusion and disorder.

Thus authority—the right to command—presupposes at least three persons, one of whom is able to join forces with another to force the third to abide by his duty. This right does not belong naturally to any one person more than to another, since it consists in the voluntary submission of those who give it to the one who is vested with it.

The society of marriage, however, is composed only of two persons, of whom one, therefore, cannot use authority and coercion towards the other. This society is not founded on fear, but on love. A man and a woman do not seek each other out fearing that one might harm the other over ownership of external possessions; rather they seek to satisfy, through the possession of their own persons, a desire which banishes all fears, which gives them the mutual consideration of the most perfect friendship and which can be fully satisfied without entering into any kind of agreement that might cause division between them. When they agree to live together it is purely voluntary, and at an age when each can have as much reason and experience as the other. Even if women had less, since the contract they make is free, it does not give men any more power than women wish to yield to them. I always except custom. Thus the authority, command, and power over body and goods is as great in the woman as in the man. As they are only two, their duties are very limited and easy to understand, so that there should be between them no more subordination and dependence than between two reasonable friends who decide between themselves how they are to behave. Thus it can be concluded with certainty that women's dependence on men rests entirely on the laws made by men for their own specific advantage.

God was trying to make Eve understand all this when he told her that she would be under the sway of her husband, warning her through these words that the sin in which she had a part would so upset him that without thinking of the equality which existed between them he would use it as a pretext to subject her to a rule of domination. This is actually the only reasonable interpretation—and one worthy of the Scriptures—that we can give the passage if taken literally: "You will be under the sway of your husband," etc., for since it cannot be interpreted either as a positive law or a formal punishment, as we have shown, then it must be a prediction of a misfortune which can nevertheless be taken as an imposed punishment, God having ordained it in a particular way. We can no more say that God, by this act, gave authority to husbands than we can say that He gave to the kings of Israel all the benefits recounted in the Bible; it is certain that in announcing to the people what the kings whom He asked against His will were sure to do, God had no intention of establishing their rights nor of authorizing their enterprises.

This passage can also be understood in perspective as can the one in the same chapter of Genesis where God says to Adam that he will eat his bread by the sweat of his brow. Here He does not include all men but only those who had the misfortune to be born poor, and He warned Adam of what was going to happen to him when, after being banished from the Garden of Eden where he would have found effortlessly all that was needful to him, he would enter a sterile and unprofitable land which would furnish him only after much toil and sweat with whatever would sustain his life for a while. Finally, if men's perverseness has indeed impelled them to try to lord it over other men and almost invariably to turn into tyranny the authority they have held, then we should not be surprised that having always had to live with women they should have used every means and opportunity to become and remain their masters.[22]

22. At the end of the seventeenth century, the most liberal preachers preferred to portray the wife's role in terms of a resigned helpmeet, companionate, understanding, and "reasonable for two" in her marriage. See J. L. Flandrin, *Familles parenté, maison, sexualité dans l'ancienne société* (Paris, 1976), 125.

Study of
passages of
St. Paul that
are used
against
women.

From the way people speak of St. Paul on the subject of women, you would think that he had written a treatise expressly against the equality of the sexes. It is true that in several places he exhorts women to be submissive to their husbands, but he does not say anywhere that they should do so because of their sex or a divine law, which he would not have failed to do, since that would be the most effective means for his purpose. Here are his own words:

> Wives, submit yourselves unto your own husbands as it is fit in the Lord. . . .
> (Col. 3:18)

> The head of every man is Christ; and the head of the woman is the man; and the head of Christ is God.
> (1 Cor. 11:3)

> Wives, submit yourselves unto your own husbands, as unto the Lord. For the husband is the head of the wife, even as Christ is the head of the church: and he is the savior of the body. Therefore as the church is subject unto Christ, so let the wives be to their own husbands in every thing.
> (Eph. 5:22–24)

Is there a single world here about inequality and natural dependence?

The purpose of the Apostle was not to prove to women that they ought to be submissive, since they already were, and they had no thought of being otherwise; but only to keep them in that state through the reasons and examples he offers them. In the same way, when he urges men, subjects, slaves to remain content in their present state of dependence, he does not mean to show that they should be there but simply that they ought to remain there and make their obedience into a sacrament. Now since it does not follow that subjection and slavery are based on divine law simply because St. Paul exhorts those who are in that state to remain content in it, it should not be assumed that he believed that the submission of women was of a similar nature, although he exhorts them strongly to accept it (Col. 3:18). This will appear still clearer if we remember that in the same place he states that there is neither male nor female, neither Jew nor Gentile nor slave in the sight of God, as if he meant that all these differences exist only in the minds of men, and that God, without respect of persons, does not take into account different states but only the manner in which each person, in his own state, fulfills the law of charity (Col. 3:11).

I grant that St. Paul says that man is the head of the woman, but he does not say that this is by a prerogative of sex; the man occupies this position as naturally as do those in any group who occupy a place of authority which they have achieved by election or some other means. And just as the title of "head in Jesus Christ" does not imply that in human terms he was of a more excellent nature than other men—according to these words of the Epistle to the Hebrews, "we have a High Priest who is like to us in all things,"[23]—he does not imply either that males who enjoy this position are more perfect than females.

Let us say therefore with St. John Chrysostom:[24]

We must understand otherwise than common men this passage of St. Paul: women be submissive to your husbands. For if he had wished to indicate by these words dominion and subjection, he would have used the example of the slave and the Lord. Although the woman is submissive to us, it is nonetheless as a woman, that is to say, as a creature who is free and as worthy of esteem and honor as we ourselves.

And lest men overestimate the comparison that the Apostle makes between their marriage and that of Jesus Christ and the church, they should be mindful of two things. First, St. Paul's sole aim is to offer married people the most perfect model for them to follow in their union by exhorting husbands to treat their wives in the same way as Jesus Christ treated the church, and urging women to submit to their husbands to the same degree as the church submits to Jesus Christ. Second, the position of head does not apply to husbands in the same way it does to Jesus Christ.

Jesus Christ is head of the church, having been destined by God to be so, and having been sacrificed for it. He is the head, but a spiritual head, who did not assume any other authority on earth than to teach truth and virtue, to lead us in order to set an example. Far from wishing to wield power, He declared that His Kingdom is not of this world and forbade His disciples to exercise domination over their brethren, warning them that all their greatness

---

23. Poullain's citation is actually a conflation of two verses, Hebrews 4:14–15: "Seeing then that we have a great high priest, that is passed into the heavens, Jesus the Son of God, let us hold fast our profession. For we have not a high priest which cannot be touched with the feeling of our infirmities; but was in all points tempted like as we are, yet without sin."

24. St. John Chrysostom (ca. 347–407) was bishop of Constantinople and a "doctor" of the Eastern church. His name "Chrysostom" means "the golden-mouthed," a name given him because of his extraordinary style of preaching. His sermons on books of the Bible establish him as one of the great Christian expositors. His plain speaking alienated him from the Empress Eudoxia, and he eventually deposed from his See. Poullain identifies the passage he cites as coming from *On the Epistle to the Corinthians*. We have not identified the passage.

consisted in their abasement and that he who desired to be first and greatest should become the least and the last. Thus the subordination of the church with respect to Jesus Christ is in no way a subordination of domination and command, but a subordination of truth, reason, and love.

The situation is wholly different with husbands. They have laid claim to the position of superiority and still cling to it. Theirs is an authority of harshness, domination, selfishness, and pride that they have established and maintained solely to satisfy their passions, for they are no less subject to ignorance and disorder than those whom they have subjugated. In sum, this authority is an advantage obtained through disregard of order and kept through custom and the laws. If they are to be worthy of the position of head in the sight of God they must earn it through qualities so like those of Jesus Christ that women would not be capable of attaining it.

It is true that Jesus Christ is not subject to the church as we have shown that husbands should be to their wives in matters of the spirit. But the reason for this difference is obvious. Not only was Jesus Christ sent from God in order to form, instruct, and govern the church, but He has always possessed and preserved the characteristics and talents with which He was vested for that purpose. Men, on the other hand, despite the advantages of the education they normally receive, are as full of blindness and faults as women. This is what should convince them of the vanity of their pretensions, for it is unlikely that if God had meant them rather than women to head their families, He would have withheld from them the qualities necessary to fulfill such a task. There is no better proof that men were not called by God to a particular estate than that they do not live as they should, which is only too common among men both in marriage and elsewhere.

Here is another passage from St. Paul which is also used against us:

> Every man praying or prophesying, having his head covered, dishonoreth his head. But every woman that prayeth or prophesieth with her head uncovered dishonoreth her head (1 Cor. 11:4–5a). For a man indeed ought not to cover his head, forasmuch as he is the image and glory of God: but the woman is the glory of the man. For the man is not of the woman; but the woman of the man. Neither was the man created for the woman; but the woman for the man. For this cause ought the woman to have power on her head.
> (11:7–10a)

This passage is neither here nor there as far as we are concerned. At the time of St. Paul and in his country, men had their heads uncovered when praying to God. Women, on the contrary, always covered their heads with a veil, especially when they appeared in public, as a mark of dependence, or refinement, or some such thing. St. Paul, who approved this practice—which has been abolished in most places as being arbitrary—is seeking a convention to support his argument. On the one hand he says that women dishonor their heads by uncovering them. This is, in fact, when usage is against it, even in the case of men who flaunt the rules of propriety when they uncover their heads in situations and countries where this is not the custom. On the other hand, he says that man is the image and glory of God, because he was created first, and that the woman is the glory of man, because she was created for man. He does not say that she is not the image of God, otherwise he would contradict Scripture itself. He does not say that she is less perfect than man, he says that she was made for man and concludes from this simply that she is in some way the image and glory of man, and not that she is not equal to him nor that she ought to be submissive to him. And as if he feared that men would see this as an opportunity to elevate themselves as they do, after saying that woman was made for man, he adds: "Nevertheless, neither is the man without the woman, neither the woman without the man, in the Lord. For as the woman is of the man, even so is the man also by the woman; but all things of God" (1 Cor. 11:11–12). Here it is clear that St. Paul unites the two sexes in God, very far from dividing them through an imaginary difference. And to end with his own words all the difficulties that might arise over the distinction between nature and custom, it is important to observe that he says in the same chapter that nature teaches women to keep their heads covered, and this is why nature gave them hair, as if it had not been given to men for the same purpose. We see, therefore, that he has mistaken long custom for nature. And as incontestable proof that he was not persuaded by all the conventions used, particularly the one on the order of the birth of Eve and Adam, here are the words with which he ends: "But if any man seem to be contentious, we have no such custom" (11:16). Thus, this last passage does not affect our subject any more than the other did.

This passage from St. Peter does not give us any greater difficulty. Here are his words:

> For after this manner in the old time, the holy women also, who trusted in God, adorned themselves, being in subjection unto their own husbands; even as Sarah obeyed Abraham, calling him lord: whose daughters ye are, as long as ye do well. . . . Likewise ye husbands, dwell with them . . . giving honor unto the wife, as unto the weaker vessel.
> (1 Peter 3:5–7a)

According to St. Peter, therefore, women ought to obey their husbands as their lords, and as persons who have the right to dominate over them, because they are weaker and consequently less capable of governing.

We do not claim that women should be dispensed from submission and obedience when they owe it, for men themselves are not exempt from it among themselves.[25] But we ought not to say that on this account those who are submissive are less perfect than those who are not, and that we are speaking here of masters, lords, and princes. The word "lord" is as often a term of politeness as of dependence. If women sometimes call their husband lord and master, husbands also often call their own wives lady and mistress. Sarah called Abraham "my lord," and Abraham called Sarah "my lady." For Sarah means my lady and my princess. And he obeyed her submissively. He received the command from God to obey her also: *"Listen to all that she shall tell you and do it."*

Women are the weaker vessel. So be it. But as the fathers we quoted above said, this infirmity, or rather this fragility, is only in the body and not in the mind (Gen. 21:12). For the word vessel means merely body as it does in St. Paul. Reason and experience teach us that even if one is frail, one is not less intelligent or less reasonable. Those who have the greater strength do not always have greater intelligence, genius, or skill. Strength of mind consists in clear and distinct knowledge, and in a strong conviction of the things one knows, and in these respects women—and anyone else who has a frail body—are not less capable than others.

Why God gave preference to males over females in the domain of public office.

The false ideas that we have in society of title and position give rise to a somewhat specious difficulty, but one which is as easily resolved as the others. Men, who are used to treating important positions with esteem and even admiration, since those positions usually confer the things that flatter greed, never fail to imbue them with their notions of excellence and nobility and to consider those who hold them as superior in merit as well as in honor and wealth. And since they judge God according to themselves, they treat Him with the same reverence they have for the men who have risen above the common people and imagine that He gave preference to males over females in ecclesiastical and civil positions because of a special esteem He has for our sex, and that this esteem is based on respect for the exceptional talents He chose to give us which make us incomparably more capable of great things than women.

I suspect that the prejudice of language contributes to this view, and that males believe also that they are closer to God and more highly

25. Poullain's views on matrimony were isolated in his time, and at least until the beginning of the nineteenth century when "marriage reforms" began to be perceived as necessary. See F. Lebrun, *La Vie conjugale sous l'ancien regime* (Paris, 1975), 81.

esteemed by Him because they make Him speak like them, saying that he is king, lord, father, etc., not queen, lady, mother, etc. Painters have perhaps also given the same impression through their images. By dint of seeing God represented in the shape of a man, we become used to imagining Him as something like men. There are very many other sleights of imagination which few people have perceived and by which we are duped.

Be that as it may, in order to correct our misapprehensions about positions and worldly greatness, we have only to reflect that they are nothing but men's particular opinions or particular external trappings, which merely give a new name to people who possess them, without effecting any change in their nature or expecting them to have a more excellent mind than others, but expecting them only to have acquired the necessary talents to perform satisfactorily in their positions. They are sometimes called the highest ranks, not that people who occupy them are more highly deserving than others, but because only those with highest personal qualities should be raised to them. It was right to name them ranks and positions of honor in order to show that those who occupy them merely change situation and that if the honors and the perquisites that go with them were withdrawn, then the loftiest and most powerful positions would become the lowliest and most insignificant. Finally, if we reflect that it is nearly always birth, wealth, and fortune that make it possible for people to rise and that all the necessary attributes are the result of education, we will realize that it is a mistake to esteem women less than men since they have no access to education.

As for the Scripture, so far from making us believe that high rank makes men more pleasing to God, it teaches us, on the contrary, that honors, power, knowledge, and wealth are but emptiness and vanity if they are not sustained by virtue which, by itself alone, constitutes true nobility of soul in His sight. He gives no thought to whether we are male or female, rich or poor, prince or subject, but whether we are righteous or sinners, which are the only two distinctions by which He values and judges men. What gives us the first place in the world sometimes gives us the last in His sight. We can drive out devils, perform miracles, be king, prophet, sacrificial priest, in a word possess everything that brings us the respect and admiration of men, yet be the object of God's hatred and abomination.

To be king in His eyes is to cause Him to reign in us, by submitting our will to His. And to be high priest of sacrifice is to offer ourselves to Him as a holy and living host, to offer up to Him without ceasing on the altar of our heart sacrifices of praise and justice (Ecclus. 35). It is certain that women have an equal part with men in this sacred order in which we are at one and the same time priest and king, where the dignity of priests is royal and royalty priestly, and where we are at the same time the sacrificial priest, the temple, altar, and victim, and where the highest rank is awarded only according to merit and not according to sex.

Finally, since the Scripture teaches us that women are capable of error and truth, of vice and virtue, that God has made them in His image, that He favors them, punishes them and rewards them as He does men, that He commands them to honor Him, to do good and not to do evil one to the other, we can conclude that He esteems them equally, and it is an indispensable obligation for us to follow His example and His judgments.

If, therefore, we ask why He has always given preference to males over females in the area of public office, we can reply in this case as in all others where the Scripture gives no reason for His conduct, that it has pleased Him to act thus; or we can say that as He orders everything with kindness, like a good father whose sole interest is that of his children, He is happy to comply with their wishes and their customs when they are not contrary to His purposes.

We do see in fact that in respect of the quality of the universal cause, He usually follows the disposition of particular causes in physics and morals, so that they will be adjusted to our temperament, habits, and usages. He allowed His prophets to speak of His acts as though He were susceptible to passion in order to accommodate Himself to the weakness of men who have difficulty in imagining Him except in coarse and material images. He adopted their language, their style, their proverbs. He explained Himself through the mouth of Moses and Isaiah who were brought up at court, in language wholly different from that of Jeremiah, who had always lived in the country; and through the mouth of St. John with a gentleness and simplicity very different from the others.

Judaic laws were for the most part national, that is to say, based on the genius and customs of the people for whom they were created. They were forbidden to use certain animals because of the diseases they might have. They were prohibited from lending money at interest, seeing that since they were extremely avaricious and self-interested, the poor would have remained without assistance. The law of retaliation allowed them to pluck out the eye of anyone who plucked out theirs, and the law which made husbands free to repudiate their wives, to fulfill or annul their vows, was based on the harshness of the Jewish people, as Jesus Christ Himself told them. Finally, the law of charity which includes all other laws, all the prophets, and all religion is a law of adaptation, of accommodation and impartiality which, as St. Paul practiced it, makes us Jews with the Jews. This is why, since males have always been masters and more highly regarded, we can say that this is the reason that the Scripture speaks only of men in the genealogies it records, that

God assumed their sex, that He spoke like them, took their titles of king and father, and spoke to both sexes under the names *man, just man, sinful man, sons or enemies of God* which, according to the usage of all languages, include equally men and women.

Thus since the Jews, like all the Orientals and the Romans, are extremely jealous of their authority and are masters of their wives, it is not to be wondered at that the Apostle, following his completely Christian precepts of accommodating himself to everyone, should have so strongly exhorted women to submission and silence for the sake of peace in the family, recommending that they wear a veil, even going so far as to say that it is shameful and a crime against nature to do otherwise.[26]

But lest it be imagined that he had something else in mind, let us examine his words. He proposed an order that should be observed in the assemblies, arguing that they would thus take place in a peaceful and orderly fashion; then he added:

> Let your women keep silence in the churches: for it is not permitted unto them to speak; but they are commanded to be under obedience, as also saith the law. And if they will learn any thing, let them ask their husbands at home: for it is a shame for women to speak in the church.
> (1 Cor. 14:34–35)

In the Epistle to Timothy he says nearly the same thing in these words:

> Let the women learn in silence with all subjection. But I suffer not a woman to teach, nor to usurp authority over the man but to be in silence. For Adam was first formed, then Eve. And Adam was not deceived but the woman being deceived was in transgression.
> (1 Tim. 2:11–14)

Does this mean that women are less capable of teaching and governing than men? The Apostle does not speak of them all in a general way, but only of those who are married, since the conduct of a marriage is the most important thing in one's life. It is the only thing that can deter them from participating in the sciences and professions. This is why he says at the end of the same chapter that they will work for their salvation through the education of their children.

26. Stuurman, "From Feminism to Biblical Criticism," 370: "Poulain's statement regarding these Biblical texts is strikingly akin to Spinoza's approach in the *Tractatus theologico-politicus* (1670). Like Spinoza, Poulain characterizes the Jewish laws as historically specific and refuses to attribute any universal validity to the social and cultural teachings of the Bible; thus, those teachings are reduced to the status of adaptations to the customs of particular times and places."

It is shameful for women to speak in the church, as it is shameful that they have their heads uncovered and that lay people speak in the church where custom forces them into silence. *If they will learn anything, let them ask their husbands at home.* This advice is excellent to avoid the confusion that would be bound to ensue if everyone tried to speak in the church. And it is to be hoped that husbands might have enough virtue and enlightenment to serve as masters and directors of their wives and that their wives might be content with this arrangement. But this does not mean that a husband should not consult his wife when she has more learning than he does.

I suffer not a woman to teach nor to usurp authority of the man. This depends only on permission and not on capacity. Not all men, however learned they may be, are allowed to teach in public. But if women understand the truth and teach it to their children, their servants, their husbands, their particular communities, only custom prevents them from doing so in public; the one is no more difficult than the other. As for domination over others, Christians should not practice it among themselves, nor—even less—should women towards their husbands, for custom is not on their side. But that does not exclude them from government.

Let women be silent, for Adam was first formed, and Adam was not led astray as was Eve. It is therefore not because they are women and that their sex is less fit to speak than ours. If this had been St. Paul's view, he would not have failed to say so, as being a better reason to force women into silence. As St. Gregory of Nazianzus says:[27] "If Eve has sinned, Adam has also sinned in the same way. Both have been deceived by the serpent, and we should not believe that the woman was weaker and that her husband showed greater strength."

Since St. Paul recognized that sin entered the world through the first man, when he says that it was Eve who was seduced, his idea is that Eve was deceived by the Devil immediately and that Adam was deceived through Eve. But how does this affect the equality of the sexes? These are not essential reasons used by the Apostle to validate custom, but are simply conventions, taken from remote history and a personal incident, which could also be used against men. For if the first man had been created after his wife and for his wife, and had been immediately led astray—something not at all impossible—and if since that time men had been under the power of their wives, then in order to keep them in a state of submission, they would have been told in the same way that they should not rule over their wives but obey them and ask them, with fear and respect, whatever they want to know. Reasoning

27. Poullain cites no source. We have not identified the passage.

of this kind does not prove anything when we examine it closely, for there is nothing it cannot destroy or establish.[28]

This is how we should reply to those who use to their advantage the fact that, under ancient law, women paid only half as much as males to redeem their vows, and that only males could be called the firstborn and offered to God, as being more acceptable to Him. For:

1. Women could pay twice as much as men and be consecrated to God if He had so ordained.

2. As this is not practiced in the new law, it is a sign that it was only a rule of discipline, no less than the repugnance with which women are viewed in the matter of ecclesiastical charges.

3. It is a proof of favor to require less of one person than of another for atonement.

4. The Scriptures teach us that God had ordered the Jewish people to make an offering of the firstborn, so that they would remember the massacre of the firstborn in Egypt, an act accomplished to bring them out of that country.[29]

Scripture does not say why some of the righteous men of the Old Testament had several wives. We do not see that Adam, who began the world, nor Noah and his children who restored it, had more than one each. The world was already populated when Jacob married Leah and Rachel and had his way with their serving maids. If celibacy is a more tranquil and happy state than marriage, if continence, as Jesus Christ teaches, is a gift from Heaven, it is difficult to believe that having several wives is a similar gift, or to believe that God chose this way to show that He loves one sex more than the other.

But finally, people say, if the sexes are equal and hence equally valued by God, and are capable of great things, it would be the final injustice in men not to give women their share in them. The prophets and apostles would not have failed to preach against such a universal and ancient confusion. There could hardly be a more erroneous interpretation than this. It is true that it is a sign of ignorance or prejudice in men to believe that they are more perfect than women; it is vain folly to despise them because they are dependent, and it is tyranny to treat them in a lordly fashion and to make laws advantageous

---

28. Stuurman, "From Feminism to Biblical Criticism," 370: "Eve's seduction is thus relegated to the status of a historically contingent event. Poulain seems on the verge of denying the universal significance of the Fall of Man, all the more so because he never dwells on the sinful condition of mankind and consistently upholds an eudemonistic vision of human nature."

29. In Exodus 12 the Israelites are ordered to slaughter a male lamb for each family or group of families. But the text does not explicitly say "first-born."

to us and disadvantageous to them. But it is in no way an injustice not to call them to share in what we possess. For in addition to the fact that, considered dispassionately, the professions, for example, are onerous burdens, [it is also true that] they do not belong to one sex more than the other—for both men and women could fill them—and that since it is not necessary for the well-being of society that these positions should be divided between men and women, it makes no difference which of them holds them, provided that whoever it is does not abuse them. In the same way, all the families in a state could have the crown, but it is not an injustice that one particular family should possess it, nor that freedom, honors, and wealth should be shared unequally among men, since only the abuse of these things is contrary to equality.

Thus, so far is religion, which occupies the strictest and most holy place in society, from condemning these sorts of institutions, that on the contrary it approves and sanctifies them, and while all the time endorsing an apparent inequality, it preserves true equality by the law of charity which makes people who possess some particular advantage consider themselves as merely its temporary stewards, so that they can share it in brotherhood with others. This is why there was no need for the prophets, apostles, and saints to speak against the inequality of possessions, but only against the abuses which can arise from it. They did so in no uncertain terms when they denounced injustice and established the maxims of Christian charity.

That according to the Scripture, women are no more prone to vice than men.

It is because they have not understood these maxims very well and have not realized that charity is the basis for our perfection, nobility, and merit in the eyes of God, that some people have thought the Scripture implies that women have a greater propensity and potential for evil than men. For since the Scripture offers everyone, indiscriminately, virtue and reward, it teaches us at the same time that we are all equally capable of both and as a result equally worthy of the love and the esteem of God.

In order to judge this more accurately, we should examine its principle and consider that there are two kinds of virtue, one of nature and the other of establishment or of custom. The first consists in the use of ourselves, of our powers, of our bodies and our mind, and all that surrounds us, according to reason, without considering the way in which men have been able to bend this usage. For example, to be sober, according to nature and reason, means to take nourishment in a quantity and quality suitable to our age, temperament, and present circumstances. To do otherwise is to sin against this virtue.

The virtue of convention consists in the use of things according to the laws, practices, and customs in force in the place one is in. The opposite vice is when one flouts custom in public without extenuating circumstances. Women, being no less capable than men of knowing themselves—as we have shown elsewhere (*On the Education of Ladies*, Fourth Conversation)— when it comes to self-knowledge are equally able to make rational use of everything that contributes to the preservation of their bodies and the perfection of their minds, which is true virtue. It cannot be denied that they are less subject than we are to a great deal of dissoluteness and crime, that they observe the most trivial customs to the point of scrupulousness, and that they have always been considered—and rightly so—as having more piety, courage, and zeal in religion than men.

Although when we consider vice and virtue in terms of nature, the same action in the same circumstances cannot be more worthy of praise or blame in one person and one sex than in another, nevertheless, custom gives a different slant to things and brings it about that an overindulgence in wine, for example, which should be equally shocking anywhere, because it is equally contrary to the laws of nature and of reason, is more offensive in men of a certain status—magistrates, for example—because we are not as used to seeing them fall into this state.

This way of reacting to things and of judging them on the basis of custom is how we have always behaved towards women. For although they have the right to think, speak, act, observe the same way men do, caprice and usage demand that the things permitted to men be entirely forbidden to women—for example that anger and drunkenness in men should be only slightly offensive whereas in women they arouse disgust.

Even if it were true that women are more swayed by passion, we could not conclude that that is a disadvantage to them, since inclinations, temperaments, and passions are instruments the soul can put to either good or bad use, depending on the circumstance and the way they are used. If there are some situations in which it is dangerous to give rein to the impulse of anger, there are others in which we should do so with prudence, in order to safeguard ourselves against the ills which beset us.

There is in our inclinations a certain complementarity of good and bad which makes them all nearly equal. For example, the inclination to love, which we all excuse or condemn depending on the cast of our imagination, is usually accompanied by gentleness, playfulness, willingness, generosity, openness, which are qualities not found in the same way in other temperaments.

We must remember that the common people almost never use moderation in judgments or in speech, always indulging in exaggeration and hyper-

294 On the Excellence of Men

bole, and making generalizations on the basis of five or six specific examples. If a man is generous, he is said to be a great philanthropist; if he is thrifty and prudent, he is accused of being a tightfisted skinflint. If we know five or six people from the same country, society, or condition who have some virtue or who possess some true or imaginary defect, then we apply these to everyone from the same group.

This behavior is the norm among poets and orators, Greeks and peoples of Asia, of whom the Jews were formerly a part. This is why, if the Scripture speaks of the defects of women in stronger terms than it speaks of those of men, it is merely imitating the way people commonly speak of women, the way they are allowed to act, and the way custom and prejudice make us view their conduct.

The strongest arguments against them are in the books of Proverbs and Ecclesiastes, in which there are the most remarkable passages, and which will give us some idea of the others.

> I applied mine heart to know, and to search and to seek out wisdom, and the reason of things (Ecclesiastes 7:25a). . . . One man among a thousand have I found; but a woman among all those have I not found. (Eccles. 7:28)

> The malice of man is nothing compared with that of woman.[30]

> There is no wrath to compare with theirs.
> (Ecclesiasticus 25:13)[31]

> I had rather dwell with a lion or a dragon, than to keep house with a wicked woman.
> (Ecclus. 25:16)

> It is better to dwell in the wilderness than with a contentious and an angry woman.
> (Prov. 21:19)

> The malicious tongue of a woman is to a peaceful man what a sandy mountain is to the feet of an old man.
> (Ecclus. 25:27)[32]

30. Poullain cites Ecclesiasticus 25:26, but the verse does not correspond. Ecclus. 25:16–26 contains a series of verses on the evils of wicked women; Poullain quotes several. Here he may be misquoting 25:19, "All wickedness is but little to the wickedness of a woman." However, the discrepancy here suggests he was writing from memory.

31. In the King James Version, Ecclesiasticus 25:13 reads: "[Give me] any wickedness but the wickedness of a woman."

32. Here Poullain's citation does not match the text. The verse is Ecclesiasticus 25:20, not 25:27, which does not exist.

A grief of heart and sorrow is a woman that is jealous over another woman, and a scourge of the tongue which communicateth with all.
(Ecclus. 26:6)

Give not thy soul unto a woman to set her foot upon thy substance.
(Ecclus. 9:2)

When women have once taken authority and advantage they become vexatious to their husbands.
(Ecclus. 25:30)[33]

Who can find a virtuous woman?
(Prov. 31:10a)

What magnifies the evil ideas that one gets from these passages is the way the Scripture speaks to men in order to turn their minds away from the dissolute acts they could commit with women.

Beware of allowing yourself to be overcome by their artifices. . . .
(Prov. 5:2)[34]

. . . sit not in the midst of women.
(Ecclus. 42:12)

Of the woman came the beginning of sin, and through her we all die.
(Ecclus. 25:24)

For from garments cometh a moth and from women wickedness. Better is the churlishness of a man than a courteous woman.
(Ecclus. 42:13–14a)

Gaze not on a maid, that thou fall not by those things that are precious in her.
(Ecclus. 9:5)

Turn away thine eye from a beautiful woman . . . for many have been deceived by the beauty of a woman; for herewith love is kindled as a fire.
(Ecclus. 9:8)

Wine and women will make men of understanding to fall away (Ecclus. 19:2a), as happened to Adam, Samson, David, and Solomon.

It is good for a man not to touch a woman.
(1 Cor. 7:1)

33. There is no Ecclesiasticus 25:30, and we have not identified the passage Poullain may have had in mind.

34. Proverbs 5:2 says nothing about women. But it does beginning at 5:3, at least up to 5:8. And although it can be said that the sentiment expressed in Poullain's citation is there, the actual words are not.

These are they which were not defiled with women; for they are virgins. These are they which follow the Lamb whithersoever he goeth.
(Rev. 14:4)

On this point, as Scripture says nothing similar to women to turn them
away from men, we imagine them as if they were the cause of all the dissoluteness in the world, and as if they had been created only to be used by the
Devil to lead our sex astray.

If we want to make a balanced judgment about all of these passages, we
should pause for reflection.

1. Proverbs and Ecclesiasticus are books of morality where the particular
inclinations of men are not discussed but rather their conduct, according to
custom, habit, and education, which often force us into actions contrary to
our inclinations.

2. As these books seem to be addressed only to men, and practically not
at all to women, we should see them as the precepts that a wise and enlightened father might offer his son, pointing out what he ought to watch for and
avoid with women. But we should remember that he speaks only on the basis
of what he has discovered through his own experience, since he says that he
"has sought wisdom," etc. and that he "has not found it," etc. Thus we should
not take him literally nor apply to the entire sex what he says of women, but
metaphorically and as applying only to some.

When he says that he has not found wisdom among women, he is speaking of an acquired wisdom, which comes less from nature than from study
and experience, which women do not have to the extent men do—particularly Jewish women who were very much more constrained than Europeans.
And it is hardly a great recommendation for men that among a thousand he
found one who was wise.

If men had to suffer women's wickedness, anger, and jealousy, as women
do men's, we could take these words literally, *there is no wickedness, anger, or jealousy like to that of a woman.*[35] If we understand this as meaning an inclination
and a power to do great evil, we can say, therefore, that women can do great
good, for the powers and means which can bring about the one can equally
bring about the other: it is the purpose, intention, and manner of using them
that create vice and virtue. But the natural meaning of the words is perhaps
that these passions, these defects, stand out and shock more in women, either
because women do not succumb to them so often or because we cannot bear
that they should be allowed the same things as we are, or, finally, because

---

35. In the preceding quotations, there is none that reads as does this one, and we have not identified its precise equivalent.

women carry their resentment very much further, thanks to the way they are brought up, which makes them much more sensitive than we are to many things. Once they have transgressed the strict bounds of propriety that are imposed on them, they put greater effort into escaping from what is inimical to them.

When Ecclesiasticus warns us not to give power over ourselves to a woman, it is speaking only of a blind and headstrong power that debauchery and baseness can give her. We certainly do not need to subject ourselves to this kind of domination either by women or men, and anyone who allows himself to be dictated to in this way usually ends up helpless before someone who is either uncontrolled or self-interested and who abuses the credulity of others. It is in no way speaking of the power and authority needed for the governance of a family or a kingdom. Sacred and secular history teaches us that there have been large numbers of women who have governed with great wisdom their husbands, their children, their families, their society, and their entire state.

Even if it were usual for them to misuse the power they hold, they would only be following the example of men; and also, when one is not used to being in command, when one has not been trained for such a role and is not expecting it, one is in danger of being overwhelmed.

If anyone says to a woman, intending to disparage her worth, *an unjust man is better than a woman who does good,* we can ask him to give his own solution to the gross absurdity he accuses the Scripture of, and make him see his ignorance or his wickedness by showing him that this passage has been altered. For the passage reads *an unjust man is better than a woman who does good and brings confusion and opprobrium.* [36] That is to say, the favors of a scheming woman whose purpose is to deceive are more to be feared than an overt act of injustice.

This shows us how unfairly we abuse Holy Scripture when we make it say the opposite of its true meaning. We see it also in the ordinary usage of these words, *who can find a virtuous woman?* As if Scripture meant by this that it is extremely rare to find one. But that is not at all what it means. The last chapter of Proverbs, from which these words are taken, contains the instructions King Solomon received from his mother; some advice she gave about finding a wife. She began by specifying the qualities she should have, exclaiming: *Who can find a virtuous woman? for her price is far above rubies.* She then

---

36. Ecclesiasticus 42:14 reads in the King James Version: "Better is the churlishness of a man than a courteous woman, a woman, I say, which bringeth shame and reproach." And in the Revised Standard Version: "Better is the wickedness of a man than a woman who does good; it is woman who brings shame and disgrace."

continued by describing the advantages a woman of this kind could bring into his family. If we attempt to change this figurative expression into another expression which is simple and without ambiguity, and which has a natural connection with what precedes and what follows, we must necessarily express it in these terms: *He who finds a virtuous woman finds an inestimable jewel,* etc.

Be that as it may, there are three or four considerations which refute anything from the Scripture that could be used against us.

1. It does not speak of all women.

2. It says at least as much good as bad. "A virtuous woman rejoiceth her husband and he shall fulfill the years of his life in peace" (Ecclus. 26:2). "A good wife is a good portion, which shall be given in the portion of them that fear the Lord" (Ecclus. 26:3). "A virtuous woman is a crown to her husband" (Prov. 12:4a). "Whoever is wise and prudent builds his house. The poor groan where there is no woman," etc. (Ecclus. 14:26).[37]

3. The amount of bad it says of men surpasses what it says about women to the same extent that we believe our sex is more excellent than theirs.

4. What it says against women could just as well be applied to men by substituting the word "man" for "woman." In fact, could not a mother who wanted to instruct her daughter say something like the following:

"My daughter, do not go among men, nor allow yourself to be deceived by their artifices, their promises, and their cajoling. Remember that sin began with them and that they are the cause of the unhappiness of all women. The iniquity of woman comes from man. The evil that a woman does is preferable to the good that a man tries to do. Do not spend too long admiring beauty, good looks, nor all that adds grace to men for fear that this will excite in you the fire of concupiscence and cause you disgrace and scandal, as it has to so many others of your sex I could mention and who were previously very wise and virtuous. Distance yourself therefore from their company as much as possible. You would do better to have no commerce with them, not even marriage. Be mindful that those who follow the lamb everywhere it goes are those who are virgins and not defiled by men.

"Nonetheless, since I do not mean to force your inclination, if it leads you to wish for a husband, mind that you choose well. For it is ex-

37. Ecclesiasticus 14:26 reads: "He shall set his children under her shelter [i.e., goodness, wisdom, and understanding], and shall lodge under her branches." There is no reference here to women, and we have not identified a passage corresponding to Poullain's passage. In any case, he has probably put together two passages and paraphrased both.

tremely rare to find a good one. It is a gift which you should expect only from Heaven. A man of virtue and good sense who loves his wife is a continual source of joy and consolation and is more to be prized than a crown and all the treasures of the world.

"But on the other hand, it is the greatest misfortune for a woman to have a husband given to quarrels, anger, and jealousy. It would be better to live in the desert with tigers, dragons, and the fiercest beasts. It is like a roof which constantly leaks in the middle of the winter and like a wild and tiresome wind that howls without ceasing. For this reason, consider it well.

"If you are blessed with children, take particular care to protect them against vice. Boys require great attention and surveillance lest they escape and go astray. And if ever you see any possibility of that, redouble your vigilance and your care, lest they yield at the first opportunity. You could do nothing better for your peace of mind and for their well-being than to give them a wife who is intelligent and virtuous to rein them in by her modesty and by her gentleness to keep them within the narrow limits they find it so difficult to observe."

In order to address all our concerns about sexual commerce between men and women, we must remember that in their relations with one another, they are like all other goods, of which we can make good or bad use, and for which blame must fall on the one who is guilty, without in any way diminishing the value or the esteem of the thing abused. Thus, although men are capable of using women badly and dishonoring themselves over them, it is no more the fault of women—considering simply the question of usage—than it is the fault of the wealth that causes the unhappiness of a prodigal, or of anyone else who does not know how to make use of it. It could even be said, if we examine dispassionately the way women contribute to the downfall of men, and men to that of women, that we have to admit that nearly all the evil is on our side. In fact, although women have at least as much need of men as men have of them, nevertheless they have greater strength to make it not appear so. It is the men who seek, solicit, and pressure them. And it seems, when they yield, that it is rather to escape the burdensome soliciting, or to recognize the services and the attention offered them, the love and esteem shown them, rather than to satisfy a desire that is as natural to them as to us. It is in fact men who reveal their weakness in all this, who abuse women, corrupt them, destroy them, and drag them to the precipice with them.

It was not Delilah who sought out Samson; it was rather he who sought her out. And it was he—with the strength to tear apart lions, to defeat single-handedly great hosts of enemies—it was he, I say, who was weak enough to be conquered by the caresses of a woman and foolish enough to reveal to her the secret on which his freedom and life depended.

Bathsheba had no thought of David on her mind, when he, the prince, who had been smitten by her beauty, sent for her; and it was he who ordered Uriah, the husband of this lady, to be exposed to danger, when he was unable to force him to return home in order to cover up the result of the adultery he had committed with his wife.

Is it the women Solomon loved, or Solomon himself, who should be accused of depravity of mind—he who had been close to the heart of God, who had received so many good things and so much wisdom from Him, he, finally, who was certainly not ignorant of the prohibition God had issued to His people against having commerce with foreign women (Exodus 36)?

We have only to consult Scripture to know who committed the greatest crimes in the eyes of God, whether it is the women who allowed themselves to be corrupted or the men who have corrupted them. Even though Bathsheba was guilty of failing to remain faithful to her husband, it was nevertheless David alone whom God reproached for the crime (2 Kings 2:12).[38] It was to him alone that He sent the prophet Nathan; it was he who did penance; all the punishment fell on him, and it was to punish him that the infant who came from his adultery was struck down dead. Scripture does not say a word against the foreign women with whom Solomon became enamored. "And the Lord was angry against Solomon, because his heart was turned from the Lord God of Israel" (1 Kings 11:9). And Scripture tells us that God, in order to punish him for his sin, roused up his enemies against him and sundered his states.

Thus when women are reproached for corrupting us, they can reply that it is we, on the contrary, who are the cause of their corruption and of their confusion; that the very men who like to think of themselves as the preeminent sex are not ashamed to become their slaves and to sink to the most utter baseness to get them to satisfy their passion; that those men who boast of having greater intelligence, strength, and courage than women have little enough of any of these not to discover their artifices nor to allow themselves to be conquered by such paltry charms; that if there are so many things said to men in the Scripture to deter them from the wickedness they may commit with women, it is not because women enjoy less esteem, but, on the contrary, because, given the weakness of men, they had to be prevented from falling by strong exhortations, without anything similar being said to women, who

38. The citation of 2 Kings 2:12 is incorrect. For the story of David and Bathsheba, see 2 Samuel 11–12.

do not succumb so easily. Finally, if God has not placed women in public, civic, or ecclesiastical positions, it is because men have caused all the evils of society and women have done nothing but follow their example, so that it is only right that men should make amends, for God prefers to find the remedy within the very cause of the ill.

These are the reflections needed to clarify passages read as being contrary to the opinion expressed in *On the Equality of the Two Sexes* and for the effective comparison we mentioned at the outset.

Regarding the *Treatise on the Excellence of Men*, it should be read as if it came from an unknown hand, zealous for the glory of our sex, in order to see whether the author has been biased in his own favor in diminishing the proofs of his adversaries and whether he has said against women all the ill that can be publicly said of them. For invectives are the usual way of attacking women, exaggerating their faults, applying to the entire sex the faults of the few, which are equally found in men, attributing to inclination what is merely an effect of custom, education, and the way they are viewed and view themselves.

REMARKS

Remarks necessary for the clarification of various difficulties about the equality of the sexes and on the excellence of the one in relation to the other.

Although what is in the book *On the Equality of the Two Sexes* should be sufficient to resolve all the considerable difficulties that arise on this subject, it may still be pertinent to add a few remarks.

I. In this case, as in all others, we should study closely the nature of the question to see exactly what is under discussion and what is the aim of the speaker in order to stay within the terms and limits he lays down. We claim simply that the two sexes, considered according to the natural advantages of the mind and body, are equally capable, equally noble, and equally estimable. In my view, therefore, it is irrelevant to ask whether there is some disadvantage in placing women in public positions. For we are not asking whether they *should* be placed there, but only whether they are *capable* of it.

Apart from the fact that an objection does not destroy a truth, those objections that could be used against us come only from custom and from the fact that civil society is considered on the basis of the actual state it is in at this moment and the way in which it is governed and controlled. But we do not reflect that even though things have not always been governed in this way, and are even today not governed in this way all over the world, they have, nonetheless, run smoothly. If women had been in control, they would have regulated privileges and positions in their own way, just as men have. For example, they might have imposed celibacy upon those women who enter positions of public service where this way of life would be more appropriate, just as it is imposed on men.

The obligation marriage imposes upon them to bear children in their womb and suckle them afterwards would have caused them no greater difficulty or obstacle than in the republics of Lycurgus or Plato,[39] where girls would have been brought up with the same discipline as boys and would, perhaps, have acquired the same strength and vigor. And indeed, we know that throughout the Americas and in the greater part of Africa, where women work alongside men, pregnancy is no hindrance to them. They give birth in the middle of the woods and fields; afterwards they wash themselves and the baby in the nearest water source, leave the baby at home unswaddled, and return to their regular work, with greater freedom than before. There are even some places where the husbands take to their beds for childbirth, the newly delivered women acting as nurses.[40]

Be all that as it may, in order for two people to be equal in a society, they do not have to do the same thing, nor do it in the same way. It is enough that they can do equivalent things. Now it is certain that the bearing and nurturing of children, which is women's work, is at least as important and as noble as anything that men do.[41] And since this in no way prevents them from fulfilling their tasks as well as men, whereas men cannot do all that women do, then the two sides are equal.

II. Those who use the consensus of all men as an argument in favor of their claim to excellence give ample demonstration that their reasoning is no more correct than their cause. For from the moment I claim that popular opinion is prejudiced and erroneous, all those who share it become my opponents and are consequently untrustworthy, for then only reason is left to decide between us. And to say that an opinion accepted by all men cannot be false is to beg the question. The paucity of people who follow reason, and the

39. See Plato *Republic* book 5, where Socrates asks, for example: "Is it possible to employ any creature for the same ends as another if you do not assign it the same nurture and education?" And responds: "If we are to use the women for the same things as the men, we must also teach them the same things." *The Collected Dialogues of Plato,* ed. Edith Hamilton and Huntington Cairns (Princeton, 1989), 691.

40. A reference to the practice of couvade reported by ethnologists throughout the world. Poullain's description is strikingly similar to that of Strabo's (ca. 58 B.C.E.–25 C.E.) in his *Geographica* 2.4.17. There is also a reference to couvade in A. Biet, *Voyage de la France équinoxale en l'Isle de Cayenne* (Paris, 1664), 389–90. See Nor Hall's introduction to the re-edition of Warren R Dawson's 1929 text, *The Custom of Couvade,* in *Broodmales* (Manchester, 1989).

41. See, in the translation of *Equality,* Part II, "in what does women's worth consist?"

difficulty we have discovering it, teach us all too well that we should distrust what is most universally accepted and practiced, since that is, perhaps, the most natural effect of men's corruption and of the passions that govern them.

This is why, since men received from the first of their kind [i.e., Adam] an example of domination over women, it is not too hard to understand that they would have kept and transmitted the same example as they spread around the world;[42] or to realize that since the world was already established and imbued with certain ideas, a new ideology would crop up, which, despite its falsity, converted half the earth and has been established now for a thousand years.[43]

It should be added that the testimony of large numbers of people and centuries has its place only in historical matters, where we need to know what was said or done about things that we ourselves cannot be witness to. But this testimony has no use in physics and the other sciences which we can elucidate for ourselves.

Women know nothing except what they are taught by men, and they tend, following the latter's example, to accept all the foolishness that is foisted upon them. This is why it is not surprising that they have always held opinions disadvantageous to themselves, nor that they are so disinclined to believe those who try to put them right; for they are like the children of aristocrats who have been farmed out to a wet-nurse and raised as peasants and who refuse to take seriously the people who come to retrieve them.

III. It makes little sense to resort to animals to judge the excellence of men. If we prize male animals more than females, it is because we do the same among ourselves, since, indeed, we cannot judge them in this respect except in relation to ourselves. Thus I prefer a dog to an ox, since it has greater intelligence. Someone else might prefer an ox to a dog for its extra flesh and strength. Which goes to show that the excellence of beasts from our point of view is quite arbitrary, since it can only be based on bodily similarities between them and us, and on the pleasure and use we get from them, each according to his needs and disposition. For the rest, they should not be seen as examples any more than men are except in one way, namely, when the things we see in them awaken our reason and make us mindful of what we ought to do; otherwise we should accept everything indiscriminately as our rule. And I think that the Emperor Sigismund's second wife[44] was right when, after the

42. See, in the translation of *Equality*, Part I, "false idea of custom."

43. "Mohamedanism" is written in the margin here.

44. Sigismund (1368–1437) acceded to the throne of Hungary through his first wife Mary, who was daughter of the previous king, Louis the Great. After the death of Mary, Sigismund married Barbe de Cilley, nicknamed "the German Messalina," and was survived by her.

death of her husband and people were urging her to follow the example of the turtle-dove and remain a widow, she asked why they did not take pigeons or some other animal as examples. There is nothing in the intercourse between males and females which gives the advantage to the former. The upper is worth no more than the lower, and what is the lower here is the upper for the antipodes. There has been such a complete revision of the opinion that the male is an active principle in generation and the female a purely passive principle, that it would be pointless to mention it. Besides the one who acts suffers in his own way and the one who suffers sometimes acts the more, although his action is imperceptible to us.

IV. We have spoken enough elsewhere about women's temperament.[45] If we put what we have already written about it together with the general idea of science that we give in the same book and with what we say about employment, it will be easy to see that whatever qualities they have, warm or cold, dry or wet, they can extend their minds as far as we can by following the method we have established for them for the conduct of the mind in the sciences and in morals. Experience teaches us to see great wisdom and good judgment in people of quite opposite qualities, and very humid women can reason with greater good sense and discernment and about more things than dry men who have studied extensively.

We must, therefore, pay no attention when people say, as they usually do, that women have a colder constitution than men. For that does not coincide with the internal warmth necessary for women to produce a creature in their womb, nor with what we observe and what everyone agrees upon, that women have a livelier, quicker imagination than we do, nor with what is generally said, that they are fundamentally coquettish by nature and that they are more prone to love than men. For all these effects come from movement and heat.

Few among them will acknowledge this, for since we make it a virtue and a point of honor in our society to persecute love and to use it to frighten the simple-minded by turning it into a bogey-man, it often happens that those who are most smitten by it pretend that they are its most mortal enemies in order to look fashionable and to appear to be immune to a disease that infects everyone.

It does seem, however, that the Creator was wise in giving women a greater enthusiasm than men for marriage, so that their imagination might dwell more on its attractive aspects and less upon its disadvantages, which

45. See, in the translation of *Equality*, Part II, "who are those best suited for science?" and "on temperament."

could well turn them away from it. What helps to persuade them of the contrary is the custom which imposes on them greater diffidence and reserve than on men, especially in matters of love; men are allowed to seek out women, to solicit them, and to show their passion in public.

The blushing emotion known as modesty, which they experience more than men, also gives them confirmation of the generally held opinion that modesty is natural to us and more so to women than to men, a view so widespread that a majority of people hold it. Modesty denies women many things that are allowed men, and since it was nature that gave it to them to act as a restraint, it is a sign that she was keeping them aloof from those same things.

For my part, I cannot see that nature should have denied them anything allowed us, since she gave them the same right to do whatever they see fit for the perfecting of their minds and the preservation and ease of their bodies. If there is any difference between them and us in this respect, it is an effect of custom which is the arbiter of glory, shame, blame, scorn, civility, and incivility. For modesty is nothing more than the fear of being blamed and scorned by men by saying or doing in front of them things that they do not choose to approve.

We should give the name natural only to what is based on nature, namely, on the interior and essential disposition of each thing. Anything of this kind is never lost and is found everywhere, at all times, and in all states and all the circumstances of life, being a necessary consequence of what we ourselves are.

Let us examine against this rule what we see as the main object of modesty. At one moment we blush at certain things which we do blithely in another; I do not believe that all women would blush in the presence of a gallant man who told them that they were more amorously constituted than ourselves. At least they should be no more ashamed of this than when they are told they are more beautiful. These two qualities—greater tenderness and greater beauty—are their great advantage and a sign of their preeminence over us, if there must be any preeminence between the sexes apart from that which comes from reason.

Here is what one of my most beautiful and intelligent friends, who neither seeks nor avoids gallantry, replied one day to a friend of hers who mentioned in conversation that she could not abide people who think that women are more tenderly constituted than men.

"No doubt you have your reasons," she said, "for taking as an insult what I hear as a compliment. For me it is no more insulting of a man to say that I have a greater penchant for love than to say that I am handsomer than he is.

"This is certainly not the attitude of ordinary women, who would give anything to be beautiful. It is not that I do not think of beauty as being very desirable. I understand its power, but it is of brief duration and is too fragile and too weak compared with the advantages that go with love.

"It is only love that gives us spirit and pleasure. He who has no spirit has no love. You know the man you met here recently. A while ago he was stupid, taciturn, unpredictable, irascible, stubborn, foul-tempered, without manners or grace, a burden to himself and to all those who had the misfortune to find themselves in his company. In short, people avoided him like the plague, and called him Mr Marjoy.

"Some time later, about a month ago, he came to see me at an hour when people do not usually go calling and found me alone. I did my best to entertain him with as much cordiality as I could manage. I told him I admired him; I praised everything about him that could be praised. I answered as civilly as I could everything he said about the feelings of his heart, and I finally realized, from his protestations, his confidences, and the offers he made me, that he had fallen in love and that I had touched his heart.

"I tell you this simply to show you what the remedy had done for him. For he has so completely changed his personality that he is hardly recognizable. He has become polite, accommodating, pleasant, eager to please, and can now hold up his end of a conversation in a way I had thought impossible before.

"What I am saying about this new conquest is something you must have noticed to some degree in all those inspired by the fair passion. If love can be so effective and so useful to people who have experienced it for only a short time, imagine what must be its effect on those who have it more as part of their nature than others, so long as it is not tainted by ill temper or by the countless fantasies that people get into their heads if they do not consult their reason. And we see, in fact, that the men whose temperament most resembles women's, and who spend most time with them, are always the most reasonable and the most polite, since they have the qualities best adapted to society and to peace.

"You will, perhaps, tell me that we use a term of disparagement to designate those who resemble us and who like to spend time with us when we call them effeminate. It is true that that is the usual term, but you understand men's disposition. You know what their rule is concerning us. They hold our sex in contempt, and by extension whatever is peculiar to us. They have a much higher opinion of their own, and everything connected with it seems to them superior. This is the reason that the faults common to both sexes are, in their estimation, much greater and more horrific in ours, and the perfections they share with us occur in a higher degree among them.

"Truth itself becomes absurd and despicable in our mouth. I have very often had the experience of quoting certain arguments as coming from women and finding that no notice is taken of what I say, or that it is greeted with 'those are typical women's arguments.' Whereas if on another occasion I quoted the same arguments in the name of a man, then they were greeted with great respect and given serious consideration.

"The most shining virtues in our sex suffer the same fate as truth. They become a vice, instead of which vice is transformed into virtue in men. For example, is there anything more contrary to natural and divine law than to expose one's own life—except in order to preserve it—and to throw oneself into obvious danger out of the sole desire for glory, which is the vainest of all the chimeras that men have invented, especially since one only acquires it after one's own death, when it is of no use. Yet this behavior is seen as the highest virtue among men; it is what makes heroes, what brings accolades, triumphs, and immortality. We, in contrast, are scorned because we follow the laws of religion and reason and prefer a life remote from armed conflict, because we are sensitive to the misery of others, and because we have no desire to plunge a sword into the breast of a man who has offended us or that of an unknown foreigner who is only our enemy because someone else has called him a foreigner and has told us that there is glory in killing him or in being killed by his hand. This is why any decent man who loves peace, tranquility, and gentleness, like ourselves, is called limp, cowardly, and effeminate.

"We were not put into the world to do evil but to do good; we are not here to hate but to love. Nature and religion both preach peace. God created the world and preserves it through love and for love. We did not enter this world nor can we be virtuous and happy in it without love, and we will be rewarded in the next world only though love, and through having loved well in this world.

"This is one of the reasons that leads me to believe that those who have a greater facility for love are more excellent than others. And you will find it easy to go along with this idea if you set aside custom, which governs the discourse and conduct of love in private as well as in public. For most people are simple-minded enough to think that we should be ruled by custom in the absence of men—or even in their presence. Custom makes them idolaters in point of fact, since they give to something which is almost always quite arbitrary, the respect and fear that we owe only to God, whom we should obey in all things, everywhere, for He sees everything.

"I would not say this in the middle of the street or in the presence of a crowd of people dead set against love, and who do not think that women have any business talking about it, any more than I would appear in public in my dressing gown. But I have no hesitation in telling you—you who like to reason and who do nothing without reasoning—that I would be happy to be even more disposed to love than I am, because then I would have more spirit. And to force you to receive a compliment—or what you would call an insult—I shall tell you an idea that will strike you as being as amusing as it is novel, about what we properly call love. It seems to me that if on the one hand we believe that women have a greater capacity for love than men, and on the other we examine how they contribute to procreation, we can say that women are more excellent than men, for they are the images of God in a more perfect way.

"Did it ever occur to you that just as we can have knowledge of God only through His creatures, in the same way we can conceive of nothing in Him except in relation to the same creatures which are His handiwork. This is why I define Him as the Being who has produced and engendered the world. If I seek the reason for this creation, I find no other, nor any other model than the love of God. Thus the whole universe in general, and each creature in particular, is at one and the same time the effect and the image of divine love.

"Indeed, since the powers we possess were given to us specifically to act since creatures cannot resemble their author in His essence as in His actions, and since love is the first and most important power to which everything we recognize in Him is connected—power to carry out the project of love, wisdom to order its effects, providence to preserve them, goodness to favor men, justice to regulate their love and their duties, mercy to bring back those who have strayed from them—we can say that love is what He wanted to make manifest in His creatures and that their nature, individuality, and nobility consist in the way each of them manifests it.

"This appears in the fact that not only does He love them, all of them, as His effects and His images, uniting with them through His presence and His action, but He also wants to be loved by them, wants them all to unite with and relate to Him, those who are capable of reason through a complete union and conformity of mind and will, and the rest through recognizing Him as the Author and end of all things and by making use of everything, that is to say, uniting with everything according to the laws He has laid down for them.

"This is why He has inspired in all His creatures the desire for union which is what I understand as love. The bodies which constitute the universe desire union so strongly that we cannot conceive that any of them could be separated from the others by a void. The parts of these bodies have a greater disposition to be joined with some than with others. The perfection and beauty of each body consists of nothing but the union and perfect adaptation of all their parts. What convinces me that this desire for union in the most inanimate bodies (based on the differences in their extent, figures, [and] movements) could well be called love, without the metaphor being too far-fetched, is that the love animals have for each other and for anything else is merely the physical instinct that makes them seek what is best adapted for them.[46]

"I will not dwell on the order that could be imagined for all things created on the basis of this principle. I will say only that it seems to me that those things that are most subtle and most active—fire, for example—should be placed ahead of the others, for as they penetrate more things, they are more capable of union, and thus better represent the action whereby God acts upon everything and is united with everything.

"But since His principal action is the love by which He produces a new being distinct from Himself, the things that most resemble Him in this respect should have preeminence. This is why man is the noblest of all animals and other creatures, for there is nothing with which he cannot be joined through his thoughts and his desires, being able, besides, to produce his like with knowledge and will.

"Now in the same way that in God everything has its reference to love, so does it also in man. He is man only through the union and the love of body and spirit. The body is perfect and whole only through the precise assembly of all its members, and it cannot maintain its state of perfection nor reach a higher one without union by means of its organs with everything that surrounds it, to approach what it loves or to retreat from what it cannot love. And the spirit, the principle of knowing and willing, which is to say, of uniting through understanding and will, cannot be content and satisfied unless it is united in both these ways with what seems to it best adapted for itself or for the body.

"So much for what concerns the desire to preserve ourselves commonly called self-love. God gave us also a second desire which has as its object union with a person of a different sex and constitution, an intercourse which is necessary to produce a being of the same nature as ourselves. Now it is in this desire that we are actually the images of God, since, as we fulfill it according to His laws, we imitate what we recognize as paramount in Him, namely, to produce through love a work separate from ourselves, which depends on us without our depending on it, which needs our help for its preservation as for its creation, to which we remain united by love, and for which it seems that everything in us was made.

46. This is in reference to Descartes's theory of animal instincts. See for example the last pages of his *Méditation*, VI.

"If we do not think during the first years of life, it is because the body needs this time to acquire the strength necessary for itself. For as soon as it has sufficient strength, the second desire begins to take possession of the heart; it detaches us, so to speak, from ourselves and from those to whom we owe our life, to attach us both to the person whose love and union are necessary to give life to another and to the person who received life from us. It seems, then, that we no longer live for ourselves but only for those we love; we make greater efforts for them than for ourselves. We are more affected by the good and bad things that happen to them than to ourselves. This desire strengthens with age; it takes up the best part of our lives; it does not cease even when the body has lost its strength, but remains in the mind, and it makes men immortal like God, insofar as the condition of a creature made to produce another allows. We die only a half death when we leave behind us other selves in whom we hope to live on in some way after death. And this is why fathers and mothers are more concerned with how their children will fare after their deaths than during their lifetimes.

"Thus love is the beginning, the end, the happiness and the perfection of man, for there is nothing which makes him more like the First Being who does everything through love and for love. There is no doubt that women are more like Him than men, for it is women who have the greater love, and this love makes them act in a way that approaches that of God in the creation of the world. For it is they—who actually form us in their womb—who give us being, growth, perfection, life, birth, and nurturing. In doing so they imitate the great divine power who, in His immensity, creates, as in a vast womb, a work different from Himself. They also imitate God's goodness, wisdom, mercy, and providence much more closely than men, who normally have less love and concern for their children, contributing to their generation in a fleeting moment, like a shower of rain necessary to the earth for the germination of the seeds it contains. This is why we belong naturally to our mothers, to whom we are primarily attached during our infancy, like the young of all other animals.

"According to the principle you have just heard, if one sex is for the other, as we commonly take it to be, then it is indubitably men who are for women, for nature has made them to serve women, endowing them with a love that is more passionate and more violent because of its shorter duration, with a mind that is more solid and more weighty, [and with] a body that is coarser and more robust to make it better able to carry out our orders, to endure fatigue, to till the soil, and to perform all the tasks necessary to sustain wives and children.

"What I find comical in men's behavior is the way they have transformed into an occasion for elevation and domination what should be for them—according to the most ordinary rules by which they are governed—a reason for humiliation and submission. They pride themselves on being the inventors of all that is grand and fine in the world and claim that it is a sign of greater intelligence, superiority, and excellence to have discovered the arts and sciences, built cities, founded empires, and always to have been the arbiters of war and peace. They are exactly like servants and subordinates who try to govern their masters by an abuse of the power and resources they have been given to perform their duties, and who overstep their mandate. I would very much like to know why the craftsmen, farmers, and merchants, who carry the main burden of the state, are held in lower esteem than the nobles who do nothing, or why, on the other hand, men, who ought to be the family retainers in their relations with women, nevertheless see themselves as superior. If those who do the lion's share of the work are forced into an inferior position, then you can tell what rank the superior men occupy, so that it must be less out of politeness than duty that they elevate us to a seat of honor. Just for fun let us look at their claims to nobility. It is only right that we should see what is their due for the discoveries they have made in the arts and sciences and for the fine institutions they claim we owe to them. We must give them their just deserts.

"As far as the arts and sciences are concerned, we should, perhaps, claim our own part in their invention. The precision and skill we exhibit in everything we undertake, the delicacy of our fingers, the liveliness and inventiveness of our imagination must have shown them quite clearly what we are capable of. And if only they remembered how feeble were the arts at their inception, how slow and uncertain their progress, how many hands it took to perfect them, how many centuries and how much effort to bring them to the state of perfection they are now in, and how big a role was played by chance, then I think that they would speak of their intelligence with greater modesty. When I consider that we did without these great and cherished inventions for such a long time, that other parts of the earth were without them as recently as a century ago without being any the less happy, and that the majority of them serve merely to provoke our desires, our ambition, our vanity, our extravagance, our greed—of which they are the effects—and to increase our needs, our worries, and our misery, then it seems to me that our high opinion of them comes merely because that is what we are used to.

"Have you never thought to judge men's intelligence by the way they rank the arts they have invented? For my own part, when I see that the most necessary ones, like agriculture, are considered as the lowliest and most despicable, and the people who perform them as the dregs of society who are trodden beneath the ground they cultivate, and on the contrary, that the most frivolous and noxious occupations are highly esteemed, I cannot help thinking that there is great emptiness in those male heads who want to be seen as the most reliable.

"After all that, we should not be surprised that women are so despised, even though they have a better understanding than men of the finest of all the arts, namely, the art of loving which is the end and rule of all the others, and even though they produce, nurture, and raise men—for which reason they alone deserve the honor and glory of the finest work and the greatest ornament in the world, for whom all the arts have been pursued.

"If a trained scientist were to hear me, he would surely take me to task about his subject and would tell me that his scientific forebears deserve particular status and recognition, since it is due to the sciences they invented that the mind can be opened up, enlightened, ordered, perfected, and made sociable and happy.

"This is, indeed, what the sciences ought to produce, but it is not, in fact, what actually is produced by the ones men usually profess, for there is no one more uncouth, more condescending, more unaccommodating, more stubborn, more irascible, more ignorant, more incapable of reason, nor more inimical to women and love at least in appearance than those we call savants.

"Men have been seeking the truth for four or five thousand years already. They are made to study it from the cradle; most of them devote to it their whole lives, wealth, leisure. They have storerooms and warehouses filled with the harvests of their learned predecessors. What have they produced with all that? Fantasy, prejudice, error, sects, division, heresy, superstition, whose only contribution has been to disturb the peace of the world. And after all these arguments and all this research through the centuries, some maintain that the truth is at the bottom of a pit inaccessible to anyone, others that all science consists in recognizing that one knows nothing, and the most modern, that hitherto we have been deceived by prejudice and that to become learned we have to return to our ABCs, as if we had learned nothing. Have you never been in a public square and seen charlatans accost foolish bystanders with their empty patter, accusing each other of poisoning their customers and peddling their elixirs by dressing up in outlandish costumes and swallowing snakes? This is the picture of savants of all kinds. Apply this image to yourselves—it is not difficult.

"Yes, men's science is pure charlatanism; only the science of love deserves such a fine name, since we cannot do or know anything else with certainty. This is why, since women are so much better at it than men, they are in no way inferior to them on that front. If you have understood the system I have described, you will have the pleasure of recognizing for yourself what I have said about the savants.

"I used to be foolish enough to believe it a great blessing to have been born in a flourishing empire where by means of the arts, sciences, and fortune one could obtain friends, pleasures, riches, sumptuous clothes, magnificent palaces, a great retinue of employees and servants, and through trade enjoy all the fine and marvelous things from foreign countries.[47] But since I have started to be guided more by reason than by custom and have come to understand how the first men lived and how men that the common people know as savages—because that is how they have heard them called, and because they live differently from us—live even today, I have seen how mistaken I was.

"At the dawn of the world, traces of which are still to be seen in the innocent loves of shepherds and shepherdesses and in the pleasures of the rustic life, which is untroubled by the fear of powers or enemies, all men were equal, just, and sincere, since their only rule and law was that of good sense. Their moderation and sobriety were the reasons for their justice; each was content if the land he had received from his father yielded the fruits of his labor. Since they were all occupied without care, envy, or ambition in such a praiseworthy enterprise, the only illness was old age from which people suffered briefly after living to be a hundred.

"But since some men took advantage of their strength and their leisure to try to subjugate others, the golden age of liberty gave way to an iron age of servitude. Self-interest and wealth were so bound together through domination that it became impossible not to have to depend on others. This combination increased in proportion to the distance from the state of innocence and peace, giving rise to greed, ambition, vanity, extravagance, idleness, condescension, cruelty, tyranny, deceit, schisms, wars, chance, worries—in short, all the infirmities of mind and body that afflict us.[48]

"I believe that it is since that time that truth and justice have been persecuted—justice being obliged to flee to the heavens and truth to hide at the bottom of a pit. Love dared not appear before such people—though it was only for love that they were gathered—because of the prejudices of custom and propriety. Love was forced to put a band over his eyes and pretend to be

47. Stock, "Poullain de la Barre," 47–48: "The apparent distaste for luxury, wealth, and position, the exaltation of the humble, the insistence on love and charity as the sustaining force of the universe—attitudes evident in the final pages of the *Remarques* following *De l'Excellence des hommes*—make [Poullain's] decision to take orders more comprehensible."

48. This account of the evolution of society will be echoed in Montesquieu's parable of the Troglodytes in his *Lettres persanes* (1721).

blind, like a sage of antiquity who had to pretend to be a madman in order to give good advice with impunity.

"Finally, to combat men with men themselves, I should point out that the few wise men among them examined what goes on in high society and could only discover two significant elements, one inspiring mockery and the other pity. I agree with them completely. And if I just consider the way men have treated women, I am not sure they do not deserve, for their wisdom and their justice, to wear on their heads, they who are heads of families, the illustrious signs of their so-called excellence."[49]

The opinion of this admirable young person coincides with my own. I see no greater sign of men's prejudice than their opinion of the value and nobility of their own sex. It was only to become better acquainted with their errors and biases that I undertook this work, which contains almost all of them. And since my only purpose was to amuse myself with my pen, I end with this second work a subject which, had I wished to deal with it in all its ramifications, could have supplied me with enough material for twenty volumes.

49. These "signs" are horns, which have a double meaning. They are signs of honor when they are like to ones that artists give to Moses, which represent the light that descended upon him on Mount Sinai. But they are also a sign of shame—sometimes, though by no means always, of being cuckolded.

SELECT BIBLIOGRAPHY

PRIMARY SOURCES

Alberti, Leon Battista (1404–72). *The Family in Renaissance Florence.* Trans. Renée Neu Watkins. Columbia: University of South Carolina Press, 1969.

Arenal, Electa, and Stacey Schlau, eds. *Untold Sisters: Hispanic Nuns in Their Own Works.* Trans. Amanda Powell. Albuquerque: University of New Mexico Press, 1989.

Astell, Mary (1666–1731). *An Essay in Defence of the Female Sex.* London, 1696.

———. *The First English Feminist: Reflections on Marriage and Other Writings.* Ed. and Intro. Bridget Hill. New York: St. Martin's Press, 1986.

Atherton, Margaret, ed. *Women Philosophers of the Early Modern Period.* Indianapolis, Ind.: Hackett Publishing Co., 1994.

Aughterson, Kate, ed. *Renaissance Woman: Constructions of Femininity in England: A Source Book.* London and New York: Routledge, 1995.

Barbaro, Francesco (1390–1454). *On Wifely Duties.* Trans. Benjamin Kohl. In *The Earthly Republic,* ed. Benjamin Kohl and R. G. Witt, 179–228. Philadelphia: University of Pennsylvania Press, 1978. Translation of the Preface and Book 2.

Basnage, Henri. *Histoire des ouvrages des sçavans.* [Rotterdam, 1687–1709]. Geneva: Slatkine Reprints, 1969.

Behn, Aphra. *The Works of Aphra Behn.* 7 vols. Ed. Janet Todd. Columbus: Ohio State University Press, 1992–96.

Boccaccio, Giovanni (1313–75). *Concerning Famous Women.* Trans. Guido A. Guarino. New Brunswick, N.J.: Rutgers University Press, 1963.

———. *Corbaccio; or, the Labyrinth of Love.* Trans. and ed. Anthony K. Cassell. 2d rev. ed. Binghamton, N.Y.: Medieval and Renaissance Texts and Studies, 1993.

Bruni, Leonardo (1370–1444). "On the Study of Literature to Lady Battista Malatesta of Moltefeltro" (1405). In *The Humanism of Leonardo Bruni: Selected Texts,* trans. and intro. Gordon Griffiths, James Hankins, and David Thompson, 240–51. Binghamton, N.Y.: Medieval and Renaissance Studies and Texts, 1987.

Castiglione, Baldassare (1478–1529). *The Book of the Courtier.* Trans. George Bull. New York: Penguin, 1967.

Cerasano, S. P., and Marion Wynne-Davies, eds. *Readings in Renaissance Women's Drama: Criticism, History, and Performance, 1594–1998.* London and New York: Routledge, 1998.

Christine de Pizan (1365–1431). *The Book of the City of Ladies.* Trans. Earl Jeffrey
    Richards. Foreword Marina Warner. New York: Persea Books, 1982.
————. *The Treasure of the City of Ladies.* Trans. Sarah Lawson. New York: Viking Pen-
    guin, 1985. Also trans. and intro. Charity Cannon Willard, ed. and intro. Made-
    leine P. Cosman. New York: Persea Books, 1989.
Crawford, Patricia, and Laura Gowing, eds. *Women's Worlds in Seventeenth-Century En-
    gland: A Source Book.* London and New York: Routledge, 2000.
Descartes, René (1596–1650). *Philosophical Essays and Correspondence.* Ed. with intro.
    Roger Ariew. Indianapolis and Cambridge: Hackett Publishing Co., 2000.
Elizabeth I. *Elizabeth I: Collected Works.* Ed. Leah S. Marcus, Janel Mueller, and Mary
    Beth Rose. Chicago: University of Chicago Press, 2000.
Elyot, Sir Thomas (1490–1546). *Defence of Good Women.* In *The Feminist Controversy of the
    Renaissance,* ed. Diane Bornstein. Delmar, N.Y.: Scholars' Facsimilies and Reprints,
    1980.
Erasmus, Desiderius (1467–1536). *Erasmus on Women.* Ed. Erika Rummel. Toronto:
    University of Toronto Press, 1996.
Ferguson, Moira, ed. *First Feminists: British Women Writers 1578–1799.* Bloomington: Indi-
    ana University Press, 1985.
Glückel of Hameln (1646–1724). *The Memoirs of Glückel of Hameln.* Trans. Marvin
    Lowenthal, new intro. Robert Rosen. New York: Schocken Books, 1977.
Gournay, Marie Le Jars de (1565–1645). *Egalité des hommes et des femmes: Grief des dames
    suivis du proumenoir de Monsieur de Montaigne.* Ed. Constant Venesoen. Geneva: Droz,
    1993.
Henderson, Datherine Usher, and Barbara F. McManus, eds. *Half Humankind: Contexts
    and Texts of the Controversy about Women in England, 1540–1640.* Urbana: University of
    Illinois Press, 1985.
Joscelin, Elizabeth (1596–1622). *The Mothers Legacy to her Vnborn Childe.* Ed. Jean
    LeDrew Metcalfer. Toronto: University of Toronto Press, 2000.
Kaminsky, Amy Katz, ed. *Water Lilies, Flores del agua: An Anthology of Spanish Women Writ-
    ers from the Fifteenth Through the Nineteenth Century.* Minneapolis: University of Min-
    nesota Press, 1996.
Kempe, Margery (1373–1439). *The Book of Margery Kempe.* Trans. Barry Windeatt.
    New York: Viking Penguin, 1986.
King, Margaret L., and Albert Rabil Jr., eds. *Her Immaculate Hand: Selected Works by and
    about the Women Humanists of Quattrocento Italy.* Binghamton, N.Y.: Medieval and Re-
    naissance Texts and Studies, 1983; 2d rev. ed., 1991.
Klein, Joan Larsen, ed. *Daughters, Wives, and Widows: Writings by Men about Women and
    Marriage in England, 1500–1640.* Urbana: University of Illinois Press, 1992.
Knox, John (1505–72). *The Political Writings of John Knox: The First Blast of the Trumpet
    against the Monstrous Regiment of Women and Other Selected Works.* Ed. Marvin A. Breslow.
    Washington, D.C.: Folger Shakespeare Library, 1985.
Kors, Alan C., and Edward Peters, eds. *Witchcraft in Europe, 400–1700: A Documentary
    History.* Philadelphia: University of Pennsylvania Press, 2000.
Krämer, Heinrich, and Jacob Sprenger. *Malleus Maleficarum* (ca. 1487). Trans. Mon-
    tague Summers. London: Pushkin Press, 1928; rpt. New York: Dover, 1971.
Larson, Anne R., and Colette Winn, eds., *Writings by Pre-Revolutionary French Women,
    From Marie de France to Elizabeth Vigié-Lebrun.* New York and London: Garland, 2000.

de Lorris, William, and Jean de Meun. *The Romance of the Rose.* Trans. Charles Dahlbert. Princeton: Princeton University Press, 1971; rpt. University Press of New England, 1983.

Marguerite d'Angoulême, Queen of Navarre (1492–1549). *The Heptameron.* Trans. P. A. Chilton. New York: Viking Penguin, 1984.

Montaigne, Michel de (1533–1592). *The Complete Works.* Trans. Donald Frame. Stanford: Stanford University Press, 1958.

Poullain de la Barre, François (1647–1723). *Les Rapports de la langue latine avec la françoise, pour traduire élégamment et sans peine. Avec un recueil etymologique et méthodologique de cinq mille mots françois tirez immediatement du Latin.* Paris: Veuve Claude Thiboust and Pierre Esclassan, 1672 (attributed to Poullain by Goujet).

———. *De l'Egalité des deux sexes: Discours physique et moral où l'on voit l'importance de se défaire des préjugez.* Paris: Du Puis, 1673.

———. *De l'Egalité des deux sexes: Opinions d'autrefois et d'aujourd'hui.* Ed. J. B. Scott. Paris: Institut américain de droit international, Editions Internationales, 1932.

———. *De l'Egalité des deux sexes.* Corpus des Oeuvres de Philosophie en Langue Française. Paris: Fayard, 1984.

———. *The Woman as Good as the Man or the Equality of Both Sexes* (1677). Trans. "A. L." Ed. with an intro. Gerald M. MacLean. Detroit: Wayne State University Press, 1988.

———. *The Equality of the Two Sexes.* Trans. A. Daniel Frankforter and Paul J. Morman. Studies in the History of Philosophy, Volume 11. Lewiston, N.Y.: Edwin Mellen Press, 1989.

———. *The Equality of the Sexes.* Trans. Desmond M. Clarke, with intro. and notes. Manchester and New York: Manchester University Press, 1990.

———. *De l'Education des dames pour la conduite de l'esprit dans les sciences et dans les moeurs.* Paris: Du Puis, 1674.

———. *De l'Education des dames pour la conduite de l'esprit dans les sciences et dans les moeurs.* Facsimile rpt. of Paris: Antoine Dezalier, 1679. Ed. with an Intro. Bernard Magné. Toulouse: Université de Toulouse le Mirail, 1983.

———. *De l'Excellence des hommes, contre l'égalité des sexes.* Paris: Du Puis, 1675.

———. *Essai des remarques particulières sur la langue françoise pour la ville de Genève.* Geneva, 1691.

———. *La Doctrine des protestants sur la liberté de lire l'Ecriture Sainte, le Service divin en langue entendue, l'Invocation des Saints, le Sacrement de l'Eucharistie. Justifiée par le Missel Romain et par des Réflexions sur chaque Point. Avec un Commentaire philosophique sur ces paroles de Jésus-Christ, Ceci est mon corps; Ceci est mon sang, Matth. Cha. XXVI, v. 26.* Geneva, 1720.

Russell, Rinaldina, ed. *Sister Maria Celeste's Letters to Her Father, Galileo.* San Jose and New York: Writers Club Press, 2000.

Sartori, Eva, ed. *The Feminist Companion to French Literature.* New York: Greenwood Press, 1999.

Teresa of Avila, St. (1515–82). *The Life of Saint Teresa of Avila by Herself.* Trans. J. M. Cohen. New York: Viking Penguin, 1957.

Weyer, Johann (1515–88). *Witches, Devils, and Doctors in the Renaissance: Johann Weyer, De praestigiis daemonum.* Ed. George Mora with Benjamin G. Kohl, Erik Midelfort, and Helen Bacon. Trans. John Shea. Binghamton, N.Y.: Medieval and Renaissance Texts and Studies, 1991.

Wilson, Katharina M., ed. *Medieval Women Writers.* Athens: University of Georgia Press, 1984.

————, ed. *Women Writers of the Renaissance and Reformation.* Athens: University of Georgia Press, 1987.

Wilson, Katharina M., and Frank J. Warnke, eds. *Women Writers of the Seventeenth Century.* Athens: University of Georgia Press, 1989.

Winn, Colette, and Donna Huizinga, eds. *Women Writers in Pre-Revolutionary France: Strategies of Emancipation.* New York and London: Garland Publishing, 1997.

Wollstonecraft, Mary. *A Vindication of the Rights of Men* and *A Vindication of the Rights of Woman.* Ed. Sylvana Tomaselli. Cambridge: Cambridge University Press, 1995. Also *The Vindications of the Rights of Men, The Rights of Woman.* Ed. D. L. Macdonald and Kathleen Scherf. Peterborough, Ontario, Canada: Broadview Press, 1997.

Women Critics 1660–1820: An Anthology. Edited by the Folger Collective on Early Women Critics. Bloomington: Indiana University Press, 1995.

Women Writers in English, 1350–1850. Fifteen volumes published through 1999 (projected 30-volume series suspended). London: Oxford University Press.

Wroth, Lady Mary. *The Countess of Montgomery's Urania.* 2 parts. Ed. Josephine A. Roberts. Tempe, Ariz.: MRTS, 1995, 1999.

————. *The Poems of Lady Mary Wroth.* Ed. Josephine A. Roberts. Baton Rouge: Louisiana State University Press, 1983.

de Zayas Maria. *The Disenchantments of Love.* Trans. H. Patsy Boyer. Albany: State University of New York Press, 1997.

————. *The Enchantments of Love: Amorous and Exemplary Novels.* Trans. H. Patsy Boyer. Berkeley: University of California Press, 1990.

SECONDARY SOURCES

Adam, Antoine. *Grandeur and Illusion: French Literature and Society, 1600–1715.* Trans. Herbert Tint. New York: Basic Books, 1972.

Akkerman, Tjitske, and Siep Stuurman, ed. *Feminist Thought in European History, 1400–2000.* London and New York: Routledge, 1997.

Albistur, Maïté, and Daniel Armagothe. *Histoire du féminisme français, du Moyen Age à nos jours.* Paris: Des Femmes, 1977.

————. *Le Grief des femmes: Anthologie des textes feministes du Moyen Age à la Seconde République.* 2 vols. Paris: Editions Hier et Demain, 1978.

Alcover, Madeleine. "The Indecency of Knowledge." *Rice University Studies* 64 (1978): 25–39.

————. *Poullain de la Barre: Une aventure philosophique.* Biblio 17. Paris, Seattle, Tübingen: Papers on French Seventeenth Century Literature, 1981.

Angenot, Marc. *Les Champions des femmes: Examen du discours sur la supériorité des femmes, 1400–1800.* Montréal: Les Presses de l'Université du Québec, 1977.

Ariew, Roger. *Descartes and the Last Scholastics.* Ithaca and London: Cornell University Press, 1999.

Armogathe, Daniel. "De l'Egalité des deux sexes, 'la belle question,'" *Corpus* 1 (1985): 17–26.

Atherton, Margaret. "Cartesian Reason and Gendered Reason." In *A Mind of One's*

Own: Feminist Essays on Reason, ed. Louise M. Anthony and Charlotte Witt, 19–34. Boulder: Westview, 1993.

Badinter, Elisabeth. "Ne portons pas trop loin la différence des sexes." *Corpus* 1 (1985): 13–15.

Backer, Dorothy Anne Loit. *Precious Women*. New York: Basic Books, 1974.

Barash, Carol. *English Women's Poetry, 1649–1714: Politics, Community, and Linguistic Authority*. New York and Oxford: Oxford University Press, 1996.

Battigelli, Anna. *Margaret Cavendish and the Exiles of the Mind*. Lexington: University of Kentucky Press, 1998.

Beauvoir, Simone de. *Le Deuxième Sexe*. 2 vols. Paris: Gallimard, 1949.

———. *The Second Sex*. Trans. and ed. H. M. Parshley, with intro. Deidre Bair. New York: Vintage Books, 1989.

Beilin, Elaine V. *Redeeming Eve: Women Writers of the English Renaissance*. Princeton: Princeton University Press, 1987.

Benson, Pamela Joseph. *The Invention of Renaissance Woman: The Challenge of Female Independence in the Literature and Thought of Italy and England*. University Park: Pennsylvania State University Press, 1992.

Berg, Elizabeth. "Recognizing Differences: Perrault's Modernist Esthetic in *Parallèls des Anciens et des Modernes*," *Papers on French Seventeenth-Century Literature* 18 (1983): 135–48.

Blain, Virginia, Isobel Grundy, and Patricia Clements, eds. *The Feminist Companion to Literature in English: Women Writers from the Middle Ages to the Present*. New Haven: Yale University Press, 1990.

Bloch, R. Howard. *Medieval Misogyny and the Invention of Western Romantic Love*. Chicago: University of Chicago Press, 1991.

Bornstein, Daniel, and Roberto Rusconi, eds. *Women and Religion in Medieval and Renaissance Italy*. Trans. Margery J. Schneider. Chicago: University of Chicago Press, 1996.

Bouiller, Francisque. *Histoire de la philosophie cartésienne*. 3d ed. Paris: Delagrave, 1868.

Brant, Clare, and Diane Purkiss, eds. *Women, Texts and Histories, 1575–1760*. London and New York: Routledge, 1992.

Briggs, Robin. *Witches and Neighbors: The Social and Cultural Context of European Witchcraft*. New York: HarperCollins, 1995; Viking Penguin, 1996.

Brown, Judith C. *Immodest Acts: The Life of a Lesbian Nun in Renaissance Italy*. New York: Oxford University Press, 1986.

Cervigni, Dino S., ed. "Women Mystic Writers." *Annali d'Italianistica* 13 (1995) (entire issue).

Cervigni, Dino S., and Rebecca West, eds. "Women's Voices in Italian Literature." *Annali d'Italianistica* 7 (1989) (entire issue).

Charlton, Kenneth. *Women, Religion and Education in Early Modern England*. London and New York: Routledge, 1999.

Chojnacka, Monica. *Working Women in Early Modern Venice*. Baltimore: Johns Hopkins University Press, 2001.

Chojnacki, Stanley. *Women and Men in Renaissance Venice: Twelve Essays on Patrician Society*. Baltimore: Johns Hopkins University Press, 2000.

Chapco, J. Ellen. "Women at Court in Seventeenth-Century France: Madame de La Fayette and the concept of *Honnêté*." *Western Society for French History Proceedings* 11 (1984): 122–29.

Cholakian, Patricia F. *Rape and Writing in the "Heptaméron" of Marguerite de Navarre.* Carbondale: Southern Illinois University Press, 1991.

———. *Women and the Politics of Self-Representation in Seventeenth-Century France.* Newark: University of Delaware Press, 2000.

Darmon, Pierre. *Le Mythe de la procréation à l'âge baroque.* Paris: Editions du Seuil, 1981.

———. *Mythologie de la femme dans l'ancienne France, XVIe–XIXe siècle.* Paris: Editions du Seuil, 1985.

Davis, Natalie Zemon. *Society and Culture in Early Modern France.* Stanford: Stanford University Press, 1975. Especially chapters 3 and 5.

———. *Women on the Margins: Three Seventeenth-Century Lives.* Cambridge, Mass.: Harvard University Press, 1995.

De Erauso, Catalina. *Lieutenant Nun: Memoir of a Basque Transvestite in the New World.* Trans. Michele Stepto and Gabriel Stepto. Foreword by Marjorie Garber. Boston: Beacon Press, 1995.

DeJean, Joan. *Ancients against Moderns: Culture Wars and the Making of a Fin de Siècle.* Chicago: University of Chicago Press, 1997.

———. *Tender Geographies: Women and the Origins of the Novel in France.* New York: Columbia University Press, 1991.

DeJean, Joan, and Nancy K. Miller. *Displacements: Women, Tradition, Literatures in French.* Baltimore and London: Johns Hopkins University Press, 1991.

Dicker, Georges. *Descartes: An Analytic and Historical Introduction.* New York and Oxford: Oxford University Press, 1993.

Dixon, Laurinda S. *Perilous Chastity: Women and Illness in Pre-Enlightenment Art and Medicine.* Ithaca: Cornell University Press, 1995.

Dolan, Frances, E. *Whores of Babylon: Catholicism, Gender and Seventeenth-Century Print Culture.* Ithaca: Cornell University Press, 1999.

Donovan, Josephine. *Women and the Rise of the Novel, 1405–1726.* New York: St. Martin's Press, 1999.

Erickson, Amy Louise. *Women and Property in Early Modern England.* London and New York: Routledge, 1993.

Ezell, Margaret J. M. *Writing Women's Literary History.* Baltimore: Johns Hopkins University Press, 1993.

Fauré, Christine. "Poullain de la Barre, sociologue et libre penseur." *Corpus* 1 (1985): 43–51.

———. *Democracy Without Women: Feminism and the Rise of Liberal Individualism in France.* Trans. Claudia Gorbman and John Berks. Bloomington: Indiana University Press, 1991.

Ferguson, Margaret W., Maureen Quilligan, and Nancy J. Vickers, eds. *Rewriting the Renaissance: The Discourses of Sexual Difference in Early Modern Europe.* Chicago: University of Chicago Press, 1987.

Fletcher, Anthony. *Gender, Sex and Subordination in England, 1500–1800.* New Haven: Yale University Press, 1995.

Fraisse, Geneviève. "Poullain de la Barre ou le procès des préjugés." *Corpus* 1 (1985): 27–41.

Frye, Susan, and Karen Robertson, eds. *Maids and Mistresses, Cousins and Queens: Women's Alliances in Early Modern England.* Oxford: Oxford University Press, 1999.

Gallagher, Catherine. *Nobody's Story: The Vanishing Acts of Women Writers in the Market-place, 1670–1820*. Berkeley: University of California Press, 1994.

Gelbart, Nina Rattner. *The King's Midwife: A History and Mystery of Madame du Coudray*. Berkeley: University of California Press, 1998.

Gibson, Wendy. *Women in Seventeenth-Century France*. New York: St. Martin's Press, 1989.

Goldberg, Jonathan. *Desiring Women Writing: English Renaissance Examples*. Stanford: Stanford University Press, 1997.

Goldsmith, Elizabeth C., ed. *Writing the Female Voice*. Boston: Northeastern University Press, 1989.

Goldsmith, Elizabeth C., and Dena Goodman, eds. *Going Public: Women and Publishing in Early Modern France*. Ithaca: Cornell University Press, 1995.

Greer, Margaret Rich. *Maria de Zayas*. University Park: Pennsylvania State University Press, 2000.

Hall, Kim F. *Things of Darkness: Economies of Race and Gender in Early Modern England*. Ithaca, N.Y.: Cornell University Press, 1995.

Hampton, Timothy. *Literature and the Nation in the Sixteenth Century: Inventing Renaissance France*. Ithaca, N.Y.: Cornell University Press, 2001.

Hardwick, Julie. *The Practice of Patriarchy: Gender and the Politics of Household Authority in Early Modern France*. University Park: Pennsylvania State University Press, 1998.

Harth, Erica. *Cartesian Women: Versions and Subversions of Rational Discourse in the Old Regime*. Ithaca and London: Cornell University Press, 1992.

Haselkorn, Anne M., and Betty Travitsky, eds. *The Renaissance Englishwoman in Print: Counterbalancing the Canon*. Amherst: University of Massachusetts Press, 1990.

Hazard, Paul. *The European Mind (1680–1715)*. Trans. J. Lewis May. Cleveland and New York: The World Publishing Company, 1963.

Herlihy, David. "Did Women Have a Renaissance? A Reconsideration." *Medievalia et Humanistica* n.s. 13 (1985): 1–22.

Hill, Bridget. *The Republican Virago: The Life and Times of Catharine Macaulay, Historian*. New York: Oxford University Press, 1992.

A History of Women in the West. Vol. 1: *From Ancient Goddesses to Christian Saints*. Ed. Pauline Schmitt Pantel. Cambridge, Mass.: Harvard University Press, 1992.

———. Vol. 2: *Silences of the Middle Ages*. Ed. Christiane Klapisch-Zuber. Cambridge, Mass.: Harvard University Press, 1992.

———. Vol. 3: *Renaissance and Enlightenment Paradoxes*. Ed. Natalie Zemon Davis and Arlette Farge. Cambridge, Mass.: Harvard University Press, 1993.

Horowitz, Maryanne Cline. "Aristotle and Women." *Journal of the History of Biology* 9 (1976): 183–213.

Hufton, Olwen H. *The Prospect before Her: A History of Women in Western Europe*, vol. 1: *1500–1800*. New York: HarperCollins, 1996.

Hull, Suzanne W. *Chaste, Silent, and Obedient: English Books for Women, 1475–1640*. San Marino, Calif.: The Huntington Library, 1982.

Hutner, Heidi, ed. *Rereading Aphra Behn: History, Theory, and Criticism*. Charlottesville: University Press of Virginia, 1993.

Hutson, Lorna, ed. *Feminism and Renaissance Studies*. New York: Oxford University Press, 1999.

James, Susan E. *Kateryn Parr: The Making of a Queen*. Aldershot and Brookfield: Ashgate Publishing, 1999.

Jankowski, Theodora A. *Women in Power in the Early Modern Drama*. Urbana: University of Illinois Press, 1992.

Jed, Stephanie H. *Chaste Thinking: The Rape of Lucretia and the Birth of Humanism*. Bloomington: Indiana University Press, 1989.

Jordan, Constance. *Renaissance Feminism: Literary Texts and Political Models*. Ithaca: Cornell University Press, 1990.

Kelly, Joan. "Did Women Have a Renaissance?" In her *Women, History, and Theory*, 19–50. Chicago: University of Chicago Press, 1984. Also in *Becoming Visible: Women in European History*, ed. Renate Bridenthal and Claudia Koonz, 137–64. Boston: Houghton Mifflin, 1977.

———. "Early Feminist Theory and the *Querelle des Femmes*." In *Women, History, and Theory*, 65–109.

Kelso, Ruth. *Doctrine for the Lady of the Renaissance*. Foreword by Katharine M. Rogers. Urbana: University of Illinois Press, 1956, 1978.

King, Carole. *Renaissance Women Patrons: Wives and Widows in Italy, c. 1300–1550*. New York and Manchester: Manchester University Press, 1998.

King, Margaret L. *Women of the Renaissance*. Foreword by Catharine R. Stimpson. Chicago: University of Chicago Press, 1991.

Knibielher, Yvonne, and Catherine Fouquet. *Histoire des mères du Moyen Age à nos jours*. Paris: Editions Montalba, 1977.

Krontiris, Tina. *Oppositional Voices: Women as Writers and Translators of Literature in the English Renaissance*. London and New York: Routledge, 1992.

Kuehn, Thomas. *Law, Family, and Women: Toward a Legal Anthropology of Renaissance Italy*. Chicago: University of Chicago Press, 1991.

Kunze, Bonnelyn Young. *Margaret Fell and the Rise of Quakerism*. Stanford: Stanford University Press, 1994.

Labalme, Patricia A., ed. *Beyond Their Sex: Learned Women of the European Past*. New York: New York University Press, 1980.

Laqueur, Thomas. *Making Sex: Body and Gender from the Greeks to Freud*. Cambridge, Mass.: Harvard University Press, 1990.

Larsen, Anne R., and Colette H. Winn, eds. *Renaissance Women Writers: French Texts/ American Contexts*. Detroit: Wayne State University Press, 1994.

Lebrun, François. *La Vie conjugale sous l'ancien régime*. Paris: Armand Colin, 1975.

Lerner, Gerda. *The Creation of Patriarchy*. New York: Oxford University Press, 1986.

———. *The Creation of Feminist Consciousness, 1000–1870*. New York: Oxford University Press, 1994.

Levin, Carole, and Jeanie Watson, eds. *Ambiguous Realities: Women in the Middle Ages and Renaissance*. Detroit: Wayne State University Press, 1987.

Levin, Carole, et al. *Extraordinary Women of the Medieval and Renaissance World: A Biographical Dictionary*. Westport, Conn.: Greenwood Press, 2000.

Lindsey, Karen. *Divorced Beheaded Survived: A Feminist Reinterpretation of the Wives of Henry VIII*. Reading, Mass.: Addison-Wesley Publishing Co., 1995.

Lochrie, Karma. *Margery Kempe and Translations of the Flesh*. Philadelphia: University of Pennsylvania Press, 1992.

Lougee, Carolyn C. *Le Paradis des Femmes: Women, Salons, and Social Stratification in Seventeenth-Century France.* Princeton, N.J.: Princeton University Press, 1976.

MacCarthy, Bridget G. *The Female Pen: Women Writers and Novelists, 1621–1818.* Preface by Janet Todd. New York: New York University Press, 1994. Originally published by Cork University Press, 1946–47.

Maclean, Ian. *Woman Triumphant: Feminism in French Literature, 1610–1652.* Oxford: Clarendon Press, 1977.

———. *The Renaissance Notion of Woman: A Study of the Fortunes of Scholasticism and Medical Science in European Intellectual Life.* Cambridge: Cambridge University Press, 1980.

Magné, Bernard. "Une Source de la Lettre Persane XXXVIII? *L'Egalité des deux sexes* de Poullain de la Barre." *Revue d'histoire littéraire de la France* 3–4 (1968): 407–14.

Marshall, John. *Descartes's Moral Theory.* Ithaca and London: Cornell University Press, 1998.

Matter, E. Ann, and John Coakley, eds. *Creative Women in Medieval and Early Modern Italy.* Philadelphia: University of Pennsylvania Press, 1994. (Sequel to the Monson collection, below.)

McNiven Hine, Ellen. "The Women Question in Early Eighteenth-Century French Literature: The Influence of Poullain de la Barre." *Studies on Voltaire* 66 (1973): 65–79.

Mendelson, Sara, and Patricia Crawford. *Women in Early Modern England, 1550–1720.* Oxford: Clarendon Press, 1998.

Molino, Jean. "Le noeud de la matière: l'Unité des *Femmes savantes.*" *XVIIe siècle* 113 (1976): 23–47.

Monson, Craig A., ed. *The Crannied Wall. Women, Religion, and the Arts in Early Modern Europe.* Ann Arbor: University of Michigan Press, 1992.

Newman, Karen. *Fashioning Femininity and English Renaissance Drama.* Chicago: University of Chicago Press, 1991.

Okin, Susan Moller. *Women in Western Political Thought.* Princeton: Princeton University Press, 1979.

Ozment, Steven. *The Bürgermeister's Daughter: Scandal in a Sixteenth-Century German Town.* New York: St. Martin's Press, 1995.

Pacheco, Anita, ed. *Early Women Writers: 1600–1720.* New York and London: Longman, 1998.

Pagels, Elaine. *Adam, Eve, and the Serpent.* New York: Harper Collins, 1988.

Panizza, Letizia, ed. *Women in Italian Renaissance Culture and Society.* Oxford: European Humanities Research Centre, 2000.

Panizza, Letizia, and Sharon Wood, eds. *A History of Women's Writing in Italy.* Cambridge: Cambridge University Press, 2000.

Perry, Ruth. *The Celebrated Mary Astell: An Early English Feminist.* Chicago: University of Chicago Press, 1986.

Pieron, Henri. "De l'Influence sociale des principes cartésiens: Un précurseur inconnu du féminisme et de la Révolution: Poullain de la Barre." *Revue de synthèse historique* 184 (1902): 153–85; 270–82.

Raven, James, Helen Small, and Naomi Tadmor, eds. *The Practice and Representation of Reading in England.* Cambridge: Cambridge University Press, 1996.

Rémy, Monique. *Histoire des mouvements des femmes: De l'utopie à l'intégration.* Paris: L'Harmattan 1990.

Reynier, Gustave. *La Femme au XVIIe siècle: Ses ennemis et ses défenseurs.* Paris: Plon, 1933.

Richardson, Brian. *Printing, Writers and Readers in Renaissance Italy.* Cambridge: Cambridge University Press, 1999.

Riddle, John M. *Contraception and Abortion from the Ancient World to the Renaissance.* Cambridge, Mass.: Harvard University Press, 1992.

———. *Eve's Herbs: A History of Contraception and Abortion in the West.* Cambridge, Mass.: Harvard University Press, 1997.

Roger, Jacques. *Les Sciences de la vie dans la pensée française du XVIIIe siècle.* Paris: Armand Colin, 1963.

Ronzeaud, Pierre. "La Femme au pouvoir ou le monde à l'envers." *XVIIe siècle* 108 (1975): 9–33.

Rose, Mary Beth, ed. *Women in the Middle Ages and the Renaissance: Literary and Historical Perspectives.* Syracuse: Syracuse University Press, 1986.

Rosenthal, Margaret F. *The Honest Courtesan: Veronica Franco, Citizen and Writer in Sixteenth-Century Venice.* Foreword by Catharine R. Stimpson. Chicago: University of Chicago Press, 1992.

Rosso Geffriaud, Jeannette. *Montesquieu et la féminité.* Pisa: Libreria Goliarca Editrice, 1977.

Rousselot, Paul. *Histoire de l'éducation des femmes en France.* Vol. 1. 1883. Reprint, New York: Burt Franklin Reprint, 1971.

Rowan, Mary M. "Seventeenth-Century French Feminism: Two Opposing Attitudes." *International Journal of Women Studies* 3 (1980): 273–91.

Schiebinger, Londa. *The Mind has no Sex? Women in the Origins of Modern Science.* Cambridge, Mass.: Harvard University Press, 1991.

———. *Nature's Body: Gender in the Making of Modern Science.* Boston: Beacon Press, 1993.

Shaw, David. "*Les Femmes savantes* and Feminism." *Journal of European Studies* 14 (1984): 24–38.

Seidel, Michael. "Poulain de la Barre's *The Women As Good as the Man.*" *Journal of the History of Ideas* 35 (1974): 499–508.

Shemek, Deanna. *Ladies Errant: Wayward Women and Social Order in Early Modern Italy.* Durham, N.C.: Duke University Press, 1998.

Simons, Margaret A. *Beauvoir and "The Second Sex": Feminism, Race, and the Origins of Existentialism.* Lanham, Boulder, New York, and Oxford: Rowman and Littlefield Publishers, 1999.

Sobel, Dava. *Galileo's Daughter: A Historical Memoir of Science, Faith, and Love.* New York: Penguin Books, 2000.

Solé, Jacques. *L'Amour en Occident à l'époque moderne.* Paris: Editions Complexe, 1976.

Sommerville, Margaret R. *Sex and Subjection: Attitudes to Women in Early-Modern Society.* London: Arnold, 1995.

Spencer, Jane. *The Rise of the Woman Novelist: From Aphra Behn to Jane Austen.* Oxford: Basil Blackwell, 1986.

Spender, Dale. *Mothers of the Novel: 100 Good Women Writers before Jane Austen.* London and New York: Routledge, 1986.

Sperling, Jutta Gisela. *Convents and the Body Politic in Late Renaissance Venice.* Foreword by Catharine R. Stimpson. Chicago: University of Chicago Press, 1999.

Stanton, Domna, and Abigail J. Stewart. *Feminisms in the Academy.* Ann Arbor: The University of Michigan Press, 1995.

Steinbrügge, Lieselotte. *The Moral Sex: Woman's Nature in the French Enlightenment.* Trans. Pamela E. Selwyn. New York: Oxford University Press, 1995.

Stock, Marie-Louise. "Poullain de la Barre: A Seventeenth-Century Feminist." Ph.D. diss., Columbia University, 1961.

Stuard, Susan M. "The Dominion of Gender: Women's Fortunes in the High Middle Ages." In *Becoming Visible: Women in European History,* ed. Renate Bridenthal, Claudia Koonz, and Susan M. Stuard, 129–50. 3d ed. Boston: Houghton Mifflin, 1998.

Stuurman, Siep. "From Feminism to Biblical Criticism: The Theological Trajectory of François Poulain de la Barre." *Eighteenth-Century Studies* 33 (2000): 367–82.

———. "Social Cartesianism: François Poulain de la Barre and the Origins of the Enlightenment." *Journal of the History of Ideas* 58 (1997): 617–40.

Summit, Jennifer. *Lost Property: The Woman Writer and English Literary History, 1380–1589.* Chicago: University of Chicago Press, 2000.

Teague, Frances. *Bathsua Makin, Woman of Learning.* Lewisburg, Penn.: Bucknell University Press, 1999.

Timmermans, Linda. *L'Accès des femmes à la culture (1598–1715): Un débat d'idées de Saint François de Sales à la Marquise de Lambert.* Paris: Honoré Champion Editeur, 1993.

Todd, Janet. *The Secret Life of Aphra Behn.* London, New York, and Sydney: Pandora, 2000.

———. *The Sign of Angelica: Women, Writing and Fiction, 1660–1800.* New York: Columbia University Press, 1989.

Toulmin, Stephen. *Cosmopolis: The Hidden Agenda of Modernity.* Chicago: University of Chicago Press, 1990.

Walsh, William T. *St. Teresa of Avila: A Biography.* Rockford, Ill.: TAN Books and Publications, 1987.

Warner, Marina. *Alone of All Her Sex: The Myth and Cult of the Virgin Mary.* New York: Knopf, 1976.

Warnicke, Retha M. *The Marrying of Anne of Cleves: Royal Protocol in Tudor England.* Cambridge: Cambridge University Press, 2000.

Watt, Diane. *Secretaries of God: Women Prophets in Late Medieval and Early Modern England.* Cambridge, England: D. S. Brewer, 1997.

Welch Maistre, Marcelle. "*De l'Education des dames pour la conduite de l'esprit dans les sciences et les moeurs (1674)* ou le rêve cartésien de Poullain de la Barre." In *L'Education des femmes en Europe et en Amérique du Nord de la Renaissance à 1848,* ed. Guyonne Leduc, 135–43. Paris: L'Harmattan, 1997.

———. "La Réponse de Poullain de la Barre aux *Femmes savantes* de Molière." In *Ordre et constestation au temps des Classiques,* ed. Roger Duchêne and Pierre Ronzeaud, 1:183–91. Biblio 17. Paris, Seattle, Tübingen: Papers on French Seventeenth Century Literature, 1992.

———. "Le Corps féminin dans la pensée de Poullain de la Barre." In *Le Corps au XVIIe siècle,* ed. Ronald W. Tobin, 67–75. Biblio 17. Paris, Seattle, Tübingen: Papers on French Seventeenth Century Literature, 1995.

———. "Les Limites du libéralisme matrimonial de Poullain de la Barre." *Cahiers du Dix-septième* 5 (Fall 1991): 41–52.

Welles, Marcia L. *Persephone's Girdle: Narratives of Rape in Seventeenth-Century Spanish Literature.* Nashville: Vanderbilt University Press, 2000.

Whitehead, Barbara J., ed. *Women's Education in Early Modern Europe: A History, 1500–1800.* New York and London: Garland Publishing Co., 1999.

Wiesner, Merry E. *Women and Gender in Early Modern Europe.* Cambridge: Cambridge University Press, 1993.

Willard, Charity Cannon. *Christine de Pizan: Her Life and Works.* New York: Persea Books, 1984.

Wilson, Katharina, ed. *An Encyclopedia of Continental Women Writers.* 2 vols. New York: Garland, 1991.

Woodbridge, Linda. *Women and the English Renaissance: Literature and the Nature of Womankind, 1540–1620.* Urbana: University of Illinois Press, 1984.

Woods, Susanne, and Margaret P. Hannay, eds. *Teaching Tudor and Stuart Women Writers.* New York: MLA, 2000.

INDEX